The Tapestry of Culture

An Introduction to Cultural Anthropology

The Tapestry of Culture

An Introduction to Cultural Anthropology

Seventh Edition

Abraham Rosman, Professor Emeritus,
Barnard College, Columbia University

Paula G. Rubel, Professor Emerita,
Barnard College, Columbia University

McGraw Hill

Boston   Burr Ridge, IL   Dubuque, IA   Madison, WI
New York   San Francisco   St. Louis
Bangkok   Bogotá   Caracas   Lisbon   London   Madrid   Mexico City
Milan   New Delhi   Seoul   Singapore   Sydney   Taipei   Toronto

McGraw-Hill Higher Education 🕸

A Division of The **McGraw-Hill** Companies

The Tapestry of Culture
An Introduction to Cultural Anthropology

Published by McGraw-Hill, an imprint of The McGraw-Hill Companies, Inc. 1221 Avenue of the Americas, New York, NY, 10020. Copyright © 2001, 1998, 1995, 1992, xxxx, 1985, 1981, by The McGraw-Hill Companies, Inc. All rights reserved. No part of this publication may be reproduced or distributed in any form or by any means, or stored in a data base or retrieval system, without the prior written consent of The McGraw-Hill Companies, Inc., including, but not limited to, in any network or other electronic storage or transmission, or broadcast for distance learning.
Some ancillaries, including electronic and print components, may not be available to customers outside the United States.

This book is printed on acid-free paper.

1 2 3 4 5 6 7 8 9 0 DOC/DOC 0 9 8 7 6 5 4 3 2 1 0

ISBN 0072321547

Publisher: *Phil Butcher*
Sponsoring editor: *Carolyn Henderson*
Editorial assistant: *Suzanne Driscoll*
Marketing manager: *Leslie Kraham*
Project manager: *Paula Krauza*
Production supervisor: *Rose Hepburn*
Supplement coordinator: *Matthew Perry*
New media: *Todd Vaccaro*
Cover design: *Oxygen Design*
Cover Image: *Tilman Reitzle*
Compositor: *Carlisle Communications, Ltd.*
Typeface: *10/12 Garamond Light*
Printer: *R. R. Donnelley & Sons Company*

Library of Congress Cataloging-in-Publication Data

Rosman, Abraham.
    Tapestry of culture: an introduction to cultural anthropology/Abraham Rosman, Paula
G. Rubel.—7th ed.
        p. cm.
    Includes bibliographical references and index.
    ISBN 0-07-232154-7 (softcover: alk. paper)
    1. Ethnology. I. Rubel, Paula G. II. Title
GN316 .R67 2001
306—dc21
                                                                                    00-036136

www.mhhe.com

About the Authors

Abraham Rosman received a Ph.D. in anthropology from Yale University. His first fieldwork was with the Kamuri of Bornu Province, in northern Nigeria. He has taught at Vassar College, Antioch College, and Barnard College, Columbia University, where he is now professor emeritus.

Paula G. Rubel has a Ph.D. in anthropology from Columbia University. She carried out fieldwork on the Kalmyk Mongol refugees who settled in New Jersey and Philadelphia in 1950. Her doctoral dissertation was published as *The Kalmyk Mongols: A Study in Continuity and Change*. She taught at Barnard College, Columbia University, where she is now professor emerita.

Abraham Rosman and Paula Rubel began their collaboration in 1971 when they published *Feasting with Mine Enemy,* a comparative study of the potlatch in six Northwest Coast societies. They have done fieldwork together in Iran, Afghanistan, and Papua New Guinea, and in 1978 they published *Your Own Pigs You May Not Eat: A Comparative Study of New Guinea Societies.* They have also published many articles on their fieldwork and comparative research. Their later fieldwork in New Ireland, Papua New Guinea, and their research on the nineteenth-century collecting of ethnographic artifacts there have been the basis for several recent articles.

v

To the memory of Daniel

Contents

Preface

In the past decade, the lives of people scattered over the world have undergone enormous change. At the same time, American anthropology has also changed drastically, responding to scholarly and political influences as well as changing generations. These influences, referred to as postmodernism, have created an anthropology much more contested and fragmented than that of 30 years ago. It is unfair to introduce students to a field of study like anthropology, which is inherently very appealing, by pointing out its disjointed, fragmented character. Yet it would be equally unfair to imply that a unified, agreed-upon approach exists. *The Tapestry of Culture* adopts a distinctive approach to anthropology, which attempts to accommodate the various viewpoints. It examines cultural differences but also seeks to establish cultural similarities that emerge as a result of comparative study. The approach also emphasizes the interpretation of symbols and the meaning of things. The task is to translate the behavior and ideas of other cultures into our culture's terms. Today the trend is to see every ethnography as a description of a unique society, not comparable to any other. However, beyond each society's uniqueness, the presence of cultural similarities is clear. From its inception, anthropology has always been comparative, enabling generalizations to be made about human behavior. At present, such generalizations may deal, for example, with the nature of ethnic group behavior and the role religion plays in many instances of ethnic conflict, whereas anthropologists formerly generalized about the nature of rules of residence and kinship terminology. In *The Tapestry of Culture* we discuss many different kinds of generalizations.

Postmodernists pay particular attention to the nature of ethnographic texts, and anthropologists today still consider ethnographies, that is, descriptions of unique societies based on field research, the heart of the discipline. One of the best ways for students to be introduced to anthropology is by reading ethnographies so that they can feel the electricity of a first-rate fieldworker engaged in his or her work. Seeing the Trobriand Islands through Bronislaw Malinowski's eyes as he describes them in *Argonauts of the Western Pacific* conveys to the students Malinowski's feeling of being a castaway on a strange shore and his sense of adventure and discovery, in addition to informing them about Trobriand culture as it was at the turn of the twentieth century. However, students must be provided with the concepts and theories that anthropologists use in order to understand and appreciate ethnographies. Students need a framework for the critical evaluation of ethnographies such as Malinowski's. *The Tapestry of Culture* provides a concise and up-to-date conceptual framework with which to understand not only classic ethnographies but also the ethnographies being written today. In teaching introductory anthropology, we ourselves have used studies of groups like the Yanomamo of the South American tropical forest, a small-scale society being forced to adapt to the modern world, as well as those describing aspects of industrialized societies, such as the multiethnic neighborhoods of Philadelphia. *The Tapestry of Culture* is organized so that it can be used with the particular ethnographies that suit the instructor's interests.

The title of our book refers to culture metaphorically as a tapestry, composed of many interconnected threads, in which the whole is more than the sum of its parts. Standing back from the tapestry, one no longer sees the individual threads, but an overall design. The anthropologist does not see "culture," the overall design of the tapestry, while doing fieldwork. Rather, he or she converses with individuals and observes their actions; this is the equivalent of the threads. From this, the anthropologist, in collaboration with members of the culture, creates a picture of that culture, which results in the ethnography. Culture is therefore an analytical concept, an abstraction from reality. Like a tapestry, each culture has an overall design, even though we do take it apart and study it, by employing categories such as kinship, economics, and religion, and then examine the interconnections between the parts.

The Seventh Edition

Today we have passed into a new millennium and are in the twenty-first century. During the past century, the world changed more than it had in the previous 5000 years. Anthropology, as the study of humans and their ways of life, has the task of dealing with and trying to understand these changes. Ethnicity and ethnic identity are crucial issues in the world today. Nation-states and empires have fractured. People of different ethnic groups who lived together in one state and even intermarried are now fiercely at war with one another. Technological advances in many fields have brought about great changes in industrial societies like our own. Automation has made many earlier types of employment obsolete, and not everyone controls the skills to ride the information superhighway. These changes have required the rethinking of the economic organization of modern industrial societies. Technology has even overtaken and transformed human reproduction and required new ways of thinking about motherhood and parenting. Ideas about gender and gender role are being reformulated, with significant consequences for family organization. Anthropology today has had to come to grips with these various issues, as have we in this seventh edition of *The Tapestry of Culture*. Though some issues have been with us since the beginnings of the discipline, contemporary commentators and critics within and outside anthropology have compelled us to confront them anew.

In this seventh edition, as is our usual practice, we have made discussions and examples in every chapter more current, in accord with present-day thinking in the anthropological literature. In this Preface, we will discuss only the major changes to the text to be found in the seventh edition.

We have reorganized Chapters 1 and 2. Chapter 1, "The Anthropological Perspective," now presents an extended discussion of the concept of culture and related concepts, such as cultural rules, cultural universals, and cultural change. Postmodernism continues to have an influence on contemporary anthropology, and Chapter 1 discusses the present state of anthropological theory and the degree to which postmodernism still has an influence. We have completely reorganized Chapter 2, which is now entitled "The Anthropological Method." It begins with a discussion of participant observation and the various aspects of fieldwork in small-scale as well as complex societies. After describing the beginnings of fieldwork and the role played by Franz Boas, we present an ethnographic description of a Kwakiutl marriage from Boas's corpus of ethnographic material on the Kwakiutl. Research in complex societies is then illustrated by a description of an American marriage. Lastly, to illuminate the comparative approach, we discuss the similarities and differences between these two ethnographic examples.

We have changed the order of chapters; the chapter on symbolic systems is now Chapter 5. The new Chapter 4, entitled "Learning Language and Learning Culture: Culture and the Individual," places much greater emphasis on language acquisition and cultural acquisition. Chapter 6 is now entitled "Marriage, Family, and Kinship." The discussion of kinship in the modern world is no longer a separate section; the information has been included in the appropriate sections. Chapter 7, on gender and age, has been expanded to include a discussion of retirement communities in Japan as well as the United States. The discussion of genital mutilation has been expanded into a new section entitled "Genital Mutilation—A Human Rights Issue."

In Chapter 10, "Religion and the Supernatural," we have expanded our discussion of religious experiences in modern Western society to highlight the comparison of Wicca and shamanism in modern society with the same phenomena in small-scale societies. In Chapter 11, "Myths, Legends, and Folktales," the discussion of legends and folktales in American culture has been enlarged to include a discussion of the *Star Wars* epic. There are now separate sections on music and dance in Chapter 12, "The Artistic Dimension," and both sections include a great deal of new material.

The title of Chapter 13 has been changed to "The Colonial and Postcolonial Periods: Globalization, Migration, Diasporas, and Transnationalism," to reflect a much greater emphasis on these phenomena, which characterize the present period in world history. There is now a separate section entitled "Internal Migration, Transmigration, and Diasporas." The section "Missionaries and Cultural Change" has been expanded to include information on the missionaries themselves and their relationship to their converts. Chapter 14 has been retitled "Ethnicity, Race, and Nationalism: Anthropology for the Twenty-first Century" and continues the discussions of *ethnogenesis,* ethnicity, race, and transnationalism, among other related topics, begun in Chapter 13. Chapter 14 also contains a discussion of the relationship between the concept of ethnocentrism, introduced in Chapter 1, and ethnic identity and ethnonationalism. A totally new Epilogue has been written for this edition, which reiterates the central themes of the book.

There are now brief summaries at the end of each chapter, and we have added new photographs to illuminate the new textual material.

Supplements

As a full-service publisher of quality educational products, McGraw-Hill does much more than just sell textbooks. We create and publish an extensive array of supplements for students and instructors. This edition of *The Tapestry of Culture* is accompanied by the following instructor supplements:

- Instructor's Manual/Testbank—chapter outlines, key terms, lecture notes, discussion questions, a complete testbank, and more.
- Computerized Testbank—easy-to-use computerized testing program for both Windows and Macintosh computers.

All of these supplements are provided free of charge to instructors. Orders of new (versus used) textbooks help us defray the substantial cost of developing such supplements. Please contact your local McGraw-Hill representative for more information on any of the above supplements.

Acknowledgments

This new edition could not have been written without assistance from many people. First of all, we would like to thank the many students in our introductory anthropology classes who, over the years, have asked us many penetrating questions. We have always learned from our students and are continuously in their debt. We are especially grateful to the professors who have continued to use *The Tapestry of Culture* in their introductory anthropology courses and have given us their pithy comments and observations. To these individuals and all the others who have helped us in the past, we owe a debt of gratitude for raising questions that have contributed to a significant improvement in the organization and clarity of this book. We would like to especially thank our friend and fellow anthropologist Aram A. Yengoyan for his thoughtful comments and many suggestions. We must also mention the following reviewers, who offered many valuable comments and suggestions:

Kenneth Ackerman, University of Delaware
Traci Ardren, Florida State University
John Fritz, Salt Lake Community College
Ilsa M. Glazer, Kingsborough Community College
Robert Hill, Tulane University
Deanna Kingston, Eastern Connecticut State University
Larry L. Naylor, University of North Texas
Steven Lee Rubenstein, Georgetown University
Dorothy Ukaegbu, Community College of Southern Nevada

We would also like to thank Carolyn Henderson for her encouragement and help. Finally, our thanks to Phil Butcher for his continuing support of *The Tapestry of Culture* through several editions.

Abraham Rosman
Paula G. Rubel

The Tapestry of Culture

An Introduction to Cultural Anthropology

Chapter One

The Anthropological Perspective

Anthropology informs us about other peoples, and in the process we learn about ourselves. The anthropologist's method is different from that of other social scientists, and that difference influences the nature of the discipline—its theories, concepts, and procedures. Anthropological research involves a journey—a journey in space, a journey through time, a psychological journey into an alien world. Anthropological investigation of a way of life other than one's own may seem at first like a trip through the looking glass into Alice's wonderland, into another universe where the rules may be turned on their heads and people behave in very different ways. Anthropologists refer to the way of life of a people, with all its variation, as their *culture,* which includes their behavior, the things they make, and their ideas. However, like the world through the looking glass, each culture has an underlying logic of its own. The behavior of people makes sense once we understand the basic premises by which they live. The anthropologist's task is to translate cultures and their premises into something that we can comprehend.

From the beginning, human beings have always moved or traveled beyond the borders of the area they called home. This was the means by which Homo sapiens eventually peopled most of the earth. When they became literate, writers from Heradotus to Marco Polo wrote about the others they encountered. Though today, the process of globalization has brought Pepsi Cola and the menus of McDonald's to the most remote parts of the world, a traveler to distant places will still be impressed with differences between cultures. Chinese people eat dogs and sea cucumbers, but Americans do not consider such creatures to be food. People in every culture think that what they eat is "the right stuff." The belief that one's own culture represents the best way to do things is known as *ethnocentrism.* Ethnocentrism emphasizes the pride a group has in its cultural accomplishments, its historical achievements, the supremacy of its religious beliefs, and the god-given virtues of its sexual and

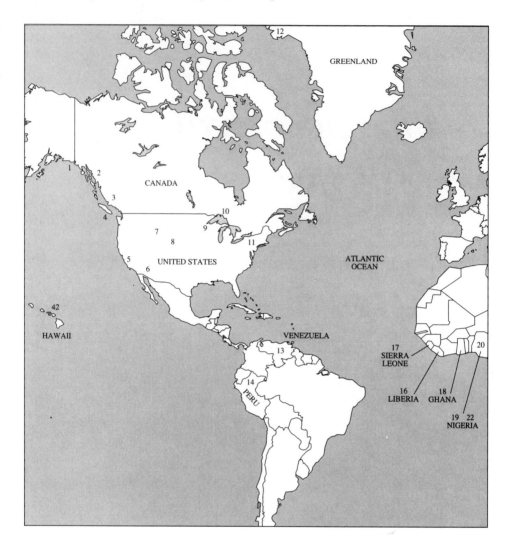

culinary practices. Ethnocentrism also includes the idea that other peoples' (often one's closest neighbors') beliefs, customs, and practices are like those of "animals." At the root of ethnic conflict and ethnonationalism, so prevalent in the world today, is ethnocentrism.

Anthropology is the study of the world of cultural differences. It examines cultural practices in their cultural contexts. *Cultural relativism* is the idea that each culture is unique and distinctive but none are superior. This is in sharp contrast to the ethnocentric point of view that one's own culture is superior to all others. However, the question of morality, what is right and wrong, presents a problem for proponents of cultural relativism. On the one hand, for example, are those who believe

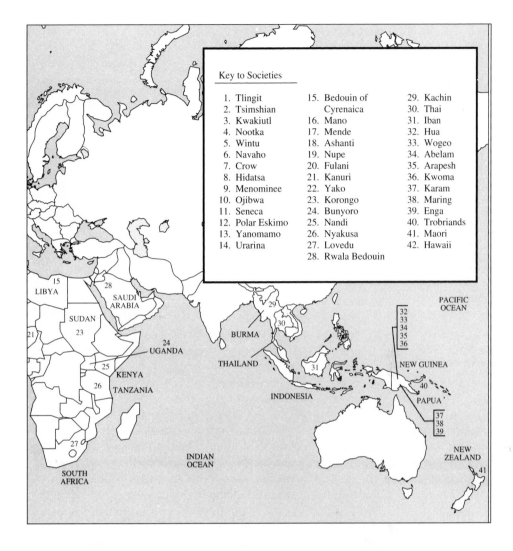

Key to Societies

1. Tlingit	15. Bedouin of	29. Kachin
2. Tsimshian	Cyrenaica	30. Thai
3. Kwakiutl	16. Mano	31. Iban
4. Nootka	17. Mende	32. Hua
5. Wintu	18. Ashanti	33. Wogeo
6. Navaho	19. Nupe	34. Abelam
7. Crow	20. Fulani	35. Arapesh
8. Hidatsa	21. Kanuri	36. Kwoma
9. Menominee	22. Yako	37. Karam
10. Ojibwa	23. Korongo	38. Maring
11. Seneca	24. Bunyoro	39. Enga
12. Polar Eskimo	25. Nandi	40. Trobriands
13. Yanomamo	26. Nyakusa	41. Maori
14. Urarina	27. Lovedu	42. Hawaii
	28. Rwala Bedouin	

that killing another human being should be universally condemned. On the other hand are those who point to killing within ceremonial or ritual contexts, as in head-hunting and cannibalism, which has, in the past, been a core feature of the societies in which it occurred. The Marquesans were cannibals and took trophy heads, as illustrated. Should those killings be condemned on the basis of a universal morality? Under this rubric, the rights of the individual are emphasized over those of the community. This is the position taken by advocates of universal human rights. Community-supported genital mutilation and arranged marriage are said, by those supporting universal rights, to be violations of the rights of the individual. Many citizens of the United States feel that the death penalty in their country, a

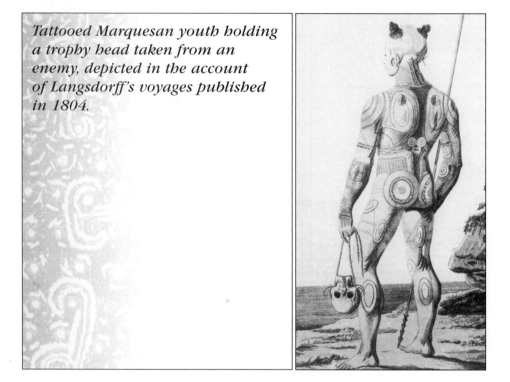

Tattooed Marquesan youth holding a trophy head taken from an enemy, depicted in the account of Langsdorff's voyages published in 1804.

practice renounced by most other Western countries, is also a violation of the universal moral principle against the taking of a human life by the state. Today there is an ongoing debate between supporters of a universal morality and supporters of moral relativism. Though universal human rights as an idea is widely accepted, what should be included as a universal human right is subject to continuing discussion.

The study of cultural differences by anthropologists also reveals what cultures have in common. Utilizing the comparative approach, anthropologists compare cultures to identify similarities of cultural patterning. For example, until World War II, the Rwala Bedouin of the Saudi Arabian desert depended primarily on their camel herds for subsistence. Until the early twentieth century, the Kazaks of what is now Kazakstan relied on their herds of horses in the grassland steppe environment where they lived. Despite the fact that the environments they inhabited were totally different, the Rwala Bedouin and the Kazaks shared a number of cultural features. They both moved with their animals from place to place over fixed migration routes during the year in order to provide pasture for them. They lived in similar sorts of communities—nomadic encampments consisting of several related groups of people, each with its own tent. In each case, the nomads depended on exchanging the products of their herds (such as milk, butter, cheese, and hides) with townspeople for commodities, such as flour and tea, that they could not provide for themselves. Because of the basic similarities in the ways of life of the Rwala Bedouin and the Kazaks, anthropologists characterize them both as a type of society called nomadic pastoralist. However, cultural differences existed between the Rwala and the Kazak. They spoke totally different languages belonging to unrelated language families, and had different beliefs and practices. But, in a more general sense, as nomadic pastoralists, both groups had lifestyles and community structures similarly constructed around a cycle of movement with their herds.

Culture

The central concept of anthropology is culture. Other disciplines study the different kinds of human activities in all societies, but each discipline studies a specific sector of this activity. Thus, economists study economy, political scientists study government, art historians study art, musicologists study music, and religion specialists study religion. Each discipline focuses on particular activities of humans as if those activities were largely autonomous. The anthropologist investigates all these fields, but the emphasis is on their interrelationship. Anthropology's holistic approach, which focuses on culture as an organizing concept, stresses the relationship among economics, politics, art, religion, and other activities.

Today, many individuals live their lives in a world of overlapping cultures. The Navajo, studied by generations of anthropologists, still retain their Navajo identity even though they are part of a much larger complex culture, American culture, participating in the larger American economy and political system. Many individuals are bilingual, speaking the Navajo language and English, and retain elements of Navajo religion and beliefs. Within the large Navajo population, there is considerable cultural variation among individuals, between communities, and between regions. Navajo people have always been very receptive to new cultural ideas. The practice of herding sheep, the weaving of blankets, and the manufacture of silver, so central to Navajo culture today, were introduced by the Spanish at the time of their conquest of the New World. Though the Navajo adopted silver working and weaving from the Spanish, the styles embodied in these arts are distinctively Navajo. However, earlier they chose not to adopt the horticulture of their neighbors, the Hopi and Zuni. What emerges from the Navajo experience is an awareness that culture as a concept exists at many levels—the individual, the community, the subculture, and the larger society or political entity. Cultures do not exist with fixed boundaries; they blend into one another. Changes are constantly taking place in culture. Lastly, individuals are not simply recipients of culture; they are active participants involved in reworking their cultures.

If the first thing one notices is that there are cultural differences, the second is that all cultures have a certain degree of internal consistency. We have called this book *The Tapestry of Culture* because the imagery of a tapestry aptly conveys the integrated nature of culture. Many strands, many colors, many patterns contribute to the overall design of a tapestry, just as many items of behavior and many customs form patterns that, in turn, compose a culture. However, patterns and regularities of culture do not remain eternally the same, but rather, change through time. While culture is integrated to a degree, there are frequently internal inconsistencies and contradictions, as will be illustrated in later chapters. Cultures should not be thought of as single monolithic entities. In most societies, there are subcultures based on regional class, ethnic, or religious differences, and the like. Feminist studies have made us much more aware that men and women have differing views of their culture. Because of the power differentials between rulers and subjects, and workers and bosses, perspectives on the culture that they share are different. The distinction between what constitutes a subculture and what constitutes a different perspective within a single culture is not so clear-cut from a definitional point of view.

Culture is learned and acquired by infants through a process referred to by anthropologists as *enculturation*. Mental structures or schema are created in the individual as a result of the process of enculturation. People who share a culture have reoccurring common experiences, which lead them to develop similar mental schema. Individuals are enculturated not as passive agents, but as active recipients. They internalize cultural practices but may change and transform those practices as a result of their experiences. Culture is transgenerational; that is, it continues beyond the lifetimes of individuals. There is a stability and consistency of cultural patterning through time, despite the fact that culture is continually being reworked and re-created. Culture is always a dialogue between past and present. As cultures reproduce themselves, changes occur; some are the result of internal developments and innovations while others represent introductions from outside. Anthropologists study the process of culture change through time by examining historical, archival, and sometimes, archaeological data deriving from the excavation of prehistoric sites. Innovators and rebels, who try to transform their societies, have a view of the society which is different from that of other members. It is a dream of a different future, of a "brave new world," which demands that present ways of doing things be changed.

Anthropologists have differing definitions of what constitutes culture. Some have focused upon culture as primarily a set of ideas and meanings that people use, derived from the past and reshaped in the present. In this view, historically transmitted patterns of meaning are embodied in symbols, by means of which humans communicate, perpetuate, and develop their knowledge about and attitudes toward life. The role of the anthropologist is then to grasp, comprehend, and translate those ideas and meanings so people of other groups may understand them. Other anthropologists, influenced by ideas about biological evolution in particular, by evolutionary psychology, see culture as the means by which human beings adapt to their environment. They argue that the repertoire of cultural traits of a particular group must have been the result of evolutionary selection. This repertoire is adaptive; otherwise, it would not have been perpetuated. In this view, individuals with adaptive cultural traits are reproductively successful and flourish, while those with cultural traits that are not adaptive die out. This perspective emphasizes what humans have in common with other animal species, which are each adapted to their environment in particular ways.

Another concept, paralleling culture, is that of society. Culture deals with meanings and symbolic patterning, while *society* deals with the organization of social relationships. Culture is distinctive of humans alone. However, all animals that live in groups, humans among them, can be said to have societies. Thus a wolf pack, a deer herd, and a baboon troop constitute societies. As in a human society, the individual members of a wolf pack are differentiated as males and females, as immature individuals and adults, and as mothers, fathers, and offspring. Individual wolves in each of these social categories behave in particular ways. That there are resemblances between wolf and human societies should not be surprising, since both wolves and humans are social animals. But human societies not only are more complex; they also have culture, which is based on symbols, is transmitted transgenerationally, and is infinitely expandable.

The Biological Basis for Culture

Human beings are cultural beings. It is the possession of culture that distinguishes humans from all other animal species. In animal species, social behavior and communication are determined primarily by instinct and are essentially uniform throughout the species. Recently, primatologists have reported that different groups of chimpanzees of the same species exhibit behavioral differences in the way that they obtain their food. For example, some groups of chimpanzees crack nuts by hammering them on wood with a piece of wood, while other groups hammer nuts with a stone on a piece of wood. Similar regional variations between groups have been observed in how they obtain ants, how they attract attention, and how they use leaves to clean or groom themselves. Though chimpanzees may use stones, sticks, and leaves as tools, they do not understand the properties of these materials and, consequently, do not have the capacity to invent new tools. Fifty years ago, Japanese primatologists reported that a young rhesus macaque on the island of Koshima started washing the dirt off sweet potatoes in water before eating them. Other macaques of his group copied this behavior, and the macaques of Koshima Island continue to do this. Other groups of Japanese macaques do not exhibit this behavior. Similarly, songbirds learn their songs from their parents and peers. They exhibit regional variation in their songs as chimpanzees do in their tool-using behavior. Some primatologists call this chimpanzee behavior cultural behavior. However, given its similarity to that of the macaques and songbirds, it falls into the category of learned behavior, with regional variations, which is short of true cultural behavior.

These behaviors are in sharp contrast to human cultural behavior, which is not only learned and transmitted from one generation to the next but also based on language and the capacity to create symbols. Human cultural behavior is not limited, as is chimpanzee learned behavior, but is infinitely expandable. Ape-human comparisons, as Tattersall notes, only provide a background for understanding the way in which human mental capacities for culture evolved (1998: 49).

The evolution of the human species from proto-human and early human forms involved a number of significant physical changes, including increase in brain size and development of bipedal erect locomotion. The evolution of the human brain was also marked by the development of cerebral asymmetry. In humans, each cerebral hemisphere has somewhat different functions. Cerebral asymmetry is connected to right- and left-handedness. The earliest stone tools were made by right-handed individuals (Tattersall, 1998: 76). Though primates have a significant level of intellectual capacity when compared with other animals, the evolution of humans was marked by a rapid

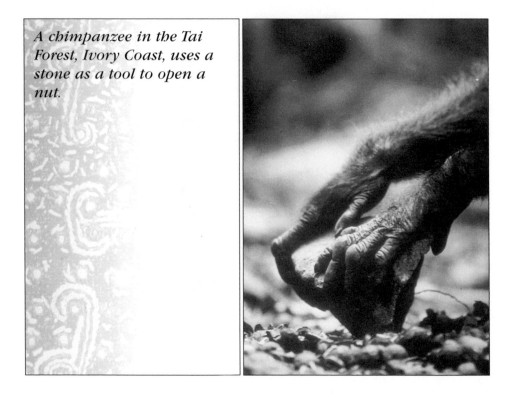

A chimpanzee in the Tai Forest, Ivory Coast, uses a stone as a tool to open a nut.

expansion of this faculty. The use of rudimentary tools by some apes was greatly surpassed even by proto-humans. This was facilitated by the retention of the hand as a generalized organ for grasping, combined with the new characteristic of erect posture. The increase in sophistication of the tools manufactured by early human beings occurred with expansion in brain size and intelligence. The early archaeological record shows the widespread geographical distribution of the same pattern or style of tool type, indicating the presence of the features that characterize culture. Though particular tool types, which would seem to embody common cultural concepts, existed in the minds of individuals living over a wide area, these tools were made for particular and often different purposes.

Human communication through language depends on the increase in human intellectual capacity noted above. Unlike the limited call systems of other animal species, every human language has the capacity to enable its speakers to produce new sentences that convey ideas never voiced before. It is clear that language and the use, creation, and manipulation of symbols evolved as did brain size and tool use. However, at this point there is no definitive information about the way in which language evolved, since there are no "linguistic fossils" representing intermediate forms of language. The central role of language in culture will be explored more fully in Chapter 3. Art and music are other systems of communication that employ symbols. They make their first appearance in the Upper Paleolithic with the people called Cro-Magnon, who were *Homo sapiens* like us.

A butcher sells glazed dog meat in the market at Guanzhou (Canton), Peoples' Republic of China.

Still another feature distinguishes human cultural behavior from animal behavior. Human behavior is governed primarily by cultural rules, not by the need for immediate gratification. The capacity to defer gratification was increasingly built into human physiology as humans evolved. Human beings do not eat the minute they become hungry or have a period of estrus during which they need to have sexual intercourse. Instead, they usually follow their culture's set of rules as to when and where to eat and when and where to have sex. Humans have developed the ability to internalize rules of behavior and depend upon other humans for approval.

Cultural Universals

The biological nature of the human species requires that all cultures solve the basic problems of human existence. As a consequence, though cultural differences do exist, all cultures share certain fundamental similarities, which are referred to as *cultural universals*. All languages are characterized by certain universal features, such as the presence of nouns, possessive forms, and verbs that distinguish between the past, present, and future. All languages have these universal features, though they are individually different from one another. All humans cook food and control the use of fire. No other animal species cooks food. Animals are biologically programmed to feed randomly or at certain times of the day, while human consumption of food follows cultural rules regarding what is eaten, when and with whom food is eaten, and with which utensils. All cultures have some kind of incest taboo, though the relatives with whom they must not have sexual intercourse vary. Rites of passage, such as birth, reaching adulthood, marriage, and death, are celebrated ceremonially, by societies, though not all of them celebrate every rite of passage. Some anthropologists have pointed out that all cultures have law, government, religion, conceptions of self, marriage, family, and kinship (Brown, 1991; Kluckhohn, 1953). These universal cultural categories are common denominators of culture, dealing with the problems and concerns that all humans face (Goodenough, 1970: 120). Ultimately, it is the nature of the human species, or more specifically, the human mind, that is the basis for cultural universals. Languages and cultures are structured in a particular manner as a consequence of the fact that the Homo sapiens' mind is organized in a certain way.

Cultural Rules

All human biological drives are governed by sets of cultural rules. What is learned and internalized by human infants during the process of enculturation are *cultural rules*. The enormous variations in culture are due to differences in cultural rules. Frequently, people from a particular culture can tell the anthropologist what the rules are. At other times, they may behave according to rules that they cannot verbalize. Defining these cultural rules is like trying to identify the rules of a language. All languages operate according to sets of rules, and people follow these rules in their speech. It is the linguist's job to determine the rules of grammar that the speakers of the language use automatically and are usually not aware of. Informants are members of a culture who help the anthropologist to explain their culture. The anthropologist's job is to determine the cultural rules of which people may also be unaware. The existence of rules does not imply that speakers of a language or members of a culture are robots who speak and act in identical fashion. Each infant learns the cultural rules in a distinctive manner, and every speaker of a language has his or her distinctive pronunciation and linguistic mannerisms. Individual variation is considerable in spoken language. Individual variation is equally present in cultural practice. Rules are meant to be flouted, and some individuals respond to rules that way. Lawyers in our society, for example, advise us on how to get as close as possible to the limit of the law, without actually crossing over the line. That is their job. Individual interpretation of rules, as well as of laws, results in such variation in observing the rules.

Rules govern sexual behavior in terms of with whom it is allowed, as well as when, where, and how. For example, in Lesu, a community in Papua New Guinea, it is acceptable for sexual intercourse to take place before marriage. The marriage relationship is symbolized by eating together. When a couple publicly shares a meal, they are married and can henceforth eat only with one another. Even though husband and wife may have sexual relations with other individuals, they may not eat with them. Until the beginning of the sexual revolution about 50 years ago in our society, couples engaged to be married could eat together, but sexual intercourse was not to take place until after marriage. The act of sexual intercourse symbolized marriage. At that time, if either spouse had intercourse with another individual after marriage, that was considered the criminal act of adultery, though either spouse could have dinner with someone of the opposite sex. From the perspective of someone in our society, the rules governing marriage in Lesu appear like our earlier rules "stood on their heads."

We noted above that workers and bosses have differing cultural perspectives. Their repertoire of cultural rules likewise may vary. Similarly, subcultures also exhibit cultural variability in their rules. In our society today, there is cultural variability with regard to sexual behavior. Christian Fundamentalists have beliefs about sex before marriage that are very different from those of members of the entertainment industry. Each of these groups represents a subculture with its own rules about a variety of cultural behaviors.

On occasion, individuals may violate cultural rules. All cultures have some provision for sanctioning the violation of cultural rules as well as rewards for obeying them. Both rewards and sanctions differ from one culture to another, in the same way that the sets of cultural rules differ. Cultural rules also change over time. When many individuals consistently interpret a rule differently than it had been interpreted before, the result will be a change in the rule itself. An example is the change that has come about in our society now that sexual intercourse is no longer solely a symbol of marriage.

Though cultural rules exist, it is individuals who interpret them in a variety of ways. Anthropologists explore the relationship between culture and the individual. These individual interpretations are a consequence of the mental schema that have been internalized during enculturation. Each person speaks his or her unique version of a language, which linguists refer to as one's *idiolect*. The vocabulary, syntax, and pronunciation one uses represent one's interpretation and use of the sets of rules underlying the language being spoken. In the same manner, individuals act according to their interpretations of the rules of their culture. This sometimes involves choosing from among a number of cultural rules that present themselves as options or alternatives.

Social Structure

The particular patterns of social relationships that characterize a society are referred to as its *social structure*. These patterns of social structure are based on cultural rules. Social structure includes the social groupings that a society recognizes, which may be organized on the basis of family, kinship, residential propinquity, or common interest. These groupings have continuity through time and are organized according to a particular pattern of relationship. The entire network of social roles, to be discussed below, constitutes another aspect of social structure. The concept of social structure may be distinguished from *social organization* (Firth, 1951). While structure emphasizes continuity and stability, organization refers to the way in which individuals perceive the structure and context of any situation and make decisions and choices from among alternative courses of behavior. Organization refers to variations in individual behavior and emphasizes flux and change. This emphasis on individual choices and decisions is also referred to as practice (Bourdieu, 1977).

In human societies, individuals occupy different positions, or *social statuses*. They usually occupy more than one social status at the same time. An individual may occupy the social statuses of father, chief, and priest at the same time. Societies, of course, vary in the number and kinds of social statuses. The behavior associated with a particular social status in a society is known as the *social role*. Social roles involve behavior toward other people, as a father to his children, a supervisor to her staff, or a headman to his followers. A headman will lead his followers to attend a ceremony sponsored by another headman and his followers. When the headman orates on such an occasion, he speaks for his group, and he is carrying out the social role of headman. Interaction of people in their social roles and interaction between groups define social relationships.

In anthropology the terms *structure* and *pattern* refer to and describe form. We may talk about the structure or form of a myth, the various aspects of the structure of a language, or the form of a type of tool or material artifact. In parallel fashion, that myth, tool, or particular aspect of language, a verb, for instance, has a use or function to perform. This tells what the parts do and how they operate. When archaeologists talk about *structure,* they are talking about the formal elements that characterize, for instance, a type of pottery or tool. This contrasts with its use, its purpose, or *function*. Similarly, a linguist will talk about the phonetic structure of a language—a description of formal relationships. This is different from the function of phonemes, the units of sound, which is to differentiate meanings. Cultural anthropologists may talk about political structure, for example, of Trobriand Island society in the South Pacific at the beginning of the twentieth century, which was made up of villages with headmen, formed into a district headed by a chief. The functions of Trobriand political structure were governmental. The village headman organized and directed village ceremonies and collected tribute to be given to the chief of the district. The chief of the entire district maintained order in his district by punishing wrongdoers, and he used his wealth and tribute to reward those who performed services for him. In similar fashion, one can describe the economic structure, the religious structure, and the kinship structure of any society, including one's own.

◼ Anthropological Theory

The discipline of anthropology has been professionalized for more than a century. To more clearly understand the work that anthropologists are doing today as well as the results of their past research, it is useful to briefly survey the significant theoretical and methodological approaches that have informed, shaped, and focused this research. When anthropology was developing during the nineteenth century, it was envisioned as a science, patterned after the natural sciences. This image was dominant until the early part of the twentieth century. At that point, a more humanistic approach began to emerge and to become dominant in American anthropology, characterized in particular by the work of Ruth Benedict. At the same time, in Britain, a strongly scientific approach emerged. After World War II, the scientific approach reemerged in American anthropology. In the 1990s, however, postmodernists launched an attack on anthropology as a science, claiming that the anthropological approach cannot be objective and that theory construction is completely inappropriate in cultural anthropology. Today, there is an ongoing debate on this subject. Anthropology and its various current theoretical positions, including the postmodernist idea of the absence of theory in anthropology, can only be understood by examining the theoretical thinking of the past.

Cultural Evolution

In the nineteenth century, a period of colonial expansion and the development of great empires by European powers, Darwinian evolutionary theory was dominant. Social Darwinism, which proclaimed the survival of the fittest, was used to justify the domination and suppression of native peoples, as well as the exploitation of the underclass in industrial societies. During this period the discipline of anthropology came into being. The significant theory of the time was *cultural evolution*. At this point, the central concept of culture, proposed by Sir Edward Tylor (1871), was defined in a broad, all-encompassing manner.

Neither he nor the American Lewis Henry Morgan, the major figures in nineteenth-century evolutionary theory, did the kind of anthropological fieldwork with which anthropology was later identified, though Morgan carried out observations on the Iroquois and on the native peoples of the Plains, and Tylor visited Mexico. Generally, anthropologists of that time remained in their armchairs and utilized the accounts of missionaries; explorers, such as Captain Cook; travelers, such as Prince Maximilian, who explored the area of the Louisiana Purchase; and others who described the native peoples they encountered. However, many of these descriptions were ethnocentric, biased accounts. Tylor and Morgan conceived of cultural evolution in terms of stages through which all societies progressed, with the simple developing into increasingly more complex forms, culminating in their own Victorian society. However, in the view of these anthropologists, not all societies evolved into complex forms. Some, the "savages" being encountered by the missionaries, travelers, and others, were believed to represent cases of arrested development, contemporary survivals of earlier stages.

The evolutionists organized their data and carried out what is clearly recognizable as the comparative approach, which we have discussed above. They looked for similarities and differences in cultures, classified them into cultural types, and ordered the types from simple to complex. As noted, they were ethnocentric in their evaluation of other societies, always making comparisons with Western civilization; that is, Western religion, family life, and so on, were all assumed to be the apogee of evolutionary development. Morgan's emphasis on the economic base as the determining factor of stages of cultural evolution caught the attention of Friedrich Engels. Engels's *The Origin of the Family, Private Property and the State* (1884) contains a reinterpretation of Morgan's *Ancient Society* (1877). Both Marx and Engels were taken with the work of Morgan, because, like Morgan, they were economic determinists and were interested in the evolution of culture.

At the beginning of the twentieth century, the weaknesses of the nineteenth-century evolutionary approach to culture began to be recognized. The data on which the theories were based were found wanting, and fieldwork by anthropologists with university training was begun, superseding the accounts of earlier amateurs. In the 1940s, however, evolutionary theory was resurrected by Leslie White (1949, 1959), a technological determinist who saw the totality of culture evolving and becoming more complex as human beings developed increasingly more efficient ways of capturing energy from the environment. In contrast to White and his universal evolutionary scheme, Julian Steward (1955) was interested in how particular societies were transformed. He saw the relationship among the environment, economic subsistence activities, and associated social and political institutions, what he called the cultural core, as the determining factor in the evolutionary transformation of particular societies. Steward developed a system of cultural types, each of which was seen as having a different line of evolutionary development. In 1960, Marshall Sahlins and Elman Service attempted to reconcile White's and Steward's theories. They proposed a distinction between specific evolution, concerned with the adaptation of particular societies to their environments as they develop through time, and general evolution, concerned with the emergence of higher forms of culture regardless of historical sequence and based upon progress in terms of energy capture. The adaptation of different societies to their environments became the focus of the ecological approach, which saw the society and its environmental setting as a single, interrelated system.

All anthropologists today would agree that complex forms of society have evolved from simpler ones. However, contemporary cultural anthropological theory, by and large, is not concerned with evolutionary questions. Many anthropologists feel that evolutionary theory does not take into account the particular and unique aspects of culture with which they are now concerned. But evolutionary questions remain important to many archaeologists. Other anthropologists, Ingold, for example, are interested in the role human consciousness plays in cultural evolution and in whether there is a cultural analogue of natural selection (1986). Some anthropologists are interested in the ideas of evolutionary psychology.

Cultural Relativism

At the beginning of the twentieth century, there was a strong reaction against nineteenth-century evolutionary thinking, particularly the view that all societies had gone through the same series of stages, and alternative anthropological theories began to appear. Though Franz Boas started out as a supporter of the evolutionary viewpoint, his fieldwork with Eskimos of Baffin Island in the late nineteenth century, known today as Inuit, and somewhat later with a variety of Northwest Coast societies, especially the Kwakiutl, led him to abandon the evolutionary approach. Boas made language a central focus of his research. After learning the Kwakiutl language, he came to respect the significant differences between the way the Kwakiutl viewed the world and the way other people viewed it. He moved away from attempts to range societies from simple to complex, considering all cultures and languages equally distinctive and complex in different ways. This emphasis on distinctiveness came to be referred to as cultural relativism. Boas saw cultures as symbolic systems of ideas rather than as entities adapting to environments. His work stressed the gathering of texts in the native language concerning all the aspects of the life of the people, especially art, mythology, and language. Boas felt that anthropologists should first concentrate on learning about the history of the development of particular societies, such as the Kwakiutl and other

Native American Indian societies, before attempting to theorize about the general process of cultural change and evolution. Boas's emphasis on cultural relativism came to be associated with the humanistic approach mentioned above and characterized the work of his students, for example, Benedict, Sapir, and Kroeber.

Functionalism

The British reaction against nineteenth-century evolutionary theory took a somewhat different form. British anthropologists at the beginning of the twentieth century rejected the theoretical framework of cultural evolution and supplanted it with a model, derived from biology, of society as a living organism. The basic organizing concepts they used were structure and function (discussed above). They spurned the speculative nature of nineteenth-century evolutionary stages and substituted for it fieldwork, that is, the empirical field observations of anthropologists who had spent a year or more in the field learning the language and doing participant observation, which will be discussed in the next chapter.

Bronislaw Malinowski, a major theorist in the development of this approach, spent an extended period of time doing fieldwork in the Trobriand Islands off New Guinea and is often cited as one of the founders of modern anthropological field-work. His method of analysis of field data involved identifying the institutions that made up the "skeleton" of society and then describing in detail how those institutions functioned. For example, in his two-volume work *Coral Gardens and Their Magic* (1935), he describes that part of the economic institution of the Trobrianders concerned with horticulture. Not only does he describe the process of planting and cultivating yams, but he also goes into great detail about the magic involved in yam cultivation, the texts of the spells used, and finally, the way the yams are used in the complex exchange system of fulfilling obligations to kin and chiefs. Malinowski saw cultural institutions functioning in response to basic human biological needs, which exist for people in all societies, as well as to what he called culturally derived needs.

Though coupled at times with Malinowski as a British functionalist, A. R. Radcliffe-Brown moved in his anthropological theorizing in a somewhat different direction. Using a comparative approach, he tried to develop typologies to sort and categorize different kinds of societies (1952). He was concerned with the "anatomy" of societies, with social structure, not with how institutions functioned to satisfy biological needs. When Radcliffe-Brown talked about the function of a part of the social structure, such as a clan, he used the term *function* to mean the contribution made by the clan to the ongoing life processes of the society. The next generation of British anthropologists became experts in the delineation of different kinds of social structures and such aspects of culture as law, political organization, land tenure, and religion, and the way these functioned. The central organizing concept for them was society and its patterns of interrelationship, and culture was merely the medium through which these relations were expressed. Radcliffe-Brown strongly opposed what he referred to as conjectural history. Real history, he argued, existed only where there were written records kept by the people themselves. The effect of Radcliffe-Brown's attitude was to inhibit all kinds of historical research by British anthropologists for one or two generations.

In the face of culture change and the breakdown of colonial empires after World War II, the functionalist theoretical framework, which emphasized unchanging societies existing in a state of equilibrium, came under attack. British anthropologists, such as A. L. Epstein and Philip Mayer, began to follow the tribal people whom they had studied as they moved into the cities and went to work in the mines. Others, such as E. E. Evans-Pritchard and M. G. Smith, turned to the historical investigation of societies based on archival material, rejecting Radcliffe-Brown's injunctions against the study of what he called conjectural history. A much more processual model, which emphasized not social structure but social organization concepts, came into play.

Structuralism

Structuralism as a theoretical approach is closely associated with the work of the French anthropologist Claude Lévi-Strauss. He has taken the way in which a linguist analyzes data as a model and applied it to the analysis of culture. Like the sounds in a language, which by themselves have no meaning but are part of a larger structure that conveys meaning, the elements of a culture must be seen in their relationship to one another as they form a structure. Meanings are conveyed through such structures. The structural anthropologist looks for the underlying structure of a culture, which corresponds to the grammar of a language in the linguist's analysis. It was Boas who first pointed out that the grammar of a language was not part of the consciousness of the speaker and, in a similar fashion, that culture also had an underlying structure and operated like language. Lévi-Strauss saw Boas as his intellectual ancestor. Structuralists analyzed cognitive systems, kinship structure, art, mythology, ritual, and ceremony, among other things. Structural anthropologists were comparative in that they looked for similarities in underlying structures in different cultures. Thus this approach may group together societies that seem to be very different at first glance. Poststructuralists and postmodernists have objected to Lévi-Straussian structuralism because its models are too abstract and deal with cultural material in an ahistorical fashion.

Historical Anthropology

Although postmodernists and poststructuralists reject the idea of theory altogether, other anthropologists today work with a variety of theoretical perspectives. Contemporary approaches are much less unified and do not share a single set of assumptions as did the theoretical points of view we have discussed up to this point. Many contemporary anthropologists work within a historical framework. Ethnohistorians, crossing subdisciplinary boundaries, use archaeological, archival, and oral history materials to trace the history of cultures where people left no written records of their own. A number of scholars have examined how European economic and political expansion during the colonial period affected small-scale societies, focusing on the colonial discourse that developed between colonizers and colonized. Bennetta Jules-Rosette, for example, has done a study of three generations of African writers living in France, which focuses on the relationship between African writing and French intellectual discourse and culture (1998).

In contrast, Eric Wolf was concerned with the impact on Europe during the colonial period of the "people without history" (Wolf, 1982). He was interested in how non-European populations reacted to the introduction of capitalism and how, in turn, these reactions determined the direction of capitalism in Europe. Leland Donald uses colonial eyewitness observations as well as subsequent ethnographic sources to detail how slavery functioned within the economic, social, and belief systems of Northwest Coast societies and how it rapidly changed in the period from 1780 to 1880, when slavery ended (Donald, 1997).

Marshall Sahlins advocates a theoretical approach that combines history and structuralism. Sahlins points out that when Captain Cook landed on Hawaii, the Hawaiians, perceiving him in terms of their own cultural categories, saw him as the god Lono. When the Hawaiians killed Captain Cook, as each year they ritually killed the god Lono, this not only affected subsequent events involving Hawaiian-European relations (i.e., history) but also resulted in changes in Hawaiian cultural rules (structure). In this theoretical framework, structure and history are seen as constantly interrelated (Sahlins, 1985). Obeysekere objected to Sahlins's point of view, accusing him of adopting an imperialist perspective in which Western white men are always seen as gods by the "natives" (1992).

Symbolic Anthropology

Over the past 20 years or more, symbolic anthropology, which is concerned with uncovering meaning, has become one of the dominant approaches in anthropology. This emphasis harks back to Boas's interest in meaning as well as to the centrality of meaning in the structuralism of Lévi-Strauss. Culture is seen as a system of symbols, and the task of the anthropologist is to decipher the meanings of the system. In the 1970s, anthropologists such as David Schneider and Clifford Geertz began to focus on the tangle of interrelated meanings that cultures encode. The task of the anthropologist then became one of translating the layers of meaning of a "thick description" into our concepts and our language. Culture is therefore viewed as a text, to be read and interpreted. This emphasis on meaning has been associated in anthropology with particularism and cultural relativism, both of which are basically anticomparative.

During the next two decades, most American anthropologists accepted many of the ideas associated with the symbolic approach. Meanwhile, Geertz and Schneider were modifying their positions. Geertz's approach has increasingly become akin to literary criticism. If anthropologists, who wrote ethnographies, were collecting texts, then anthropological analysis was the analysis of texts. In the mid-1980s, in *Works and Lives,* Geertz argued that understanding an anthropologist's ethnographic writings is like understanding a fictional body of work by Melville, or Mark Twain. The meaning of a text is found in the author's voice, and the anthropological material contained therein must be interpreted in that light. In contrast, Schneider viewed culture as a symbolic system, and each ethnography represented the symbolic system of a particular and uniquely different culture. There no longer was any room for a comparative approach in Schneider' s anthropology. As we shall see, postmodernism borrowed heavily from the later writings of both Geertz and Schneider.

An interesting example of the combination of the symbolic and the historical approaches is Raymond Bucko's *The Lakota Ritual of the Sweat Lodge: History and Contemporary Practice* (1998). He shows how symbolic meanings and usages in the contemporary sweat-house ritual draw upon memories and texts from an earlier time when economic and political conditions were different.

Postmodernism in Anthropology

Anthropology, along with the other human sciences, has recently been undergoing a reassessment, which has been labeled *postmodernism*. Anthropologists' study of the meanings of the culture of others and the analysis of how those cultures operated was deemed insufficient and inadequate to the task of translation and complete understanding. Up to the present, anthropology has been considered as belonging to both the humanities and the social sciences. In its stance as part of the humanities, anthropology emphasized cultural uniqueness and relativism. As a social science, anthropology emphasized generalization, analysis, and the comparative approach. Postmodernism in anthropology has found fault with generalization and a more scientific approach, arguing that anthropology should totally embrace humanism, striving to capture the uniqueness of each cultural situation, which postmodernists see as lost when one generalizes. Because anthropology depends on the interaction of one human being with others, they argue that a science of anthropology is impossible. The observation of human subjects and their behavior by an anthropologist from another culture is no longer viewed as the foundation upon which to build social science conclusions based upon the conceptual framework of anthropology. Instead, the ethnographer and his or her informants are to be seen as part of the same social time and space, with the ethnographer's task being that of an interpreter or translator. His or her understanding of the culture along with the understandings of the informants are to be presented in the ethnography for the reading public to make their own conclusions about the people and their way of life. The focus should be on the life of everyday people to demonstrate that they are not the passive instruments of elite domination but actors making decisions and choices within the structure of constraints, able, if they desire, to modify their patterns of relationships. The radical political agenda of postmodernism is sometimes more, sometimes less evident as its practitioners focus on how the global affects the local and vice versa.

Some have seen the product of the dialogue between informant and fieldworker as not sufficiently representative of the variety of points of view or ideas held by individuals in the culture. They have argued that segments of a society may have contested views regarding cultural meanings. They have advocated representing these different views by including the informants' ideas in their own words in the ethnography itself. In the book by Richard Price, *First Time: The Historical Vision of an Afro-American People,* his picture of the history of the Saramaka is presented alongside the versions of several elders in the culture (1983). In other instances, in order to pay more attention to the views of informants, anthropologists have presented their analyses to their informants for comment, as Steven Feld did to his Kaluli informants to see if they agreed with his conclusions regarding the meanings of sounds in their culture

(1987). Some postmodernists prefer that the informants' voices take center stage in telling their story, utilizing the life history approach, which has traditionally been part of anthropological methodology. This approach is in response to the feeling that in the past the voices of ethnographic subjects have been marginalized or displaced by the sole authoritative voice of the ethnographer. Still another approach to the matter of representation is the role of the native ethnographer, that is, the individual who is a member of the culture who has received training as an anthropologist. Such individuals are seen as having intuitive understanding of the culture and greater ability to empathize with and understand their culture than an anthropologist who is a member of another culture. However, there are those who argue that greater empathy comes at the expense of the perspective and understanding that an outsider can bring. Anthropologists studying their own culture cannot be objective, tend to justify behavior in an ethnocentric way, and often have their own political agendas.

When anthropology is seen as a science, observation plays an essential role. However, to postmodernists who emphasize the humanistic view of anthropology, observation plays a secondary role to dialogues with informants and the recording of the information informants present as an ethnographic text. In the ethnographic accounts that postmodernists applaud, analytic conceptual frameworks are played down or completely absent, since it is felt that in each society, which is considered a unique entity, the categories must be understood in their own terms and cannot be equated with categories in other societies, as is done in comparative cross-cultural research.

Postmodernists have forced anthropologists to rethink the nature of fieldwork. The emphasis they have put is upon knowing how the ethnographer felt as a person in the fieldwork situation, and how important it is to convey the experiential aspects of the field in the ethnography. Postmodernist anthropologists have considered the writing of ethnographic descriptions to be so central that one of them defines anthropology as "a discursive category, a type or group of types of writing that have important filiations to other modern cultural and academic fields" (Manganaro, 1990: 5). They are interested in learning what rhetorical devices are being used to convince the reader that the fieldworker was "there" and that his or her observations and conclusions are accurate representations of the lives of the "others" whom anthropologists have traditionally studied. When culture is seen as a text, as in Geertz's view, and ethnography becomes a type of writing, then anthropology moves much closer to literary theory. Anthropology becomes part of a new humanistic interdisciplinary approach, which also includes philosophy, history, art history, and architecture, which has come to be called cultural studies.

At the present time, many of anthropology's older assumptions have been called into question, and anthropologists have been forced to rethink the basic concepts and the purpose of the discipline. Not only are basic premises of the field being reconsidered, but postmodernist anthropologists have also made central the self-critical aspects of anthropology, in which readers of ethnographies are compelled to reflect on their own culture. In this respect, they are continuing Boas's earlier concern with racism in the modern world and Mead's discussion of Samoan adolescence in order to illuminate American adolescence. The postmodern emphasis on uniqueness has meant that the comparative aspect of anthropology, which pays attention to what cultures have in common as well as how they differ, has been left by the wayside. Further, in this vein, the legitimate anthropological focus on what can be observed, and sometimes quantified, has been played down. The postmodernist argument has been that even the physical world is not characterized by deterministic regularities— so why should we expect such regularities to characterize social behavior? However, this viewpoint ignores the fact that because of the constraints of culture, there is no absolute freedom of action or complete randomness in human behavior. People do behave in ways that demonstrate cultural regularities, and the concept of culture remains a powerful conceptual tool for organizing anthropological data. Despite the postmodern emphasis on plurality, fragmentation, and subjectivity, the comparative dimension is reemerging as relevant and important in anthropology.

———————

The journey to another place or another time, which we defined at the beginning of this chapter as the hallmark of anthropology, is recapitulated by each fledgling anthropologist as she or he embarks on fieldwork. Lévi-Strauss, in his personal memoir, *Tristes Tropiques* (1955), saw his own fieldwork in terms of just such a journey. His journey to the field took him from the Old World to the New World, from the cold North to the tropical South, to a world that contrasted in every respect with his own. His goal was to find a simple form of society, since he felt that to understand how societies work, it is best to study one that is elementary in its organization. As in all fieldwork situations, he was first struck by what appeared to be great cultural differences. However, in time, Lévi-Strauss, the sophisticated French student of philosophy, saw a common humanity behind the painted faces of the Nambikwara. He wrote, "I had been looking for a society reduced to its simplest expression. The society of the Nambikwara had been reduced to the point at which I found nothing but human beings" (Lévi-Strauss, 1961: 310). The pages that follow also represent a journey—a journey into the world of anthropology.

Chapter Two

The Anthropological Method

Historically, the methodology used by nineteenth-century anthropologists, focusing on the evolution of culture, involved examining the ethnographic information collected by missionaries, colonial officials, and others who visited or lived for a time in the parts of the world where societies of interest to anthropologists were located. However, as noted in the previous chapter, it was the fieldwork and participant observation pioneered by Franz Boas and Bronislaw Malinowski that became the defining ethnographic methodology for anthropology after the turn of the century.

Participant Observation

How does one gain perspective on another society? The answer for the anthropologist has always been to step outside the web of his or her own cultural world to closely examine another, often vastly different, way of life. This is what anthropologists do when they carry out fieldwork. Over the years, we have separately carried out fieldwork, Rosman with the Kanuri in northern Nigeria and Rubel with a Kalmyk Mongol emigré community in New Jersey, and we have jointly carried out fieldwork in Iran, Afghanistan, and Papua New Guinea. The heart of fieldwork is *participant observation*—living with other people, learning their language, and coming to understand their behavior and the ideas that are important to them. It usually includes living in their kind of house, be it the black goat-hair tent that we lived in when we did fieldwork in Afghanistan or the mud-brick house used by Rosman in the Nigerian town of Geidam; donning their dress on ceremonial occasions (see Rosman in Kanuri garb in the illustration on page 22); and eating their cuisine—nan, or flat bread, in Iran, or the roast pig and taro at a New Ireland

A participant in another culture often will don its clothing while doing fieldwork. This is Abraham Rosman doing research among the Kanuri.

funerary celebration. Fieldworkers celebrate the birth rites of the people with whom they live and mourn with them at funerals.

The anthropologist, while learning the language, is also learning the culture of the people. When first immersed in a different culture, the fieldworker experiences *culture shock,* which is similar to the experience of plunging into an ice-cold bath, on recognizing that his or her own culture is not "natural." As the anthropologist learns the culture, he or she is in the position of a child in that new culture. American anthropologists, who have learned as children to eat with knives, forks, and spoons, may need to learn to eat with their fingers from a common bowl, as Rosman did during fieldwork with the Kanuri. When, because of inexperience, bits of food fell from his hands and soiled his clothing, people discreetly turned away so that their laughter would not embarrass him. It was the fate of Rubel to eat boiled lamb (the Mongolian dish served on festive occasions) and horse meat steaks in New Jersey. In attempting to present himself or herself in the best possible light to gain rapport and acceptance, the fieldworker engages in what has been called impression management. She or he consciously constructs the persona of someone friendly, helpful, interested, and eager to learn about the culture, suppressing his or her feelings and opinions if they appear to jeopardize developing relationships.

However, participant observation involves an inherent contradiction. A participant operates inside a culture, while an observer is like a stranger, looking in from outside. As one learns how to participate as a member of a culture, one becomes engaged in that culture and identifies with it. On the other hand, an observer is expected to remain detached and to report objectively what he or she sees and hears. Because it involves this basic paradox, participant observation is difficult to carry out.

Participation in another culture means learning how to view things from the natives' point of view. When anthropologists do fieldwork, they bring along their own cultural categories, or ways of seeing things, which need to be overcome. This necessitates that fieldworkers be consciously aware of those cultural categories and make the effort not to order their perceptions by them.

In addition to observations, anthropologists gain information by interviewing individuals in the culture, who are referred to as informants. In the interaction between informant and anthropologist, the informant increasingly learns what her or his fieldworker-colleague is interested in finding out and also gains a certain amount of knowledge about anthropology. In the process, informants begin to see things about their own culture in a different way. In trying to explain their culture to the questioning anthropologist, informants start to understand it in a way they did not before. They may become conscious of cultural rules in their own society that they had not previously recognized.

The personal relationship between anthropologist and informant is a complex one. Individuals who become intimate friends of as well as mentors to the anthropologist are referred to as key informants. The key informant for Rosman while he was doing fieldwork among the Kanuri was the District Head, a titled aristocrat (pictured in the illustration on page 22) much older than the fledgling anthropologist, whom he adopted. This relationship was crucial since many people trusted and were willing to talk to the anthropologist as a result of it. However, because of this connection, other sources of information were closed because they were in opposition to, or belonged to another faction of the community. Key informants are often individuals who straddle two cultures. They may have mixed parentage. Stoller has suggested that the ethnographer should be like the West African *griot*, who narrates the history, myths, tales, and stories of his people so that they can cope with the present. Like the griot, the ethnographer should spend long periods of time apprenticed to elders, mastering knowledge in order to respectfully and poetically evoke the tales of a people in his or her ethnography (Stoller, 1994: 354).

Fieldwork involves reciprocity on the part of the anthropologist. However, the nature of what the anthropologist returns to his or her informants is highly varied. In rural as well as urban areas, the anthropologist with a vehicle often reciprocates by becoming chauffeur for the entire community, as Rubel did for the Kalmyk Mongols with whom she worked in New Jersey. Frequently, anthropologists identify with the people among whom they have lived and worked. They become partisans and take on the causes of the community as advocates in the media or become expert witnesses for them in the courts. When legal conflicts between the Hopi and the Navajo

Author Paula Rubel recording details of a ceremony in New Ireland.

arose concerning land ownership, anthropologists who had done research with the Navajo advocated their side of the case, while those who had worked with the Hopi took their part. Anthropologists have shared tobacco as still another way of reciprocating. It is curious that the sharing of tobacco seems to occur in cultures all over the world. In Papua New Guinea we always presented tobacco to people with whom we talked.

Fieldwork involves the anthropologist in a moral dilemma. It could be said that anthropologists use informants for their own ends, since the anthropologists return to their own societies with the information gathered. The publication of this information, in a dissertation or book, helps the career of the anthropologist, but in what way does it help the people whose way of life has been recorded? As indicated above, the anthropologist tries in a variety of ways to make some return for what has been given. Often, research done by anthropologists in the past may be of use to the subjects of that research today. For example, the Kwakiutl as well as other Native American peoples have found that ethnographies written at the turn of the century, like those of Boas, and historical studies of Native American tradition are of value as written records of traditions, the knowledge of which by this time may have been lost. Such information has also proved important for Native Americans in pursuing claims regarding fishing rights and land rights. In a more general way, the product of the anthropologist's work makes a contribution to the wider understanding of human behavior.

In the field, anthropologists observe and record peoples' actions and with the help of informants seek to understand the meanings of those actions. This is illustrated in the photograph of Rubel collecting information from informants on New Ireland (see page 24). These observations by anthropologists are a very important component of fieldwork, as are discussions with informants. But neither alone is sufficient. When informants attempt to explain their culture to anthropologists, the informants are objectifying their own cultural experiences. In order to understand the informants' experiences and thereby grasp their point of view, anthropologists, as noted above, strive to go beyond their *own* cultural categories. In their interactions, informants and anthropologists are, in a sense, operating in an area between their two cultures. The data are thus produced through the mutual efforts of anthropologist and informant. This process is repeated with other informants, and a pattern begins to emerge. The data are checked against the anthropologists' own observations, as well as with other informants with whom contacts are more limited.

Ultimately, the problem for the anthropologist is to translate the cultural categories of the society being studied into the language of anthropology, that is, the conceptual framework to be set forth in *The Tapestry of Culture*. The basic assumption is that cultures have characteristics in common, above and beyond those aspects which are unique, and that this can be revealed through comparative research using anthropological concepts. The final product of fieldwork is an ethnography, which embodies the results of fieldwork and analysis.

In the past, anthropological fieldworkers investigated societies that were small both in scale and in population size, where all the spheres of human activity could be explored by a single investigator. They often selected small islands for study, where the unit of analysis was bounded in a most distinct manner. Other anthropologists went off to study societies in Africa and elsewhere, selecting a village or a camp on which to concentrate and from which they generalized about the culture. This unit, sometimes referred to as a *community*, had a name, and the people within recognized themselves as members. The community was bounded, in the sense that its members concentrated their interactions within it, and it had an internal social structure that could be discerned. The interaction of the community with other communities was always of concern to the anthropologist. Today, the community remains the starting point for field research.

From Small-Scale to Complex Societies

In the study of small-scale societies, the community had been taken to represent the culture as a whole. When anthropologists began to study complex societies in the 1930s, it was clear that a single community could not be considered representative of, for example, India, France, or Japan. Such complex societies could not be encompassed in their totality at the level of detail at which the anthropologist worked. As a result of regional, class, occupational, religious, and ethnic differences, complex societies are very heterogeneous and culturally diverse. Such diverse groups have subcultures of their own that may become units of analysis for the anthropologist, who must keep in mind that what is happening locally must always be related to what is happening on a broader national, international, or even global level. Anthropologists working in complex societies may also focus on particular problems, such as rural-urban migration, or the effects of the closing of a mine or factory in a company town. The unit of analysis here is dictated by the problem. It may be a farming community, a labor union, a corporation, or a social movement. In the United States, for example, an anthropologist might focus on some aspects of American culture—what we have in common—or choose to examine cultural aspects or particular problems among the different racial and ethnic populations that are the subgroupings of our society.

Earlier, anthropologists tended to work in areas where their nations had established colonial empires. American anthropologists worked with American Indians, and British and French anthropologists worked in British and French colonies. Some of the entities that anthropologists in the past assumed were indigenous groupings were, in reality, colonial constructs. After contact with Europeans, these small-scale societies were increasingly brought under the jurisdiction of larger political entities, typically European colonial empires. Colonial administrations imposed a structure consisting of tribes and districts in order to govern more easily. At first, anthropologists paid little attention to the nature of the articulation of these small-scale societies to the colonial empire. Today they are interested in the process of how these societies were incorporated into the newly formed nation-states of which they are now a part. Often they constitute ethnic groups in conflict with one another and with the nation-state. Modernization and industrialization have made small-scale societies part of a world system, and anthropologists now investigate how they have responded to those changes.

In recent years, postmodernist anthropologists have begun to rethink exactly how fieldworkers obtain their data and the way ethnographic texts are produced. They talk about making visible the discovery practices and procedures, that is, making explicit the actual fieldwork experience, which earlier had not been part of the published ethnography. This involves describing the way in which the highly personal experience of fieldwork is reconciled with fieldwork as a method of data collection with specific procedures. As fieldwork procedures were made more explicit, postmodernists began to feel that scientific goals could not be achieved. However, being explicit about one's procedures is also part of the process of being scientific. At first, the concern was with being more reflexive, that is, informing the readers of the ethnography about the experiential aspects of the fieldwork, not just the anthropological conclusions of the field research. Then the rhetorical devices used by anthropologists in the writing of ethnographies became the subject of concern, with the emphasis on how ethnographers convinced their readers that they were actually "there" in the field and that their ethnographic reports were accurate and truthful. More recently, some postmodern anthropologists have advocated the production of confessional ethnography. In this new type of ethnography, the fieldworker is at the center of the stage and the focus is on how he or she came to know a particular social world, not on that world itself—that is, the way of life of the people being studied. These new ideas about the ethnographic enterprise have had an impact on the field, if only to make anthropologists more explicit about what they are doing when they do fieldwork and how the various aspects of the fieldwork and other types of research related to the project at hand are translated into conclusions that accurately reflect the social world that the anthropologist has chosen as a subject of research.

It is typically the case that anthropologists come from powerful industrialized nations to conduct research in Third World countries, and the initial relationship in the field may be perceived in terms of dominance and subordination, or power differentials, between anthropologists and informants. Often, anthropologist and informant use one another. The anthropologist may be at the mercy of the informant's desires, sometimes being used to further the political ambitions of the informant. Informants may see the anthropologist as exploiting them in that he or she is "taking away" their myths, rituals, and traditions and erroneously representing and portraying them as violent or helpless victims to the outside world. All these factors, which are involved in the interaction, influence the nature of the information that is obtained and must be taken into account when the data are being analyzed.

In addition to fieldwork, anthropologists utilize other techniques to collect data, such as historical and archival information, as well as data from archaeological and linguistic investigations and census materials. Research on a culture's past, the ethnohistorical approach referred to in Chapter 1, has become particularly significant as anthropology has moved to a processual model. As anthropologists study new kinds of problems and the unit of analysis is no longer necessarily a community, many supplement the central methodology of anthropology—participant observation—with a variety of additional techniques, such as questionnaires and statistical analyses. The anthropologist then translates these data into the language of anthropological concepts.

The Beginnings of Fieldwork

Earlier, we described the way in which anthropological fieldwork had been developed in the early twentieth century as a reaction to the armchair anthropology of nineteenth-century anthropologists. In 1883 to 1884, Boas carried out fieldwork among the Eskimos of Baffinland in Labrador. Before he embarked on his voyage to Canada, he familiarized himself with all the literature on the area, including accounts of voyages of discovery, and missionary accounts of Eskimo ways of life and the cultural traditions in the area. He also acquired some knowledge of the Eskimo language from missionaries' word books and grammars. While in Baffinland, he traveled by dogsled from village to village, living with the Eskimos in their igloos, or snow houses. He focused his attention on the geography of the region and the way in which the Baffin Islanders exploited it economically, and migrated over the terrain. He worked extensively on the language, collecting texts of Eskimo myths, tales, and sayings. Living with and interacting with the people and learning the language become the hallmarks of anthropological fieldwork.

Within a few years, Boas shifted his area of interest to the peoples of the Northwest Coast of Canada. After doing a survey of the various indigenous peoples of the area under the auspices of the British Association for the Advancement of Science, he began to concentrate his research on the Kwakiutl. They were to occupy much of his attention for the rest of his life. Over the decades, Boas accumulated what has been described as the "five-foot shelf" of ethnographic data on the Kwakiutl. In addition to short visits, Boas did three months of participant observation during the Kwakiutl Winter Ceremonial of 1894 to 1895. The rest of this enormous bulk of ethnographic material was collected by means of informant interviews or by George Hunt, whom Boas trained to be an ethnographic field researcher and to record texts in phonetic transcription. Though Hunt's mother was Tlingit and his father was Scottish, he grew up at Fort Rupert, the home of a number of Kwakiutl tribes, and was a native speaker of Kwakw'ala, the language of the Kwakiutl. Most of the thousands of pages of Kwakw'ala text, which Boas published in his 1910 volume of texts, were collected and composed by Hunt. As Berman notes, "Hunt was not simply an informant, not simply Boas' guide and interpreter in the field. Although he might not have perceived of his activities in such a light, he was a fieldworker in his own right, an ethnographer and author" (Berman, 1991: 15–16). Hunt was an individual who straddled several cultures, Scottish, Tlingit, and Kwakiutl, the culture of the area where he grew up and into which he married. His relationship with Boas also illustrates the way in which, as we described above, an informant becomes more and more familiar with what anthropologists do and the kinds of data they collect, as the native point of view is conveyed.

Boas described how the Kwakiutl, a Native American society, lived along the coast of British Columbia, subsisting on fishing, hunting land and sea mammals, and collecting wild plants and berries. They did not practice any form of agriculture. They were famous for their expert carving of totem poles and many other items of wood. Because the environment was rich, they were semisedentary and shifted from winter to summer villages. They built large plank houses in which many people who were kin to one another dwelled. A number of such houses were joined through kinship into a larger family-type grouping, which the Kwakiutl called a *numaym*. The Kwakiutl had chiefs and an elaborate system of ranking in which each person had a different rank position. One of their most distinctive ceremonies was the *potlatch,* at which the host distributed large amounts of property to individuals of other groups. By doing this, the host acquired prestige and enhanced his rank. Among the Kwakiutl, various rites of passage, ceremonies which marked significant points in the life cycle, were the occasions for a donor to hold a potlatch. The marriage of a child was one of the most important occasions.

■ A Kwakiutl Marriage*

The following description of a Kwakiutl marriage rite is an example of an ethnographic account. It was based on a combination of informants' accounts collected by Boas and George Hunt as well as some participant observation by Hunt. These sources were organized into a description of the marriage rite by Boas, which was included in a manuscript that remained unpublished until after his death. This description is of marriage rites in the nineteenth century, on the occasion of the marriage of the children of chiefs. It is a generalized description combined with accounts of specific events. To the reader, this may appear to be more a description of several elaborate exchanges of property rather than a description of a marriage.

There were three stages to a Kwakiutl marriage. The first stage was the initiation of negotiations and agreement on the size of the bridewealth payment to be made by the family of the groom to the family of the bride. The second stage was the formal wooing and the transfer of the bridewealth payment from the groom's family to the bride's family at a potlatch. The third stage constituted a repurchase of the bride by her family when goods, names, and privileges went from the family of the bride to that of the groom, also at a potlatch. When children of important chiefs married, invariably two different Kwakiutl tribes were involved. In such a marriage, the tribe of the groom had to come to the village of the bride to symbolically seize or capture her to take her to their village. The bride was "moved" from her village to the village of the groom through the magical power that the chiefs of the groom's group had obtained from their ancestors and through the payment of property by the groom's side. Since the major events of a marriage were accompanied by the distribution of large amounts of property and were witnessed by many people from many tribes, they constituted Kwakiutl potlatches. All the property distributed was eventually reciprocated, and payment was made for the services performed by various chiefs. The giving away of property enhanced the prestige of the donor. The advance in social rank that derived from the potlatch aspects of a marriage often entirely overshadowed the marriage's primary purpose—the establishment of a family.

The parents or those responsible for the young people arranged the marriage, sometimes without even the knowledge of the young couple. The first messengers

*This section is based on *Kwakiutl Ethnography* by Franz Boas, edited by Helen Codere, adapted by permission of The University of Chicago Press.

The groom's party arrives by canoe at an early stage of a Kwakiutl marriage. A crest belonging to the groom's numaym *decorates the front of the canoe. Edward L. Curtis took this photograph before 1914.*

were formally sent by the groom's side to the bride's side. They delivered speeches to her father requesting the bride in marriage, and he rewarded them with a pair of blankets. When they returned to the groom, he too rewarded them with a pair of blankets. Then a second group of messengers was sent, this time, chiefs, to deliver messages to the bride's father concerning the marriage proposal. He gave them each two pairs of blankets in return for the messages. That night, the groom went to eat in the bride's house, sitting next to her. The bride's father talked to the groom about the bride's father's expectation of receiving 500 blankets. The groom's father assembled the 500 blankets, and they were piled in front of the door of the bride's father's house. The groom's father, accompanied by several chiefs, then went to the house of the bride. To one chief he said, "It is your office given to you according to the earliest myths to speak about the blankets given away." As the formal Speaker, this chief received two blankets for his service from the father of the groom. The blankets were officially counted by the counter from the groom's side and then were handed over to the bride's father by still another officeholder. On receiving the blankets, the father of the bride expressed his thanks.

Several months later, a second ceremony was held at which 550 additional blankets were handed over, this time to "move" the bride. The men of the groom's *numaym* and those of other *numaym* blackened their faces and dressed like war-

A Kwakiutl wedding party stands before the bride's house. The house posts are carved with the crests of her numaym.

riors as they went to the house of the bride with the final payment of blankets, which would move her. Often, the bride's doorway was protected by fire against the "invading warriors" of the groom. They might have had to run a gauntlet of flaming torches held by men of the bride's side or, as in another account by Boas, go through a ring of burning cedar bark soaked in oil. After the groom's men proved they were not afraid of fire and the fire burned down, the bride's father "called forth the Devourer of Tribes, who had devoured all those who had tried to woo his daughter. It was a large mask of a sea bear attached to a bear skin (worn by a man). Seven skulls and a number of long bones were hidden under the bear skin. As soon as the man wearing this masked dress came forth, the bride's father poked its stomach with a pole and it vomited skulls and bones."

Then the chiefs from the groom's side make their traditional wedding speeches. In these speeches, the chiefs called upon their supernatural powers, which came from ancient mythological times down through their family lines. These powers were said to be used to "move the bride." For example, Made-to-Be-Tied, chief of the Kwa'wadilikala *numaym,* on being called upon, said, "In the beginning of myth times I was the great supernatural Kwa'wadilikala, the only owner of the great wolf ceremonial that came down to me from heaven. Now I will go and lift the princess."

The Speaker for the chief distributes blankets at a Kwakiutl wedding potlatch held in 1894.

After going out, he returned to the doorway, wearing the great wolf mask of Walking Body, the chief of the wolves. For this he received five blankets from the official Speaker representing the groom's side. At a really great wedding, many chiefs who bore illustrious names made speeches, detailing how their privileges descended to them from ancient times. These privileges included a particular name, the animal designs worn on clothing or in the shape of masks, the songs they sang, and the dances they were privileged to perform. Each received a payment of blankets for, as the Kwakiutl say, "the weight of his breath," referring to the speech that was delivered at the wedding. Their combined breath acted as a weight upon an imaginary scale used to move the bride. The metaphor operated such that the greater the names of the bride, the more speeches, or "breath," were needed to move her to the groom.

After the last of the chiefs had spoken, the ceremony of giving out the blankets brought by the groom's side for the bride's side took place. Blankets were counted and ceremonially brought into the bride's house. Then the bride's side piled up 200 blankets with the bride sitting alongside them. A chief from the bride's side said, "Come to your wife and take her into your house with these two hundred blankets as her mat." The groom's side sang the traditional song of thanks while the bride walked between two officials to the groom's side. Then the new wife was led to the seat she was to occupy, and the 200 blankets were distributed to the guests from other Kwakiutl tribes on the groom's side, but not to members of the groom's own tribe. In the evening, all the distinguished young men of the Kwakiutl tribes assembled to sing love songs and led the bride and groom back to his father's house. The bride's father brought 50 blankets to exchange for food for the young men in order to thank them for bringing the groom. The groom sat alongside his new wife, and this part of the marriage ceremony came to an end.

Some time later, usually after a child was born to the couple, the wife's side began preparations to make a large return payment of goods to the husband's side, a transfer of property that constituted what Boas refers to as the repurchase of the wife by her own *numaym*. The Kwakiutl term for this payment means payment of the marriage debt. Since the wife's group was the recipient of the marriage potlatch given by the groom's group, it was in debt until a return in kind was made. Repurchase at another potlatch constituted this return. The return did not consist of blankets, but of objects known in Kwakiutl as "trifles, bad things." As we shall see from the list of items included, trifles and bad things meant just the opposite. What was returned was far in excess of what the wife's father received. In one of Boas's examples of a repurchase, the items included were 120 box covers set with sea otter teeth, 100 abalone shells, copper bracelets, horn bracelets covered with dentalia shells, miniature coppers, 1000 strings of dentalia one fathom long, 200 dressed deerskins, 500 cedar bark blankets, 200 mats, an equal number of wooden boxes, 2 neck rings of twisted copper, and hammered copper objects of great value, "as mast of the marriage debt canoe." A large amount of food was also provided, as well as the horn and wooden spoons with which to eat it. Names and privileges were also given to the son-in-law as part of the repurchase payment.

When everything was ready, the wife's father called together his *numaym* to announce that he was going to hold a potlatch to repay the marriage debt. The song leader of the *numaym* was asked to write a new song to commemorate the occasion, which he did. The song described the privileges and the copper that were to be given to the groom. The next morning father-in-law and son-in-law each invited their respective *numayms* to attend. After breakfast, the men of the father-in-law's *numaym* carried the goods to the son-in-law's house. There they arranged the box covers in a square or rectangle, which was called the catamaran because it was supposed to represent the boat upon which the father-in-law came to repay the debt. All the goods were piled on top, and the *numaym* of the father-in-law "went on board," where they then sang the song of repayment of the marriage debt. In keeping with the symbolism of warfare, the younger brother of the son-in-law, his face blackened as a warrior, rushed out and split one of the box covers with an ax, thereby "sinking the catamaran." The box containing the symbols of the privileges to be given to the son-in-law was carried out from the father-in-law's house, and the wife who was being repurchased emerged from the house bearing the copper that was to be transferred. The young wife and her father both danced to the accompaniment of the new marriage repayment song. The father-in-law's Speaker presented the box of privileges to the son-in-law and then presented the copper. The Speaker of the husband's *numaym* expressed his thanks. Then the Speaker of the father-in-law arose and bestowed names that traditionally belonged to the wife's family upon the husband and his two sisters. These names constituted the final part of the marriage repayment, all the other items having already been transferred. The husband's *numaym* sang songs of gratitude, and this ended the ceremony of marriage repurchase.

Marriage for the Kwakiutl was clearly not a single event, but a series of events that extended for years, since the repurchase of a wife was normally not held until after the birth of a child. When the wife had been repurchased by her father and her own *numaym,* she was really free to return to her father unless her husband purchased her for the second time. This was followed by a second repurchase by her own group. These exchanges of property via potlatches could take place up to four times, after which the wife's rank was so high that she could "stay for nothing." Since the giver of the potlatch fed the great numbers of guests who came to witness these events and thereby enhanced his prestige with each potlatch, the families of both groom and bride respectively increased their standing with each potlatch and its transfer of goods.

The ritual of marriage among the Kwakiutl embodies many of the central ideas in Kwakiutl culture. The Kwakiutl emphasis on rank was reiterated again and again throughout the course of the marriage potlatch. The high rank of the bride demanded that there be large payments for her. At the same time, such payments enhanced the rank of the giver, the groom. The importance of making a return for what one has received was reflected in the repurchase payment made by the bride's side. Seating of guests at the potlatch and the order in which they received gifts revealed their ranking with respect to one another. The political power and legitimacy of sponsoring chiefs was also demonstrated in the potlatch. The claim to rightfully own a title or name was made by a chief at a potlatch when he recited the line of ancestors through whom the title was passed on until it reached him. Lastly, the marriage ceremony was symbolically conceptualized as a form of warfare, in which warriors demonstrated their bravery in capturing the bride and the return purchase was conveyed by a symbolic war canoe.

In Boas's time, the aim of the anthropologist was to record as much of the traditional culture as possible before it disappeared. As a consequence, his description did not take account of the fact that the Kwakiutl at that time were part of the larger Canadian economic and political systems. The blankets they were distributing were blankets sold by the Hudson Bay Company. The enormous amount of material goods involved were obtained with money earned from working locally in canneries and from employment in Victoria, British Columbia, and elsewhere.

■ An American Marriage

When anthropologists began to do fieldwork in complex Western societies in the 1930s, of necessity their fieldwork methods and the nature of their analyses and conclusions changed. This development can be illustrated by an ethnographic example from our own society. As noted in the previous chapter, complex societies such as our own are composed of different social classes and subgroups with differing perspectives. American weddings, for example, are differentiated according to religion, ethnic background, occupation, and social class. The factor of personal preference, absent in the earlier Kwakiutl wedding rituals, plays an important role in the wide range of American weddings that occur each year. Each Sunday, the *New York Times* has a column describing innovative weddings, which illustrates their wide diversity. Individuals marry while skydiving, on water skis, and in other uncommon settings. Weddings are conducted by male and female rabbis, priests, and ministers, Wiccan ritualists, swamis, and so on.

Kwakiutl marriage rituals had kinship, economic, religious, political, aesthetic, and performative dimensions, a characteristic that led Marcel Mauss, the French anthropologist of the early twentieth century, to refer to such rituals as "total social phenomena" (1925). In contrast, in complex societies, in addition to the variegated nature of social groupings, there are complex political economies and institutional specialization. As a consequence, when one examines weddings in American, one finds that there is a wedding industry, with wedding planners and individuals who specialize in providing distinctive commodities and specialized services. An American wedding is less than what Mauss referred to as a total social phenomenon. However, just as the Kwakiutl wedding informed us about Kwakiutl culture, an analysis of an American wedding provides information about the particular American subculture of the individuals who are marrying.

How does one go about doing an anthropological investigation of the pattern of weddings conducted by members of a particular American subculture or class? One could do participant observation at several weddings. This would include observing and recording information about all the preparations of the families of the individuals marrying, as well as interviewing all the various participants to determine the economics of the wedding and to obtain background information on the families for each wedding. What were the considerations that led to the decisions about the date of the wedding, the degree of its elaboration, the kind of wedding dress the bride would wear—her mother's or other relative's, or one purchased in a store specializing in such dresses—and the responsibility for payment of the various expenses of the wedding? One would try to participate in as many events as possible leading up to and including the marriage ceremony. Accurate information on the expenditures for each category as well as the total cost of the wedding might be difficult to obtain because this information is considered private.

Books on etiquette, such as *Good Housekeeping's Book of Today's Etiquette,* provide guidelines on how to conduct an American wedding. They can be considered statements of the ideal pattern or set of guidelines. We have chosen to describe the wedding of two well-known celebrities in American society to parallel the Kwakiutl marriage of the children of high-ranking chiefs. We will describe the wedding of Maria Shriver and Arnold Schwarzenegger, which was held on April 26, 1986. Since the authors did not attend this wedding, the following description is not based on participant observation. Instead, it is based upon information provided in *Time* magazine, the *New York Times,* and the *Cape Cod Times.*

Just as the daughter of a Kwakiutl chief belongs to the highest ranks of her society, Maria Shriver, a member of the Kennedy clan, belongs to the moneyed American elite. Her mother, Eunice, is a sister of the late president John F. Kennedy. Her father, Sargent Shriver, was the first director of the Peace Corps, a former ambassador to France, and the Democratic nominee for vice president in 1972. The bride is a television celebrity, who, at the time of her marriage, was co-anchor of the *CBS Morning News*. The Austrian-born Schwarzenegger, originally a bodybuilder and now a film superstar, is the son of a local Austrian police chief, now deceased. The two first met eight years earlier, a year after her graduation from Georgetown University, at a tennis tournament sponsored by the Kennedy family and named for Maria's late uncle, Robert F. Kennedy. At that time she was working for a small television station. She interrupted her own career to work on her Uncle Ted's presidential bid in 1980. In 1981, breaking with the East Coast family tradition, she moved to Los Angeles to continue her career on her own and to be near her boyfriend, Arnold. She worked as a magazine reporter for two years and then returned to television as a reporter for CBS. Schwarzenegger, who has a degree in business and marketing from the University of Wisconsin, became famous as a bodybuilder. He subsequently became a movie star after starring in the movie *Pumping Iron*.

Arnold proposed to Maria during a trip to Austria in August 1985, and they then purchased a $3 million house in Pacific Palisades. After their decision to marry, Maria was offered the anchor position at *CBS Morning News,* which required her to move to New York and be apart from her future husband. The couple did not marry until she was 30 and he was 38, eight years after they first met. This may have been due to the demands of their two careers. Career women now tend to marry when they are in their thirties, though this was not the case in American society at an earlier time.

The wedding was held at the summer residence of the Kennedys in Hyannis, Massachusetts. The Roman Catholic wedding mass, performed by the Reverend John Baptist Riordan, was held at St. Francis Xavier Roman Catholic Church, the Kennedy family's parish church in Hyannis. Since the couple wanted their wedding to be a "private" affair, details of the wedding were kept from the media, except for information provided by a publicist hired to handle wedding press coverage. Kennedy influence was used to maintain tight security and keep gossip columnists and journalists away from the wedding party. Provincetown-Boston Airline, which flies to Hyannis, was "persuaded" to lock up its computer a day before the wedding so that the guest list would not be revealed. The bride, ever career-oriented, told her viewers she would be off for several days, without mentioning her forthcoming wedding, and the groom arrived the day before the wedding from Puerta Vallarta, where he had been filming a new movie, *Predator,* the film that subsequently launched him as a superstar.

The bride wore a white muslin, silk, and lace gown with an 11-foot train. The gown was designed by Christian Dior, who had designed the wedding dress of the bride's mother in 1953. The groom wore a classic gray cutaway coat, pleated white shirt, gray vest, and gray-striped ascot. A fellow bodybuilder, Franco Columbu, served as his best man. The 13 ushers included the bride's four brothers, the bridegroom's cousin and nephew, and bodybuilder friends of the groom. The maid of honor was the bride's cousin Caroline Bouvier Kennedy, daughter of the late President Kennedy. Among the bridesmaids were several other Kennedy cousins. Some 60 women, guests and members of the bridal party, had their hair coiffed at the local beauty salon on the morning of the wedding, but the bride's hair was done by her own hairdresser from Los Angeles. Besides members of the Kennedy family, the more than 450 guests included television celebrities Diane Sawyer, Tom Brokaw, and Barbara Walters; advice columnist Abigail Van Buren; pop artist Andy Warhol (wearing a black leather jacket over a black tuxedo, and black Reebok sneakers); and singer/actress Grace Jones. Proclaiming the most recent fashions, female guests wore dresses sporting geometric designs from the art deco period and from pop art. Since reporters were barred from the church itself, a viewing stand was erected across the street for them.

The bride and her father walked up the aisle to the familiar wedding march, Wagner's "Bridal March" from the opera *Lohengrin* ("Here comes the bride . . ."). The details of the religious ceremony had been planned by the bride and groom themselves. The couple exchanged traditional Roman Catholic vows, which had been rewritten to remove sexist language, replacing "man and wife" with "husband and wife." Short selections from the New Testament were then read by Senator Ted Kennedy and by a friend of Schwarzenegger. Intercessions written by the wedding couple and read by the bride's parents and brother called for an end to terrorism and war, proclaimed the bride and groom as a model couple, honored deceased Kennedys, and discussed the meaning of Passover. These topics were a reflection of themes important in America at the time. Discussing the meaning of Passover, which was taking place that month, demonstrated the ecumenical feelings of the bride and groom. Oprah Winfrey, the television host, then read Elizabeth Barrett Browning's poem "How Do I Love Thee?"—a choice of the bride. After a series of musical selections, the ceremony concluded with the bridal couple's walking together down the aisle to Rodgers and Hammerstein's "Bridal March" from *The Sound of Music.*

After the ceremony, limousines and buses took the guests to the Kennedy compound for the reception. All air traffic within a 2-mile radius of the compound was prohibited from cruising below 2000 feet for the entire day. The reception was held in two huge white tents, with heaters to keep out the chill winds. Fruit trees in pink and white blossoms decorated the tents. The guests danced to music played by Peter Duchin's band, which often plays at society occasions. An elaborate lunch (including cold lobster in the shell and chicken breast with champagne sauce) was concluded with the cutting of an eight-tier, 425-pound wedding cake, topped by traditional figures of a bride and groom, baked by the Shriver family chef and modeled after Maria Shriver's parents' wedding cake.

The couple took a brief honeymoon before returning to work, he to his filming in Puerta Vallarta, she to her anchor position at CBS in New York.

The above account is a description of a single wedding taken from the published sources, not based on participant observation and fieldwork. Many things occurred that were not reported by the press. When the families of the bride and groom are strangers to one another, there is usually a formal meeting of the two sets of parents before the wedding. There is no information on whether or how the Shrivers met Mrs. Schwarzenegger. Often, the bride receives an engagement ring, and an engagement party is held. Wedding gifts may be publicly displayed at the bride's home. According to *Good Housekeeping's Book of Today's Etiquette,* "the expenses of the wedding are divided in a time-honored way." The bride's family pays for the following: invitations; reception cards and announcements; rental of the place where the ceremony is to be held; fee for the organist, choir, and sexton; transportation of the bridal party from house to church or temple and from there to the reception; bridesmaids' bouquets; the bride's gifts to the bridesmaids; the bride's wedding dress and trousseau; and all the expenses of the reception. The groom pays for the engagement and wedding rings, marriage license, contribution to the clergyman, flowers for the bride's mother and groom's mother, and the bachelor dinner. No information was provided regarding the financial arrangements of the Schriver-Schwarzenegger wedding and who paid for which expenses. The financial status of the parties involved is not the sole factor in determining which of these features of an American wedding will be present or absent. Today, couples often live together, sometimes for several years, before getting married. Despite this, they may elect to go through some or all of the ceremonies associated with an American wedding. The bride wears a white gown, a symbol of virginity, even though the couple may have lived together for several years.

Just as a Kwakiutl wedding reveals themes and patterns central to Kwakiutl culture, so does an American wedding illuminate symbolic themes in American culture. The bride in her white gown symbolizes purity and virginity, though she in fact may not possess these attributes. The hall bedecked with blossoms and the wedding march with its all-too-familiar lyrics echo the same themes. In American society, the powerful, moneyed elite frequently reiterate their familial connections. Thus we are reminded in various ways of Maria Schriver's connection to her mother, Joseph Kennedy's daughter, and to the rest of the Kennedy clan. Like her mother's, her gown was designed by Dior; and her wedding cake was a replica of her mother's. This extravagant wedding was characterized by the couple as a "private" affair. However, though they called it a private affair, Maria and Arnold meant just the opposite. The fact that there was a publicist controlling information dispensed about the wedding attests to its public nature. The Kwakiutl wedding represented a very different symbolism of marriage, with an enormous audience witnessing the capture of the bride by warriors of one *numaym* and her movement to her husband's *numaym.*

The Comparative Approach—Examining Similarities and Differences

Earlier we noted that fieldwork and participant observation were the hallmarks of anthropological methodology. In the same manner, the comparative approach is central to the discipline. A comparison of Kwakiutl and American weddings reveals that in an American wedding, even that of a member of an important family, the focus is almost exclusively on the bride and groom. The Shriver-Schwarzenegger wedding more or less conformed to the ideal pattern of an American wedding, though much larger in scale. American weddings are less a matter of two kin groups establishing a relationship, as was the case in a Kwakiutl wedding, and more a matter of bringing to-

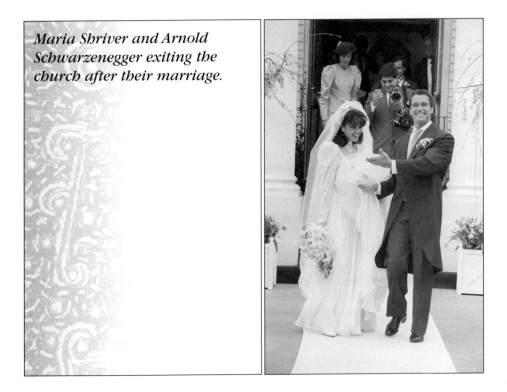

Maria Shriver and Arnold Schwarzenegger exiting the church after their marriage.

gether and displaying the groom's and bride's personal network of friends and colleagues. Because, in the wedding just described, both bride and groom had established careers and were such well-known celebrities, their personal network was large and studded with famous personalities, making this wedding different from other American weddings. Celebrities like Oprah Winfrey and Andy Warhol used the occasion of the wedding to draw attention to themselves. The bride and groom planned the wedding themselves. They acted as the centers of all activity, though other individuals from their respective families as well as friends and relatives played some part. This emphasis on the couple themselves demonstrates the importance in American culture of the newly formed family as autonomous and separate from other families. The Kwakiutl wedding, on the other hand, was a total social phenomenon in which the entire community was involved and in which elements of economics, politics, and political maneuvering concerning transfer of a whole series of privileges as well as property were at issue. In fact, Boas, the observer, noted that these things overshadowed the purpose of the wedding—to establish a new family. In the American wedding, economics were involved, in that goods were purchased and there were many expenditures. But the Kwakiutl marriage itself was an institution for transfers of large amounts of property. Religion was involved in the American wedding, in that a priest officiated and Roman Catholic vows were exchanged. Similarly, in the Kwakiutl marriage the rights and privileges exhibited demanded the recitation of myths linking people to their ancestors, a cornerstone of Kwakiutl religious belief. In a Kwakiutl marriage the whole underlying structure of Kwakiutl society is played out. In contrast, in America, where there has been more institutional separation, an entire wedding industry exists. A wedding really focuses on the couple who are establishing the new family, and other aspects are only tangentially related.

In addition to the differences, there are some interesting similarities that should not go unnoticed. In both Kwakiutl and American societies, all weddings are public ceremonies witnessed by guests. In both instances, the guests who attend the ceremony and communally eat the food perform the function of publicly witnessing a rite of passage. In the American wedding described, an attempt was made to keep it "a private affair," limited to just 450 witnesses. However, as celebrities, the bride and groom also wanted the entire society to witness their wedding, but they wanted to control the information that was made available. In both societies, prestige is determined by the size of the outlay, which, in turn, relates to the social status of the families involved. The more lavish the display, the greater the standing and renown of the participants and their families. In these respects, the display exhibited at the Schriver-Schwartzenegger wedding—the lavish hair-dressing activities, the art deco costuming of the guests, for example—resembled that of a potlatch, at which prestige derives from conspicuous extravagance.

———————

Anthropological methodology, with participant observation at its core, has undergone, as we have pointed out here, a long developmental trajectory since Boas's time. Methodology has changed in keeping with the transformations that have occurred in the focus of anthropological research. There is a fundamental contradiction in participant observation, which the anthropologist always must overcome, between participating in the culture while maintaining the stance of the observer and outsider. However, the anthropologist in the field works with his or her informants as colleagues reflecting on their own culture to produce an ethnographic description to overcome this dilemma. The anthropologist also uses historical analysis, statistical research, and other techniques, especially in the study of more complex societies.

As we have tried to demonstrate here, the rich, detailed ethnographic description has been and will continue to be the objective and goal of anthropological research. Such descriptions, applied in the comparative approach, reveal certain basic similarities between American and Kwakiutl weddings, along with the differences in symbolic meanings.

Chapter Three

Language and Culture

Language is a part of culture, and yet it is more than that. It is central to culture since it is the means through which most of culture is learned and communicated. As we shall see below, when a group begins to lose its language, its cultural tapestry starts to unravel. Infants learn the language and simultaneously acquire the culture of the society into which they are born, and we will discuss these processes in Chapter 4. In our earlier discussion of fieldwork, we described the way in which anthropologists carrying out field research learn the language as they study the culture, just as a child does in that culture. Only humans have the biological capacity for language, which allows them to communicate cultural ideas and symbolic meanings from one generation to the next and to constantly create new cultural ideas. The capacity for language separates humans from the other primates. In any language, a limitless number of possible sentences can be constructed and used to convey an infinite number of cultural ideas. Because of this, human language is significantly different from any other system of animal communication.

The Structure of Language

Like culture, language is patterned. However, language is primarily arbitrary in nature. As the Swiss linguist Ferdinand de Saussure (1915) pointed out in his study of language, the units that carry meaning are two-sided. One side is the physical characteristics that make up the word. These characteristics consist of sounds, or vibrations of the vocal chords, transmitted through the air, which emanate from one person and are received by another. The other side consists of the word's meaning or what it stands for. For example, the word *tree* is made up of a particular series of sounds—t/r/e—and it stands for:

The same object is referred to as *arbre* in French and *Baum* in German. Thus the connection between any combination of sounds that make up a word and its meaning is mostly arbitrary—that is, there is no intrinsic and natural connection between the sounds of a word and its meaning. The same meaning—tree—is conveyed by a different combination of sounds in each language. Occasionally, there is some natural connection between sound and meaning, as occurs in words that imitate natural phenomena, such as *buzz* and *hiss*. Language is therefore not completely arbitrary.

Phonemic Structure

We have mentioned that language is patterned. Let us begin at the level of sound, the building blocks of language. Each language has a small number of basic sounds, usually between 20 and 40, which are used in various combinations to make up the units of meaning. These basic sound units are called *phonemes*. All languages are constructed in the same way. From a small number of phonemes, arranged in different ways, an infinite number of words can be produced. For example, the English word *pin* differs in meaning from *pan* since /i/ is a different phoneme from /a/. Add /s/ to *pin* and you get the plural form of *pin*, that is, *pins*. But if the /s/ is added to the beginning of the word, rather than the end, the result is *spin*, a word with a totally different meaning. Thus, the same phonemes in a different order produce a word with a different meaning.

If the reader has been paying close attention, he or she will have noted that the /p/ in *pin* is different from the /p/ in *spin*. If you hold a sheet of paper in front of your mouth and pronounce *pin* loudly, the paper will flutter because the /p/ in *pin* is aspirated (air blows out). Pronounce *spin* and the sheet of paper remains still, because the /p/ in *spin* is not aspirated. The two /p/'s are said to be *allophones* of the same phoneme. They are variant forms of the single English phoneme /p/, which vary because of their environments, that is, the contexts in which they are found.

The phonemes of a language form a structure or system. The phonemes of English can be divided into vowels and consonants. For a native speaker, English consonants seem independent and unrelated to one another. However, let us examine the following list of some English consonants:

t	d
p	b
f	v
s	z
k	g

When one makes the sounds /t/ and /d/, the tongue, teeth, and lips, known as the points of articulation, are in the same position for both. This is also true for the other paired sounds on the two lists—/p/ and /b/, /f/ and /v/, /s/ and /z/, and /k/ and /g/. There is a relationship between the group of consonants in the left-hand column and the group of consonants in the right-hand column. The consonants in the column on the left are all pronounced without vibrations of the vocal cords. They are voiceless consonants. The vocal cords vibrate when those in the right-hand column are pronounced. These are called voiced consonants. The distinction between voiced and voiceless consonants is one of the several kinds of distinctions characterizing English phonemes. All these features organize the set of English phonemes into a structure and serve to differentiate them. If the phonemes of a language are structured, then what is their function? Phonemes serve to differentiate words like *pin* and *pan*. Though phonemes themselves do not carry meaning, their function is to differentiate words in terms of their meanings.

Morphemic Structure

The units of language that carry meaning are called *morphemes*. Morphemes are not equivalent to words, because some words may be broken into smaller units that carry meaning. For example, the word *shoemaker* may be subdivided into three separate morphemes: *shoe, make,* and *-er,* each with its own meaning. Each of these morphemes is in turn made up of phonemes. Some morphemes, like *shoe,* can stand independently. These are called free morphemes. Others, like *-er,* meaning "one who has to do with," are always found bound to other morphemes (as in *speaker, singer,* and *leader*) and are referred to as bound morphemes. Sometimes two or more forms, that is, combinations of phonemes, have the same meaning. The form *-er* has the same meaning in English as *-ist* in the word *pianist.* These two forms, *-er* and *-ist,* are known as *allomorphs* of the same morpheme.

Syntax and Grammar

The rules by which larger speech units, such as phrases and sentences, are formed compose the *syntax* of a language. English, like all other languages, has rules about the order of words in a sentence. Word order conveys meaning. Thus, "man bites dog" has a meaning different from "dog bites man." In the film *E.T. The Extra-Terrestrial*, E.T.'s sentence "Home phone" is undecipherable; when he says "Phone home," however, his hearers understand. The ways in which a language indicates singular and plural are also part of its syntax.

The complete description of a language is known as its *grammar.* This would include the phonology (a description of its phonemic system), the morphology (a description of its morphemic system), and the syntax. In addition, a complete description of a language would also include a lexicon, or dictionary, that lists all the morphemes and their meanings.

Linguistic Relativity

Early in the nineteenth century, European philologists made the discovery that ancient Sanskrit, Latin, and Greek, and most of the languages of modern Europe belong to a single language family—Indo-European—meaning that all these languages had evolved from a single ancestral language and are basically similar to one another. When linguists began to encounter the languages spoken by native North Americans, unrelated to Indo-European, they assumed (incorrectly) that these languages could be analyzed in terms of Latin grammatical categories. Like the nineteenth-century anthropologists interested in evolutionary theory, these linguists were ethnocentric in their approach and ranked languages as more or less advanced. They termed languages "advanced" if they were spoken by people who were "civilized." Hunters and gatherers, who were considered at a lower cultural level, were said to speak "primitive" languages.

The intensive study of American Indian languages, spearheaded by Franz Boas at the beginning of the twentieth century, demonstrated the fallacious reasoning behind this nineteenth-century evolutionary approach to language. Boas's own work concentrated on the Kwakiutl, as we noted in Chapter 1, and he encouraged his students to go out and study other American Indian languages. As a result of these studies, it became evident to Boas, and later to others, that languages could not be rated on a scale from simple to complex and that there is no one-to-one relationship between technological complexity or cultural complexity, and linguistic complexity. All languages known to linguists, regardless of whether the society had writing, are equally complex. Languages spoken by bands of hunters and gatherers are as systematically patterned as English or Latin. This is known as *linguistic relativity,* paralleling the concept of cultural relativity. Furthermore, Boas convincingly demonstrated that it was necessary to analyze each language in terms of its own structure. This is not to say that there are no universals in language. Indeed there are. All languages have a phonemic system, a morphology, and syntax. The American linguist Noam Chomsky has taken a position against linguistic relativity. He argues that there are a great many other shared characteristics in all languages. These he claims are due to the underlying structure of the human brain.

Historical Linguistics and Language Change

As noted in Chapter 1, cultures are continually undergoing some degree of change. Since language is a part of culture, it too is always changing. Of course, during one's lifetime, one is not aware of linguistic change, except for changes in vocabulary, particularly slang words and expressions. (How many Americans under age 60 would understand the meaning of "The Flat Foot Floogie with the Floy Floy," the title of a popular song of 1940?) If we compare our language usage with that of the language of Shakespeare's plays, the extent to which English has changed over the past centuries is obvious.

It is apparent that present-day dialect differences represent developments from an earlier form of the language. How do such dialect differences arise in the first place? Speech communities are made up of members of a group within a society who interact and speak frequently with one another. One speech community that is very similar to a neighboring speech community will develop slight differences in pronunciation or vocabulary, differentiating it from its neighbor. As these differences increase, they become the basis for greater dialect differentiation. Dialect differentiation, over time, leads to divergence and to the development of two separate languages.

If one examines French, Spanish, Portuguese, and Italian, one can immediately recognize a host of similarities. Some languages, such as Spanish and Portuguese, are more closely related than others, such as French and Portuguese. Because of the high degree of mutual intelligibility between Spanish and Portuguese, one could argue that these two languages are more like different dialects of a single language. All these languages, along with certain other languages, such as Rumanian, are daughter languages, descendants of the vernacular Latin spoken during the time of Julius Caesar. Vernacular Latin was the language spoken by the common people, and it differs from the literary Latin familiar to us from the scholarly works of that time. Dialects of the Latin language spread over large parts of Europe and the Mediterranean world as a result of Roman conquest. These dialects of Latin later developed into separate languages. The vernacular Latin of the Roman period is referred to as the *proto-language,* and the present-day languages descended from it are known as Romance languages. In parallel fashion, English, Dutch, German, and the Scandinavian languages compose the Germanic language family—all descended from a common proto-language called Proto-Germanic. Similarly, all the Slavic languages (Russian, Polish, Czech, Serbo-Croatian, for example) are descended from Proto-Slavic. The European languages we have just mentioned, along with other European and Asian languages, such as Persian, Hindi, and Bengali, form a large family of related languages called the Indo-European language family. All these languages are descended from a common ancestor, Proto-Indo-European.

Recent research on the identity of the language community of Proto-Indo-European speakers, and where and when they lived, demonstrates how useful a convergence of linguists and archaeology can be (Anthony, 1996). Since the Proto-Indo-European speakers had words for beaver, otter, birch, and aspen, and used euphemisms for the ritually important bear, they must have lived in a temperate climate—now thought to be the Ukraine and western Russia. Archaeologists identify them with the Yamna people who lived in this area about 3500 B.C. and who were among the earliest to domesticate and ride horses and to use wheeled vehicles. The latter enabled some Yamna people to migrate into western Europe, while others moved south into Iran and southeast into India, resulting in the diversification that produced the various branches of Indo-European.

Not all languages spoken in Europe are part of this family. Finnish and Hungarian belong to the Finno-Ugric family, while Basque, which is completely unrelated to any other language, is called a language isolate.

For the languages of Europe, where written records have existed for millennia, the historical sequence of language development is known. The written record going back to Latin enables us to know what Proto-Romance was like. Languages thought to be related are systematically studied, using the comparative method. This can be illustrated with a simple example from the Germanic languages. The English word *dance* has as its equivalent the German word *Tanz,* and the English word *door* has as its equivalent the German *Tur.* The forms that have been paired have the same meaning, and their phonemic structures are similar but not identical. These pairs are referred to as *cognates.* The initial *d* in English regularly corresponds to the initial *t* in German. These two forms represent modern divergences from the original phoneme in Proto-Germanic. This correspondence operates throughout the two languages, so that everywhere one finds an initial *d* in English, one would expect to find an initial *t* in German. This is just a single example of the many sound correspondences to be found between German and English.

As a result of their traditional association with small-scale societies, anthropologists studied the languages of the indigenous people of North and South America, Africa, and Oceania. Until studied by anthropologists, these languages had not been recorded in written form. These languages are organized in terms of language families in the same fashion as the European languages discussed above. Some of these language families are very large, encompassing many languages, whereas others may be very small or may even be isolates, like Basque.

If one systematically compares cognates in two unwritten languages, such as Navajo and Apache, and finds similar sound correspondences, this demonstrates that the two languages were genetically related to one another and belonged to the same language family, Athapaskan. It also enables one to reconstruct a tentative picture of the phonemic structure of the proto-language from which these present-day languages have descended. The morphemic structure of the proto-language could be determined through the same comparative approach. This also provides information about what the culture of the speakers of this proto-language was like. Words in the proto-language for plants, trees, and animals are used to pinpoint the possible location of the speakers' original homeland before they dispersed. This type of research enables us to say that the original homeland of the Navajo and the Apache was in the forest area of northwestern Canada where many speakers of other Athapaskan languages still live. The Navajo and Apache migrated from this area to their present home in the Southwest more than a thousand years ago.

Languages also change as a result of diffusion, or borrowing from speakers of one language by speakers of another language. This may be the borrowing of words, sounds, or grammatical forms. Contact and borrowing come about in a number of different ways, some of them peaceful, others not. An excellent example of language change as a consequence of military conquest occurred after the Norman conquest of England (A.D. 1066). The Norman invaders, the conquering class, were speakers of an earlier version of French, while the subjugated English spoke Anglo-Saxon, a Germanic language. The effects of that invasion are present today in our own language. The French, famous for their cuisine, introduced a series of terms referring to different kinds of cooked meat into the Anglo-Saxon language. The *cow* (Saxon), when cooked, became *beef* (*boeuf* in French); *calf* (Saxon) became *veal* (*veau* in French); sheep (Saxon) became mutton (*mouton* in French); and *swine* (Saxon) became *pork* (*porc* in French).

Contact Languages—Pidgins and Creoles

One consequence of the European exploration and colonization of many parts of the world was to bring indigenous languages into contact with European ones. The result was the development of new languages known as contact languages, or pidgins and creoles. *Pidgins* are created by social conditions, like trade, that require communication between two or more language communities. The most important characteristic of pidgins is that they have no native speakers. For all speakers, they are second languages. Governed by rules, they have vocabularies and grammars that are simpler than their source languages. They are sufficiently different from their source languages so as not to be mutually intelligible with them (Sebba, 1997: 15).

Pidgin English, widely used in the Far East and the Pacific, developed out of a nautical jargon during the nineteenth century. As a consequence of historical circumstances, several varieties of this pidgin developed, which have since become national languages. Bislama, the official language of the Republic of Vanauatu (formerly the New Hebrides, ruled jointly by the French and the English), developed during the period of trade in bêche-de-mer, edible sea slugs. It originally was known as Bêche-de-Mer English. Solomon Islands Pijin, or Neo-Solomonic, is an important lingua franca in the Solomon Islands, where there are 80 local languages. Tok pisin is the Melanesian variety of pidgin in this area. It originated among workers in the German colony of New Guinea, especially from the islands of New Ireland and New Britain, who were recruited to work on German-owned plantations in Samoa. They brought the pidgin back with them on their return. Fifteen percent of the vocabulary of Tok Pisin derives from Tolai, spoken in the area around Rabaul, on New Britain, the early headquarters of the German colonial government (Lynch, 1998: 223–224).

When a pidgin language is the native language for the next generation and no longer a second language, then it becomes a *creole*. For over 100 years, Tok Pisin remained a second language for its speakers. However, in the twentieth century, during the postwar period, Tok Pisin began to become the primary language for families in the urban areas of Papua New Guinea, where the adults came from different language areas, as a consequence of increasing rural-urban migration and social mobility (Sebba, 1997: 107). Tok Pisin is in the process of becoming a creole. Since independence in 1975 it has been the official language of the nation of Papua New Guinea.

Language Imperialism versus Language Renewal

Among the topics subsumed under linguistic change is what Muhlhausler has called *linguistic imperialism* (1996). Before the arrival of Europeans in the late fifteenth century, the Pacific area was one of marked linguistic diversity. Up to 4000 languages were spoken there, most of them in Melanesia, where 2 million people speak (or spoke) one-quarter of the world's languages (Muhlhausler, 1996: 10). This intensive language diversity existed side by side with bi- and multilingualism. As a consequence of European colonization and language imperialism, English, French, or German became the dominant language in the respective colonial areas, and a trend from linguistic diversity to monolingualism and language death was established. There were many changes in the indigenous languages, including losses of lexical items and changes in grammatical forms. The question of indigenous language maintenance in a new nation-state like Papua New Guinea pits multilingualism against the need of the nation-state to build a national culture and to have a single national language, in this case, Tok Pisin. In urban areas of Papua New Guinea intermarriage is more common, and Tok Pisin is the language of the household as well as the public arena. In rural areas, however, older people often speak only the indigenous language, while others are bilingual, speaking the indigenous language and Tok Pisin. In some states in the United States, there have been attempts at legislation to make English, and only English, the official language. The argument advanced for doing so is, as in the case of Papua New Guinea, that the use of English alone would reinforce the notion of a single American culture and nation and have a unifying effect. This represents a kind of linguistic imperialism in the face of the current multilingual nature of education in our school system and the use of a multiplicity of languages in the courtrooms and the voting booths of the United States.

A large erosion of indigenous languages took place after the conquest of North America. The recent response of some groups, like the Kwakiutl, was to attempt to maintain and rejuvenate their language by developing Kwakiutl language materials using the phonetic alphabet to teach the language to their children in a school setting.

When a language dies, does that mean that the culture has died along with it? Language is often used as an important marker of cultural or ethnic identity. But it is not the only such marker. When a community is bilingual, and members speak their indigenous language along with the dominant language spoken by the much larger language community of the nation-state, we find that each language may have its own functions and that switching from one language to another follows predictable patterns. Even when the trend toward monolingualism progresses, and only the grandparental generation really speaks the indigenous language, underlying patterns may be perpetuated in the way the dominant language is employed. Woodbury cites a fascinating example of this in an Alaskan community, in which college students from Inupiaq and Yupik (Eskimo) communities use a variety of devices as qualifiers in written English essays to avoid sounding assertive, since such circumspection is part of the way an individual in their native culture should behave (Kwachka and Basham, 1990, cited in Woodbury, 1996). This way of nativizing a replacement language is fragile and tentative since it is likely to disappear under pressure from the mainstream community. Woodbury concludes that while we cannot assume that a culture has died when a language dies, a fundamental way of organizing the surrounding world eventually disappears when a language dies, because it simply cannot be translated into the words and phrases of the dominant language that has replaced it. According to Woodbury, "loss of a language leads to an unraveling, or restructuring, or reevaluation of cultural tradition" (1996: 14).

Language and Cognition

There is a close and intimate relationship between language and experience. Boas's study of the Kwakiutl language, which led him to his concept of linguistic relativity, includes a discussion of how, in Kwakiutl, the speaker must indicate how she or he knows about an action other individuals are performing. For example, in the sentence:

The lady was washing clothes

it is necessary in Kwakiutl to make the following distinctions: Did the speaker actually see the lady washing clothes? Did the speaker infer that she was washing clothes from the sound that was heard? Did a third party tell the speaker that she was washing clothes? In the Kwakiutl language, these distinctions must be made as part of the grammar of the language. In some languages the grammar includes forms by means of which the speakers must specify how they acquired the information they are imparting. English does not have this feature as part of its grammar, though the information can be provided by the speakers, if they wish to give it, with additional words. Boas made the general point that in all languages, grammatical rules, such as the one in this example, are obligatory. Just as Kwakiutl speakers are obliged to use a grammatical category that specifies how they know what they know, English speakers must use one or another tense form to indicate whether they are speaking about the past, the present, or the future. The speakers of a language are not usually aware of these grammatical rules, though they guide all utterances. Boas pointed out that such grammatical rules remain unconscious.

People speaking different languages organize what they experience differently. Thus a Kwakiutl person always attends to how he or she receives information, because this is necessary in conveying information to others. Since a vital issue is how you know what you know, one can imagine the comparison between the precision of a Kwakiutl speaker as a witness at a court trial and the lack of specificity of the equivalent English-speaking witness at the same trial. The relationship between language and how society organizes experience was also explored by Boas's student Edward Sapir. He argued that language was a guide to social reality, and that the "real world" was, to a great extent, unconsciously built upon the language habits of a society. This line of argument was carried to what many people considered an extreme position by Benjamin Lee Whorf, who considered that the conception of the world by a member of a particular society was determined by the language or "fashion of speaking."

Ethnosemantics

The way in which a particular language organizes experience for its speakers can be seen most clearly by examination of a specific cultural domain, such as the organization and classification of the world of animals, the world of plants, the system of colors, or the realm of relatives or kin.

In all languages, there is a set of terms used to refer to animals. The world of animals is separable from other domains in the world. It is distinct from the domain of plants, though they both share the characteristic of life in contrast to the inanimate world of rocks and soils. People using different languages will sort this world of animals in ways different from our own. For example, the Linnaean system of classification, which we use, groups human beings, bats, and whales as mammals on the basis of such criteria as being warm-blooded, suckling their young, and having hair. Whether these animals fly, live on the land, or swim in the sea is not important. Other peoples use different criteria for their animal classifications. For example, the Karam of Papua New Guinea, studied by Ralph Bulmer, distinguish birds from other animals in their language. However, the cassowary, a flightless bird like an ostrich, which stands over 5 feet tall, is not placed in the category of birds (where we place it). Rather, the Karam place it in an anomalous category. Unlike birds, it does not fly. It walks on two legs and is seen as related to humans.

We have noted above that our category of mammals is distinguished by a series of criteria, distinctive features or components, which differentiate the category from that of reptiles. The categories are hierarchically organized into successively more inclusive groupings, from species to genus to class. When anthropologists like Bulmer study Karam language and Karam culture, they not only collect the meanings of all animal terms and the categories in which the Karam place them but must then determine the Karam basis for the classifications as well. They ascertain the distinctive features the Karam employ when they classify forms such as the cassowary. Each language employs its own cultural logic in making its classifications. The anthropological investigation of this topic is known as *ethnosemantics*.

In Chapter 6, we will discuss the way in which societies over the world use kinship terms to sort their relatives into different categories, but here we will examine kinship terminologies from the point of view of their semantic content—that is, as language. A kinship terminology is parallel to a system of animal classification. It is characterized by sets of components or distinctive features and is hierarchically ordered in the same fashion as the system of animal classification. Our kinship terminology is hierarchically organized in that at the highest level of organization, the *affinal,* or "in-law," category contrasts with that of consanguineal, or "blood," relatives.

All kinship terminologies may be analyzed in terms of eight features, and specific terminologies employ some of these features but not others. For example, the kinship terminology of the Yanomamo, who live in lowland South America, recognizes the features of sex of relative (whether the relative referred to is male or female), generation (to which generation the relative referred to belongs), and sex of linking relative (whether the relative is related through one's mother or one's father). It does not take into account the distinction between consanguineal relatives (blood relatives) and affinal relatives (relatives by marriage) or other features that occur in kinship terminologies over the world. In every language there is a kinship terminology that represents a set of terms for relatives and sorts them in a particular way by using certain components and ignoring others. Each kinship terminology is invariably much simpler than it might be if every possible relative were distinguished with his or her own term or label. Thus, in every kinship terminology each kin term represents several different kinds of relatives—the English term *uncle* is a category that includes mother's brother, father's brother, mother's sister's husband, and father's sister's husband; the Yanomamo term *haya* is a category that includes father and father's brother, and so on.

Still another cultural domain that has been studied in this manner is the set of linguistic terms used for colors. Every language has a set of terms for colors, though the number of these terms varies from one language to another. Viewers looking at a rainbow see an undivided series of colors, one color grading into another, while as speakers of different languages they will divide this spectrum differently. Boas used the example of color categories to illustrate the principle of linguistic relativity mentioned earlier. Later, Brent Berlin and Paul Kay did a comparative study of basic color categories in many different languages throughout the world that shows that the classification of colors in different languages is not completely arbitrary (1969). In some languages, there are only two basic color terms, bright and dark (which can be equated to white and black). More common are languages with three terms, and those terms will always be red, bright (white), and dark (black). Still other languages, with four color categories, add either yellow or green. Other groups of languages through time will successively add blue, brown, purple, pink, orange, and gray. What Berlin and Kay have demonstrated is that the color spectrum is not randomly divided. There is order and regularity in the way in which languages add to the number of color terms. In recent research, color categories have been further divided into the dimensions of brightness and hue in order to explain the findings of Berlin and Kay in terms of cognitive processes.

This does not mean that people over the world who lack terms for particular colors cannot in a descriptive fashion express in their language the colors they see (without a term for blue they might say "it is the color of a robin's egg"). What it does mean is that the color categories their language possesses will organize their experience in a particular way.

In this general discussion of ethnosemantics, we have shown the way in which the concept of distinctive features is used. A common way of distinguishing two categories from one another is for one of the categories to possess an attribute that the other category lacks. In the Linnaean classification, mammals are warm-blooded animals while reptiles are not. Thus, one might say that the category of mammals is the "plus" category. The linguist Roman Jakobson identified this principle of classification, which he called *markedness*. The category in which the attribute was present he called the marked category, and the category in which it was absent, the unmarked category. Jakobson pointed out that in linguistics, the unmarked category is the more general and inclusive of the two. For example, in English, we have the words *lion* and *lioness*. The marked category is the word *lioness* (*-ess* is added to *lion*—thus marking it). *Lion* includes *lioness,* as in the sentence "Christians were thrown to the lions." The unmarked category is also often the dominant category, while the marked category is subordinate. The presence of marked and unmarked categories is found in all languages (Greenberg, 1966).

Sociolinguistics

Saussure, the linguist referred to earlier, made a distinction between *langue* and *parole,* that is, between language and speech. To obtain information about a language, the field-worker observes and records many examples of speech. These examples are analyzed in order to obtain a picture of the grammar, or underlying structure, of that language. *Sociolinguistics* deals with the analysis of parole, or speech, and its social functions. Recently, anthropological linguists have been interested in a more integrative way of understanding how language channels social life. Language is an integral part of the construction of social life; it also provides a window on the social process. Language forges shared cultural understandings and acts as a medium of social exchange and connection between people (Mertz, 1994: 441). This perspective in sociolinguistics is equally concerned with speech as well as with its ethnographic setting, which includes social relations, spatial aspects, cultural meanings and beliefs, and material objects.

Male and Female Speech

In many societies, distinctions between male and female speech have been observed, though men and women interact with one another as members of the same speech community. As infants and young children learn their language and their culture, they are simultaneously learning female-specific and male-specific behavior, and appropriate gender-related forms of speech. In a survey of differences between male and female speech in Great Britain, Coates noted that men and women have different interactive styles (1993). In mixed-sex conversations, men dominate the conversation by interrupting women, by controlling the topics of the conversation, and by becoming silent. Men talk more, swear more, and use imperative forms to get things done. In contrast, women use more tentative speech, use more linguistic forms associated with politeness, and make greater use of minimal responses (like "uh-huh") to indicate support for the speaker. These characteristics are sometimes termed men's and women's styles of speech. In single-sex conversations, a different pattern emerges. Whereas men disagree with or ignore each other's utterances, women, in conversations with other women, meld or blend their talk, arriving at a collaborative account satisfactory to all participants. In this way, men pursue a style of individual assertion and power, while women's style is based on solidarity and support (Jones, 1980, in Coates, 1993; Coates, 1996: 64). These different styles sometimes result in miscommunication between the sexes.

Investigations of male and female speech in American society reveal the same hierarchical pattern of dominance and subordination. In a study by Fishman, it was found that men do most of the interrupting and talking, and they also often choose what to talk about (1983). According to Tannen, different ethnic interactional styles need to be factored into the discussion of interruptions (1994). Poynton (1989) adds to the list of features distinguishing male from female speech. While women will talk on topics raised by men, men may and do reject women's topics in mixed conversations. When men make commands, they use the imperative form. Women tend to use interrogatives ("Would you mind closing the window?") and declarative forms ("I wonder if you would be so kind as to shut the door"). Poynton argues that men and women use different forms of a common language, which encodes an ideological opposition between the sexes. That ideology maintains that males and their activities are of great importance and value, while females and their activities are of less importance and value.

Gender differences in speech are found in other cultures in the world, but sometimes the forms contrast with what we have described for Great Britain and the United States. In a study of a Malagasy-speaking community of Madagascar, Keenan (1974) has observed that men tend not to express their sentiments openly, are not confrontational, do not show anger, and behave with discretion. This is reflected in men's speech. They favor subtlety in speech and more indirect and circumspect forms of expression, especially on ceremonial occasions. In contrast, women tend to speak in a straightforward manner, directly expressing anger and criticism that may insult the person being addressed. Since direct speech is characteristic of the marketplace, women do much of the bargaining, buying, and selling in this society. Men usually sell goods that are more or less fixed in price. When they do bargain, it is an elaborate and circumspect procedure, in which confrontation is to be avoided. In Japanese the marked differences between male and female speech are so strong that some observers talk about a "true" women's language. In contrast to Malagasy, in Japanese, it is the women's speech in Japanese that is characterized by the more frequent use of polite forms. Japanese women's speech is also distinguished from men's speech by the presence of different sets of first- and second-person pronouns and special terms of self-reference and address. In a study of Pohnpeian speech interactions, Keating shows how the use of honorific language by chieftesses not only concretizes existing status differences but also can constitute a creative force to challenge authority, since it accords prestige to the addressee, referent, and user (1998: 153).

Language is always politically important. The way in which speech is used to express power varies from culture to culture. As Gal notes, "Extensive ethnographic case studies have demonstrated that in some societies it is the holders of greatest power who must restrain themselves physically, linguistically, and often in the expression of emotion exactly because it is superior restraint that culturally and ideologically defines their power, enabling them to properly exercise it" (1995: 413). For example, among the Kanuri, speaking in a low and unexcited tone demonstrates control and exercise of power. In contrast, in Western cultures, demonstration of power is often achieved by cursing, screaming, and ignoring the personhood of others present, as, for example, Hitler and former president Nixon did.

People in the underclass and in positions of powerlessness express their opposition and resistance by means of certain linguistic styles. In a bilingual community in Hungary, Gal has found that "any single villager expresses many and often conflicting opinions about the value of the two languages he or she speaks, including opinions that show evidence of resistance to official languages and ideologies" (Gal, 1995: 412–413). Abu-Lughod's discussion of Bedouin love poetry, which we will examine later, demonstrates how this form of expression is associated with women and young men expressing defiance and rebellion toward male tribal hierarchy.

Other kinds of variations in speech within a language correspond to class differences—that is, to vertical differences that structure a society. Such class-correlated linguistic differences are found in the United States. In contrast to speech differences based on class, differences in speech due to geography and region may be conceptualized as horizontal differences. Speakers in different geographical areas speaking different versions of a language are said to speak different *dialects*. Different regions of the United States are characterized by different patterns of speech, including differences in pronunciation, vocabulary, and syntax. One can immediately recognize a Boston accent, a Midwestern accent, or a Southern accent. Some of these differences are a consequence of the immigrant populations from different countries who settled in these areas. In the film *Fargo,* the local population in Minnesota and adjoining South Dakota employed an excessive number of "you betchas" and substituted "yah" for "yeah" (or "yes") in their usage of American English. These usages are markers of their ethnic identity as Scandinavian Americans.

African-American Speech

Differences in language usage in the United States also parallel racial differences. The speech of the African-American community, referred to in the past as Black English but now referred to as African-American Vernacular English (AAVE), in contrast to Standard English (SE), is the subject of much scholarly research and debate (Morgan, 1994; Mufwene et al., 1998). (The Oakland School Board, in 1996, proposed that the term *Ebonics* be used to refer to African-American English.). AAVE was originally viewed by some as a collection of mistakes and deviations from Standard English, which reflected deficits in the cultural behavior of its speakers. However, Labov, in his several decades of work, and others have demonstrated that AAVE should be viewed as a system, with an invariant core, that should be analyzed without reference to other dialects (Labov, 1972, 1998). Labov's findings marked the beginning of serious consideration of the linguistic attributes of African-American Vernacular English, the range of its usage, and its origins. There are phonological, syntactic, and lexical features that mark African-American English as different from American English, though some of these differences are also present in other American English dialects. Most recently, Labov has proposed that AAVE represents the coexistence of two distinct components, General English (GE), which is similar to the grammar of Other American Dialects (OAD), and the African-American (AA) component (1998:117 ff.). The General English component, consisting of a fairly complete set of syntactical, morphological, and phonological structures, provides speakers with the same grammatical and lexical machinery as Other American Dialects. The African-American component is a subset of grammatical and lexical forms that are combined with part of the grammatical inventory of GE, permitting the development of a specialized semantics and the construction of sentence types not available to OAD. The main grammatical work is done by the General English system of AAVE, permitting a semantic efflorescence in the AA component. One of the most important points made by Labov in his recent work regards the continuing divergence of AAVE from OAD and the fact that "many important features of the modern dialect are creations of the twentieth century and not an inheritance of the nineteenth" (Labov, 1998: 119). Though AAVE is also seen as having creole affinities and creole roots, it is not viewed as a full-fledged creole such as Gullah, the language spoken on the Sea Islands, off the coast of Georgia. In its early form Gullah was structurally related to the creole languages that developed on the islands in the Caribbean owned by the English, where English was the colonial language (Rickford, 1998: 191).

Originally, it was believed that African languages and cultures were completely destroyed by the experience of slavery. However, today scholars have challenged this opinion and have come to the conclusion that the African heritage continues to exist in both African-American language and culture. According to Smitherman, the uniqueness of AAVE is to be found in the following three areas: "(1) patterns of grammar and pronunciation; (2) verbal rituals from the oral tradition and the continued importance of the word as in African cultures; and (3) the lexicon, developed by giving special meaning to English words, a practice that goes back to enslavement and to the need for a system of communication that only those in the slave community could understand" (1998: 207). Many studies have analyzed the African-American male style of speech referred to as signifying, sounding, or playing the dozens. This kind of verbal skill, which is an echo of the verbal rituals of the African language tradition, is most frequently associated with adolescent males and involves taking a serious topic that is culturally significant and playing with it in an ironic, sarcastic, and humorous fashion (Morgan, 1994: 333).

Language is an important aspect of the construction of cultural identity. African-American Vernacular English is seen by some as a symbol of slave mentality, in particular by members of the Nation of Islam, and by others as a symbol of resistance to slavery and oppression (Morgan, 1994: 338–339). More significantly, today African-American Vernacular English plays a role in the construction of African-American identity in a multicultural America. However, as Mitchell-Kernan points out, both African-American Vernacular English and Standard English are necessary to improve one's life chances, since lack of Standard English harms one in school and in the workplace while absence of African-American Vernacular English deprives one of status within one's ethnic group (Mitchell-Kernan, 1972, in Morgan, 1994). In recent years, there has been an increase in the size of the African-American middle class and a greater stratification of the African-American community in general. Studies have noted that for African Americans, the higher the class, the greater the consciousness of racial identity (Morgan, 1994: 337–338). This is illustrated by African-American students in elite college campuses who employ African-American lexical, phonological, and grammatical features of African-American Vernacular English in both formal and informal contexts in order to reinforce their ethnic identity (Baugh, 1987, 1992, in Morgan, 1994: 338). During the last decade of the twentieth century the curious spectacle of crossover, in which white people have begun to use aspects of African-American Vernacular English lexicon in their own speech, has been observed. As Smitherman notes, "This is a historical moment in which Rap and other forms of Black language and culture are used to sell everything from Coca-Cola and Gatorade to snow blowers and shampoo for White people's hair" (1998: 223). Of course, sounding "hip" is not a new phenomenon, as Norman Mailer observed in 1957.

––––––––––

Since culture is structured much as language is, procedures and concepts from linguistics have been utilized by anthropologists in their studies of cultural problems. In subsequent chapters dealing with symbolism, mythology, and art, we will again be discussing some of the concepts and ideas we have presented in this chapter.

Chapter Four

Learning Language and Learning Culture: Culture and the Individual

It is now appropriate to pause and consider the ways in which individuals born into a particular society learn its language and its culture and the behaviors which individuals in that culture consider appropriate. In the course of this discussion, we will also be talking about the relationship of the individual to his or her culture, the range of personality variation within cultures, and the ways of dealing with individuals whose behavior is outside the norms of their culture. This will take us into a consideration of how mental illness is defined in particular cultures and how innovators and rebels, whose societies sometimes consider them mentally ill, are dealt with.

Language Acquisition and Cultural Acquisition

Language is the primary tool by which children acquire cultural knowledge. It is the medium of socialization and the means by which children acquire the meanings, beliefs, and world view that characterize their culture. Enculturation and language acquisition are interactive processes. It is by means of interaction between the child and those taking care of the child that he or she comes to internalize cultural and linguistic norms and to acquire the ability to perform appropriately in various cultural contexts.

A normal child is born with the ability to learn language, since that is part of every human being's genetic endowment. It is an aspect of the cognitive structure that all humans have inherited from their ancestors. According to Chomsky, "we assume that the language faculty has an initial state, genetically determined, common to the species . . . , and apparently unique to the human species. We know that this initial stage can mature to a number of different steady states—the various attainable languages as conditions of exposure vary" (1999: 41). If the infant is exposed to one language, let us say English, the "mind/brain" will incorporate knowledge of English, not Japanese. An infant as young as 4 days old can distinguish between the sounds of its own language and those of another, and will suck harder while nursing in order to hear the language of the parents rather than another language (J. Mehler et al., cited in Pinker, 1994: 264). Babies several months old become aware of the stress patterns of their language. At 9 months of age, English babies paid attention to words with the predominant stress patterns of English but not to words with other stress patterns (Bavin, 1995: 376). Though language capacity is innate, it flourishes in a stimulating environment and languishes in an impoverished environment. Child language acquisition is more importantly a matter of elaboration of the structure that is present from birth, rather than the accumulation of knowledge (Ritchie, 1999: 10). The interaction with people and the early experiences of a child, linguistic and otherwise, are necessary for the development of language. Chomsky's underlying premises are that there is a universal mental schema and that all languages have a series of fundamental properties, or linguistic invariants, in common. These linguistic invariants are another way of talking about the language universals discussed in Chapter 1. This mental schema comes with a number of open parameters of variation, which correspond to the differences between the languages of the world. During the acquisition of language, children learn the particular parameters of the language spoken around them. For example, an Italian child learns that pronoun subjects may be dropped while an English child learns that they may not (Bavin, 1995: 375).

Derek Bickerton has worked on the problem of the development of pidgins and creoles and the evolution of languages. He has suggested that the child until the age of 2 utilizes a kind of proto-language that is primarily devoid of syntax. Phylogenetically, it resembles an earlier stage of language evolution; it also has the properties of pidgin, which develops when direct linguistic communication between speakers of different languages is not possible. Around the age of 2, a developmental explosion occurs in the quantity and quality of the child's utterances. This is a consequence of an innate "language biogram," hypothesizes Bickerton, that specifies an increase in language complexity at that point of maturation. When children of speakers of pidgin acquire pidgin as a first language, this innate mechanism creates creole language. In Bickerton's provocative hypothesis, language ontogeny recapitulates phylogeny.

Researchers have studied how children learn color terms, and some have proposed that the sequence of learning terms for colors mirrors a universal color hierarchy of the type developed by Berlin and Kay, to which we have referred in the previous chapter. However, research on English-speaking children by Gleason and Ely reveals that the terms *blue* and *red* appear between 22 and 23 months of age, while *white* and *black*, which Berlin and Kay proposed are the most basic of terms, do not appear until 27 months of age (1998: 177). Since parents also used *red* and *blue* more frequently than *white* and *black*, parental input is clearly a factor in the child's acquisition of color terminology.

Researchers' opinions differ regarding the role played by innate cognitive factors, cognitive development and general learning mechanisms, and to the cultural setting within which language acquisition occurs. Some scholars see the characteristics of the language being acquired as playing a much more significant role in the process of acquisition than the innate capacity for language postulated by Chomsky. Their interest is on which linguistic categories are acquired, in which order, and how they are encoded in particular languages.

Scholars like Schiefflin and Ochs see language acquisition and its cultural context as being inextricably tied together, with learning of linguistic forms closely interrelated to the cultural setting within which learning takes place (1986). Sociocultural information is encoded in the organization of conversation, and from earliest infancy, children acquire knowledge as they are involved in such interactions. Cross-culturally, those caring for children provide explicit instructions to children on how to speak and what to say in a range of recurring situations and events (Ochs, 1986: 5). However, the mode of instruction is variable. In most cultures, it is typically by means of explicit prompting with particular phraseology, modifying voice quality or intonation, repeating utterances, and simplifying semantic content or grammatical structure. In our culture, this instructional language is referred to as baby talk.

At the same time that children acquire language, they are also acquiring knowledge of the statuses and roles that constitute the social order of their society. In Samoa, children use the word for "give" earlier and more frequently than the word for "come," though the former is semantically more complex. The use of "give" is more appropriate for small children in directing older siblings and adults, while "come" is used solely for animals and younger siblings (Platt, 1986). Clearly these usages relate to the hierarchical nature of Samoan social structure.

The learning of the affect, attitudes, feelings, and emotional sets characteristic of a culture is also connected to language acquisition and varies from culture to culture. Schiefflin has investigated the range of linguistic forms that Kaluli children can use to perform the act of requesting. It is necessary for children to learn the appropriate request forms in order to operate successfully in the all-important reciprocity and exchange activities that organize Kaluli society (Schiefflin and Ochs, 1999: 255, 256). Kaluli adults tease and shame children, using name-calling, formulaic expressions, rhetorical questions, or "turned-over words" to teach children how to become adult Kaluli who are individually autonomous, assertive, and direct (Schiefflin, 1986). In contrast, the Japanese communicative style, which is somewhat depersonalized, is inculcated in children by Japanese mothers by using indirect forms of communicating and correcting children's use of direct utterances, which are considered improper. Children learn a variety of greetings and polite expressions, as well as other linguistic forms of politeness used to indicate particular roles and situations (Nakamura, 1999: 248).

As children learn language from those surrounding them, those who care for them, and those with whom they interact, at the same time, they learn social roles, politeness and deference toward elders, autonomy, assertiveness, and initiative. They are learning cultural values and what is appropriate behavior for a child in their culture. While Kaluli children learn that autonomy and assertiveness are valued in their culture, Samoan children learn that assertiveness toward elders is bad, and Japanese children learn that indirectness and circumscribed behavior are valued over directness. Particular forms of language as they relate to correct forms of behavior in each society are taught to children.

Gender roles and the kinds of persons men and women are expected to be are also acquired during the socialization and language acquisition processes. If boys are expected to be more assertive than girls in a particular culture, they are taught by the individuals around them to be that way, and their use of language reflects this. The people who inhabit the Kerkennah Islands, 12 miles off Tunisia, think of males and females as having sharply different ideas of self, which are basically different by nature (Platt, 1988). They think that a female fetus rides "in the lap" and a male fetus "astride the hips" during the mother's pregnancy. After birth, babies of both sexes are swaddled to avoid any external influences or dangerous forces. Beyond two months of birth, Kerkenni males are treated differently from females, based on the belief that they are different by nature. The mother behaves toward the male child as if he were an adult male, playfully referring to him as "oh, Daddy" or "oh, Sir." This results in an earlier and fuller development of a sense of self on the part of male infants as compared with female infants. The female infant instead is treated as an extension of the mother herself. Male infants are seen as more demanding and requiring more attention. They are the foci of much more ritual activity. After circumcision, between the ages of 3 and 4, the male child moves beyond the sphere of the mother and into the world of male peers. There is no equivalent sharp break for the female child, who remains close to her mother. Older boys are expected to express aggression outwardly, and they are teased to foster this, while girls turn their anger inward upon themselves. Two different kinds of selves, one for males and another for females, are characteristic of this society. However, as noted earlier, the Kerkenni themselves see these differences in the expression of self as attributable entirely to nature, not to cultural learning.

In the United States and Australia, studies of the interaction of parents and children and of children themselves demonstrate that gender is a social construct that is constantly being modified as a consequence of the interactions in which children and their parents and teachers engage. Earlier there was a view that children were not consciously taught but merely absorbed information about appropriate behaviors. However, now educators think that "children constitute and structure a gender position in response to the discourses within which they participate, and this position is dynamic with the child taking an active part" (Lowe, 1998: 206). The enculturation process takes place in the interaction of children with their families at home, with other children and teachers in school and on the playground, when they are out in the larger community, and through the many forms of media, such as television and films, to which they are exposed. For example, the mass toy market presents a sexual division of toys, with Barbie and GI Joe as just two examples (Farrell, 1998: 105). In a study of Australian parents and children, male and female gender roles are presented as mutually exclusive and are seen in that manner by most children. It was clear that the chores that mothers and fathers, and girls and boys, performed at home were primarily complementary, with fathers and boys concerned with tidying the yard, washing the car, and working on the periphery of meal preparation, and mothers and girls concerned with domestic tasks. The study further showed that in play situations at school "girls felt at home in home corner setting, where they were

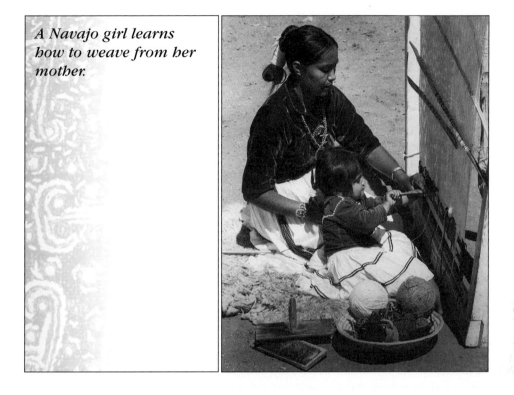

A Navajo girl learns how to weave from her mother.

familiar with the rituals and positions involved. The boys, on the other hand, were more comfortable exploring the boundaries of socially acceptable behavior and developing the skills they felt they would need as adults to work outdoors and outside the home" (Lowe, 1998: 209). It is apparent that children enter school with gender roles already clearly defined. Not only are they aware of the complementarity of roles but observation of the interaction of children in play settings in school reveals that in their behavior, they also enact male domination of space and language and female submissiveness (Lowe, 1998: 214). It is interesting to conjecture what such a parallel study in the United States would reveal, given the movement to make gender roles more similar rather than complementary. Some educators in the United States and Australia have made deliberate efforts, in their organization of the classroom and class activities, to make children aware of the possibility of roles that are more egalitarian in nature, rather than those roles that suggest male dominance and female subordination.

In a study of Venda children in South Africa, Blacking (1988) investigated how children learn to understand and eventually perform the music and dances of their culture, and how learning to understand music relates to learning how a Venda should think, act, feel, and relate to others. During infancy, a Venda child spends most of the time on his or her mother's or a sibling's back, hearing the songs and feeling the movements as the mother or sibling dances and sings during ritual performances and other social contexts. When a child starts spontaneous banging with an object, the adult converts this behavior into musical action by adding a second part in a different rhythm. As is characteristic of the music of many African societies, Venda music is polyrhythmic. The Venda view of personhood is that it is created through interaction with others. When Venda children sing as they play with adults and later with other children, the polyrhythms in which they sing assert their own person and create a sense of community at the same time.

Studies of socialization in different types of societies indicate that while teaching is the predominant method for learning economic and social roles in urban-industrial societies, societies dependent on horticulture, and on hunting and foraging, rely much more on children's observing and imitating elders, and on honing such skills by playing games. Such devices for socializing the child do not seem to be used as much in industrial societies (Munroe and Munroe, 1996).

Culture and Personality

Not only do individuals in a society learn a language and a culture; the personality structure characteristic of their culture is also inculcated in them. In all societies, people exhibit individual personality differences as a result of genetic differences, upbringing, and particular life experiences. Each individual has a certain personality, a certain character, which is more or less stable over his or her lifetime. This is not to say that individuals never change. An individual's personality can change, sometimes through his or her own efforts and sometimes with the assistance of a therapist. But most frequently, individuals demonstrate stability of personality. They act consistently in different kinds of situations. The stability of individual personality is the result of the interaction of genetic, biological predispositions and the individual's life experience from birth on. A range of personality types exists in our society, as well as in every other society in the world.

Though there is a range of personality types in every society, in any one society there is a preponderance of individuals with a particular kind of personality. This range of personality types differs from one society to the next. The attempt to characterize the dominant personality types of different societies and tribes goes back to ancient times. Tacitus, the Roman historian, in his work, *Germania: On the Origin, Geography, Institutions, and Tribes of the Germans* written at the end of the first century A.D., characterized the Germans as "a race without either natural or acquired cunning, they disclose their hidden thoughts in the freedom of the festivity." He also notes that they represent a strange combination of idleness and sloth and readiness to go to war. Tacitus tried to capture what was distinctive about the personality characteristics of the Germans as a people. Throughout history, such characterizations of different peoples have been made. One must always be wary of stereotypes based on prejudice, as distinguished from accurate characterizations based on data and observations.

In the 1930s and 1940s, anthropological studies of personality and culture focused on personality differences between various cultures, the measures for determining and verifying these differences, the investigation of the cultural institutions that bring about the development of these particular personality types through time, and the other aspects of culture to which these personality differences are related. In American anthropology, investigations of the relationship between personality and culture were strongly influenced by the ideas and concepts of Sigmund Freud, especially those concerned with child-rearing techniques, the socialization of the child, and the way in which these affected the development of the adult personality. Margaret Mead and Ruth Benedict, both students of Franz Boas, took Freud's emphasis on early childhood experiences and combined it with Boas's theoretical point of view of cultural relativism. In separate works written in the 1930s, Mead and Benedict applied this point of view to personality, maintaining that cultures varied in terms of patterns of child rearing, personality development, sex-role behavior, and types of mental disorder. In her first important work on Samoa, Mead demonstrated that while adolescence in America involves a period of crisis and search for identity, in Samoa there is no equivalent period of crisis. In her subsequent fieldwork in the Admiralty Islands off New Guinea, she focused upon the specific ways in which children were reared, weaned, and toilet trained; how and when they learned to walk and to swim; how infants were handled; and how children were taught and encouraged to become adults and develop the kind of personality valued by the Admiralty Islanders. In *Sex and Temperament,* published in 1935, Mead demonstrated how male and female roles, and the personality characteristics associated with them, were culturally determined in three New Guinea societies. Mead claimed that in Tchambuli society, the females were assertive, usually a male characteristic, and in Arapesh, the males were passive, gentle, and sensitive, characteristics usually associated with female roles.

Child Rearing and Personality

We have discussed how children acquire language and learn the rules of their own culture. In the process, the particular personality characteristics favored in that culture are also inculcated in them. Through the process of enculturation, children learn not only the rules of their culture, but also, as noted above, the values of their society. In addition, they increasingly become motivated to act according to those values. The motivations that have been built in during the enculturation process are what lead most people to conform to those rules. To act otherwise—to violate rules—produces guilt in the individual. As the psychoanalyst Erich Fromm (1944) long ago noted, stable individuals in a well-integrated culture will want to do the things that they have to do. This applies not only to cultural behavior, but to emotion as well, which is also culturally determined. Though the form in which emotion is expressed varies from one culture to another, there are certain aspects of emotional states, like happiness and grief, that are universal.

The psychoanalytic approach conceived of personality development as proceeding through a series of developmental stages, such as weaning and toilet training. Erik Erikson (1963), a psychoanalyst strongly influenced by anthropologists, broadened Freud's stages of psychosexual development in order to make them applicable to non-Western cultures. He was impressed by the cultural differences among the Yurok, the Sioux, and the American patients whom he was treating, and he saw these differences in culture and in child rearing as being related to differences in the adult personality.

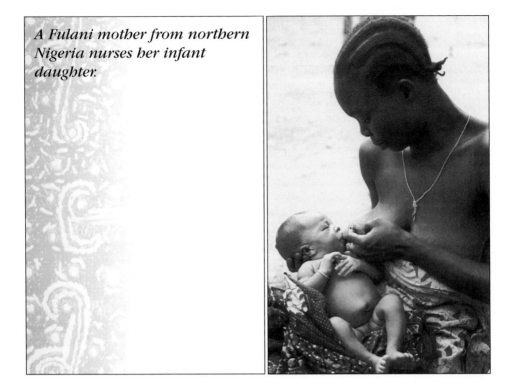

A Fulani mother from northern Nigeria nurses her infant daughter.

Among the Sioux of South Dakota, children were freely breast-fed up to age 3, and there was no systematic weaning. The Sioux child was toilet trained by imitating older children, and the matter of toilet training was treated in a very relaxed fashion. Erikson saw a clear relationship between the way in which the Sioux handled these two developmental stages and the value that the Sioux placed on the generous adult individual, as expressed, for example, in the economic institution of the "giveaway." In contrast, among the Yurok of California, a child was breast-fed for only six months, and weaning, which was called "forgetting the mother," could be brought about by the mother's leaving the house for a few days. Autonomy was encouraged very early. With respect to toilet training, the Yurok were particularly concerned that the child not urinate into the Klamath River, which each year brought them salmon on which they depended. In Erikson's view, these aspects of child rearing were tied to an adult Yurok personality characterized by retentive hoarding, suspicious miserliness, and compulsive ritualization. It was Erikson's interpretation that the Yurok, who had their own kind of money in the form of shells, adapted well to American economic institutions since their personalities and their own economic system were already very similar to those of American culture. Sioux culture and Sioux personality were quite different; thus the Sioux did not adapt well to American culture.

The Relationship of Culture and Social Structure to Personality

Individuals who make up a society occupy different social positions, different statuses in the society. In all societies, people are minimally differentiated according to age and sex. Beyond this, there are many other bases for differentiation. Individuals who occupy different statuses within the same society are likely to have different personality characteristics. For example, shamans in a society will have somewhat different personalities from nonshamans in the same society. The Big Man, a type of political leader that we will discuss in Chapter 9, will have a somewhat different personality from his followers. There are two ways to view this relationship between social status and personality. In the first view, individuals with certain kinds of personality characteristics will gravitate toward those social roles or occupations that suit their personalities. These differences in personality characteristics result from individual differences in socialization. For example, in our own society, individuals who are self-confident, assertive, and willing to take risks often gravitate toward entrepreneurial positions in the business world. Others, with different personality traits, such as a tendency to intellectualize and a curiosity about the world but a sense of uneasiness in dealing with other people, are more likely to become scientists and to do research. In the second view, people moving into particular social roles will undergo personality changes brought about by the demands of the role. A classic example of this is Thomas à Becket, who, as chancellor of the exchequer in the twelfth century, was a free spirit and caroused with King Henry II. When Becket was appointed archbishop of Canterbury, he proceeded to behave according to that role. He changed from a frivolous, pleasure-seeking individual to the committed defender of a moral cause who chose martyrdom at the command of his former friend, the king, rather than surrender his principles.

■ Culture and Mental Illness

If, in our society, a man said one day that a guardian spirit had come to him and told him that it would protect and watch over him throughout his life as long as he followed certain commands and obeyed certain taboos, we would consider him mentally ill. If he reported that he had actually seen and spoken to the spirit, we would say that he was having hallucinations. However, adolescent boys among the Crow of the Plains were expected to go on a vision quest to seek such a spirit. Seeing visions was very common among the Crow, as well as among many other Native American societies who also had the vision quest. What is regarded as a symptom of mental illness in one society may be merely one aspect of normal, healthy life in another.

The anthropological definition of *mental illness* takes the normal, expected, and acceptable behavior in a culture as a baseline and views deviance from this baseline as abnormal behavior or mental illness. Seeking a vision was normal and expected behavior for Crow boys, and they might torture themselves and undergo deprivation until the vision came to them. But visions of spirits are not considered normal behavior in our society. Someone who sees them and hears them is exhibiting abnormal behavior. Another instance of exhibiting signs of abnormal behavior is the belief in witchcraft. Among the Navajo and the Basseri, individuals who believed that someone was practicing witchcraft on them would not be considered abnormal. However, in most segments of our society, individuals who came into the emergency room of a hospital complaining of internal pains because they had been bewitched would be considered mentally ill.

This approach to abnormal behavior and mental illness is essentially a relativistic one. Nevertheless, anthropologists who study forms of mental illness cross-culturally use certain general categories. They distinguish between disorders caused by brain damage and behavioral disorders, where there is no apparent brain damage. The latter category is subdivided into psychoses, such as schizophrenia, depression, and paranoia, and neuroses of a variety of types. Recently, depressive illness has been examined cross-culturally (Kleinman and Good, 1985). Bereavement is experienced in all societies, and grief is the emotion that accompanies it. The relationship between the normal experience of grief and pathological grieving or depression has yet to be investigated. Depression as an emotion or affect seems to be similar experientially in many different cultures. However, the boundary line between a depressed state as normal behavior and abnormal depressive disorder has not yet been established. Depressive illness has a psychophysiological syndrome of behaviors that can be recognized by clinicians cross-culturally. At the same time, the cultural meanings of depressive illness and the cultural expression of the symptoms differ from one culture to another. Universal aspects of other mental illnesses, such as schizophrenia, neuroses, and personality disturbances, have also been recognized (Draguns, 1980). However, these illnesses are also culturally shaped. Variations in their manifestations are related to social, economic, technological, religious, and other features of the societies in which they are found.

Some kinds of symptoms seem to be specific to a particular culture. These culturally shaped symptoms have been viewed in two quite different ways. One view is that there are universal psychopathological disease categories (such as schizophrenia and depression) that are manifested in different kinds of behavior from one culture to another. The opposing view is that universally stressful situations produce different kinds of diseases in different cultures. The Windigo psychosis, which occurred among Algonquian Native Americans in the Northeast, was characterized by feeling persecuted by supernatural spirits and having cannibalistic fantasies. Though its symptoms were specific to Algonquian culture, Windigo psychosis is much like paranoid schizophrenia. In Western society, the symptoms of paranoid schizophrenia include ideas of persecution by other human beings, such as people in the government, people in the telephone company, or men from Mars, as well as anxiety over homosexual impulses. *Amok* is another mental illness, found in Malaysia and Indonesia, that has a specific set of symptoms. The central feature of *amok* is that the victim kills people while in a temporarily deranged state. Some researchers consider *amok* a disease specific to these particular cultures, while others consider it a culturally determined form of depression psychosis produced by extreme stress. We get our expression "to run amok" from this mental illness of Southeast Asia. Arctic hysteria is a form of mental illness found in Central Asia and among Siberian peoples, in which the victim shouts obscenities, acts in an immodest fashion, and senselessly imitates the behavior of others. An illness similar to arctic hysteria, *latah,* is found in Malaysia. In a recent survey of *latah,* Winzeler (1995) indicates that it occurs in association with societies where there is familiarity with trance states and which practice shamanism. He also notes the similarities of *latah* to certain symptoms in Western illnesses, namely startle reactions and imitative behavior. Winzeler is unable to conclude whether it is a specific form of illness related to Malay culture or a symptom of a universal category of illness. These forms of behavior are recognized as abnormal by the peoples of the cultures themselves, and the terms *amok* and *latah* are the native terms used to describe them. *Amok* and *latah* are identified by virtue of the symptoms exhibited. Good has pointed out the profound role that culture plays not only in the expression of symptoms but also in the course the illness takes (1992).

Mental illness has been defined as abnormal behavior, that is, behavior that is different from the cultural norm in a particular society. It is important to differentiate deviant behavior that represents mental illness from deviant behavior that does not. Not all those who violate the rules of a society are, by definition, mentally ill. Some are criminals; some are rebels; some are innovators.

Rebels and Innovators

From time to time, individuals appear who renounce important aspects of their own culture and propose that a radically different way of doing things be substituted for the old way. They are frequently considered mentally ill by the members of their society, but when they are successful in attracting followers and in overthrowing the old order, they are called innovators and revolutionaries. These individuals are often central in bringing about changes that result in significant transformations in the design of the tapestry of culture. Their conceptualization, which may come to them in the form of a vision or a dream, is often a new organization for society.

The typical personality type of the well-adjusted individual in all cultures incorporates the motivations and values of the culture. Such an individual will want to do the things considered desirable in the society and will not think of changing them. This individual is very different from the rebel and innovator. The rebel, therefore, must differ in personality in some significant way from the typical person. These differences in personality between the rebel and the typical person reflect a difference in early life experience on the part of the rebel. Erik Erikson (1958, 1969) explored the relationship between successful rebels and their cultures in a series of biographical case studies of individuals such as Martin Luther and Gandhi. Erikson has stressed the significance of these individuals to the historical process of cultural change. His emphasis is on the psychological characteristics of innovators as these relate to the cultural setting within which these individuals lived and their effect on history. This approach might be seen as ancestral to psychohistories being done by some historians today.

Culture and the Structure of Emotion

Today, anthropologists also talk about the structure of emotion and how it relates to other aspects of culture, sometimes going on to make cross-cultural comparisons. Differences in the expression of emotions such as anger have been related to differences between what Rosaldo (1984) called bride-service societies—those societies that are predominantly hunting and gathering societies—and bridewealth societies—more complex, sedentary, agricultural societies. In bride-service societies, anger, if expressed, is quickly contained or forgotten. It is not allowed to fester. People in these societies see the expression of anger as destructive to social relationships. In a society like the foraging Hadza, discussed in Chapter 9, if anger cannot be contained, the only way to settle disputes is by the dispersal of the disputants. In bridewealth societies, it is expected that anger will be publicly expressed in words, since holding anger within can lead only to its expression in other ways, such as witchcraft. The implication of Rosaldo's suggestion is that small-scale, foraging societies do not have the social mechanisms to deal with overt expressions of violence and anger, while more complex societies have a variety of institutions to deal with such expressions. However, these institutional devices in more complex societies are not always successful in dealing with violence and anger. The failure of our own court and prison system to contain explosive anger attests to our inability to handle violence and expression of anger.

In the Faeroe Islands, men in particular must control their anger, since expression of anger is considered harmful to ongoing social relationships. In this characteristic, they parallel the bride-service societies discussed by Rosaldo, though the Faeroe Islanders have a different type of society. They live on some 20 islands in the north Atlantic and until recently have preserved much of their distinctive cultural identity as a consequence of limited trade and contact with the outside world. Faeroe women, whose lives are confined to the domestic sphere, can express their anger and it is not thought to be threatening, since their activities are limited to the domestic sphere. On the other hand, Faeroe men should be unemotional or, at least, less expressive of anger. A strong value is placed on male emotional control because men work outside their homes, often in cooperative endeavors in close quarters, and under such circumstances the expression of anger is socially destructive (Gaffin, 1995: 161).

The structure of emotion that characterizes Faeroe Island society is a dynamic creation that sometimes involves the "intentional production of emotional states in others" (Gaffin, 1995), which develop as a result of taunting and teasing. These are deemed undesirable and are negatively sanctioned, but they occur to test an individual's emotional mettle, as well as to demonstrate that anger must be controlled. Particular men seem more susceptible to taunting and teasing. The teasing of these men not only is an emotional sport but also channels community ideas about male behavior. The provoking behavior, by eliciting undesirable and negatively sanctioned behavior, not only tests the taunted individual's self-control, but at the same time serves as a form of social control. If the victim controls his anger and can tolerate the teasing, he is viewed in a positive manner. If he loses his temper, then he is the target of ridicule. The lesson to be learned is that a man must maintain an even temperament because loss of control damages the man's ability to be an effective member of the community.

The Person and the Self

The socially constituted person, as distinguished from the individual self, is a concept with a long history in anthropology. Individuals learn to perform a repertoire of social roles, and those roles constitute a major component of the social person. The conception of the person varies from one society to the next. Each society has its own conception of what emotions persons can appropriately express and when they can be expressed, as well as its own ideas about what is right and wrong and what characterizes the good person and the bad person.

Clifford Geertz (1974) examined differences in personhood in Java, Bali, and Western societies. Geertz, whose theoretical approaches were discussed in Chapter 1, was concerned with the methodology used by the anthropologist to see things from the native's point of view. Rather than putting himself in the place of the other or conducting psychological tests, as did earlier psychological anthropologists, Geertz preferred to analyze the series of symbolic forms that people in a culture use to represent themselves to themselves and to others. Like Margaret Mead, he begins his analysis with the Western conception of the person, which he described as "a bounded, unique, more or less integrated motivational and cognitive universe, a dynamic center of awareness, emotion, judgment, and action organized into a distinctive whole and set contrastively both against other such wholes and against its social and natural background" (1984: 126).

The sense of personhood in Java, according to Geertz, is different from the Western conception of the person. It is based on two sets of contrasts: inside/outside and refined/vulgar. The ideal for a person is, through religious discipline, to achieve a state of stilled emotion in the inner realm (he "thins out his emotional life to a constant hum"), while in the outer realm, the same kind of purity and refinement is achieved through elaborate etiquette. Refinement is desired both inside and outside, and vulgarity is to be avoided. The Javanese concept of person is a bifurcated one, in contrast to the Western concept, which emphasizes integration.

The Balinese view of the person is as an appropriate representative of a category, rather than a unique individual. People attempt to mute individual personal characteristics and to emphasize, in contrast, features of status. Geertz, who frequently used the dramatic or theatrical metaphor to describe Balinese culture, likens Balinese persons to a cast of characters. In Bali, the face itself is considered a mask. Geertz's point is that the Western concept of the person as an autonomous, bounded entity operating in his or her own way vis-à-vis other like entities is not shared by other cultures. Since Geertz is a cultural relativist who emphasizes the unique features that differentiate cultures, he also views personhood as being distinctive for each culture.

While the person may be conceived of in different ways in various cultures, there are certain universal characteristics of the person. These universal features are present in the early stages of the process of development of the person. Developmental psychologists are of the opinion that the boundedness of self and self-motivation are found in children in all societies. During the enculturation process in some societies, such as Java and Bali, a different notion of self is inculcated. All infants share boundedness and act as autonomous entities who are in contrast with others. However, as the child develops in some non-Western cultures, he or she learns to suppress this autonomous self.

Conceptualization of the self in Western cultures like that of the United States differs from conceptualization of the self in Eastern cultures like those of Java, Bali, Japan, and China. This difference is expressed in language. Roger Brown argues that the self is conceptualized differently. In order to use the proper linguistic forms in Javanese or in Japanese, the speaker must know his or her relationship to the listener (or receiver). Misperceiving the relationship and using the wrong or impolite form disgraces one. Thus, the speaker must know certain information, for example, whether the person being addressed is a professor, is of a higher social class, or is older than the speaker. Relative age is always a factor—one is either a younger brother or an older brother. One must always use the appropriate form of address. In discussing the Japanese concept of the self, Brown suggests that it is basically relational—the self constantly viewed in relation to others (higher or lower, more respectful or less respectful, older or younger). In contrast, the American self is bounded (rather than relational), autonomous, and individualistic (Brown, 1996: 47–48). The anthropologist Dorinne Kondo observed, "I was always defined by my obligations and links to others" when she conducted her research in Japan (Kondo, cited in Brown, 1996: 47). Because it is necessary for the Japanese child to learn the complexities of the social structure, and his or her place in relation to all others within that structure, learning the proper forms of linguistic expression may take hard work and years of training.

In recent research in a north China village, Kipnis found that the Chinese villagers saw the self as socially determined. As in the Japanese example discussed above, one's relationships to others constitute one's self (1999: 8). *Quanxi* refers to the formation of social relationships and *ganqing* refers to the human feeling constituted in those relationships. *Quanxi* is produced and reproduced in social actions such as visiting, helping out, using kinship terms, attending and properly behaving at various ritual gatherings, including official village banquets, weddings, and the like. The feelings embodying *ganqing* are produced on such occasions. *Quanxi* also refers to the material aspects of social relationships, such as gift giving at various rites of passage, and providing food and drink at a broad range of social events (Kipnis, 1997: chaps. 2 and 3).

Cultural Psychology

Recently, attempts have been made to integrate the approaches of anthropology and psychology, which are somewhat different from the earlier debate concerning the relationship between culture and personality. This new approach involves moving away from the idea that the fundamentals of mental life are fixed, universal, and abstract by nature, to a concern with cultural psychology, which is "the study of the way cultural traditions and social practices regulate, express, transform, and permute the human psyche, resulting less in psychic unity for humankind than in ethnic divergences in mind, self and emotion" (Stigler, Shweder, and Herdt, 1990: 1). A basic premise of cultural psychology is intentionality. That is, individuals are perceived as actors who seize meanings and resources from their cultural environment and by this process are transformed. In turn, the sociocultural world is a human product that is changed as a result of human action. Culture and human psyches are seen as interdependent and dialectically interrelated to one another. This point of view has been influenced to some extent by Bourdieu's theory of practice and its emphasis on everyday experience.

Shweder, Mahapatra, and Miller (1990), in a study that focuses on cultural distinctions in moral development between Brahman and Untouchable families in Orissa, India, and Judeo-Christian families in Chicago, Illinois, illustrate how the Indian child is socialized regarding moral understandings relating to pollution and purity. Menstruating women must remove themselves from physical contact with other people. A menstruating mother exclaims, "I am polluted (*mara*). Don't touch me!" when her young child tries to sit on her lap. She will get up and walk away if the child comes closer. These women explain that their state of menstrual pollution is due to their having stepped in dog excrement. Children soon learn that when their mothers are *mara*, they will avoid others, sleep alone on a mat on the floor, stay out of the kitchen, eat alone, and not groom themselves. According to the authors, "most six-year-olds think it is wrong for a 'polluted' (*ëmaraí*) woman to cook food or sleep in the same bed with her husband; most nine-year-olds think that *ëmaraí* is an objective force of nature and that all women in the world have a moral obligation not to touch other people or cook food while they are *ëmaraí*" (Shweder, Mahapatra, and Miller, 1990: 196). In the social interaction and communication between the young child and his or her cultural world, the child learns about the moral tenet of pollution experientially.

Learning language and learning culture are the means by which an infant becomes a part of human society. Human beings live according to the precepts of their culture, but they are also unique individuals. Most anthropologists see the relationship between the individual and his or her culture as a dialectical one. While individuals themselves are cultural products and change as their culture changes, at the same time, they also remake and change their culture.

Chapter Five

Symbolic Systems and Meanings

In their fieldwork, anthropologists observe and record what people say and do. The next step is to understand and interpret the meanings of these words and actions. This is accomplished by discussing the material with informants and examining the words and actions in a number of other cultural contexts. People's behavior is framed according to a set of symbols or cultural ideas that constitutes the overall design of the tapestry of culture. To understand people's economic behavior, political behavior, and social behavior, one must understand the system of cultural meanings that permeate these institutions. From another perspective, people in their day-to-day actions create and re-create their culture. As they do this, they are also creating and conveying cultural meaning. How they walk, how they dress, how they talk—all convey meaning. Sometimes people change their behavior, and then its meaning also changes. To understand the meaning of cultural behavior, one must "read" culture like a text.

73

The analysis of symbols deals with the meanings of things in a culture—the meanings of words, the meanings of actions, and the meanings of objects. In addition to involving meaning, symbols are also expressive and convey emotion. This is especially true with regard to symbols in art and in religion. As noted in Chapter 3, language itself is a system made up entirely of symbols. All symbols, like the morphemes of language, operate as if they are two-sided coins. On one side are the physical characteristics, and on the other side are the meanings, or what the symbols stand for. Symbols are manifested in behavior as well as in ideas. Symbols and their meanings guide people's actions and also motivate such actions. Further, people's behavior itself has symbolic meaning to those who observe it.

Metaphor, a kind of symbol, is an important analytical concept used by anthropologists in the study of symbolic systems. A metaphor is an idea that people use to stand for another set of ideas. The meaning of the metaphor is the recognition of the connection between the metaphor itself and the "something else" it represents. In the Kwakiutl marriage ceremony described in Chapter 2, many of the activities described were also characteristic of warfare, such as blackening the faces, dressing like warriors, and running through a gauntlet of fire in order to demonstrate courage. Among the Kwakiutl, marriage is metaphorically a form of warfare. Warfare is apt as a metaphor to symbolize marriage among the Kwakiutl because both involve competition. The competitive aspect of marriage is also seen in the potlatch, which pits one side against the other.

In our society, games are often used as metaphors for life. Games involve struggle and competition. Sometimes you win and sometimes you lose, but games must be played according to a set of rules. Games demand from the players strategic ability, risk taking, stamina, and courage—virtues in our culture. During Nixon's presidency, White House officials talked about "playing hardball" and used the expression from baseball, "When the going gets tough, the tough get going." Baseball was being used to stand for something else—politics—because both have competition, struggle, and some element of danger in common, though they may differ in many other respects.

Competition or struggle can be physical or mental. The chessboard is a miniature world peopled with a feudal society. In the classic movie The Seventh Seal, the White Knight plays against Death, represented by the black pieces. The White Knight plays for his life against death, which represents the Black Death—the plague sweeping Europe. The moviemaker, Ingmar Bergman, talks about life and death using the chess game as a metaphor.

Another type of symbol is a *metonym*. Like a metaphor, a metonym is also based upon a substitution of one thing for another, but in this case the symbol standing for the something else is one of the several things that constitute the something else. Thus the monarch can be referred to as the head of state, and the crown or throne can stand as a symbol for the monarchy. The capital of any type of government can be referred to as the seat of government. In each case, a part has been taken and used to stand as a symbol for the whole.

One category of symbols, *public symbols,* constitutes the cultural system for a society. Much of that body of cultural symbols is known, understood, and shared by all the members of the society. However, some symbols, often the most important ones, are more esoteric and may be known only by religious practitioners. Individuals also create symbols out of their own experiences, which are not commonly shared by others. Known as *private symbols,* they are the symbols of our dream life and fantasies. In the creative process, the artist, novelist, or filmmaker uses private symbols. The process of interpretation of artistic works by the public and the critic involves trying to decipher what the private symbols mean. We will discuss how the creative artist uses private and public symbols in Chapter 12.

At the beginning of this chapter we referred to the two-sidedness of symbols and the arbitrary relationship between the two sides, as occurs in language. For public symbols, the connection between the two is culturally, not individually, determined. The symbols and the meanings, which are connected, differ from culture to culture, as words do from language to language. Thus there are two ways in which the study of symbolism can be approached. The first is to examine a particular symbol and the different meanings that are attached to it in various cultures. The second is to begin with the other side of the coin—to study the thing symbolized and the different symbols used for it.

The Symbolism of Food

As an example of how a symbol may have various meanings attached to it in different cultures, we will examine the symbolism of food and its ingestion. From the utilitarian or materialist perspective, food is ingested by the human animal to sustain life. It is made up of calories, protein, fats, minerals, and carbohydrates and is introduced into the human animal by eating. This aspect of food is equivalent to the physical manifestations or sounds that make up a word. Not to go beyond this aspect of food in terms of one's investigation would be like analyzing words without considering their meanings.

Eating is a metaphor for sexual intercourse in a great many societies, including our own. Why is one a metaphor for the other? What do the two actions have in common? These two acts are completely different physiologically; nevertheless, they are tied together in their symbolic significance. In many societies "eating" can be used figuratively for sexual intercourse and "to hunger for" as a metaphor for sexual desire. As McKnight notes, among the Lardil of Mornington Island, Australia, "there is a strong identification between food and sex, sexual intercourse and eating" (1999: 23). In discussing eating practices among Americans, Lukanuski has pointed out the same equation and intertwining of eating and sex (1998: 114).

Eating as a metaphor is sometimes used to signify marriage. In many New Guinea societies, like that of the Lesu on the island of New Ireland in the Pacific and that of the Trobriand Islanders, marriage is symbolized by the couple's eating together for the first time. Adolescent boys and girls freely engage in sexual intercourse without commitment to marriage or any gossip or criticism from the community. But eating together constitutes a public announcement that they are now married. Eating symbolizes their new status as a married couple. In our society, it is just the reverse. One can take a date to dinner, but engaging in sexual intercourse used to be and frequently still is a sign of marriage. In other New Guinea societies, such as the Wogeo, if a man eats with a woman, then she is like his sister and he can't marry her. Here, eating is equally symbolic but has a different meaning. Instead of marriage, eating symbolizes a brother-sister relationship—those who cannot marry.

In some New Guinea societies the nuclear family is not the unit that eats together, as is the case in American society. The men take their meals in the men's house, separately from their wives and children. Women prepare and eat their food in their own houses, and take the husbands' portions to the men's house. This pattern is also widespread among Near Eastern societies, where men usually eat with other men and women with other women, and husbands and wives do not eat together. This is the case among the Marri Baluch of western Pakistan, where the family arranges marriage between close relatives, and husbands never eat with their wives. But in adulterous relationships between a man and a woman, illicit eating together symbolizes their love for one another. In Lesu, the symbolic meaning of eating is exactly opposite from its meaning among the Marri Baluch. In Lesu, betrothal and marriage are symbolized by a man and woman sitting down and eating together, but a woman never eats with her lover.

Recognition of the metaphoric connection between eating and sexual intercourse can also help explain some other cultural rules that have to do with taboos against eating certain things. In some societies, members of a clan are not allowed to eat the animal or bird that is their totemic ancestor. Since they believe themselves to be descended from that ancestor, it would be like eating that ancestor or eating themselves. This would be equivalent to sexual intercourse within the group, which is incest. For the Siuai of Bougainville in the Solomon Islands, eating the totemic animal is equivalent to having intercourse with a person from one's own clan. There is another incestlike prohibition involving food among the Abelam and the Arapesh of New Guinea. The Arapesh express it in the form of an aphorism:

Other people's mothers

Other people's sisters

Other people's pigs

Other people's yams which they have piled up

You may eat,

Your own mother

Your own sister

Your own pigs

Your own yams which you have piled up

You may not eat.

The pigs that a person raises are considered his children, and the owner of a pig is referred to as its father. The Arapesh explicitly recognize the symbolic connection between eating and sexual intercourse, as evidenced in the prohibition against eating one's own pigs and yams and the prohibition against incest with one's sister and mother. In Abelam and Arapesh, the taboo against eating one's own pigs and yams compels social groups to exchange their pigs and yams with other groups, resulting in ongoing exchange relationships with those groups.

It would be unthinkable to eat with one's enemies. Even in our own society, one may be compelled to say a polite good morning to one's enemy, but the line is drawn at breaking bread together. This is generally true in societies around the world. Eating together symbolizes goodwill and peaceful relations. What happens when enemies accidentally find themselves together for one reason or another? Among the Pathans of Swat, great stress is placed upon the giving of hospitality. Food symbolizes this hospitality. Even if the host learns the guests are enemies, with whom he would normally not share food, the rules of hospitality dictate that as guests they must be fed. When the guests are ready to leave, the host escorts them to the border of his territory. His obligations of hospitality having ended, and he is free to treat them like enemies and kill them.

As noted above, food is used to distinguish various social categories of people. It can also be used to distinguish different categories of rank. Among the Trobrianders, the highest-ranked chiefly subclan is not allowed to eat stingaree (a kind of fish) or bush pig, while low-ranking subclans may. Should members of the highest-ranked group eat these things unknowingly and then be told, they would become nauseated and would regurgitate them. The association between food prohibitions and rank is found in the most extreme form in the caste system of India, but there, the association is coupled with the idea of pollution. A caste system consists of ranked groups, each with a different economic specialization. Members of highly ranked groups can be polluted by coming into contact with the bodily secretions, particularly saliva, of individuals of lower-ranked castes. Because of the fear of pollution, Brahmans and other high-ranked individuals will not share food with, not eat from the same plate as, nor even accept food from an individual from a low-ranking caste. In Sri Lanka and India, rules about eating as well as rules about sex relations serve to keep castes apart. Higher-caste women do not marry men from lower castes, and people of high caste do not take food from people of lower castes. Once again, rules about eating and rules about sexual intercourse parallel one another in serving to keep social groups apart. However, among the Tharu of Nepal, a society also organized according to a caste hierarchy, where diet and commensality are important markers of caste, the food associated with caste is changing. This group is somewhat different from other castes in that they are seen as tribal or having an aboriginal past (McDonough, 1997: 156). Buffalo meat was taboo to them according to caste strictures. However, beginning in the last decade, Tharu men began to travel to a nearby town and to eat buffalo meat, even though it had not been fully accepted. Political developments, giving the Tharu a new sense of confidence and optimism, economic changes shifting them from sharecroppers to tenant farmers, and ideological challenges to caste have emboldened them to begin to eat buffalo without lowering their caste status (McDonaugh, 1997: 161–165).

The relationship between eating and sexual intercourse may be carried one step further in that men may be prohibited from eating foods that have metaphoric associations with women's reproductive functions. Meigs (1992), writing about the Hua of Papua New Guinea, relates the series of prohibitions to which men are subject. These include foods that are red, identified with menstrual blood; foods associated with holes, such as birds and possums that live in holes in trees; foods that are hairy, like furbearing animals and birds with facial plumage; and foods that smell like a menstruating woman, such as certain species of possum and two species of yam. Among the Hua, sexual intercourse, though initiated by men, is thought to be debilitating for males while it increases the vitality of females because of what is viewed as a transfer of *nu,* or grease. Feeding, its metaphorical opposite, is the quintessential female activity and is viewed positively because, by the transfer of *nu,* feeding produces strength and vitality.

Cultural rules determine every aspect of food consumption. Who eats together defines social units. As noted above, in our society, the nuclear family is the unit that regularly eats together. The anthropologist Mary Douglas (1972) has pointed out that for the English, the kind of meal and the kind of food that is served relate to the kinds of social links between the people who are eating together. She distinguishes between regular meals; Sunday meals, when relatives may come; and such occasions as when guests come for drinks or acquaintances are invited to a cocktail party. The food served symbolizes the occasion and reflects who is present. For example, only tidbits and snacks—finger foods—are served at a cocktail party. It would be inappropriate to serve a steak or hamburgers. The distinctions among cocktail parties, regular meals, and special dinners mark degrees of social distance and the social boundaries between those guests who are invited for drinks, those who are invited to dinner, and those who come to a family meal. In this example, the type of food symbolizes the kind of guest with whom it is eaten.

A similar analysis would apply to American society. As previously noted, individualism is prized in American society; nevertheless, when Americans eat alone, they feel uncomfortable. Eating is primarily a group activity. "Eating alone is a stigmatized behavior because it defies the expectations we have of eating. It will probably continue to be thought of as an unfortunate activity of the social outcast" (Lukanski, 1998: 119).

Food has a great many meanings in present-day American society. For example, regions are symbolized by different foods. Grits, fried chicken, black-eyed peas, collards, and mustard greens represent the South. Boiled dinners, clam chowder, and lobster immediately symbolize New England. Some American foods, like the Big Mac and Classic Coke, have become international and can be found in almost every part of the globe. On the other hand, ethnic foods and ingredients, such as bagels, pita bread, and oriental condiments, are on the shelves of supermarkets in small towns and large cities across America. This reflects the fact that ethnic identity has become increasingly important as a component of American identity. Particular dishes distinctive of a national cuisine are used to create an ethnic identity; but beyond that, members of other ethnic groups have become familiar with such foods. For example, the principal characters in *The Godfather* films are constantly signaling their Italian-American identities by what they cook and eat ("Take the cannoli; leave the gun"). Americans of other ethnicities also eat cannolis.

Social Groups, Social Categories, and Their Symbols

In the previous section, we selected something tangible, food, and then discussed the various meanings attached to it in different cultures. Group identity may be symbolized in a number of other ways in addition to its cuisine. For example, a social group such as a clan may be represented by a totemic animal, with pictorial representations of the animal being used to signify that clan. The Kwakiutl, whose wedding ceremony was discussed in Chapter 2, as well as other tribes of the Pacific coast of Canada, painted the specific totemic animal of the group on the facade of the house and carved it on the totem pole standing before the house. These tribes were like many other societies of the world, in that personal names given to members of the group belonged to the entire group. When a person died, his or her name returned to the pool of names, to be used again when a child was born. There was also the belief that a name carried an identity, and that identity was perpetuated through the names handed down from generation to generation. In this way, individual identity was linked to clan identity, since, to the outside world, the name symbolized membership in the group.

In general, the clan as a social group may be associated with particular spirits, including spirits of the clan ancestors, who are said to dwell in a specific location in the clan territory. The spirits and the territory represent the clan. Strangers crossing the territory, or hunting in it, are in danger from the spirits that protect it. In such a

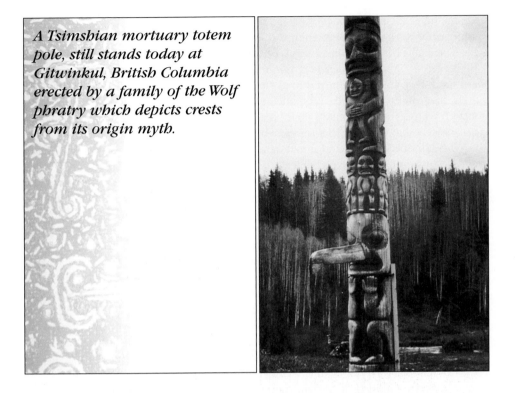

A Tsimshian mortuary totem pole, still stands today at Gitwinkul, British Columbia erected by a family of the Wolf phratry which depicts crests from its origin myth.

situation, where the land symbolizes the continuity of the social group (the clan) from mythical times to the present, the land could not be sold for money without destroying the identity of the group itself. Thus, as food stands as a symbol for the group, so too can an animal, a painting, a carving, a name, or a territory.

Fairly common forms used to symbolize social groups are birds, fish, and animals. One may ask why it is that animals are used to stand for people. Though the animal world exists apart from the human world, people use the animal world to talk metaphorically about the human world. The world is seen as a jungle or referred to as an animal farm. Though the world of animals and the world of people are very different, there are links between them. The world of animals is divided into species; the world of people, into social groups. Some animal species are more like others and share a certain number of characteristics: There are those that fly, those that swim, and those that walk or crawl. Societies use these different characteristics to make systems of classification of animals, like those discussed in Chapter 3. This classification will differ from one society to the next, because each society may single out a different series of characteristics upon which its classification is based. For example, among the Karam of New Guinea, the cassowary, an enormous flightless bird like an ostrich, is not classed as a bird, but is in a separate class. In a society with clans, each clan is different from the others, just as the animal species differ from one another. This is why differences among animal species are used to express differences among groups of people.

Sometimes society is conceptualized as being divided into halves, which may be symbolically represented as higher and lower, sun and moon, or right side and left side. The Yafar of New Guinea think of the two parts as male and female. Each village is divided into two sides, one side referred to as "male" and made up of several clans, and the other side referred to as "female" and also comprising several clans. In rituals, men of the male half of the village use objects conceptualized as male and associated with plants designated male, while men of the female half of the village use ritual objects that are female and connected to female plants (Juillerat, 1996: 48, 49, 71). The symbols of male and female are used by the Yafar to designate the halves, each with its own distinctive character, which are nevertheless complementary.

The animal world may be ordered in still another way. Some animals live very close to humans, even under the same roof; others live under human protection in the barn; still others live in the forest, where humans hunt them; and finally, certain exotic, inedible animals live in the zoo. Edmund Leach (1964) has pointed out that this particular series of animal categories corresponds to categories of social distance in English society. Sisters make up the closest category. Next come first cousins. The third category is neighbors who are not kin, and the fourth category is complete strangers with whom one has no social relationship. The significant aspect of Leach's analysis of these corresponding categories is the connection between edibility and permissible sexual relationships. The first category of animals—pets—is equivalent to the first category of females—sisters. Pets may not be eaten, and sisters are not permissible as sex partners. Farm animals make up the second animal category, and these are eaten only if they have been castrated or have not reached physical maturity. The corresponding category of women is cousins, with whom one might have sexual relations but whom one cannot marry. The third category is made up of game animals, which are edible; they correspond to neighbors, who are very marriageable. The fourth category is composed of exotic animals, which are not edible, and, correspondingly, exotic women, who are not marriageable. Leach's analysis demonstrates that the cultural domains of animal classification and of degrees of social distance of females are organized in the same way; at the same time, the parallel between edibility and permissible sexual relations becomes apparent.

Another common way to symbolize social groupings and social relationships is to use the human body. Among the Teutonic tribes at the dawn of history, close and distant relatives were symbolized by close and more distant parts of the body, reckoned from the head. The father and mother were symbolized by the head; brothers and sisters were at the neck; first cousins at the shoulders; second cousins at the elbows; third cousins at the wrists; and fourth, fifth, and sixth cousins at the knuckles and finger joints. At the cutoff point of kin were seventh cousins, who were called nail relatives. Individuals beyond seven degrees of relationship were not considered kinsmen.

The internal skeletal structure of the body is also used as a metaphor for the internal structure of society. The word *bone* was used for clan among the Mongols, and the aristocracy were referred to as *White Bone* to distinguish them from commoners, who were referred to as *Black Bone*. A slightly different metaphor is used by the Riff of Morocco, who refer to their clan as a *vein*. Just as the Mongols used a skeletal metaphor, the Riff use the metaphor of blood vessels to represent the interconnection between the parts of their society.

Americans use the metaphor of blood to represent kinship. In thinking about the biological facts of conception, we can see that the sperm from the father and the egg from the mother, which unite to form the new individual, have nothing to do with blood. Yet Americans say that the blood of their fathers and mothers flows in their veins. This is our symbolic way of talking about kinship.

The Symbolic Meanings of Space

Arrangements of space also make important symbolic statements about social groupings and social relationships. Among the Nuchanulth (Nootka) of the Pacific coast of Canada, each of the large plank houses in the winter villages in which they lived in the nineteenth century represented a social group. The floor plan of the house was divided into spaces that were ranked with respect to one another (see Figure 1). The place of honor, the left corner of the rear of the house, was occupied by the owner, who was the highest-ranking person in the house and held the highest title, and his family. The next most important man and his family occupied the right rear corner of the house; the third most important man and his family occupied the left front corner of the house; the fourth most important man and his family were in the right front corner; the least important titled man lived with his family on the left-hand side of the house. Untitled commoners and their families lived in the remaining spaces along the sides of the house. Each location had its own hearth. Each nuclear family in the Nuchanulth house was ranked with respect to the others, and this rank was symbolized by the location of each family's hearth and its living space in relation to the others. The house floor plan was like a seating plan according to seniority.

Figure 1   Nuchanulth house floor plan.

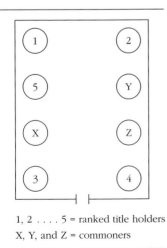

1, 2 . . . . 5 = ranked title holders

X, Y, and Z = commoners

Figure 2   Thai house floor plan.

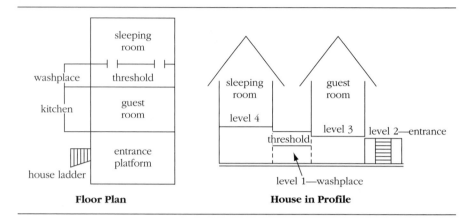

Floor Plan   **House in Profile**

In a peasant village in northeastern Thailand, space in a house is divided to symbolize not rank, but rules about marriage and sex (see Figure 2). The sleeping room is the most sacred part of the house. First cousins, with whom sexual relations and marriage are not permitted, may enter that room but may not sleep there. More distant relatives, whom one may marry, are not allowed to enter the sleeping room and must remain in the guest room. S. J. Tambiah (1969), who has analyzed the Thai material, also relates categories of animals and their edibility to relatives whom you may and may not marry. First cousins, whom you cannot marry, are equivalent to your own buffalo, oxen, and pigs, who live under the house. You may not eat them and must give them to other people. More distant relatives, whom you can marry, are equivalent to other people's domestic animals, which you can eat. The same logic that connects edible and inedible animals with marriageable and unmarriageable relatives (as pointed out in English society by Leach) is also found in Thai society. Since social space symbolizes degree of social relationship, and edibility also signifies social relationships, then the meaning of social space is also related to edibility.

Gender differences are also symbolized in the use of space. As noted earlier, husbands and wives in Papua New Guinea not only do not eat together but also live in separate houses. Women will take their husband's food to the door of the men's house but will not enter it. Space is also gendered in the Middle East, where men who are not members of the family may not enter the women's quarters.

The way in which people use social space can also reflect social relationships and ethnic identity. Early immigrants to America from Europe brought with them a communal style of living, which they retained until late in the eighteenth century. Historical records and archaeological findings document a group-oriented existence, in which one room was used for eating, entertaining guests, and sleeping (Dietz, 1977, in Pader, 1993: 18). People ate stews from a communal pot, shared drinking cups, and used a common pit toilet. With the development of ideas about individualism, people soon began to shift to the use of individual cups and plates; the eating of meals, which included meat, starch, and vegetables, served on separate plates; and the use of individual chamber pots. They began to build their houses with separate rooms to entertain guests (living rooms), separate bedrooms for sleeping, separate work areas (kitchen, laundry room), and separate bathrooms.

In Mexico, the meaning and organization of domestic space is strikingly different. Houses are organized around a patio, or courtyard. Rooms for sleeping, dressing, talking when the weather is inclement, cooking, and storage open onto the patio, where all kinds of domestic activities, such as socializing, child play, bathing, and doing laundry, take place. Individuals do not have separate bedrooms. Children often sleep with parents, and same-sex siblings share a bed, emphasizing familial interdependence. Rooms in Mexican houses are locations for multiple activities that, in contrast, are rigidly separated in the United States.

The households of Mexican Americans in Los Angeles represent a transition between Mexican and American usages. According to Pader, they "blur the lines between the U.S. coding system, with its emphasis on greater bodily privacy and the individual, and the Mexican system, with its emphasis on sharing and close daily interconnection" (Pader, 1993: 130–131). As Mexican-American children mature, they change their ideas about family, become more individuated, and desire their own beds and bedrooms.

Gypsies, who are found in every major American city, have retained important elements of their own culture, including extended families, which form households, and their ideas about pollution and space utilization. When the Gypsies of Richmond, California, move into a house previously occupied by non-Gypsies (*gaje*), the house must first be ritually cleansed of the polluting effects of *gaje* by a thorough cleaning with disinfectants and the burning of incense. Then the inner walls are torn down and the doors removed to create communal living space, which is divided by hanging drapes. One space is devoted to palm reading, the major source of income; the other space is used as a living area for the extended family that will live there. The head of one Gypsy family moved into what had formerly been a bar and dance club in order to house the 28 members of his family and the many guests the family entertained (Sutherland, 1986).

Space may also be symbolically conquered and inscribed with new meanings. In recent decades, many Muslims, members of Sufi regional cults centered in the North-West Frontier Province of Pakistan, have migrated to England, extending and expanding cult influence (Werbner, 1996). At first, Muslim religious and ritual observances were conducted in mosques and in the home, where immigrants' religious observances were protected from external hostility. Expansion and conquest of new space is a significant aspect of Sufi cult organization. As Werbner notes, "the moral conquest of alien space is a test of the charismatic authenticity that legitimizes the rise of new 'living saints' " (1996: 310). Muslim men march and chant, twice a year, in the *julus* ceremonial procession through the Manchester, Birmingham, or London Pakistani immigrant neighborhoods, "sacralizing and 'Islamazicizing' the very earth, the buildings, the streets and the neighborhoods through which they march" (Werbner, 1996: 312). The "new order" with its own "living saints" is established in a foreign place, but these diasporas are still connected to home, creating a transnational network encompassing the East and the West. The march is also "an expression of the rights of minorities to celebrate their culture and religion in the public domain within a multicultural, multifaith, multiracial society" (Werbner, 1996: 333).

Symbols, Politics, and Authority

Just as clans can be represented by such things as totems, houses, and personal names, so too may an entire nation be represented by an array of symbols. The combat between symbolic animals—the eagle and the bear—was used by political cartoonists to portray the conflict between the United States and the former Soviet Union. In the same way that the Nuchanulth house and the Thai house symbolize those who live within them, so also do two buildings represent the United States and Russia. News reports often indicate that the White House says this and the Kremlin says that. National flags, anthems, and food also symbolize nations. Trees sometimes are used to symbolize the nation-state, as exemplified by the cedar, which symbolizes Lebanon.

Individuals in positions of authority are associated with particular objects that become symbols of the office they hold. Sometimes the object is something, such as a crown or imperial regalia or insignia, that the officeholder alone may wear. The installation ceremony for a successor usually involves putting on the garments or in-

A Fante chief from Ghana with his symbols of authority, which include his "cloth of gold" cloak, headdress, jewelry, and fly wisk.

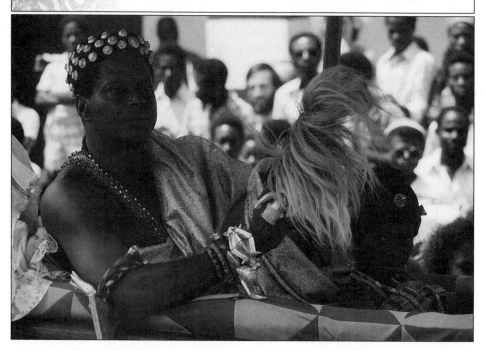

signia of office. Sometimes the officeholder carries a staff, wand, umbrella, or fly whisk. In our definition of *metonym,* we pointed out how the crown or the throne could alternatively stand for the monarchy. A parallel is found in the term referring to the leader of an academic department at a college or university. He or she is referred to as either the chair or the head. These symbols of authority are metonyms. Use of the term *head* draws attention to one end of the human anatomy, while use of the term *chair* draws attention to the opposite end.

In a number of African societies, the ruler or paramount chief represents the entire society. Thus the health of its members, as well as their fertility and the fertility of their crops, is dependent on the ruler and his health. Among the Aluund of southwestern Zaire, the paramount chief is linked metaphorically not only to the entire body politic of Aluund society but also to the kapwiip tree (De Boek, 1994). Trees in general serve as Aluund metaphors for the sexual joining of male and female, and, therefore, trees serve a unifying and purifying function. Just as the chief is the elder at the center of the community around whom the populace gathers, the kapwiip tree is the elder among trees. The chief is perceived as the trunk, and the people are the fruit surrounding the trunk. The chief rarely leaves his compound; instead, he listens (a mark of wisdom) to the people who come to him there, like the wise kapwiip tree, which remains in one place and "listens." By listening well, the chief mediates and resolves disputes. He is seen as asexual, with both powerful masculine and nurturant feminine characteristics, and is portrayed as Janus-like in carvings—one face male, and the other female. The staff he holds, made from the wood of the kapwiip tree, is carved to represent three levels—a bird (usually the fish eagle) symbolizing heaven, a female human symbolizing earth, and a snake and crocodile symbolizing the underworld. The chief is seen as mediating between these three worlds. He is "lord of the soil," responsible for all regenerative aspects of Luunda culture (De Boek, 1994: 457). Since fertility and reproduction depend on the state of the paramount chief, he must not show signs of disease, decay, or old age. The Aluund have a complex symbolic system in which metaphors are simultaneously extended in many different directions.

If authority is represented by a series of symbols, opposition to that authority is symbolically represented by an inversion of those symbols. In the 1960s in the United States, all men in authority had short hair. Young men created a symbol of opposition when they allowed their hair to grow long. If authorities have short hair, then long hair is a symbol of opposition to that authority. However, today, wearing one's hair long is acceptable. Long hair is no longer a symbol of opposition to society, but dyeing one's hair fuchsia, blue, or orange is. During the seventeenth century, the Cavaliers of Charles I of England wore their hair long, while those who opposed them, the Puritans led by Oliver Cromwell, wore short hair. The Puritans' hairstyle became the focal symbol of their opposition, and so they were called Roundheads (as depicted in a cartoon of the period on page 86). These examples relate to the general principle that those who oppose the established authority will select as their symbol something that is the reverse of the symbol of those in authority. Political symbols may seem trivial, but, in reality, people will die rather than deny them or give them up. People's identity as members of a group is powerfully bound up with such symbols. To deny or reject them is to deny one's identity and worth.

The Cavaliers of seventeenth-century England wore their hair long, while their Puritan opposition wore their hair short. In this cartoon of the period, both men and their dogs are characterized by their respective hairstyles.

In our society, love poetry is seen solely as the expression of feeling and sentiment toward another person. However, among the Awlad ʿAli Bedouin of Egypt, love poetry, in addition to expressing personal sentiments, is a symbolic means of proclaiming opposition to authority and the social order, as noted in Chapter 3 (Abu-Lughod, 1990). This authority is exercised by male elders within the family and the lineage, who make all major decisions concerning such things as resource allocation and the arrangement of marriages. Love poetry, a highly developed art, represents a challenge to that authority since any form of sexuality or desire for marriage outside of what the elders approve is perceived as a threat to the system of family and lineage. There is an inherent contradiction in Bedouin society between the hierarchical system of lineage and family and the wider sphere of tribal politics with its ideal of autonomy and freedom. Love poetry reflects this fundamental tension. According to Abu-Lughod, there is ambivalence and discomfort concerning love poetry, and yet it is also glorified since it represents a refusal to be dominated, which echoes the wider tribal ideology emphasizing freedom. It is a discourse of defiance and rebellion recited by young men and women, those dominated by the hierarchical system, and yet it appeals to both the oppressed and their oppressors and is widely admired by all segments of Bedouin society.

The Symbolism of Sports

As noted earlier, games in a culture are often metaphors for life. Sports in American society are children's games played by adults, but they are much more than just games. They make symbolic statements about the society, which explains their enormous popularity. Individual sports, such as tennis, pool, and even chess, whether they are physical or intellectual activities, have certain aspects in common that relate them to American culture. They involve situations of head-to-head competition in which each person relies only on himself or herself to win. This is the rugged individualism of American society. In such one-on-one sports, it is important to establish a reputation, which is often not an accurate reflection of the individual's true abilities, but rather an attempt to create the impression that the individual is much better or much worse than he or she really is. This is done either to frighten an opponent or to create overconfidence in the opponent. In pool, this is referred to as one's speed, and one should never let an opponent know one's true speed. In many Western films of the past, these same features of individualism and reputation characterized the gunfighter. These same symbols, rugged individualism and a reputation that will create fear in others, are also operative in American business, where the people at the top are perceived as having gotten there on their own by beating out their opponents in head-to-head competition.

In American team sports, such as football, individual achievement is subordinated to team effort. Here, the symbolism is different. Football is an exclusively male activity in which male bonding ties individuals together in a collective effort. In this aspect, it is similar to male initiations in other societies, in which a ritual separates men from women and binds them together into a male peer group. As in such male initiation rites, in professional and college football during the training period and before games, male players are separated from women. In his analysis of American football, entitled "Into the Endzone for a Touchdown," Alan Dundes examines the folk speech involved in football and observes "that American football could be a ritual combat between groups of males attempting to assert their masculinity by penetrating the endzones of their rivals" (1978: 86). He likens football, as a form of symbolic homosexual behavior, to the initiation rites of aboriginal Australia, which also have a homosexual aspect. The male bonding of American football sets males, the participants, against females, the outsiders. This would also explain why the New England Patriots had strong feelings that the presence of a female reporter in their dressing room was completely inappropriate. In their eyes, she was intruding into a male ritual. The team aspect of football is also a recapitulation of the value of teamwork, pulling together for a common goal, in American society.

When a sport that originated in one culture spreads to another culture, it may take on a completely different set of symbolic meanings. With the expansion of the British Empire, cricket moved into the colonial areas that the British conquered, and today it is enthusiastically played from the Caribbean to the Pacific, especially on the Indian subcontinent. During the colonial period, it personified the quintessence of British colonialism. In fact, the expression *not cricket* means not acting like a proper

Englishman and refers to stretching the rules. Nowhere is cricket played in a more spirited fashion than in the Trobriand Islands, where it was introduced by English missionaries at the beginning of the twentieth century. Over the years, the Trobrianders transformed the English version of the game, which represented colonial domination, into a cultural creation that has a multiplicity of meanings in their own Trobriand culture. In contrast to English cricket, where all the players wear white, in Trobriand cricket the players dress in the traditional regalia for warfare, and each team may have up to 40 players. The cricket game is usually part of the competition when one village challenges another to a *kayasa,* a competitive period of feasting and exchange of yams. Magic that was used in warfare, which was outlawed by the colonial authorities, is used during the cricket game, since the game of cricket is symbolically like warfare as well as like competitive exchange. When the bowler pitches the ball, he recites the magic formula that was formerly used to make a spear hit its target. In Trobriand cricket, the home team always wins; this is not supposed to happen in Western sports. The symbolism of Trobriand cricket may be seen as more like that of competitive exchange—first you "win," then I "win"—than the way sports are played in the United States, that is, to decide the "ultimate" winners.

Universal Symbols

It can be argued that certain symbols are found universally and carry similar meanings in all cultures. Colors are frequently associated with emotional states and sometimes with other meaningful messages as well. Some have argued that red brings about emotional arousal on the part of the viewer. In American society red means danger and is used for stop signs in traffic control. Green is the complementary color to red and is used to symbolize the opposite of red. Since traffic lights, like all symbols, are arbitrary, the question of whether they might have originally been put forth in reversed fashion, so that red meant go and green meant stop, could be asked. Because these symbols are part of the larger category of color symbolism in our society, in which a red dress symbolizes a prostitute, the red-light district signifies a den of iniquity, and red hair means a fiery temper, it seems likely that the colors could not have been reversed. The question of whether red has the same meaning in other cultures remains to be systematically explored. In our society, black is the color of mourning; at a funeral, people wear black clothing. In contrast, white, the color of Maria Shriver's wedding gown, represents purity and virginity. A bride wears white when the relationship is established and black if the relationship is terminated by the death of her husband. In China the color symbolism for death and mourning is exactly the opposite; there, white is the color of death and mourning, so mourners wear white clothing. It is clear that the meanings of colors vary from one culture to another.

Other symbols have been suggested as ones that have universal meaning. Hair is one of these. As noted above, long hair can be a symbol of rebellion when everyone else is wearing short hair. However, Edmund Leach (1958) has pointed out that, in a number of widely separate cultures, long hair, especially unkempt long hair, is a symbol of sexuality. Short hair symbolizes restraint, while a shaved head often indicates celibacy. Rituals that involve the cutting of hair are seen as symbolic forms of castration. The symbolism of hair is quite overt. We are not dealing here with private symbols of the type referred to earlier in the chapter, but rather with a culturally accepted and widely understood symbol. It is not a symbol whose meaning is unconscious.

Symbols and their meanings are crucial to understanding what a culture is all about. The term *metaphor* refers to the relationship in which one thing stands for something else, as eating is a metaphor for sexual activity. *Metonym* refers to a part of something standing for the whole, such as the crown that stands for the political authority of the Queen of England. Symbols are two-sided—the physical properties of the symbol as distinct from what the symbol stands for. For example, food has many different meanings in different cultures, as does space. Political authority is also symbolized in a variety of ways. Sports activities resonate symbolic meanings, which are often unconscious. In the chapters to come, we will discuss different cultural domains, such as kinship, economics, political organization, and religion, which are all imbued with symbolic meaning. To understand how these institutions work, one must understand the symbols and the cultural meanings through which they are organized.

Chapter Six

Marriage, Family, and Kinship

In the weaving of the tapestry of culture, kinship plays a fundamental role. In the societies anthropologists first studied, most of daily life was organized on the basis of kinship relationships. In these small-scale societies, all religious, economic, and political behavior took place within the context of a single social structure. This social structure was organized on the basis of kinship, which is why the study of kinship was so important. In Chapter 2, we described weddings in two different societies. In each case, groupings of kin played significant roles in the course of the event. The Kwakiutl have groups based on kinship that they refer to as *numayms*. How does one become a member of a numaym? What are one's responsibilities toward other members of the numaym? What are one's rights and privileges as a member of a *numaym?* What is one's relationship with people in different numayms? Are all one's kin in one's own numaym?

In contrast to the Kwakiutl wedding is the American wedding described in Chapter 2. Once again, groupings of people based on kinship participated—the bride's side and the groom's side, immediate relatives and distant relatives. In addition, there were those who were not relatives at all but who attended as friends, neighbors, and fellow workers. What are the differences between the ways relatives are grouped in Kwakiutl society and the ways they are grouped in our own society? What do these differences mean? This chapter will present concepts that anthropologists have developed to answer these questions.

In Chapter 2, we pointed out that a Kwakiutl wedding is an example of what are called *total social phenomena.* This means that political, economic, religious, and aesthetic aspects of the society, as well as kinship, are brought into play simultaneously. Despite the interwoven nature of all these aspects of culture in a Kwakiutl wedding, kinship can be disentangled from the rest for the purposes of analysis. The discussion of marriage, family, and kinship that follows will deal with the cultural rules to be found in a variety of societies. It is important to note that in every society, there will always be variations in behavior and deviations from these cultural rules. In the succeeding chapters on religion, politics, economics, and art, we will see that kinship plays a crucial role in these areas in small-scale societies.

Such societies were shaken to their roots as they were incorporated into colonial empires and then into new nations. However, kinship and kin groups have continued to be very significant in people's lives, whether they remained in their rural villages or migrated to look for work in expanding cities like Lagos, Nigeria, or Port Moresby, Papua New Guinea.

Until recently, it was widely believed by anthropologists that kinship relations withered in modern industrial societies. The sociologist Lewis Wirth had hypothesized that with the growth of urbanism, kinship bonds would weaken and decline in importance. As we shall see later, research on kinship in America has revealed just the opposite. Though relatives may not be living in the same town or city, they maintain contact by letter and phone.

Marriage

All known societies recognize marriage. The ritual of marriage marks a change in status for a man and a woman and the acceptance by society of the new family that is formed. Marriage, like all other things cultural, is governed by rules. Just as the rules vary from one society to another, so does the ritual by which society recognizes and celebrates the marriage. In the American wedding, the bridegroom places a ring on the third finger, left hand, of the bride and repeats the ritual formula, "With this ring, I thee wed." In the Kwakiutl wedding, the bridegroom comes as a member of a feigned war party to capture the bride and "move" her from her father's house with the payment of many blankets. These represent just two of the many ways that societies recognize and accept marriage and the formation of a new family. At both Kwakiutl and American weddings, large numbers of guests are present who represent society, serving as witnesses to the marriage. The presence of these witnesses signifies that marriage is more than a private affair and that it is recognized publicly by society. Sometimes, the ritual may be as minimal as in the Trobriand case mentioned in the previous chapter, where marriage is signified merely by the couple's publicly eating together.

Marriage Prohibitions

Societies also have rules that state whom one can and cannot marry. Rules about whom one cannot marry are directly related to the *incest taboo*. Like marriage, the incest taboo is found in all societies and is therefore a cultural universal. The incest taboo forbids sexual relations between certain categories of close relatives. Almost universally, forbidden categories include mother and son, father and daughter, and brother and sister. If sexual partners cannot be sought within the immediate family because of the incest taboo, then they must be sought elsewhere. The incest taboo that forbids sexual relations also necessarily forbids marriage, since marriage almost always includes sexual access. In many societies, there are people with whom one can have sexual intercourse but whom one cannot marry. Marriage prohibitions, therefore, are wider in scope than the prohibitions against sexual intercourse. Both the incest taboo and prohibitions against marrying certain close relatives have the effect of compelling individuals to seek sexual partners and mates outside their own group. Beyond the immediate family, there is great variation from one society to another in the rules regarding which categories of relatives one is forbidden to marry. Even within the United States, there is variation among the states in the laws regarding which relatives one may not marry. Some states permit marriage between first cousins while others prohibit it; still others prohibit marriage between second cousins.

There are a few striking examples of marriage between members of the immediate family that seem to violate the universality of the incest taboo. Among the pharaohs of ancient Egypt, such as Tutankhamen, the boy king, as well as among the royal lineages of Hawaii and the Incas in Peru, brother and sister married. In each instance, the ruler had to marry someone equal in rank, and who could be better qualified than one's own brother or sister?

Endogamy and Exogamy

In anthropological terms, marriage within the group is called *endogamy* and marriage outside the group is called *exogamy*. A rule of exogamy, like the incest taboo, requires that members of the group seek spouses outside their own group. A rule of exogamy is frequently conceptualized as an extension of the incest taboo in that the same term is used for both. For example, among the Trobriand Islanders, the term *suvasova* is used for the incest taboo and is also extended to forbid sexual relations and marriage with women of one's own larger kin group, or *dala,* all of whom are called sisters. A rule of endogamy requires individuals to marry within their own group and forbids them to marry beyond it. Religious groups such as the Amish, Mormons, Catholics, and Jews have rules of endogamy, though these are often violated when marriages take place outside the group. As noted in Chapter 5, castes in India are also endogamous. Rules of endogamy preserve separateness and exclusivity, and are a means of maintaining boundaries between one group and other groups. In this sense, the brother-sister marriages referred to above reach the absolute limit of endogamy in order to preserve sanctity and power within the ruling families of those societies. More typical are those cases where the immediate family is exogamous, while the larger group, frequently an ethnic group or religious sect, is endogamous.

Sister Exchange

Since a rule of exogamy demands that spouses come from outside one's group, relationships are created through marriage with other groups. If a man cannot marry his own sister, he gives his sister to someone in another group. According to the basic principle of exchange, something given, if accepted by the receiver, must be returned with its equivalent. If a man accepts another man's sister, he must therefore return his own sister as the equivalent. After all, the receiver, too, may not marry his own sister. In fact, in a number of societies over the world, there is a rule requiring that two men exchange sisters; anthropologists refer to this as *sister exchange*. If a man does not have a biological sister, he returns a woman for whom he uses the same kinship term that he uses for his sister. Recently, feminist anthropologists have argued that this form of marriage could just as easily be conceptualized as brother exchange. However, where men are dominant in a society, this is seen as sister exchange "from the native point of view." When Margaret Mead went to study the Mountain Arapesh in New Guinea, she asked them why they didn't marry their own sisters, expecting a response indicating revulsion at the very thought. Instead, Mead's informant stated, "What is the matter with you anyway? Don't you want a brother-in-law?" (Mead, 1935: 68). This is because one hunts, gardens, and travels with one's brother-in-law among the Arapesh. Thus a marriage creates a link not only between husband and wife but also, through the wife, between two men who are brothers-in-law to each other.

Marriage Payments

In many societies marriage involves a transfer or exchange of property. Sometimes, payments are made by the groom and his family to the family of the bride. This payment is known as *bridewealth*. In other instances, the bride brings property with her at the marriage. This is known as *dowry*. When dowry is paid, goods move in the opposite direction from bridewealth payments. In societies that practice sister exchange, there may be an option to give bridewealth if one does not have a sister to exchange. However, it is also common to find sister exchange accompanied by the payment of bridewealth, so that groups are exchanging both women and bridewealth payments. In China both bridewealth and dowry were present.

Shell rings are presented as bridewealth at an Abelam marriage.

Sometimes the groom exchanges labor for his bride, in lieu of the payment of bridewealth. When the groom works for his wife's family, this is known as *bride service*. It may be recalled that in the Old Testament Jacob labored for 7 years in order to marry Leah and then another 7 years to marry Rachel, Leah's younger sister, thus performing 14 years of bride service for his father-in-law. Bride service is also practiced by the Yanomamo, a people living in the lowlands of Venezuela. During this time, the groom lives with the bride's parents and hunts for them. Since the Yanomamo also have sister exchange, one might say that during this period of bride service, when men live with the bride's parents, they really are practicing brother exchange. However, since men determine whom women will marry, the Yanomamo do not conceptualize this as two women exchanging their brothers. After the period of bride service is over, the husband takes his wife back to his group. Yanomamo women prefer to marry within the same village rather than into some distant village; that way they can remain close to their families after marriage so that their brothers can offer them a degree of protection from husbandly abuse.

Number of Spouses

Another set of rules concerning marriage is exemplified by the biblical case of Jacob—rules regarding number of spouses. Some societies, like our own, practice *monogamy;* that is, only one spouse at a time is permitted. However, according to the Bible, husbands could have more than one wife. This is known as *polygyny* and is still permitted in many societies in the world, particularly Islamic societies. Sometimes, as in the case of Jacob, a man marries several sisters. This practice is known as *sororal polygyny*. In the societies in which it occurs, it is usually explained by saying that sisters have a good relationship with one another, and this will help overcome the inevitable jealousy that arises between co-wives. On the other hand, many people, such as the Trobriand Islanders and the Kanuri of Nigeria, explicitly forbid sororal polygyny. The Kanuri explanation for this prohibition is that the good relationship between two sisters should not be undermined by the unavoidable friction that arises between two co-wives. This simply demonstrates that whatever rules are in effect, the people will offer an explanation for their existence that is perfectly rational in their eyes. An alternative form of marriage, known as *polyandry,* in which one woman may have several husbands, occurs but is rather rare. In almost all cases, a woman marries several brothers; this is known as *fraternal polyandry*. Today, among ethnic Tibetans in northwest Nepal, the ideal form of marriage is fraternal polyandry, in which the eldest brother is the primary husband and nominally the father of all the children, whether or not he is the biological father (Levine, 1987). Sometimes, anthropologists wish to refer to plural spouses in general, either husbands or wives. In that case, they use the term *polygamy,* in contrast to the term *monogamy*. Because of the frequency of divorce and subsequent remarriage in the United States, it is sometimes said that Americans practice *serial monogamy*. We may not have more than one spouse at a time, but some people have numerous spouses, one after the other.

Levirate and Sororate

The exchange of a woman for another woman or the exchange of a woman for bridewealth is an indication that more than the bride and groom are involved in a marriage. Marriage is even more significantly the concern of the kin groups of the marrying couple. A further demonstration of this is found in the customs of the *levirate* and the *sororate*. Under the levirate, if a man dies, his widow then marries one of his brothers. The brother of the dead man steps into the deceased's place, thereby continuing the relationship between the two kin groups established by the first marriage. In the levirate, a woman marries one brother after the death of another brother; in fraternal polyandry she can be married to two brothers simultaneously. When a deceased wife is replaced in the marriage by her sister, usually an unmarried younger sister, this is known as the sororate. It is like sororal polygyny, but in the sororate a man marries two sisters, the second after the death of the first. The levirate and sororate illustrate what the British anthropologist Radcliffe-Brown referred to as the equivalence of siblings (1952), where one same-sex sibling can be substituted for another in certain societies.

Dissolution of Marriage

Stability of marriage varies from one society to another. Almost all societies provide a means for divorce or the dissolution of a marriage; however, this may be very difficult in some societies. Divorce is invariably more difficult after children have been born to the couple. Where bridewealth has been paid, it would have to be returned if the wife leaves her husband. This may be difficult to achieve if the bridewealth, paid several years before, has been spent, dispersed, or consumed. Some anthropologists have argued that the higher the bridewealth payment, the more stable the marriage and less likely a divorce, since it would require the return of bridewealth, which is so difficult in such societies. Others have said that frequency of divorce and stability of marriage are related not to the amount of bridewealth but to the degree of incorporation of a wife into her husband's family or kin group. Among the Manchus of Manchuria, who conquered China in the seventeenth century, the wife went through a fire ceremony in front of the hearth in her husband's house. This ritual served to conceptually incorporate her permanently into his kin group. In contrast, as noted in Chapter 2, at marriage, the Kwakiutl paid bridewealth to the bride's family. At a subsequent ceremony, the bride's family paid a large amount of goods to "repurchase" her, thereby reiterating her membership in the kin group of her birth. The husband must make a new bridewealth payment if he wishes her to continue to be his wife. The bridewealth and repurchase payments of the Kwakiutl, which were integral parts of Kwakiutl marriage, symbolize how two people may be joined in marriage and yet retain an identity in their own kin groups. The difference in these ceremonies indicates that divorce was more difficult among the Manchus than among the Kwakiutl.

Postmarital Residence

Societies have *postmarital residence* **rules** concerning where the new couple should live after marriage. In the North American wedding described in Chapter 2, the newly married couple set up their own household. In the case of a couple with two careers in two different cities, two households may be created, though it would appear that the primary residence of the Schwarzeneggers was in their Pacific Palisades home. The postmarital residence rule in American society is that the new couple form an independent household. This is referred to as *neolocal residence* (see Figure 1). It is clear that this is a rule in American society, since breaching it brings sanctions. If the newly married couple live for an extended period with the family of either the husband or the wife, this move is typically explained in terms of economic hardship or the couple's student status. Gossips will make snide comments about the lack of independence of the couple, since they continue to live as though they were children, and gossip is a strong sanction. If the

Figure 1.   Rules of residence.

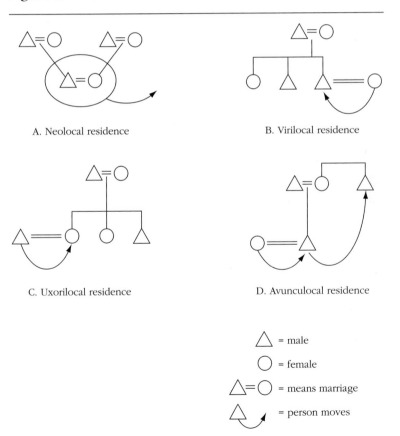

A. Neolocal residence

B. Virilocal residence

C. Uxorilocal residence

D. Avunculocal residence

$\triangle$ = male

$\bigcirc$ = female

$\triangle=\bigcirc$ = means marriage

$\triangle$ = person moves

newly married couple move in with the husband's parents, comments are made about two women in the same kitchen and the mother-in-law problem; if they move in with the wife's parents, the result is inevitable difficulties between father-in-law and son-in-law. Neolocal residence is not only characteristic of our society. It is found in other societies as well.

Probably the most common form of postmarital residence is the situation in which the newly married couple live in the household of the groom's parents. This is known as *virilocal residence* (also referred to as patrilocal residence). With a rule of virilocal residence for the new couple, the wife is incorporated, to a greater or lesser extent, into the household of her husband's kin, since it is she (the bride) who must leave the family in which she was born and raised. The groom merely remains in his household.

Less frequent is the case in which the newly married couple live in the household of the bride's parents. This is called *uxorilocal residence* (also referred to as matrilocal residence). In this instance it is the husband who must be incorporated into his wife's family. In the past, in some Pueblo societies of Arizona and New Mexico that had a rule of uxorilocal residence, the degree of incorporation of the husband into his wife's family was so slight that the wife could divorce him simply by leaving his belongings on the doorstep. Today in the Pueblo area, neolocal residence prevails, reflecting adaptation to the larger American society. When a groom performs bride service for his wife's father, as Jacob did for Laban in the Bible, he lives uxorilocally for the period of the bride service (see page 95). Then, like Jacob, he usually returns with his wife to live virilocally, with his own family.

Still another rule of postmarital residence is the arrangement in which, after marriage, the wife joins her new husband, who is living with his mother's brother rather than his own father. This is called *avunculocal residence*. This rule of residence involves two separate and distinct moves. The earlier move occurs when a man, as an adolescent, leaves his father's house to go to live with his mother's brother, from whom he will inherit later in life. The incorporation of the young man into the household of his mother's brother is associated with matrilineal descent, discussed below. After the marriage, the wife joins her husband at his maternal uncle's house. The Trobriand Islanders have an avunculocal rule of postmarital residence.

Sometimes a society will have a rule of residence stating that after marriage, the couple can live either with the bride's family or with the groom's family. In contrast to our own society, they cannot establish an independent household. This is called *bilocal residence*. On Dobu, an island near the Trobriands, the married couple spend one year in the bride's village and the following year in the groom's village, alternating in this manner between the two villages every year. Among the Iban of Borneo, however, a choice must be made at some point after marriage between affiliation with one side or the other, and this choice becomes permanent.

Lastly, there is a postmarital residence rule in which husband and wife live with their respective kin, apart from one another. This is known as *duolocal residence*. The Ashanti of Ghana, who traditionally lived in large towns, have this form of postmarital residence. Husbands and wives live in the same town, but not in the same household. At dusk, one could see young children carrying the evening meal from their mother's house to their father's house for their father to eat.

Family Types and Households

The rules stating where a couple should live after marriage result in different types of family structures. People who are related by kinship to one another constitute a family, while people living together under one roof form a household. All the members of a household may not necessarily be related by kinship to one another. Family and household units, therefore, may or may not coincide. In the Ashanti example just discussed, the family unit of husband, wife, and children live in two separate households.

With neolocal postmarital residence, as exists in America, the family that is formed is the *nuclear family* (see Figure 2). It consists of the husband, the wife, and children until they marry, at which point those children will establish their own nuclear families. The nuclear family is an independent household that operates autonomously in economic affairs, in the rearing of children, and in other phases of life.

What happens when there are plural spouses, as in societies that practice polygyny or polyandry? Among the Kanuri, where polygyny is practiced, though only a small proportion of men actually have more than one wife, each wife must have her own house and hearth. This situation is typical of a number of African societies. The husband must visit each wife in turn, at which time she cooks for him, and he must stay the night with her. Though he may favor one wife over another, he must treat them equally. A man's house and those of his wives form a single compound or household. Even though they have separate hearths and separate houses, they are all under the authority of the husband, who is the head of the household. Such a household might also include slaves belonging to the head of the household. In polyandrous societies, like Tibet, a woman and her several husbands, usually brothers, live in the same house and form a single household.

When several related nuclear families live together in the same household, they form an *extended family*. When there is a rule of virilocal residence, the household consists of an older married couple, their married sons and wives, and the unmarried children of both the older couple and their married sons. These all form one extended family. Their married daughters will have left the household to join the households of their husbands. The center of this type of extended family is a core of related men. Their in-marrying wives come from many different places and are not related to each other.

Uxorilocal postmarital residence results in extended families of a very different sort. In this case, a core of related women remain together, and their husbands marry into the extended family. With avunculocal residence there is once again a core of men forming the basis of the extended family, but this core of men is linked through women. Avunculocal residence occurs when a young man moves to his mother's brother's house during adolescence.

Extended families vary in the composition of the core of the family, as discussed above. They also vary in their extent. They may consist of parents and married children and their families. Some extended families consist only of parents and one married son and his family. Such a family is known as a *stem family* and occurs in parts of rural Ireland. Since the amount of land inherited is small and cannot be profitably

Figure 2.   Family types.

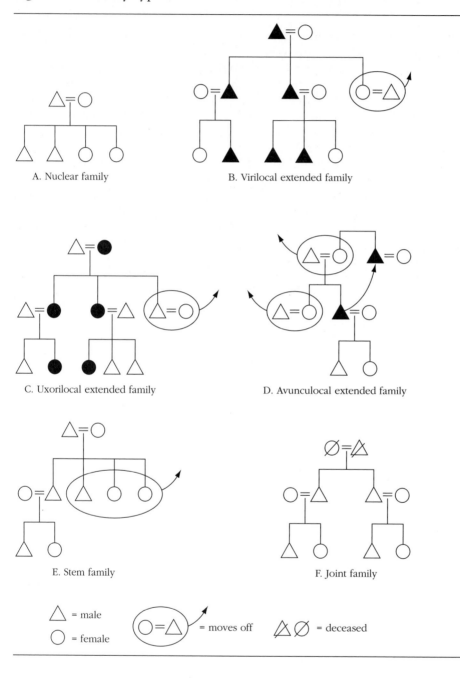

A. Nuclear family

B. Virilocal extended family

C. Uxorilocal extended family

D. Avunculocal extended family

E. Stem family

F. Joint family

△ = male
○ = female
(○=△)↗ = moves off
⧄ ⦰ = deceased

A Kirghiz extended family from the Pamir Mountains posing in front of their yurt.

subdivided, only one son, typically the youngest one, inherits the land, while his older brothers go off to the cities, become priests, or emigrate to Boston or Hong Kong. Another type of extended family is the *joint family,* which includes brothers and their wives and children who stay together as a single family after the parents have died. In most of the examples discussed above, family type and household coincide and perform a variety of functions, including the socialization of children, cooperation in economic activities, and political decision making.

Descent Groups

The kinds of family groups that we have just described are based upon both kinship and common residence. In many societies, there are groups based upon shared kinship or descent where the members need not live in the same place. These groups are usually called *clans* by the anthropologist. Members of a clan believe they are descended from a common ancestor who lived many generations ago. We have previously discussed exogamy, that is, the rule that one must marry outside one's group. In most societies that have clans, though certainly not in all, clans are exogamous, and one must marry outside one's own clan. This means that one's mother and one's father come from different clans. A child cannot be a member of both the mother's clan and the father's clan (see Figure 3). Going back two generations, that child has four grandparents, each of them likely to come from four different clans, and eight great-grandparents from as many as eight different clans. Just as the child could be a member only of the clan of one parent, that child's father could be a member only of one of his parents' clans.

Patrilineal Descent and Matrilineal Descent

Societies have rules that state that the child belongs either to the mother's clan or to the father's clan. A rule that states that a child belongs to his or her father's clan is called a *patrilineal rule of descent*. This means that children belong to their father's clan, the father belongs to his father's clan, and so forth, as illustrated in the diagram (see Figure 3). A daughter belongs to her father's clan, but her children do not. Children share common clanship with only one of their four grandparents; however, the other three grandparents are still their relatives and kinsmen. As one goes back through the generations, ties of kin relationships form a web of kinship. A rule of descent carves out of this web of kinship a much smaller segment, which comprises the members of one's own clan. Clans continue to exist through time, beyond the lifespan of individual members, as new generations continue to be born into the clan.

A *matrilineal rule of descent* states that a child belongs to the clan of his or her mother, not that of the father. The Trobriand Islanders have such a rule of descent. Among the Trobrianders, as in all matrilineal societies, the continuity of the clan is not through a man's own children but through those of his sister.

In societies where either matrilineal or patrilineal clans are present, the clans have certain functions; that is, they carry out certain activities. Some of the activities of clans concern rituals. For example, the matrilineal clan of the Trobrianders serves as host at the ceremonial distribution *(sagali)* accompanying a funeral when a member of their clan dies. Ritual objects and spells are owned by clans. Clans also have political functions and may compete with one another for power, and even fight with one another. Each clan has some kind of leadership, almost always male, to organize these political activities. The chief (the leader) of a Trobriand clan directs the accumulation of large amounts of food to be given away at a Trobriand *sagali*. Finally, what has frequently been seen as the most important function of the clan is its ownership of land. Members of a clan have the right to use its land by virtue of the fact that they are born into the clan. Clan members may work together at tasks, such as building a communal house or canoe, that benefit the clan as a whole. The common ancestor from whom all the members of a clan believe that they are descended is sometimes conceived of as an ancestral or clan spirit. This ancestral spirit may be thought of as having a nonhuman form, perhaps that of an animal. In that case all members of the clan are thought of as having a special relationship to that animal, and they may be forbidden to eat it. Such an animal is called the *clan totem,* and, as noted in Chapter 5, it is a symbol that represents the clan and could be graphically represented, as depicted in the totem pole on page 79.

Figure 3. Descent and clan membership.

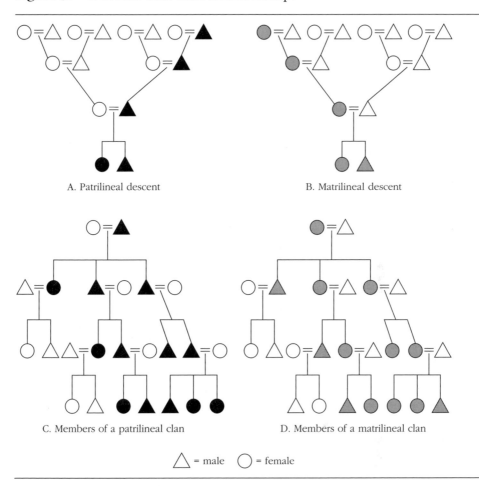

A. Patrilineal descent

B. Matrilineal descent

C. Members of a patrilineal clan

D. Members of a matrilineal clan

△ = male ◯ = female

The clan is frequently referred to by anthropologists as a *corporate descent group*, because it has many of the characteristics of a modern corporation. Like a corporation, it has an existence independent of its individual members. Old clan members die and new ones are born, while the clan continues to operate through time. The corporation owns property, and so does the clan. However, anybody can buy stock in a corporation and become an owner, but membership in a clan is restricted to certain kinds of kin, as defined by the rule of descent.

In Chapter 5 we noted the way in which elements of the human body can be used metaphorically to discuss kinship. They can also be used to contrast relationships through the mother and relationships through the father. The way in which the contrast is symbolized differs in patrilineal and matrilineal societies. In many patrilineal societies, the connection between the child and the mother is seen in terms of mother's milk and menstrual blood. In these societies, milk or blood symbolizes the maternal relationship. Connection to the father is seen in terms of semen or bone. The Arapesh of New Guinea believe that a child is created through the semen contributed by the father and the blood of the mother. The Arapesh are patrilineal; the child belongs to the father's clan. The child is seen as linked to the mother's clan through the blood she provided. The mother's clan continues to "own" the blood, and whenever the child's blood is shed through injury or cutting initiation scars, the child's mother's clan must be paid.

Since the Trobrianders are a matrilineal people, one would expect them to conceive of their kinship system in a different way than the Arapesh do. Among the Trobrianders, children belong to the clan of their mother, sharing common substance with their mother and other clan mates. The father is considered an affine, a relative by marriage only, in contrast to a consanguine, a blood relative. When a child is conceived in the mother's womb, the Trobrianders believe that an ancestral spirit from the mother's clan has entered her womb. The creation of a child is not seen as the result of the merging of substance from mother and father, and therefore they do not believe that sexual intercourse has anything to do with the conception of a child. The father, by repeated acts of intercourse, not only makes the child grow, but molds the child so that the child resembles him in appearance. The child is like a piece of clay pressed between two palms that takes on the shape of the hands that mold it. But this has nothing to do with the conception of the child in the first place, which is all the doing of the maternal ancestral spirit of the mother's clan. The child cannot be claimed by the father's clan, which had nothing to do with its creation. Though the Trobriand father is a very important relative, he is still an affine, as are all the members of his maternal clan.

Cognatic Descent

Up to now, we have discussed clans based upon either a patrilineal or a matrilineal rule of descent. Anthropologists refer to these as *unilineal descent groups.* There are also societies that have groups based upon descent from a common ancestor, where individuals belong to the group because either their father or their mother was a member of that group. This is called a *cognatic rule of descent.* Individuals have the choice of belonging to either their father's or their mother's group, or they may have rights in both groups, though there is usually active membership in only one since a person can live in only one place at a time. Individuals may even have rights in all four kin groups of their grandparents. Although the kin group created by a cognatic rule of descent is based upon descent from a common ancestor, the links through which individuals trace their descent are through either males or females. The kin group that the Kwakiutl refer to as a *numaym* is a cognatic descent group. A Kwakiutl boy could claim membership in both his mother's and his father's group. He usually became a member of the *numaym* of the parent of higher rank, from whom he hoped to inherit the highest titles and the most property. In addition, he inherited rights in the *numaym* of the other parent.

Cognatic descent groups have the same functions as unilineal descent groups (patrilineal and matrilineal clans), though their structures are different. For example, the Kwakiutl *numaym* owned houses, fishing sites, berry-picking grounds, and hunting territories. The chiefs of a *numaym* acted as political leaders in potlatching and in warfare. The *numaym* acted as a unit on ceremonial occasions, such as the marriage and repurchase of the bride, as described in Chapter 2. Kwakiutl myths describe how the supernatural ancestors of present-day *numayms* acquired magical powers that were transmitted down the generations to their descendants.

Double Descent

In some societies in the world, each person belongs to two descent groups, one patrilineal, where descent is traced through the father and father's father, and the other matrilineal, where descent is traced through the mother and mother's mother. Anthropologists call this *double descent* (see Figure 4). The two groups to which an individual belongs do not conflict with one another, since each group has its own distinct functions. For example, the Yako of southeast Nigeria had patrilineal clans called *yepun,* which owned land in common and possessed a single shrine and an assembly house, and whose men and their families resided together and farmed together. At the same time, each Yako individual also belonged to the matrilineal clan, or *lejima,* of his or her mother. The matrilineal clans carried out ritual and religious activities, such as funerals and periodic rites during the year aimed at maintaining fertility and harmony. While land is inherited patrilineally, movable wealth, such as valuables and household goods, is inherited through the matrilineal line. Thus, the two types of kin groups, patrilineal and matrilineal, serve different functions.

Figure 4   Double descent.

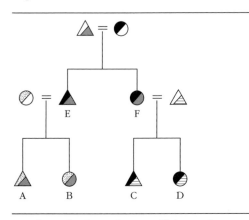

A and B are brother and sister and belong to the same two descent groups, gray from their father and stippled from their mother. Similarly, C and D belong to the same two descent groups, striped from their father and black from their mother. E and F are also brother and sister and share the two descent groups that they get from their two parents, gray from their father and black from their mother. But their respective children, A and B, and C and D, do not have any descent groups in common.

▊ The Structure of Descent Groups

Though patrilineal clans, matrilineal clans, and cognatic descent groups have the same kinds of functions, they are structured very differently. Because of the rule of descent, the structure of the patrilineal clan is that of men linked through their fathers, along with their sisters who marry into other clans. The patrilineal clan is almost always associated with virilocal postmarital residence. Sisters who marry out and wives who marry in are incorporated in varying degrees into the patrilineal clans of their husbands. In the discussion of marriage and the family in the earlier part of this chapter, we pointed out the variations in the degree of incorporation of the wife into her husband's clan. Matrilineal clans are composed of women related through their mothers and the brothers of these women. The brothers remain members of the clan into which they were born throughout their entire lives. Though they marry into different clans, in matrilineal societies, men are never incorporated into the clans of their wives. Matrilineal clans are usually associated with avunculocal or uxorilocal postmarital residence. With a rule of cognatic descent, both men and women have membership in several cognatic descent groups, since they can trace multiple lines of descent. In this situation, husbands and wives, regardless of where they reside, are never incorporated into the descent groups of their spouses; this is the case among the Kwakiutl. As can be seen, the different kinds of descent structures are associated with particular rules of postmarital residence, and have consequences for the degree of incorporation of one spouse into the other spouse's kin group.

One can see the different ways in which descent groups are structured when one looks at the way in which political leadership operates. The political functions of descent groups are carried out under the direction of leaders. In patrilineal societies like that of the Mongols, inherited leadership is usually structured in the following manner: It passes from father to son and from brother to brother (see Figure 5). Leadership in matrilineal societies, like that of the Trobrianders, is handed down from mother's brother to sister's son or from brother to brother. In a matrilineal society, a son can never directly inherit a position of leadership from his father. In such societies, though the line of descent goes through women, the women themselves are rarely the heads of their clans. One may contrast the nature of the relationship of a man to his father in patrilineal societies and to his mother's brother in matrilineal societies. In patrilineal societies, a son will replace his father in the position of leadership and is perceived as a competitor and antagonist of his father. His mother's brother, who is not in his clan, is a source of support. In contrast, in matrilineal societies, a sister's son will succeed to the position of leadership held by his mother's brother. The relationship between these two parallels that of the father-son relationship in a patrilineal society. The relationship between father and son in a matrilineal society has all the elements of antagonism and potential conflict between them removed. In societies with cognatic descent groups, like that of the Kwakiutl, a man can succeed to political leadership by virtue of descent through his mother or through his father; thus he can be the heir of his father or of his mother's brother. The contrast between the father-son relationship and the mother's brother–sister's son relationship is therefore of no importance in societies

Figure 5. Passage of political leadership.

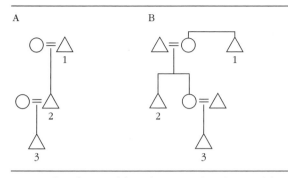

In a patrilineal society (A), and in a matrilineal society (B).

with cognatic descent. An important structural feature of cognatic societies is that brothers are not equivalent. The optional nature of the descent rule permits the possibility that brothers may be in different descent groups. Among the Kwakiutl, it frequently happens that two brothers are in different *numayms,* which can even fight each other. In patrilineal and in matrilineal societies, which are unilineal, this can never happen, since brothers are always in the same clan.

Clans

Clans come in many shapes and forms. In some societies, you belong to a clan simply because your father or your mother belonged to that clan. Other people belong to your clan, but you may not be able to trace a kin relationship to them. Nevertheless, they are fellow clan members. Anthropologists say that descent is *stipulated* in such a clan system. Where stipulated descent is found, lengthy genealogies are not kept and people usually remember back only to their grandfathers. Where long genealogies are kept, written or oral, each member of a clan can trace his or her kinship back to the founding ancestor of the clan and by this means to every other member of the clan. Anthropologists call this *demonstrated* descent. In societies where clans include large numbers of people living dispersed over a wide area, each clan may in turn be divided into smaller units. These are referred to as subclans.

   Clans based on unilineal descent continued to exist, assuming a variety of roles, even long after the emergence of complex societies and states. Patrilineal clans in twentieth-century prerevolutionary China carried out religious functions in connection with ancestor worship, maintaining ancestral shrines and cemeteries. They also had some economic functions and assisted clan members in obtaining education and other such endeavors. These patrilineal clans continue to function in the form of clan associations among overseas Chinese in San Francisco and New York within an urbanized, industrialized society moving into the second millennium.

When peasant societies were incorporated into nation-states, even Communist states, larger-scale kin units continued to exist. As recently as 1987, ethnic Albanian clans in Kosovo continued to feud with one another, answering one murder with another. As is the case in clan-based societies, when ongoing feuds are involved, all clan members are held responsible for the actions of a single member. The progress of this feud was reported on Yugoslavian television. After the Turkish earthquake, which occurred in the summer of 1999, *The New York Times* reported that 40 members of a clan had traveled 600 miles from their home to try to rescue 5 trapped relatives. They brought their own equipment, including jackhammers, drills, electrical equipment, generators, and lights. This illustrates that members of a clan feel it absolutely necessary to come to the aid of fellow clan members in distress (*New York Times,* August 22, 1999: 12). In South Korea today, individuals still cannot marry if they have the same family name, and marriages within the same clan are legally banned, despite the fact that the Korean Civil Code on kinship was amended in 1990 to reflect a more bilateral system (Lee, 1999).

Lineages

Anthropologists refer to unilineal descent groups where descent is demonstrated as *lineages*. Sometimes all the people in the society believe themselves to be descended from a single ancestor. This founding ancestor may be historical or mythical, or a little of both. The kin groups of various sizes are related to one another in an extensive genealogy.

The Bedouin Arabs of Cyrenaica in eastern Libya, studied by Emrys Peters (1960), provide us with an example of such a society. They are nomadic pastoralists who keep herds of camels and sheep in the desert areas of their territory and cows and goats in the wooded plateau areas. All the Cyrenaican Bedouin alive today consider themselves descended from the single ancestor Sa'ada, who heads the genealogy (see Figure 6).

Sa'ada was the mother of the two sons, who are said to be the founding ancestors of the two largest groups of tribes—Baraghith and 'Aqqara. The genealogy in the diagram provides a set of ideas that the Cyrenaican Bedouin use to talk about how they are related to one another and how their group is related to all other groups. The genealogy is like a branching tree, extending out to its many twigs. Several twigs, or lineages, are part of a branch, and several branches, or groupings of lineages, are part of a larger limb. The larger limb represents a still larger grouping of lineages. This kind of descent system is called a *segmentary lineage system*. It is found in societies with patrilineal descent such as the Cyrenaican Bedouin. The constant branching out represents levels of segmentation. The branching out of the genealogy also has a close relationship to the occupation of geographical areas. The two groups of tribes, descended from each of the sons of Sa'ada, occupy the eastern and western halves of Cyrenaica. Lineages descended from brothers a few generations back graze their herds on lands adjacent to one another. Lineages that are further away genealogically occupy lands farther apart. In political action, lineages closely related to one another unite to oppose a threat from a more distantly related lineage. How segmentary lineage systems operate politically will be discussed more fully in Chapter 9.

Figure 6.   Genealogy of the Cyrenaican Bedouin.

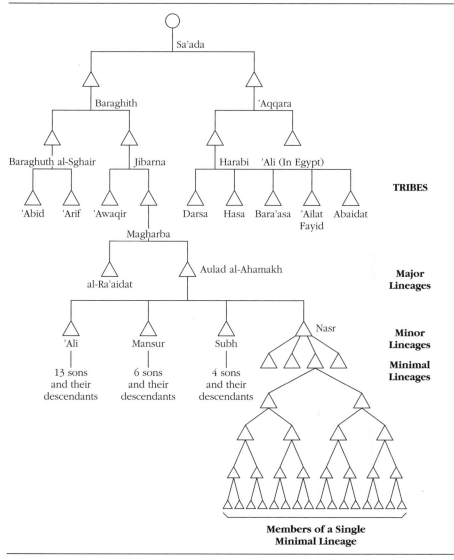

Diagram illustrating a segmentary lineage system.

Moieties

Another kind of grouping based on descent is one in which the entire society is divided into two halves, which are referred to as *moieties*. Moieties may be based upon a patrilineal or a matrilineal rule of descent. Sometimes in societies with moieties, a village site was divided in half, each half being occupied by the members of one moiety. As noted in Chapter 5, the two parts of a moiety are often referred to in oppositional terms, such as *left* and *right*. The Abelam of the Sepik River area of New Guinea have patrilineal moieties referred to simply as "us" and "them." Among the Tlingit of the Pacific coast of northern Canada and Alaska, the two moieties are known as Raven and Wolf and are based on matrilineal descent.

Kindreds

The descent groups examined above are all based on a rule of descent from a single common ancestor and are said to be *ancestor-oriented. Kindreds,* on the other hand, are reckoned in an entirely different way. Earlier, we described kinship as a web. Like a spider's web, it extends out from the center. Each person is at the center of his or her web of kinship. Anthropologists refer to the individual at the center as the ego, and the relatives who make up that web of kinship constitute ego's kindred. The kindred includes relatives on both ego's mother's and father's sides. Individuals who are descendants of ego, as well as ego's ancestors and everyone descended from those ancestors, are included in ego's kindred. The kindred is *ego-oriented.* The kindred as a unit does not own land or any other property; it only has coherence as a group around the ego at its center (see Figure 7). Societies with kindreds but without unilineal descent groups are known as *bilateral societies.* American society is an example of such a society. On an occasion such as the American wedding described in Chapter 2, the kindreds of the bride and groom attend. If any of the first cousins of the groom, for instance, his father's brother's son, get married, a different set of relatives will be present, though there will be an overlap with his kindred. This overlap occurs since the two egos share a certain set of relatives. Kindreds do not have continuity through generations as do corporate kin groups based on a rule of descent.

Relations between Groups through Marriage

We introduced our discussion of marriage by talking about exogamy, which compels groups to give their women to someone else, receiving the women of the other group in return. This is called sister exchange. Arapesh men state that they marry their sisters outside the group in order to obtain brothers-in-law. In general, marriages not only create links between brothers-in-law but also serve to link their respective kin groups. Groups that give women to and receive women from one another also exchange goods and services such as bridewealth, bride service, and other kinds of services at rites of passage after children are born from the marriage. These links between kin groups established by marriage are called *affinal links.* During warfare, kin groups frequently use these affinal ties and turn to their in-laws for assistance. For this reason, marriage is the basis for what is referred to as *alliance.*

Figure 7.   The kindred.

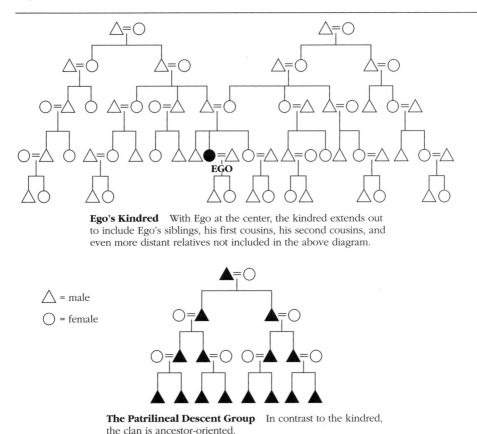

Ego's Kindred   With Ego at the center, the kindred extends out to include Ego's siblings, his first cousins, his second cousins, and even more distant relatives not included in the above diagram.

△ = male

◯ = female

The Patrilineal Descent Group   In contrast to the kindred, the clan is ancestor-oriented.

Although affines may be in opposition to one another and may even fight one another, the concept of alliance is nevertheless used by anthropologists to refer to linkages between kin groups established by marriage.

In our society, marriage is based upon the decision by the bride and groom to get married. Parents and other individuals are rarely involved in this decision. However, in other societies there are rules stating that one should marry a certain category of relative. These rules have the effect of continuing alliance over time between the groups. When groups continue to exchange sisters over generations, then women of one's own group are always marrying into the group from which wives come. This marriage pattern, which we have called sister exchange earlier, is also referred to as a system of *reciprocal exchange* (see Figure 8). In such a system, the prospective husband and the prospective wife will already be related to one another. Since their parents are brother and sister, they will be first cousins. Anthropologists refer to two

Figure 8. Sister exchange, or reciprocal exchange.

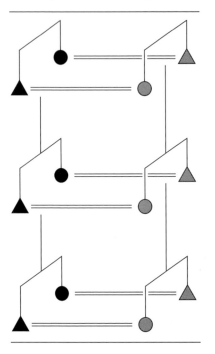

kinds of cousins: *parallel cousins,* who are the children of the mother's sister or father's brother, and *cross cousins,* who are the children of the mother's brother or father's sister (see Figure 9). In a system with reciprocal exchange, parallel cousins, who are members of one's own group, are frequently referred to as siblings. Therefore they cannot marry. Cross cousins are never in one's own group but rather, are members of the other group with which one has been intermarrying. These cross cousins are known as *bilateral cross cousins,* since they are simultaneously mother's brother's children and father's sister's children. Sister exchange continued over the generations has the same effect as marrying one's bilateral cross cousin. The Yanomamo of southern Venezuela have such a marriage system of direct reciprocal exchange. Every Yanomamo man must marry a woman whom he calls by the kinship term for female cross cousin (the Yanomamo term is *suaboya*), and this term is at the same time the term for wife. Among the Yanomamo, the terms for female cross cousin and wife are identical, as are those for husband and male cross cousin. Female parallel cousins, among the Yanomamo, are called by the same term as sisters. If a Yanomamo man has no biological sister to return to the man who gave him his wife, as we noted earlier, he returns a sister who is really his parallel cousin.

There are societies where the two kinds of cross cousins, mother's brother's children and father's sister's children, are referred to by different terms. These two types of cross cousins are not equally marriageable, as is the case for the

Figure 9. Types of cousins.

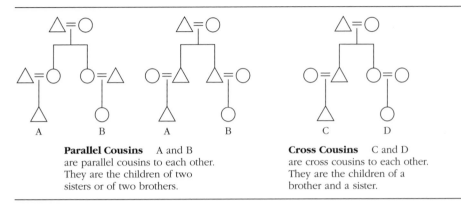

Parallel Cousins A and B
are parallel cousins to each other.
They are the children of two
sisters or of two brothers.

Cross Cousins C and D
are cross cousins to each other.
They are the children of a
brother and a sister.

Yanomamo. Some societies have a rule that a man ought to marry the daughter of his mother's brother, but he may not marry the daughter of his father's sister. Ideally, if every man married his mother's brother's daughter, in every generation, the result would be a picture like that in Figure 10. In Figure 10, the groups labeled A, B, and C, linked by the marriages, are patrilineages. This marriage rule occurs much more frequently in societies with a patrilineal rule of descent, though it also occurs in societies with matrilineal descent. If a man does not have a real mother's brother's daughter to marry, he may marry a classificatory mother's brother's daughter. A classificatory mother's brother's daughter is a woman whom a man calls by the same kinship term as his real mother's brother's daughter, and she is a member of the mother's brother's daughter's patrilineage. As one can see from the figure, lineage B gives its sisters to lineage A, and lineage C gives its sisters to lineage B, in every generation. From the perspective of lineage B, lineage A is always wife-taker and lineage C is always wife-giver. This system is very different from sister exchange in that you never return a woman to the lineage that gave you a woman. Since wife-giving lineage and wife-taking lineage are always different, a minimum of three groups is required. (However, it is usually the case that more than three groups are tied together in this kind of marriage alliance.) If there are three groups, then they can marry in a circle, with lineage A giving its women to lineage C. If, for example, the royal family of Great Britain gave its daughters in marriage to the royal family of Denmark in every generation, and the royal family of Denmark gave its daughters in marriage to the royal family of Sweden in every generation, and the royal family of Sweden gave its daughters in marriage back to the royal family of Great Britain in every generation, all intermarrying in a circle, then they would have this kind of marriage system. The Kachin of Burma, whose political organization will be discussed in Chapter 9, actually do have this kind of marriage system. It produces a structure of alliance between groups that anthropologists refer to as *generalized exchange*.

Figure 10. Mother's brother's daughter marriage, or generalized exchange.

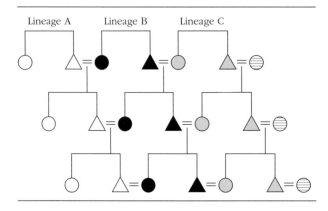

In the village of Lamalera in East Timor, this type of marriage system involving generalized exchange continues to be practiced, despite the adoption of Catholicism and substantial transformations of village economy (Barnes, 1998: 106). Though there is considerable variation in practice, 52 percent of marriages are with a man's mother's brother's daughter, and the hierarchical distinction between wife-givers and wife-takers remains significant today. Although the village of Lamalera is involved in the Indonesian national economy, economic cooperation in whale hunting, owner-ship of fishing and whaling boats, and the organization of fishing crews are still based on clan membership.

Some societies have the opposite form of the preferential rule of marriage with mother's brother's daughter. In those societies, a man cannot marry his mother's brother's daughter but should marry his father's sister's daughter. If every man married in this fashion, the result would be what is pictured in Figure 11. In the figure, groups A, B, C, and D are matrilineal subclans. This kind of marriage rule always oc-curs in societies with matrilineal descent. A man marries either his real or his classi-ficatory father's sister's daughter. This marriage rule involves the return of a wife one generation after a wife has been given. In the first generation, subclan D gives a woman to C, C gives to B, B gives to A, and A gives to D (if the subclans are mar-rying in a circle). In the next generation, the flow of women is reversed. Now sub-clan D gives to A, A gives to B, B gives to C, and C gives to D. In the third generation, the flow is reversed once again. Every generation, women move in the direction op-posite from the way they did in the previous generation. This resembles sister ex-change in that a woman is returned to the group that originally gave a woman, but the return is made a generation later. Because the return is delayed one generation, there must be more than two groups operating in the system. A minimum of four groups is required. The Trobrianders are an example of a society with a rule for mar-riage with father's sister's daughter and have this form of *delayed exchange*.

Figure 11.   Father's sister's daughter marriage.

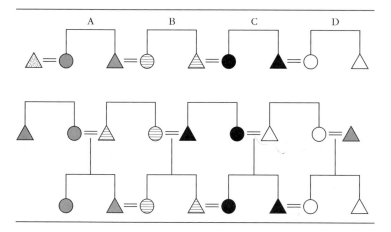

Each of these two marriage rules produces a different structure of alliances among groups, and both are different from the kind of alliance produced by bilateral cross-cousin marriage. Marrying one's cross cousins, either mother's brother's daughter or father's sister's daughter, begins with a rule of exogamy stating that one must take a wife from outside one's group. By specifying which relatives one should marry, different patterns of alliance among groups are created. Figures 8, 10, and 11 represent models of these different patterns to which particular societies conform to a greater or lesser extent.

Some societies, particularly in the Middle East, have a preferential marriage rule that is structurally opposite to this rule of exogamy. The rule states that a man should marry his parallel cousin, in this case, his father's brother's daughter. Since the societies of this area, like the Bedouin of Cyrenaica discussed above, are all patrilineal in descent, this marriage rule results in endogamous marriages. The Riff of Morocco, who have this marriage rule, say that they prefer to hold on to their daughters and marry them within their own group to avoid becoming entangled in alliances with other groups. This is an example of a point made earlier: Every group presents rationalizations of why they do things in a particular manner.

When one views marriage as an alliance, marriages may be contracted in which the procreative and sexual functions are not relevant. The Lovedu, a Bantu-speaking people of southern Africa, had a queen to whom women were given in marriage. The purpose of such marriages was to create political alliances, and sexual intercourse and procreation did not occur. Among the Kwakiutl, where privileges were transferred as a result of marriage, one man could "marry" the foot of another, become son-in-law to the man whose foot he married, and obtain privileges through this fictive marriage at the repurchase ceremony described in Chapter 2.

Figure 12.   American kinship terminology.

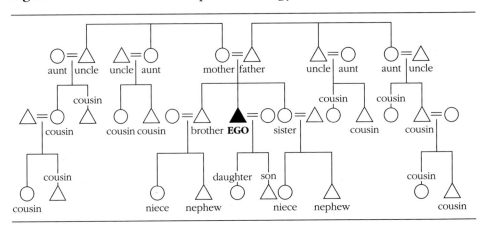

Kinship Terminology

Each society in the world has a set of words used to refer to relatives. This set of words or terms is called *kinship terminology*. Of course, the terms differ in every society since all their languages are different. However, anthropologists have been able to sort the terms used in all societies into a few basic types. Americans accept their own kin terminology as being the "natural" way of classifying relatives. Both your father's brother and your mother's brother are referred to as *uncle* in American usage. *Uncle* is also used to refer to your mother's sister's husband and father's sister's husband. Though the term *uncle* is used for these four relatives, two of them are blood relatives on different sides of the family, while two are relatives by marriage. Each of these four relatives is related to you in a different way, but our kinship terminology ignores these differences and groups them under one term. Anthropologists diagram kinship terminologies such as our own in the method depicted in Figure 12.

The Yanomamo of Venezuela have a very different way of sorting their relatives. They use the same term for both father's brother and mother's sister's husband, while they use a different term for mother's brother and father's sister's husband. The Yanomamo kinship terminology is pictured in Figure 13.

You can see that the two societies sort the terms for kin in different ways. For the parental generation, both the Yanomamo and Americans have four terms. The Americans use *father, mother, aunt,* and *uncle;* the Yanomamo use *baya, naya, yaya,* and *shoaiya.* In the Yanomamo system, father's brother and mother's brother have different terms, whereas in our society the same term is used for both. Conversely, the Yanomamo class father and father's brother together, while we use different terms. In your own generation, we have a single term, *cousin,* for all the children of uncles and aunts. This term is unusual in that it is used for males and females. The Yanomamo are also consistent in their usage. The children of all relatives called by the same term

Figure 13. Yanomamo kinship terminology.

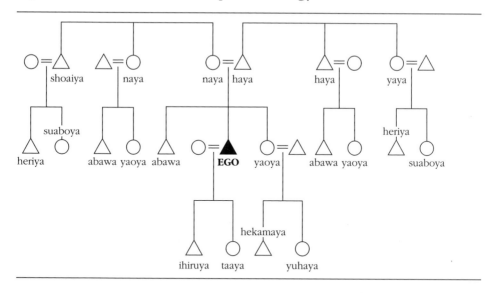

as father and mother are referred to by the term for brother and sister. This means that parallel cousins are grouped with siblings. In contrast, the children of *shoaiya,* who are one's cross cousins, are referred to by terms different from brother and sister, *suaboya* and *heriya.* Which is more complicated? Neither. Which is more natural? Neither. Each of these kinship terminologies is different because it is related to a different type of social structure. The terms in a kinship terminological system group some relatives and set apart other relatives in a way that reflects the relation of these relatives according to the rules of residence, marriage, and descent.

As a result of analysis, anthropologists have recognized that kinship terminologies around the world fall into a limited number of types. The American and Yanomamo kinship terminologies conform to two of these basic types. Strange as it may seem, American kinship terminology is classified as *Eskimo* since it is identical to that of the Eskimos—or Inuit, as they now prefer to be called—not in the words for the terms but in the pattern of organization. Its major characteristics are that it distinguishes between the generations and it distinguishes *lineal relatives* from *collateral relatives* (see Figure 14). Lineal relatives are those in the direct line of descent, that is, grandfather, father, son, grandson, grandmother, mother, daughter, granddaughter. The rest of the relatives are referred to as collateral and can be distinguished in terms of *degree of collaterality,* meaning that second cousins are more remote than first cousins, and first cousins are more remote than siblings. The Eskimo type of terminology emphasizes individual nuclear families, and it is found in societies with a particular cluster of characteristics, such as neolocal rules of residence, kindreds, bilateral descent, and the absence of descent groups. Though Inuit society and our own differed in degree of complexity, subsistence pattern, and environmental setting, the pattern of organization of kinship terms and other kinship features was the same.

Figure 14.   Degree of collaterality.

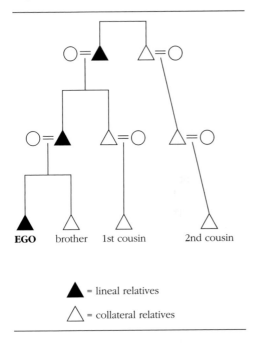

EGO   brother   1st cousin   2nd cousin

▲ = lineal relatives

△ = collateral relatives

The kinship terminology of the Yanomamo is classified as *Iroquois*. The Iroquois type of terminology distinguishes between father's side and mother's side. However, the difference between lineal and collateral relatives is ignored; father and father's brother are classed together, as are mother and mother's sister. Generational differences are always recognized, as in Eskimo terminology. The social structure with which this terminology is usually associated is one in which one's own kin group is distinct from the kin group from which one's mother came. The group from which one's mother came is the same group into which one's father's sister marries. In other words, the Iroquois terminology goes with sister exchange, which is the type of marriage pattern the Yanomamo have. This is why, in Yanomamo, the term for father's sister's husband is the same as that for mother's brother, and the term for mother's sister's husband is the same as that for father's brother. Female cross cousin is classed with wife and male cross cousin with brother-in-law. In every generation, "sisters" are exchanged between the two groups, and the kinship terminology reflects this. Iroquois terminology is associated with virilocal or uxorilocal residence, but not with neolocal residence. Instead of independent nuclear families, extended families are present. This type of terminology is also generally associated with unilineal descent, but not with cognatic descent or bilateral kinship reckoning. Iroquois is by far the most common type of kinship terminology found in the world. It should be noted that societies that have Iroquois kinship terminology may not have all these social structural features, but only some of them.

Besides Eskimo and Iroquois terminologies, four other major types of terminologies are distinguished by anthropologists. The *Crow* type, found, for example, among the Trobriand Islanders, is almost always associated with matrilineal descent groups, avunculocal residence, and extended families. Unlike Eskimo and Iroquois terminologies, the same term may be used for members of different generations. *Omaha* kinship terminology is the mirror image of Crow. It is associated with patrilineal descent groups and, like Crow, ignores generational differences in some terms. The simplest terminology, the one having the fewest terms, is the *Hawaiian* type, in which only generation and male-female distinctions are made. It is usually associated with cognatic descent groups. Despite its simplicity, it has been found in association with some societies, like the Hawaiian, that have complex political economies. In the last type of kinship terminology, *Sudanese,* every category of relative is distinguished by a different term. It is frequently associated with patrilineal descent and economically independent nuclear families, such as those found among certain nomadic pastoral societies of the Middle East.

Studying kinship terminology can help the anthropologist gain insights into how societies operate. Kinship terminology is a subject that has a long history in anthropology, and the regularity of its patterning was first noticed by Lewis Henry Morgan (1877). Continued study has revealed the general association of types of terminology with particular kinds of social structure, as pointed out above. However, some terminologies correspond only in part to the types of social structure described above, and sometimes particular terminologies are associated with different social structural features. For example, Iroquois kinship terminology may be found in association with kinship systems that have patrilineal descent but do not have sister exchange, such as the Enga in Papua New Guinea.

Some anthropologists, for example, David Schneider (1984), have been critical of the use of the anthropological concepts for analyzing kinship presented in this chapter. They see this set of analytic concepts that has been developed by anthropologists as the imposition of Western social science categories on indigenous ideas. Instead, they prefer to utilize only the native categories that people in each society use to conceptualize kin relationships. In our view, the analysis must begin with indigenous categories. These can and must be translated into anthropological concepts. These concepts have made possible the cross-cultural comparisons that have revealed the same regularities or patterns in social structural features in societies in many parts of the worlds. The kinship variables discussed so far in this chapter, including number of spouses, degree of incorporation of spouse, type of descent rule, and structure of descent group, do not operate independently. They fit together into the particular patterns that have been revealed cross-culturally.

■ Fictive Kinship

People also rely on social relationships established by means of ritual observances, which are known as *godparenthood,* or *compadrazgo.* Godparenthood creates a set of relationships that, though nonkin in their derivation, utilize a set of terms based on kinship. The English labels for these relationships use kinship terms such as *father,* *mother, daughter,* and *son,* plus the prefix—*god*—differentiating them from real kinship. This is not simply an extension of kinship, but a different kind of relationship, which uses kinship as a metaphor. This kind of relationship is found in many parts of Mediterranean Europe and in Latin America. It also occurs among Hispanic populations in the United States (Segura and Pierce, 1998: 302). The ritual occasions upon which godparenthood is established are baptism, confirmation, and marriage, at which the godparent serves as a kind of sponsor. Real parents never carry out the role of godparents. Sometimes more-distant relatives may serve as godparents, while in other cases they may not. The *compadrazgo* relationship is frequently established between individuals of different classes for social, political, and economic reasons. In peasant communities, for example, a patron who is a wealthy or powerful member of the community and probably the landlord may serve as godparent to the children of clients who are economically and politically dependent upon him. In the relationship between godparent and godchild, the godparent is expected to protect and assist the godchild, while the godchild honors the godparent, just as the patron receives support from the client when it is needed and the client receives favors from the patron. Among the Quichua-speaking Otavaleno of the Ecuadorian Andes, *compadrazgo* has not been squeezed out by the expansion of capitalism, as some anthropologists in the 1960s had predicted (Colloredo-Mansfeld, 1998: 50). These indigenous people have become prosperous weavers and traders, and they now select *compadres* as they extend their handicraft business. When their children are confirmed or marry, they select *compadres* on the basis of their need to connect with sweater-factory owners, transport operators, and shopkeepers with whom they do business (Colloredo-Mansfeld, 1998: 52).

In Serbia, godparenthood, or *kumstvo,* described by anthropologist Eugene Hammel (1968), which could only be established between nonkin, was continued from one generation to the next. The word *kum* can be translated as "sponsor." Members of one group (A) stood as godparents to another group (B), and the children of those godparents in A served as godparents to the next generation of godchildren in B. Godparenthood was not reciprocal, since the group of godchildren in B did not return the favor and act as godparents to A, but instead, acted as godparents to children in still another group (C). This created a structure of alliances between groups by means of godparenthood, which is the same as the structure of alliances created by marriage with mother's brother's daughter, which we referred to as generalized exchange.

Kinship in America Today

The symbolic meanings that Americans attach to kinship were investigated by David Schneider (1980). He pointed out that Americans conceive of two kinds of relatives, blood relatives and relatives by marriage. Americans think that a child receives half of its blood from the mother and half from the father, while more distant relatives have smaller shares of that blood, depending on the degree of distance. People think that such relationships can never be terminated because the symbolic carrier of the relationship is blood, which is always present. On the other hand, relatives through marriage are different from blood relatives in every respect. The relationships are established by people making choices rather than as the result of a natural process. Such kins are termed relatives-in-law. Relationships that are made by people can also be terminated by people, through divorce. When this happens, the person is no longer considered a relative.

Perhaps as a result of what have come to be known as reproductive technologies, Americans recently have begun to rethink the meaning of kinship in their own culture (see Strathern et al., 1993; Strathern, 1992). The meanings of *motherhood* and *fatherhood* have been called into question by these new reproductive technologies. When an egg in a surrogate mother is fertilized with sperm from a man who, with his wife, have contracted to be the child's parents, there may be conflict over the child between the couple and the surrogate mother. Test-tube fertilization of an egg from the would-be mother and sperm from the would-be father, with the developing embryo then implanted in a surrogate mother, has also called motherhood into question. If the sperm comes from an unknown donor, who is the real father—the man who has provided the sperm or the man who has acted as father in raising the child? What formerly had been seen as a natural tie of kinship between father, mother, and child is clearly much more complicated. Twenty years ago, when children were adopted, the adoption papers were sealed by the court and knowledge of their biological parentage was kept from adopted children. If Schneider's principle—that biological blood ties to parents can never be severed—is valid, then one can readily understand the need that such children, now adults, often feel to know who their biological parents are. This desire frequently invades the privacy that these biological parents sought. At present, many of these adopted children have gone to court to have the sealed adoption papers opened. Adoption has now become such an open process that the adoptive parents may establish a relationship with the biological parents even before the child is born. A recent *New York Times* article revealed the way in which a prospective adopting mother moved in with the biological mother weeks before the child arrived, and was fully involved in all the activities leading up to the birth (October 25, 1998). The adoptive parents indicated that they intended to continue to involve the biological parents in raising the child. Children conceived by artificial insemination are seeking the identity of their donor fathers, often medical students who had donated their semen merely to help infertile parents have children.

One might argue that this represents a greater emphasis on the biological and genetic aspects of kinship, a reinforcement of the idea of blood in the minds of Americans. The bodily process of procreation is very significant, since birth creates a social identity. For Americans, kinship represents ties of substance. When there is a question of where the substance is coming from, this raises questions about kinship and identity. In recent years, what social scientists have come to call a new biologism has been added to biological conceptualization of family for Americans. The primordial conceptualizations of gender, race, ethnicity, and genes as representing the "true essence of a person" have become important in shaping the identity of Americans (Skolnick, 1998: 240).

Two highly publicized court cases, both settled in 1993 after extensive litigation, highlight these issues. In Florida, two female babies were switched at birth. One of them died in early childhood, and genetic tests then revealed that she was not the biological offspring of the parents who raised her. They sued for custody of their living biological daughter, and a settlement was reached giving them visitation rights. The girl herself, who felt a strong tie to the father who had raised her, sued some time later and was permitted by the court to terminate her relationship with her biological parents, to "divorce" her parents. A biological or blood relationship was treated as if it were equivalent to an in-law relationship.

In another case, in Michigan, a baby was given up for adoption by her mother soon after birth. Then the mother, who later married the child's biological father, regretted the decision and sued for custody. After a two-year court battle the biological parents won out over the adoptive parents, who were forced to relinquish the little girl. These two cases reveal the extent to which parentage and kinship have become contested. Biological relationship in one case has been reinforced, and the other case hinges on whether one can divorce one's parents. As Skolnick notes, "In some states today, unless a parent is found to be unfit or to have abandoned the child, the rights of biological parents are all but inviolate" (1998: 239).

Until the mid-twentieth century, the usual family type for Americans was the nuclear family that lived neolocally after marriage. Immigrant families, which included three generations for a time, were an exception. As the age at which Americans married became later and later, the single-individual household became more frequent. A variant on this form is the household consisting of several unrelated young people, both men and women, who live together for financial reasons. The recent TV show *Will and Grace* portrays this form. Another household form consists of one or both grandparents and grandchildren. This occurs when the parents of the children are unable to care for them. Grandparents assume custody and responsibility instead of the state.

The high rate of divorce and the subsequent remarriage of the divorced spouses has created a new type of family—the stepfamily. The stepfather is more likely to be living with and raising young children than the biological father, though the latter may continue to be involved in child rearing and child support. Stepmothers are rarely in this position, though they may spend a great deal of time with their stepchildren (Mason, 1998: 96). Mason notes that, in contrast to the *Cinderella* story, adolescent stepchildren experience less conflict with residential stepmothers than do adolescent children with their own mothers in nondivorced families (1998: 98). The modern stepfamily has brought about a variety of sibling relationships, including full siblings, half-siblings, and stepsiblings. However, half-siblings are considered blood relatives, while stepsiblings are not. But the law has not kept up with this changing family phenomenon in America. The federal government usually views the stepparent as an individual who supports stepchildren, and provides benefits accordingly, while most states frequently consider the residential stepparent a stranger to the child (Mason, 1998: 101).

The increasingly public lifestyles of gays and lesbians today have also challenged American views on the definition of marriage and the family, as well as contributing to the debate on biological versus other forms of parentage. Sexual relations between two men and between two women are still outlawed by statute in many states.

At a lesbian marriage ceremony in San Francisco, both parties chose to dress as brides.

Gay couples and lesbian couples, who see themselves as equivalent to heterosexual couples, may go through a ritual they refer to as a marriage or commitment ceremony. A *New York Times* Op-Ed column on August 11, 1993, dealt with the publication of an announcement of the wedding of two men in the *Salina Journal,* published in Salina, Kansas. The wedding ceremony had been performed by a Presbyterian minister. While gays and lesbians from all over the country wrote the newspaper, congratulating it, 112 subscribers canceled their newspaper subscriptions in protest, and some advertisers grumbled. The story gained a nationwide audience when the couple and the writer of the *Salina Journal* story were flown to New York to appear on a nationwide TV program.

In some places, homosexual couples can legalize their relationship by registering—as, for example, at City Hall, in New York City. In *Lesbian and Gay Marriage* (Sherman, 1992), lesbian and gay couples detail not only how they view their relationships but also the various kinds of public ceremonies they have used to make a public commitment to one another. These included a Jewish religious ceremony in which rings were exchanged and a *ketubah* (traditional wedding document) was signed, followed by a formal catered affair and wedding cake. Other examples included an elaborate "wedding" on a yacht beyond the 3-mile limit; and a *Wiccan* ("early female spiritual tradition, or witchcraft") "handfasting," or betrothal ceremony (Sherman, 1992).

Homosexual couples demand legal status as married couples, but much of American society does not yet seem to have accepted the validity of their claim. In California, which has a large homosexual community, the surviving member of a couple can inherit the deceased member's pension. Mention of the surviving member of a homosexual couple in an obituary is often contested by the biological family of the deceased. Recently, in Hawaii, there has been discussion about the passage of legislation that would permit gays and lesbians to legally marry. There has been much consternation about this issue throughout the country, since laws about marriage and divorce passed by one state must be recognized by all other states. The backlash to this proposed legislation was the passage, in 1996, of the *Defense of Marriage Act,* signed by President Clinton, though he supported the rights of gays in the military. The campaign for the legalization of gay and lesbian marriage continues nevertheless.

Homosexuals not only "marry," but also create three-generation families in a variety of ways. Lesbians previously in heterosexual marriages often try to bring their biological children into the new family. In such a situation, the mother must also deal with the children's father (Lewin, 1993). Though some states prohibit lesbians and gays from adopting children, independent adoption was often a route followed if possible, particularly by gay couples. Some married lesbian couples have used artificial insemination to have children. They prefer to call it alternative insemination to emphasize that it is as natural as insemination through sexual intercourse (Weston, 1991: 171). Stacey notes, "Numerous lesbian couples solicit sperm from a brother or male relative of one woman to impregnate her partner, hoping to buttress their tenuous legal, symbolic, and social claims for shared parental status of the 'turkey-baster babies' " (Stacey, 1998: 120–121). The issue then is: What will be the relationship of the other woman in the couple to such children who are the results of artificial insemination? That woman may attempt to adopt the children of her "spouse." In several states, including California, New Jersey, and New York, this kind of adoption by lesbians has been approved by the courts. Other states, such as Florida and New Hampshire, have statutes prohibiting adoptions by a second female parent, under the reasoning that a second female could not adopt a child until the natural mother surrendered her rights to that child. Sometimes, each woman will have a child to produce a more equally balanced family. When gays and lesbians terminate their familial relationships, they sometimes end up in court arguing over the custody of the children, and challenging the court system since there are no precedents for such situations. As one might expect, biological claims of relationship are usually those that are recognized. The court has favored "the parental claims of donors who had contributed nothing more than sperm to their offspring over those of lesbians who had co-parented from the outset, even when these men [the sperm donors] had expressly agreed to abdicate paternal rights or responsibilities" (Stacey, 1998: 122).

Recently, several studies have focussed on the distinctions between heterosexual and homosexual families. In terms of compatibility, same-sex couples seem to get along better than heterosexual couples. They share more interests and spend more time with one another. Heterosexual couples have the least egalitarian relationships, and lesbian couples, the most. Child rearing is more nurturant, children more affectionate, parental relationships more cooperative and egalitarian among gay parents than among heterosexual parents. Gay parents prefer to live in communities that support the diversity of family life. As Stacey concludes, "Perhaps what is truly distinctive about lesbian and gay families is how unambiguously the substance of their relationships takes precedence over their form, emotional and social commitments over genetic claims" (Stacey, 1998: 138).

In American kinship, the term *family* refers to an infinitely extendable unit. It can be used to refer to the family group living together as a single household or, in its widest sense, to all the descendants of a single couple who gather at a family reunion. The anthropologist Kath Weston has studied the formation of lesbian and gay families in the San Francisco area (1991). When homosexuals come out to their biological families, they are often rejected and left to feel that they have no families. In response, a gay kinship ideology has emerged, which proclaims that "love makes a family." These are families that people create by choosing one another, providing a great contrast with their own biological families. The composition of such families is highly varied, and the only consistent kinship terminology in use is in reference to generational peers as *sister* and *brother*. These "sisters" and "brothers" become "aunts" and "uncles" when their "siblings" have children. Within the lesbian family, kin terms used by children for their parents are still highly varied.

David Schneider's work on American kinship was conducted among middle-class Americans, and he assumed that their value system was the ideal for the entire society, including the lower class. Lower-class kinship was seen as an adaptation to the world of racism and poverty. Carol Stack (1974) has described a kinship system among poor black people in a small Midwestern city that is quite different from the one described by Schneider. In this situation, relatives form a wide support network within which there is reciprocation, which Stack calls "swapping," of money, child care, food, clothing, shelter, and emotional support. Those biological relatives who choose not to be involved in a support network thereby renounce their status as kin. The core of this network is a cluster of linked households, usually two or even three generations of women. Relatives such as aunts and grandmothers may carry out the role of mother for children. Males are present, but they are usually boyfriends and mothers' brothers, rarely husbands or fathers. If a young couple should marry, the newly formed nuclear family draws the individuals away from their kin and out of their support networks. Should the young husband lose his job, the marriage has little chance to survive, since the couple always falls back on the resources of their respective kin networks, destroying the marriage. In this situation, ties between brother and sister are stronger than those between husband and wife. In the film *Do the Right Thing,* Spike Lee captures this contradiction when he contrasts the close emotional ties between the hero and his sister with the hero's antagonism toward his girlfriend, the mother of his child. In the kinship system described by Stack, mother's brothers more frequently serve as role models for young male children than fathers, giving the system a matrilineal cast. In writing about the way in which the criminal justice system should deal with juvenile offenders from the kinds of families Stack describes, Lund proposes that mother's brothers rather than fathers be made responsible for the supervision of such young offenders (Lund, 1995).

In contrast, a support network does not come into play in times of distress for the American middle class. Each nuclear family is separate and independent. Women with teenage children who are divorced after years of marriage are not reintegrated into their natural families, nor do they receive regular financial assistance from their parents (Newman, 1988). They therefore inevitably experience downward mobility as a result of divorce. When middle-level managers lose their jobs, they rarely seek and cannot expect help from close relatives and often keep the information about job loss secret. Brothers rarely seek financial help from one another, since the primary responsibility of each is to his own nuclear family. The obligations one has toward a relative are ambiguous in middle-class American society. When asked whether they would prefer to borrow money from relatives or from the bank, one American said, "From the bank! That's what banks are for." Another stated, "From your brother! What are brothers for?"

The migration of men and women from the Caribbean to the United States within recent decades has created the phenomenon of the international family (Ho, 1993). Ho's study of Afro-Trinidadians living in Los Angeles reveals the way in which the households of women who migrate from Trinidad may include kin, fictive kin, friends, and the children of kin and friends. Family and the network of kinship are dispersed internationally. For individuals living in Los Angeles, the family includes people in such far-flung places as Trinidad, Tobago, Jamaica, Barbados, St. Vincent, the United States Virgin Islands, New York, and cities in Connecticut and Canada. Such networks of kin and family, out of which households potentially may be formed, include up to four generations of kin and fictive kin. These individuals constitute a network of support and exchange like the network described by Carol Stack. They may own property in common and provide child support, "childminding," and informal adoption. Ties are maintained by telephone contact, letter writing, visits during vacation, and even family newsletters. The international family represents a globalization process, the result of migration for economic reasons, but a process with cultural outcomes, specifically, the "Caribbeanization" of America and the "Americanization" of the Caribbean (Ho, 1993: 39). The advent of the Internet has enabled such families, with members scattered across the globe, to keep in close touch with one another. In the summer of 1999, the *New York Times* reported that such a family, scattered over five continents, went online to hold a wake. One member delivered a eulogy online while the rest of the family watched it on their computer screens.

The family reunion in the United States, which involves kin relations beyond the nuclear family, has also been the subject of anthropological research. Neville (1987) recounts how every summer many Southern Protestant families attend such gatherings. The descendants of a male ancestor, who are now living dispersed over the United States, come together at the same time and place each year (like the Worthy family, which meets at an old camp meeting ground in north Georgia on the third Sunday in July). The descendants of the common ancestor, both male and female, constitute a constantly expanding group of descendants, which doubles with each generation. However, not all these descendants choose to come to the reunion. All such reunions include a shared meal cooked and contributed by the women of each family as well as visiting and telling of stories about the common ancestor and the kinship connections that bind them all together. They may also include church services, introduction of members, business matters, and the election of officers. When the descendants come together at the reunion, they are reenacting the Protestant biblical ideal of family and kinship. Exchanging food and partaking of a meal together once a year symbolize the solidarity of the kin group. Neville also points out a tendency to emphasize connections through women over those through men in the Southern Protestant families. A nuclear family is more likely to attend the reunions of the mother's family than the father's. Such family reunions have become common among various ethnic and racial groups in the United States. In sharp contrast to the Afro-Trinidadian and African-American kin networks described above, the family unit that comes together at family reunions has only expressive and symbolic functions.

This chapter presents the basic concepts of kinship that anthropologists have used to analyze the small-scale societies that were the focus of their attention as anthropology first developed as a discipline. These include descent, family, postmarital residence, and marriage. The incest taboo and marriage prohibitions compel individuals to marry beyond the family. Societies have rules regarding number of spouses and postmarital residence rules, which result in the creation of a variety of families. Societies also have rules regarding how marriage is contracted. Bridewealth, dowry, and bride service are the alternatives. The web of kinship rules of descent creates different kinds of kin groups or clans. Though their structures may differ, the functions of such groups—land ownership, economic and ceremonial functions—remain the same. Different types of marriage rules result in different structures of relationship or alliance between descent groups. The kinship terminology in different societies reflects the pattern of descent, family type, and marriage found in those societies. Some societies use kinship as a metaphor to create the important relationships of godparenthood. Americans have their own cultural ideas about kinship, which are currently being rethought in light of surrogate parenting, artificial insemination, stepparenthood, and adoption by gay and lesbian couples. Kinship continues to be important not only in our own complex industrial society but also in other societies all over the world. As Parkin notes, "many societies still think in terms of lineages, affinal alliance systems, residence rules and marriage payments, while virtually all are still organized in families of some sort and use kin terms to identity and classify relatives" (1997: ix–x).

Chapter Seven
Gender and Age

Every society makes social distinctions according to age and sex, and these distinctions form one of the bases for the differentiation of social roles within a society. As pointed out in Chapter 1, age and sex distinctions also form the basis for role differentiation in animal societies, like the baboon troop and the wolf pack. Human societies always distinguish between male roles and female roles, and the relations between the sexes are always culturally patterned. Gender roles differ from one culture to another, and the nature of their patterning forms a powerful motif in the tapestry of culture.

Male and Female

The relationship between males and females and the way in which male and female roles are culturally construed are topics that have received a good deal of attention in the last two decades. Before that time, anthropologists, male and female, focused primarily on male roles in their field research. In doing so, they were unconsciously reflecting the cultural bias of their own society, which emphasized the significance of male roles, and projecting its gender ideology onto the society they were studying. Sometimes this focus on the primacy of male roles reflected the male bias of the society being studied. Margaret Mead and one or two other female anthropologists were exceptions to this male bias. With the growth of the feminist movement within the past 30 years, many anthropologists of both sexes began to pay attention to female as well as male roles and to the female as well as the male point of view of society. They focused attention on the cultural construction of gender roles and how these related to other patterns in the culture. The cultural constructions of what is male and what is female are much more than natural categories based on biological differences. As Errington puts it, "Culture does not lie on the surface of the anatomical and physiological base as decoration, the way icing lies on a cake. If human social life were compared to a cake, we would better say that 'biological givens' are analogous to flour, eggs, and sugar, and the socializing process of human interaction 'cooks' them into their final form: cake" (Errington, 1990: 14).

While all societies construct female roles as different from male roles, the nature of the contrast differs from one society to another. In a society like Wogeo, an island

off New Guinea, the difference is based on the belief that men and women live separately in two different worlds. But realistically, men and women must come together
to reproduce the society as well as to carry out the usually complementary social and
economic roles upon which their society depends. Politics and power are controlled
by men. Associated with these ideas about the separateness of the sexes is the belief that sexual intercourse is polluting to both sexes and that menstrual blood is
harmful to men. While women menstruate naturally, in Wogeo the men incise their
penises to rid themselves of the bad "menstrual" blood (Hogbin, 1970).

The people of the islands of Kerkennah, as noted in Chapter 5, believe that there
is a fundamental difference between males and females, which is manifested in the
fetuses in the womb. This distinction continues during the child's development and
throughout his or her life.

In contrast to Wogeo and Kerkennah, other societies play down the differences.
The Wana on the island of Sulawesi, in Indonesia, conceptualize gender relationships
very differently from the people of Wogeo. Differences between male and female are
minimized; male and female are seen as almost identical anatomically. Husband and
wife are equally involved in procreation. The Wana say that the man carries the child
for the first seven days of gestation and then puts the child into a woman. It is believed that in the past men menstruated. Men's menstrual blood is said to be "white
blood" and to contain the essence of humanity, which solidifies in the womb as a fetus (Atkinson, 1990: 75, 76). Both the national state organization and the wilderness
surrounding the village lie outside the Wana communities. These areas are dangerous, but they are also the source of spiritual knowledge and power. The Wana believe that men are braver than women. This is one area in which there are gender
differences. Men obtain knowledge from the spirits of the forest and become
shamans. The overwhelming majority of Wana shamans are men. Even in a society
where men and women are seen as fundamentally the same, gender does make a difference when it comes to the public realm of politics. Atkinson also reports several
cases of gender shifting. In one of them, a woman, who had borne and lost a child,
lived like a man "married" to another woman and performed as a shaman (Atkinson,
1990). Among the Wana, even though most shamans are men, both men and women
may become shamans, while among the Yanomamo only men may become shamans.
On the other hand, in Korea most shamans are female (see Kendall, 1996).

In all societies, cultural constructions of gender are the bases of economic roles.
The difference is not an outgrowth of the biological differences between men and
women. A specific task may be associated with men in one society and with women
in another. Milking herd animals (cows, goats, sheep), for example, may be a female
task in some societies and a male task in others, as is also the case with making pottery and weaving cloth. Men's economic tasks invariably have greater prestige, even
though women's tasks, such as horticulture and collecting plant foods, may provide
the bulk of subsistence. Whatever the economic role of the man, it is that role which
the culture values, because in many societies what men do is usually more valued
culturally than what women do.

Earlier, we discussed the ways in which space takes on different symbolic meanings. Particular spatial areas may be associated respectively with males and females.

Because women are identified with mothering, the hearth, and the home, women are associated with the domestic realm. Men in contrast, are identified with the public realm. This distinction between domestic and public is an analytical tool that aids us in comparing male and female roles in different societies. The association of males with the public sphere and females with the domestic was widespread in the past; today this distinction is not always the case.

In a number of New Guinea societies, the men's house and the ceremonial plaza are male turf, while women are associated with their own dwelling houses. Women in many Middle Eastern societies are restricted to certain parts of the house and may only come into contact with males who are members of their own family. When they leave the house, they must veil their faces. In such societies, the coffeehouse and the market are defined as male domains. However, markets are not universally male domains. As mentioned in Chapter 3, Malagasy women conduct the haggling that takes place in the market, while in some West African societies, women actually control the marketplace.

Greek society shares a number of gender-related characteristics with Middle Eastern societies, in that women are restricted to the domestic realm, leaving the world of politics and the public sphere, including coffee shops, to men. Herzfeld examines the manner in which this particular division is reflected in the respective ways in which men and women use language in a village in Crete (Herzfeld, 1991). Men are expected to be verbal and to use language effectively in debate and argumentation with other men. The female stereotype is that women are rather inarticulate. Herzfeld finds that they are laconic, often silent. How does one interpret silence? When they do talk, women outwardly support their menfolk, but they often use irony when they privately poke fun at shows of masculinity on the part of men. In the "poetics" of women's speech (and in their silences) Herzfeld finds evidence of their attempts to subvert the existing order rather than simply to submit to it. In Greek society, men have special friendships with other men. These "friends of the heart" have a symmetrical relationship, which includes strong emotional ties, commensality, comradery, and sharing. Such friendships are symbols of masculinity, being fused with male sentiment. While women's emotionality is invested in the making of domestic structure, men's emotionality is articulated primarily outside the home and outside kinship. Male friendships are a central part of the male self (Papataxarchis, 1991).

The discussion above of the island of Wogeo made note of the fact that menstrual blood and sexual intercourse are seen as harmful to men. Menstrual blood is a substance that, perhaps more than any other, is associated with femaleness and also with pollution. We saw this in Chapter 4, where young children from India had to keep their distance from their menstruating mothers. In the course of interaction between male and female in Wogeo, as in some other societies, men may perceive women as dangerous, and this danger is often projected onto menstrual blood. Among the Mae Enga, a highland New Guinea society, men always take wives from enemy groups, and consequently, wives are seen as dangerous. They believe that a man can be harmed if he has sexual intercourse with a menstruating woman or when menstrual blood is introduced into food. The belief that menstrual blood is a dangerous substance is found in other societies in the world where wives do not come from enemy groups. A comparative study of beliefs about menstruation points out that this idea about the polluting effect of menstrual blood on men tends to be part of a male vision of society (Buckley and Gottlieb, 1988: 35). There are few studies of how females in particular societies view menstruation. Menstrual blood can be used symbolically in harmful ways in witchcraft and in a positive fashion in the manufacture of love charms.

In the previous chapter, we pointed out that Americans have their own cultural conceptualizations of kinship based on blood as a natural symbol. They also perceive differences between males and females as natural differences. Americans consider the differences in genitalia to be signs of differences in fluids and substances that naturally divide the population into two different, mutually exclusive, categories (Errington, 1990). Behavior, dress, and demeanor are viewed by Americans as determining membership in one of these two categories. Clearly, this idea of what is considered natural by Americans is a culturally constructed category that is continually expressed and enacted.

Shifting Gender Categories

As noted earlier, masculinity and femininity are culturally construed concepts. We have pointed out that gender shifting occurs among the Wana. As in the Wana case, women in Western society who carried out masculine roles, such as the author George Sand and Joan of Arc, usually dressed and acted like men.

In Native American Plains societies, the term *berdache,* a term of French derivation, was originally used to refer to men who dressed like women and sometimes lived in homosexual relationships with other men, a kind of "third gender." We now recognize that there were also women in these societies who dressed like men and assumed male roles, who constituted a "fourth gender" (Roscoe, 1998). Perhaps the most famous *berdache* in American Indian history was We'wha, a Zuni *berdache* who was accepted as a woman during his trip to Washington, D.C., in 1886, where he met many dignitaries, including President Grover Cleveland. He lived as a woman and was skilled at women's crafts. When he died, he was dressed in a dress, with a pair of pants beneath the dress, the pants symbolizing his "raw state," as a biological man, and the dress his "cooked state," that of a woman (Roscoe, 1998: 145). It would appear that the Zuni used the same metaphor employed by Errington above, that the biological state is the raw state and the cultural construction is the cooked state. *Berdaches,* who were known as *nadleehi,* were also to be found among the Navajo. Roscoe notes that the *nadleehi* tradition still continues in parts of the Navajo Reservation (1998: 65).

Roscoe gives a number of examples of female *berdaches* who were warriors. He notes that Cheyenne female warrior chiefs "dressed like the male members of the Hohnuka, or Contrary society, who fought wearing only their breachcloths" (Roscoe, 1998: 75). Some of these Cheyenne female warriors sat with the Chief Council and their opinions had weight. Similar cases occurred among the Pend d'Oreille and Flathead Indians, both from Montana, as well as the Crow and the Blackfoot. Running Eagle, a female warrior of the Blackfoot in the early nineteenth century, became a

The berdache *We'wha,*
wearing the ceremonial
costume of a Zuni woman.

legendary subject. Her story was reprinted and given new meaning in 1984 as a positive image for young women today. The Navajo also had female *nadleehi,* masculine females or female *berdaches,* giving them four culturally identified genders. Today some male *nadleehi* may use that label to identify themselves, being Navajo traditionalists in their belief. Younger acculturated and assimilated Navajo homosexuals use the Western categories gay and homosexual, and may be completely unfamiliar with the *nadleehi* tradition (Thomas, 1998: 162, 169).

A form of male transvestism occurs today among Samoans (Mageo, 1992). In the past, it was part of the sexual ribaldry and buffoonery that took place during ceremonial competition between kin groups, when both men and women performed sexually provocative dances. If a girl referred to as "sister" (in the real or extended sense) was present, no one was allowed to use coarse and sexually suggestive language in joking. Therefore, girls of one village needed to perform their suggestive dances before boys of another village to ensure that brothers were not present. As a result of the introduction of Christianity, women in general had to cease such ribald sexual banter and dancing and become modest and circumspect in their behavior. Only old women are still involved in teasing, sexual banter, and sometimes lewd dancing. The behavior of male transvestites, or *fa'afafine,* as performers and the objects of sexual joking has replaced the sexually suggestive talk and performances that young women formerly performed. Many *fa'afafine* are to be found in bars in urban areas today, and there are at least one or two in each rural village. When male transvestites perform at a beauty contest for *fa'afafine,* sexual ribaldry can occur because they are not really women. In the role of *fa'afafine,* there is a complete reversal of the normal male role. The sexually expressive *fa'afafine* is also the virginal sister turned on her head. We therefore see in Samoa the construction of a gender that is different from the present constitution of male or chaste female roles and patterned upon a ribald version of a female role from the past. This is, of course, a completely cultural construction made up of inversions of other gender roles in the culture.

Changing Gender Roles

In our own and other industrial societies, economic, spatial, and behavioral separation of the sexes was present until the beginning of the twentieth century. Ginsburg (1989) points out that in preindustrial America, the home was basically the workplace for both men and women. With increasing industrialization during the nineteenth century, men were drawn into the factories and businesses while women remained in the home, an essentially female domain. Women were identified with an ideology of nurturance and domesticity, despite the fact that some women worked in stores and factories for wages. Politics, the courts, businesses, banks, pubs, and so forth were male bastions; so too were the social clubs, where real business was carried out.

At the beginning of the twentieth century, women who questioned the assignment of these male and female roles formed the suffragist movement and began to agitate for the right to vote, which had been denied them heretofore. Men perceived the pioneers in this movement as very masculine women. World War II brought many women into the workforce, and since that time, ever-increasing numbers of women have become part of the American labor force. It took the feminist movement of the 1970s and affirmative action legislation to begin to raise both female and male consciousness and bring about the transformations that we see today. As women have moved into occupations like law and medicine, formerly occupied almost exclusively by men, the society at large has come to accept women as well as men in those roles. In this way, women in American society have invaded the public realm of men, and as this has occurred, men have increasingly had more to do in the domestic realm, taking on cooking and child care.

Another example of how gender roles have changed in America concerns childbirth. In the nineteenth century, American women gave birth in the home, which, as we noted, was identified as a female sphere. At the beginning of the twentieth century, with the increasing professionalization of medicine and the growth of hospitals, the medical profession, then male-dominated, took control over the process of giving birth, and by the 1930s more births occurred in hospitals than at home. Under these conditions, birth was defined as a medical procedure, and the female reproductive process was taken over and placed in the hands of male physicians.

With the significant changes in gender roles in our society, this process is being reversed. There are more female physicians now. Interest in natural childbirth has brought about changes, and home birth is a possibility that some feminists advocate.

Other aspects of the new reproductive technology, such as amniocentesis, genetic counseling, and the use of various birth control techniques, for example, intrauterine devices and birth control pills, have also been seen as giving women more choices and greater control over their lives in regard to reproductive functions. However, the introduction of these procedures does not really empower women, but rather, increases the control of technology and technologists over women and their reproductive processes (Rapp, 1993).

The change in gender roles just described is in no way an inevitable progression through which all modernizing societies will pass. Anthropologists have described all sorts of changes affecting gender roles in different parts of the world in recent decades. Many women in parts of the Middle East and Asia have left their traditional domestic domains to go to work outside the home with varying consequences. For example, in Hong Kong in the 1970s, in families where fathers were unemployed or underemployed, daughters went to work, becoming semiskilled factory workers (Salaff, 1995). Their incomes played a prominent role in the household economy, though their personal gain was limited. There was some loosening of family ties, and they were freed from household duties and received small amounts of spending money. Their marriages were no longer arranged and they could choose their own spouses. However, core family values of paternal rule and filial obedience were still maintained.

The constitution of gender roles often swings back and forth like a pendulum in response to political changes. In Iran, Riza Shah Pahlevi, who ruled for several decades during the mid-twentieth century, tried to modernize and industrialize the country on a grand scale. He invited foreigners, particularly businessmen, to come and set up factories and transform Iran into a Western-oriented country. He introduced universal education, and women were encouraged to seek occupations outside the home. The wearing of veils was outlawed and Family Protection Laws were passed stipulating that wives had to give their consent to all the aspects of the marriage contract, including the taking of another wife by the husband. When the shah was overthrown, the new regime, led by the Ayatollah Khomenei, turned the society 180 degrees, replacing the Shah's Westernization efforts with strict Islamic social norms and morality, especially with regard to the position of women. The sexes were viewed as having very different roles, with men being seen as more rational, brave, conquering, and aggressive in sexual urges. Women were viewed as emotional and sexually conniving (Nakanishi, 1998: 88). The Family Protection Laws were abolished, giving men the primary role in the stipulation of the conditions of the marriage. Women were required to wear the *hijab*, a scarf covering the head and shoulders, to enable men to control their sexuality.

Women have reacted to these new edicts in several ways. A moderate position has been proposed by the Women's Society of the Islamic Revolution of Iran, which sees itself as reformist but not feminist. The political writings of the group describe and critique the two extreme responses. Those still favoring the Western orientation introduced by the Shah are characterized as the "west-toxicated" women who "blindly" accept Westernization and modernization, who do not wear the *hijab* and who have lost their "true" Muslim identity (Nakanishi, 1998: 87). Traditional women, who blindly accept what the religious leaders promulgate about their inferiority, who do not take the initiative about their own lives, and who wear the *chadar,* a black

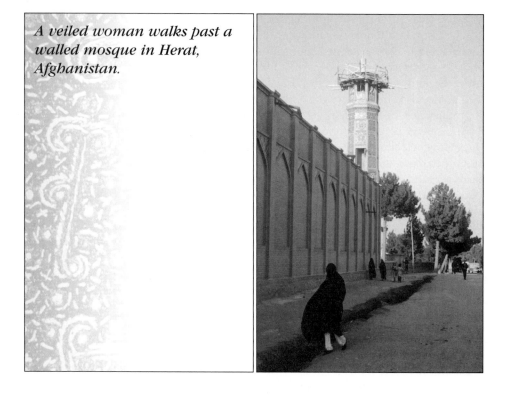

A veiled woman walks past a walled mosque in Herat, Afghanistan.

garment which covers them from head to foot, are also criticized. The proper path, advocated by the society, is that of "ideal Muslim women" who accept their identity as Muslims, demonstrated by the wearing of the *hijab,* but who are independent, participate in politics, and are not passive and subordinate to men (Nakanishi, 1998). Though the government has established councils on women's affairs in 1987 and 1992, little legislation has been passed to ensure women's rights within the context of the Islamic tradition.

Another Muslim society, the Minangkabau, who live on the island of Sumatra and are part of the Indonesian nation-state, provide us with an interesting example of the way in which the contemporary women's role is sensitive to political currents. The Minangkabau have a matrilineal rule of descent and the wife's relatives play a significant role in social and economic affairs. *Adat,* the unique body of traditions related to this social system, has melded with the Qur'an since Islam was introduced in 1600. The laws of the Qur'an developed in the context of patrilineal societies. Since the Minangkabau are matrilineal, this necessitated making compromises between *adat* and the Qur'an. These traditions have survived more than 300 years of Dutch colonial rule, as well as the development of the Indonesian nation-state after the country won independence in the mid-1950s (Whalley, 1998: 229).

The Minangkabau began to move to the urban areas of Sumatra and to educate girls as part of the modernization and transformation of Indonesia that took place under the aegis of President Suharto. This presented many challenges to both Islam and *adat*. The response, in the 1980s, was an Islamic renaissance parallel to that occurring in other Islamic countries. The government itself then began to fund the building of mosques. Soon major religious events and family celebrations were emphasized, and girls began to wear Muslim dress to school. In terms of *adat* tradition, as early as the beginning of the twentieth century, there had been a shift from uxorilocal residence, when the husband moved to live with the wife's relatives, to nuclear family households, though the families still lived on her lineage land and in close proximity to the wife's female relatives (Whalley, 1998: 233). Despite the continuation of the matrilineal tradition, husbands began to invest more time and interest in their wives and children and less on their own matrilineage, as had been the case in the past. The growing importance of the nuclear family household has resulted in the husband's providing more subsistence for his family, as well as providing for the education of his children, allocating inheritance of personal property to them, and having more of a voice in whom his daughters marry. However, mother's brother and matrilineage relatives, especially older women, still play a significant role in deciding schools to attend, professions to pursue, and marriages to be arranged. With the growing importance of Islam in the 1980s combined with the efforts at modernization, young women had to tread a narrow line to resolve the dilemma of career and family (an issue not unfamiliar to young American women). However, in contrast to traditional Islamic thinking in Iran, for example, Minangkabau women are seen as being of equal moral worth with men. Islamic scholars proclaimed women to be the pillars of society given their critical roles as mothers and wives. Women's education was encouraged, in order to enable them to better raise and educate their children. The educational choices of young women today may necessitate making decisions that do not always fit with the cultural traditions of the senior generation. Young Minangkabau women have continued to wear more modest Western-style dress, though they wear traditional Muslim Minangkabau dress for ritual occasions. Islamic traditions were being aggressively taught in contrast to the Western-style education of the 1960s and 1970s. Islam was being promoted as an answer to reestablishing order in a country threatened by Westernization. Recently, however, as a counter to the threats to the traditional *adat*, children in school are being exposed to programs emphasizing this tradition. In addition, urban middle-class Minangkabau are hosting large-scale marriage festivals that mix rock music with "all the intricate observances of high *adat*" (Whalley, 1998: 245).

It is clear that gender roles must be viewed in relation to each other since no society consists solely of males or solely of females. The two are necessary for society. But how their roles are culturally defined varies enormously and is subject to many different kinds of influences.

■ Categories Based on Age

Aging is a continuous process, from birth to death. However, the way in which this continuum is divided will vary from society to society, as well as over time within a single society. Every society has terms for different age groups, but the number of terms varies. In our own society, for example, we use such terms as *infant, child, adolescent, adult,* and *senior citizen.*

Age Grades

In some societies, when the age categories are formally named and recognized and crosscut the entire society, they are referred to as *age grades.* In a number of primarily herding societies in East Africa, from Ethiopia in the north to Tanzania in the south, formalized male age grades play an important role in the social structure. One such society is the Nandi of Kenya, studied by G.W.B. Huntingford (1953). The Nandi have a system of seven age grades that correspond to divisions of a man's life cycle. Every 15 years or so, men move from one age grade to the next, more senior, age grade. This change takes place at a ceremony that is held simultaneously at several places throughout Nandi territory. All the boys born between one ceremony and the next form a single *age set,* which is given a permanent name. Since there is a 15-year period between one change in grade and the next, there is a 15-year range in the ages of members of a single set. When the last man of the oldest set dies, the name that was assigned to that age set is free to be used for the age set of male infants being born. There is thus a set of seven names, each of which is recycled every 105 years (7 grades $\times$ 15 years, the period of time between changes of grade).

The most junior of the age grades consists of young boys. The second grade consists of initiates, averaging 15 years in age, who will be circumcised at some point while they are in this grade. Boys, during their time in this grade, learn the role of warriors, which they will take over when they move into the next grade. The third age grade is that of the warriors, the "set in power," who carry out all military actions in Nandi society, including raids against neighboring peoples. The warriors live in special bachelor houses and are allowed free sexual access to uninitiated girls. They have primary responsibility for organizing the circumcision of the younger age grade of initiates and for testing the younger grade for bravery and valor. Before the official movement into the next grade, the oldest group of warriors take wives and retire from active participation as warriors. On leaving the grade of warrior, a man and his set pass into the first of the four grades of elders. At the ceremony that marks the change from warrior to the first grade of elder, the retiring warriors remove their clothes and put on old men's fur cloaks.

There is no elaborate system of age grades, nor age sets, for women. Instead, they are divided into two categories—girls and married women. A rite, corresponding to male circumcision, is performed upon older girls, which involves an operation on the clitoris. This elaborate system of age grades among the Nandi coexists with other kinds of social groupings based on family, lineage, and clan. The age grade system divides the society like a seven-layer cake, and assigns particular functions to each of the grades.

The Nyakyusa of Tanzania, who were studied by Monica Wilson (1951, 1977), use divisions according to age as the basis for a different kind of age grade system. Age mates, as they mature, join to form a new village. When they are 10 or 11 years old, boys build huts and establish a village at the edge of their fathers' village. They sleep and spend time in their fledgling village but return to their mothers' huts for meals and assist their fathers in agriculture. The Nyakyusa emphasize that boys at this age should move out because they should not be aware of the sexual activities of their parents. Where other societies, such as the Trobriand Islanders, have the institution of the bachelor house to which adolescent boys must move, the Nyakyusa have extended the idea of the bachelor house to the formation of an entirely new village. When the original founders of the village reach the age of 15, the village becomes closed to new members. At about the age of 25, the boys, now young men, marry and bring their brides to live with them virilocally in the new village, and now each wife cooks for her husband. Once in a generation a great ritual is held, at which time administrative power and military leadership are handed over by the older generation to the younger. The men of the retiring generation move to one side, and the new villages of young men are formally established on their own lands. At this ritual the old chief retires, and his sons are recognized as chiefs of the small chiefdoms into which the Nyakyusa are divided. The retiring old chief reallocates all the land and selects a headman for each new village.

All over Nyakyusaland, at any time, there are three kinds of age grade villages. There are the villages of the grandfathers, who have retired from leadership positions but who still perform certain ritual functions. There are the villages of the fathers, who rule and are responsible for defense and administration. Finally, there are the villages of the sons, who have not yet "come out" but when necessary, fight under the leadership of men of their fathers' generation. The Nyakyusa have an intense fear of sexual relations between a young man and his father's co-wives, who are his stepmothers. Similarly, possible sexual relations between father-in-law and daughter-in-law are dreaded. The age villages are a way of keeping the generations apart and thus avoiding intimate contact between these categories of people. On the positive side, the Nyakyusa stress the friendship and fellowship within one's peer group, which promotes the solidarity of the village. Though the Nyakyusa have a rule of patrilineal descent and patrilineages, the members of a lineage are dispersed over a number of villages. In contrast to the Nyakyusa, most societies with patrilineal descent have villages based on lineage and clan organization, where the lineage or clan owns the land. However, in these societies the tension between the generations may undermine the solidarity of the clan. The Nyakyusa say that they prefer to live with people of their own generation with whom they can have easy communication, since relations between members of the same lineage but of different generations are governed by the formal respect required of juniors for their seniors. Under the recent pressure of economic change, the Nyakyusa have been moving away from their traditional age villages. When men migrate from their homes for wage labor, they leave their wives with their mothers, thereby negating the traditional value of separating a daughter-in-law from her father-in-law. Furthermore, individuals seeking economic advancement for themselves create a conflict with the traditional value of sharing between members of an age village (Wilson, 1977). This situation is in contrast to that of the Samburu, a pastoral society in nearby Kenya that also has an age grade system. Though some Samburu have moved to town, many of them still retain their herds. Their age grade system is still intact (Bilinda-Straight, 1997: 68).

Retirement Communities

We pointed out earlier how the cultural construction of gender has been changing in North America. A significant change has also taken place in the construction of the category of senior citizen. The existence of Social Security and pensions has made retirement a twentieth-century institution. There is no longer a retirement age and therefore no longer a clearly defined point at which an American moves into the category of senior citizen. However, that fact that the law has changed does not necessarily mean that peoples' attitudes and behavior have also changed. By law, a person need not retire at any particular age, but individuals may begin to consider themselves senior citizens, join the American Association of Retired Persons, and retire from their employment as early as age 55. However, the movement toward early retirement, which characterized the 1980s and 1990s, seems to be passing. The trend now is for people to continue to do some type of work.

Some people "age in place" while others, upon their retirement, migrate elsewhere, usually to a retirement community in the Sun Belt. Those retiring south are usually younger, more affluent, and healthier than older people in general. Many retirement communities are self-contained and focus on leisure activities (Rieske and Holstege, 1996: 252). These communities, whose residents must be over 55 years of age and which do not allow children to live there, resemble a Nyakyusa village of grandfathers. As a consequence, they have no schools and therefore pay no school taxes.

Retirement communities are sometimes built around religious affiliation or ethnic identity. They may also be constructed on the basis of social class, some consisting of mobile homes, while others contain condominiums or private homes. As a result of chain migration, when earlier migrants attract later ones from the same community, clusters of individuals having long-term relations develop. A Finnish-American retirement community of this sort exists in southeast Florida, though very few other Finns live and work in this area (Stoller, 1998). The community began to develop in 1940 when Finnish Americans living in New England and the Midwest, particularly Minnesota, first came to this area to retire. Some members of the community are second-generation Finnish Americans, while others were born in Finland and came to the United States after World War II. This is not a planned retirement community, like the ones described above, but rather, consists of residents scattered through a large metropolitan area and linked through informal networks and organizations. The ethnic identity manifested by the Finnish Americans in this community is the basis for informal ties and the development of solidarity and support among these older people (Stoller, 1998: 289). The community contains two "Finn Halls," which sponsor cultural and social programs. Other Finnish institutions include two churches that conduct weekly services in Finnish, a Finnish-language newspaper, and a Finnish-American rest home. In the community, 123 merchants and service providers identify themselves as Finnish.

Retirement communities are not exclusive to the United States. They have begun to be established in Japan. Traditionally, elderly parents lived with the family of one of their children in a family form known as *dokyo*. In the rural areas, 62 percent of senior citizens still live this way while in the urban areas only 33 percent do so. A recent ethnography describes Fuji-No-Sato, an example of a community or "life-care" facility, located near a small fishing and farming village, which is also an upper-class summer resort area (Kinoshita and Kiefer, 1992). Those desiring to live there purchase a right to live in the community rather than an apartment. They must be 60 years of age, live independently, pay an endowment fee when they move in and then a monthly operating fee. This community, located a day trip away from Tokyo, includes primarily individuals who remain there full-time, though a quarter of the individuals use their apartments as second homes. The well-educated inhabitants are from the middle or upper middle class. The community is self-contained, consisting of two-story buildings in a wooded environment with a shuttle bus to the village, because most of the residents do not have cars. There is a residents' association, which all must join, and a wide variety of hobby groups; Christian groups, which hold prayer meetings; and volunteer groups. Gardening is a very important activity. Since the community is an unfamiliar, unstructured, newly constituted social situation with few guidelines for behavior, people's relationships are primarily formal in nature, which characterize Japanese behavior in such unstructured situations. Since Japan is relatively homogeneous compared with the United States, ethnicity cannot serve as a basis for Japanese retirement communities; only social class can function in this way.

Male and Female Rites of Passage—Moving between Age Categories

The movement of individuals from one stage in the life cycle into another is often marked by ritual, the most important *rites of passage* being celebrated at the most significant points of change. In Chapter 2 we saw how important rites are performed at weddings. Initiation rites for boys, widely celebrated, mark the change in status from boy to man. In our discussion of Kerkennah gender roles in Chapter 4, we saw the way in which, after circumcision, the Kerkennah boy moves beyond the sphere of his mother into the world of men. The corresponding rite for girls typically occurs at first menstruation, but is less common than boys' rites. In fact, Kerkennah girls have no initiation rites and remain close to their mothers. Girls often assume female social and economic roles while still young, helping their mothers and assuming child care responsibilities for their younger siblings. For boys, there is a much sharper break between boyhood and manhood. For one thing, they must be removed from their mothers. At initiation rites, boys are often reborn "through" men.

Male and female initiatory rites are found in societies with matrilineal as well as patrilineal descent rules; however, there is a difference at boys' initiation between patrilineal and matrilineal societies. For example, the Arapesh, a patrilineal society whose rites of passage will be discussed more fully in Chapter 10, go to great lengths to "remove" the mother's blood and milk, which she contributed to a boy's conception and growth, so that he can now belong solely to his father's clan. Lesu, in New Ireland, is a matrilineal society. Before the colonial period and missionary activity, boys were initiated and circumcised. But even in this matrilineal society, boys were forcibly removed

A boy's initiation ceremony among the Mungonge of Zaire.

from their protesting mothers and turned into men. This initiatory rite, as well as girls' initiation, was performed in conjunction with mortuary rites. Young girls were secluded, fed special foods, and tatooed during this period of seclusion. Both boys and girls emerged as men and women during the final stages of the mortuary ceremony.

Girls' initiation often takes place when they menstruate for the first time. In Wogeo, menstruation is considered a natural process through which women get rid of "bad blood." Wogeo men imitate women's menstruation by incising their penises so that they too can rid themselves of the "bad blood." This process of incising the penis is taught to boys during their initiation.

In societies with age grades, like the Nandi described above, all the boys in an age grade are circumcised at the same time—while they are in the second age grade. During this time, these initiates learn how to become warriors and men. Correspondingly, Nandi girls have a female ritual, during which the clitoris is excised, turning them into women.

Genital Mutilation—A Human Rights Issue

In the past few years, first female genital mutilation and now what has come to be called sexual mutilation—the new term for circumcision and female genital cutting—has become a topic of concern and discussion internationally. The International Symposium on Sexual Mutilation has been held four times since 1989 (Denniston and Milos, 1997). Sexual mutilation, of girls as well as boys, is now seen as a worldwide problem. Female genital multilation, which is part of the initiatory rites described above, has become a topic for headlines in American newspapers. Groups such as Nurses for the Rights of Children, in the United States; the National Organization of Circumcision Information Resources Centres, in Australia; and Doctors Opposing Circumcision, functioning in the United States, Australia, and Canada, have taken up the cause of stopping all genital mutilation (Denniston and Milos, 1997). Male circumcision practiced by Jews and Muslims for religious reasons became a practice advocated by physicians in the late nineteenth century for all American males for health reasons. These reasons ranged from prevention of epilepsy and sexually transmitted diseases, at the beginning, to prevention of cancer and HIV infection today (Hodges, 1997: 36–37). Immigration, primarily by African people, who traditionally practice female genital mutilation, brought that custom to the United States and several European countries after World War II. The advocacy groups mentioned above propose eliminating all genital mutilation. They see it as a violation of human rights. A petition, named in honor of the anthropologist Ashley Montagu, "To End the Genital Mutilation of Children Worldwide" has been sent to the Secretary General of the United Nations and presented to the World Court at the Hague, but as yet there has been no response. Many human rights and feminist organizations have taken up the cause of eliminating only female genital mutilation. They view it as "a form of child abuse; as an infringement of human rights, that is, as gender-based violence; and in terms of gender dynamics, as a deliberate attempt to curtail the sexuality of women in some patriarchal societies" (Kassamali, 1998: 39). Britain and France have already passed laws making female genital mutilation a crime, and such legislation has recently been passed by the U.S. Congress. There is also pressure on African and Middle Eastern countries by international human rights organizations to prevent girls from having to forcibly undergo this procedure in order to be socially acceptable and marriageable. In Sierra Leone, the ritual of female genital cutting is considered by women an important aspect of moving into womanhood. The procedure was necessary for a girl to become marriageable. It is mothers and grandmothers who are the enforcers of this practice. Opposition to the cessation of this practice has also become an issue of women's rights. Haja Sasso, leader of the Muslim Council of Muslim Women, has led marches and protests in support of the continuation of the practice "to protect our culture." However, women from Sierra Leone, Nigeria, and Togoland have come to this country and sought asylum to escape such operations. In these societies, as well as many others from Africa to the Pacific, clitoridectomy is always coupled with male circumcision as significant rites of passage for girls and boys. In America, for the most part, discussion of genital mutilation refers to female genital mutilation, and the male practice of circumcision is not viewed in the same way, but as a matter of freedom of religion and hygienic practice. Clitoridectomy is characterized by American feminists and human rights activists as "barbaric genital mutilation," but most Americans ethnocentrically accept male circumcision as civilized practice. It should be apparent that this is not a clear-cut issue.

Age and sex are the most common bases for distinction between social roles. It would appear, initially, that cultural categories based on age and sex simply build upon biological differences. However, in human societies, where culture defines these categories, this is not the case. The cultural expressions of age and gender vary from society to society. One must also look at relationships between the categories. Females are always defined in terms of relationship to males and vice versa. The young are defined in relationship to the old. All such relationships are always subtle and complex, and these categories and their relationships change over time.

Chapter Eight

Provisioning Society: Production, Distribution, and Consumption

The British author and socialist George Orwell characterized capitalist industrial society as one in which the economy dominated all other aspects of life. Paraphrasing Paul the Apostle, Orwell mocked our contemporary life, stating, "Though I speak with the tongues of men and angels and have not money . . . I am nothing. And though I bestow all my goods to feed the poor, and though I give my body to be burned, and have not money, it profiteth me nothing. . . . And now abideth faith, hope, and money, these three; but the greatest of these is money." The point that Orwell was making is that money has become the medium by which all things—labor, land, services, sex, time, art, votes, and even love—have come to be measured, bought, and sold in our society. This increasingly has come to be the case, as the cultural principle referred to as market mentality has spread through every aspect of modern society. This is true even more today than it was in Orwell's time. For example, in a recent discussion of campaign financing, Senator Mitch McConnell argued that money equals free speech, and that when one restricts campaign distributions, one is restricting freedom of speech. As Western ideas and industrialization have spread to other parts of the world, so has the Western idea of market mentality. As we shall see, market mentality was not characteristic of the societies that anthropologists used to study, nor of Western society at an earlier time.

In this chapter, we will discuss how societies provision themselves. In the course of the discussion, we will describe how kinship groups and societies are linked to one another by systems of exchange and distribution, like the potlatch, the *kula*, and the market. Kinship groups and societies can never be looked at as isolates except for purposes of analysis. Most of the societies we will be discussing in this chapter have become part of the world system, in one way or another, as we will describe in more detail in Chapter 13.

The economic organization of a society is how that society, in a regularized fashion, goes about providing the material goods and services it needs to reproduce itself. The economic organization is a cultural construction that operates according to sets of cultural rules and arrangements that bring together human and animal labor, man-made technology, and natural resources to provide for the provisioning of society. Rules relating to economic organization are similar to rules that govern the other aspects of culture. Individuals may interpret the rules to their own advantage—in economic terms, this is known as *maximizing*. In small-scale societies economic behavior operated to a large extent within the context of their kinship structures. In such situations, rules governing who owns the resources, how the work is organized, who uses or eats the product, and so forth are aspects of kinship. The economy is embedded in the social structure, within the tapestry of the culture itself. As societies expanded in scale, the separation of economic behavior from the realm of kinship increased, and economic institutions became more and more delimited as separate systems. Though we deal with economic organization, in this chapter, separately from our discussion of political organization, the subject of the next chapter, the two topics are intertwined, as we shall see below. Economic decisions always have political implications, and political decisions likewise have economic implications, as reflected in the term *political economy*.

For purposes of analysis, economic organization may be divided into three parts: production, distribution or exchange, and consumption.

Production

Production is the process whereby a society uses the tools and energy sources at its disposal and the labor of its people and domesticated animals to create the goods necessary for supplying society as an ongoing entity. There are a number of different types of systems of production.

Hunting and Gathering

For the greatest time of their existence on earth, some 5 million years, human beings subsisted by means of a combination of hunting wild animals; gathering roots, seeds, and plants; and fishing and collecting sea life along the shores. This mode of exploitation of the natural environment is referred to by anthropologists as *hunting and gathering*. We know a good deal about hunting and gathering societies from the work of archaeologists, though today this mode of subsistence continues only as an adjunct to other modes.

By the nineteenth century, societies dependent primarily on hunting and gathering were to be found in a wide range of marginal environments. The Inuit (or Eskimo) of the Arctic region, the Pygmies of the Ituri Forest in Zaire in Central Africa, the San (or Bushmen) of the Kalahari Desert in southern Africa, and the Washo of the Great Basin on the California-Nevada border are examples of societies that used to depend on hunting and gathering for their subsistence. These hunting and gathering societies occupied very different kinds of environments with very different flora and fauna. Nevertheless, several generalizations can be made about their mode of subsistence. All these societies had sparse populations with very low population densities. The plants and animals they depended on were scarce or abundant according to the seasons. Migratory animal species were absent for much of the year and then present for a short time in superabundance. Similarly, nuts, fruits, tubers, and seeds ripened during a particular time of the year, at which point they needed to be harvested. At other times, these foods were not available. Hunters and gatherers typically had to exploit all the resources available in their environments to deal with variations in availability.

As a consequence, these societies followed a migratory cycle during the course of the year. People had to move during much of the year because it was necessary to be in particular areas to harvest what had become available in those areas at that time. While there were regular sites to which they returned every year, they did not have year-round, permanent village settlements. Larger agglomerations of individuals came together when greater amounts of food were available in one locale. This was usually the case when some single food resource was abundant (migratory caribou, spawning salmon, ripening pine nuts, and the like). Religious festivals were frequently held at such times. At other times of the year, small dispersed groups of one or more nuclear families migrated as a unit. Julian Steward noted that the kind of animal upon which a hunting and gathering society was dependent determined the organization of the social group or band that hunted it. Societies that concentrated on hunting small mammals, such as rabbits, were organized into patrilineal, patrilocal bands so that the husband could stay in the hunting territory where he had grown up and with which he was familiar. The hunting of large migratory animals, which required a bigger labor force, was performed by large composite bands with flexibility in affiliation, where membership was acquired through either father or mother.

Technology is that part of culture by means of which people directly exploit their environment. Technology encompasses the manufacture and use of tools according to a set of cultural rules. In fact, archaeologists identify prehistoric cultures primarily through the shape and design or style of their tools. The technology of hunting and gathering people is simple in that natural materials taken directly from the environment, such as stone, bone, wood, and sinew, were used; additionally, the manufacturing techniques were relatively simple, involving only a few kinds of operations. Hunters and gatherers combined intimate knowledge of the environment, including animal behavior and the growing patterns of plants, with the development of a variety of techniques for the appropriation of animals and plants. For example, the Inuit hunted seal in many different ways, depending upon climatic conditions, seasons, and seal species. Hunters put to use every part of the animals they captured for food and for the manufacture of a whole variety of goods. Many hunters in Africa and South America discovered and used various kinds of poisons for fishing or for making the points of their arrows more effective in hunting. These poisons affected

Buffalo hunters, disguised as wolves, stalk their prey on the Great Plains. The "hunter" on the right is actually the artist George Catlin, sketching the scene in 1832.

the prey but not the eaters of the flesh. In hunting and gathering societies, people made the tools they used in subsistence; there were no specialists whose only occupation was to make tools. The education of a child included teaching that child how to manufacture tools. People who still pursue a hunting and gathering mode of subsistence today as a part-time endeavor use such modern tools as rifles, steel traps, and snowmobiles.

The differentiation of tasks in production was primarily between males and females. The usual pattern was that men hunted and fished and women gathered plants, collected shellfish, and took care of the domestic tasks, such as clothing manufacture, food preparation, and child care. Children began to learn tasks at a young age and at puberty assumed adult economic roles. Individuals who excelled at their tasks (successful hunters or fishers) were accorded respect and prestige, and their advice was often sought. The hunting of certain species of mammals and certain types of fishing were performed by the entire group under an informal leader. Hunting and gathering societies tended not to have social class divisions. Nor did they usually rank individuals, that is, distinguish their social statuses as higher or lower. Earlier, many had thought that hunting and gathering was a very difficult mode of life, since food acquisition was seen as arduous and time-consuming. Marshall Sahlins (1972) has pointed out, however, that hunters and gatherers spent relatively little time in active pursuit of game, and in their use of leisure, they constituted the "original affluent society."

It should not be assumed that the environment remains constant while culture interacts with it. The environment itself changes as a result of human exploitation. Ecological balance is altered as people harvest those species they utilize. In some societies, an effort was made to limit exploitation of the environment by imposing some controls on the hunting of certain species or animals of young ages, thereby maintaining the ecological balance. In other cases, the environment became permanently degraded. For example, at an earlier period in New Guinea, since fire was used as an aid in hunting, the primary forests were destroyed and replaced by grassland, totally altering the ecosystem and the fauna of the area. Today, in the United States, we are suffering the consequences of having overfished halibut and cod on the Grand Banks off Nova Scotia and the New England seacoast.

Hunting and gathering populations were never isolates; they have always had long-term exchange relationships with agriculturalists and pastoralists of the same or different ethnic groups, once these other modes of production developed (Headland and Reid, 1989; Bird-David, 1992; Shott, 1992). This was true of hunters and gatherers in North America, Africa, and Asia. For example, Mbuti hunters of Zaire exchanged meat and other forest products with regular exchange partners among their agricultural neighbors. This was an exchange between equals. The Twa of Ruanda were hunters who were part of a hierarchical, castelike structure. They exchanged with Hutu agriculturalists and Tutsi pastoralists.

The Kwakiutl of British Columbia, whose wedding ceremony was described in Chapter 2, are an interesting exception to what we have said about this mode of subsistence and the presence of ranked differences in a society. In the past they were hunters and gatherers, but their environmental resources were so rich, particularly in sea life, that they were able to support a much denser population than is usual in hunting and gathering societies. They had permanent villages with plank houses, though they migrated from these villages at certain times of the year to exploit particular resources in other areas. They had full-time craft specialization, large wooden houses, winter villages, and elaborate, stationary artwork (totem poles). Titles, including chiefly positions, were inherited. Their political system was more complex than was found in other hunting and gathering societies. There are several reasons for this series of differences between the Kwakiutl, along with other Northwest Coast societies, and other hunting and gathering societies. The rich environment of the Northwest Coast provided game, both mammal and bird; many species of edible plant life; sea resources, including numerous varieties of fish, shellfish, and sea mammals; and lastly, but importantly, the several species of salmon that annually spawned in the rivers. In addition, the Kwakiutl had highly developed techniques for the preservation and storage of the wide range of products they obtained. This enabled them to produce surpluses; maintain large, permanent village communities; and support more complex cultures. We will discuss how they utilized the surplus that was produced for social purposes in the section on distribution below. Another technological factor important in enabling Northwest Coast societies to reach a level of complexity that included ranking and chiefs was the development of large, oceangoing plank canoes (Arnold, 1995). These plank canoes, for example, among the Nuchanulth (Nootka), who live on the west coast of Vancouver Island, enabled social interchanges and exchange of goods to take place over wide areas, were extremely useful in raiding and warfare, facilitated the hunting of sea mammals and fishing for various kinds of ocean fish, and permitted the ease of movement of household goods and house planks from one village site to another.

Contemporary hunting and gathering is always combined with a variety of other economic endeavors. Today this modified mode of subsistence is integrated into national and international economies. Though the Kwakiutl and Nuchanulth still fish, their catch of halibut or salmon goes to the cannery or fish market, since they are now an integral part of the Canadian economy. Most of the food they eat is purchased at the store with money they have earned. The Misstassini Cree of eastern Canada still spend part of the winter season in multifamily communal dwellings in the forest, trapping animals with modern steel traps. The skins of the marten, lynx, mink, and weasel they trap end up in the fur markets of New York. When protesters demonstrate against the wearing of fur coats because it represents what they see as the needless killing of furbearing animals, this directly affects the livelihood of Cree families. This controversy is similar to the Inuit problem with animal rights groups who are against the "large-scale industrial" harvesting of seals, particularly harp seal and hooded seal pups in the North Atlantic. These groups argue that the Inuit should use only traditional technology and should restrict use of the products of the hunt to subsistence only. The Inuit argue that their tradition centers on maintaining a way of life in the same environment as in the past; hunting seals is important for their subsistence and their way of life. To be Inuit today means to maintain traditions, such as sharing field products within kinship networks, as well as religious beliefs and practices within an economic system that includes modern hunting equipment. They use rifles and sell part of their harvest for cash to purchase store-bought items that are now important to them in their present mixed cash-subsistence economy (Hovelsrud-Broda, 1998). Maintaining such a subsistence economy in today's world requires the use of modern hunting equipment.

In times of recession in industrialized nations like the United States, hunting and gathering may become an important way of supplementing the family larder or even a full-time occupation. The *New York Times* (March 24, 1996) reported that in Trinity County in northern California, an occupation called "wildcrafting" has developed, involving the gathering of wild plants. It has replaced jobs lost in the lumber industry of the area. This foraging and collecting in the forest of pharmaceutical herbs like ginseng; of mosses, grasses, and shrubs used for medicinal purposes and decoration; of edible mushrooms; and of burls used for furniture can provide a decent income without despoiling the environment.

Agriculture

The domestication of plants and their use for subsistence, beginning some 8000 to 10,000 years ago, represented a significant transformation in human society. This change depended upon the development of a new corpus of information by which human beings acquired much greater control of the environment and, in turn, transformed it in a much more significant way than had been done by hunters and gatherers. Social groups were tied to territories differently than they were with hunting and gathering. Sparsely populated groups of hunters and gatherers moved over wide areas during the course of the seasonal cycle. With a shift to dependence for subsistence upon domesticated plants, social groups utilized a smaller area, population was more dense, and a tendency emerged for concentration into hamlets and villages. Agriculturalists are much more in control of their own destiny than are hunters and gatherers. We have noted that the exploitation pattern of hunting and gathering societies was seasonal. Agriculturalists also operate on the basis of a seasonal cycle, especially where there is a marked climatic difference between winter and summer or rainy and dry seasons. The year is usually divided into planting time, growing time, and harvest. Audrey Richards (1961), the British social anthropologist, pointed out that the several months before harvest are known as the "hungry months" for the Bemba of Central Africa, who depend primarily upon their crop of millet. Even when they are under the threat of starvation, agricultural people must restrain themselves from eating their seed or they will have no crop the following year. How people utilize their labor, how they work the land, how they use water resources, and which crops they grow are the factors to be considered in an examination of different economic systems based on agriculture.

Horticulture

Throughout lowland South America and Melanesia, the mode of production is based upon crops that are grown through vegetative propagation, using a part of the plant itself, rather than through the planting of seeds. Since these crops are grown in gardens, this form of cultivation is known as *horticulture*. Systems of production based upon horticulture vary in terms of how the land is used and whether there is a means for controlling water necessary for plant growth.

Horticultural practices among the many New Guinea societies may be ranged on a continuum that reflects greater and greater complexity of techniques for cultivating gardens, which results in higher crop yields and more permanent gardens. This can be illustrated by the range of horticulture in societies in Papua New Guinea. The simplest form of horticulture, known as the *swidden* type, or *shifting cultivation,* involves making gardens by burning down the forest and planting the garden in the ashes, which constitute a kind of fertilizer. No other means of fertilizing is used. Because the soil is rapidly exhausted, a new garden in a new location must be planted every few years. Thus, it is called shifting cultivation. Gardens contain many kinds of plants on a single plot, and a digging stick may be the only tool used for cultivation. This kind of horticulture is supplemented by both hunting and the collection of wild plants. In lowland New Guinea, the sago palm, a wild plant whose pith is used for food, is an important supplement to what is produced in the gardens. For example, as much as

90 percent of the diet of the Tor in western New Guinea may come from wild sago. Their population is almost as sparse as that of a hunting and gathering society, though they live in villages surrounded by their yam gardens.

An intermediary type of horticulture is characterized by the mode of subsistence of the Abelam of New Guinea. Many varieties of short yams, taro, sweet potatoes, and a range of other plants are grown in gardens that are used several times and then allowed to remain fallow and uncultivated. The Abelam also grow a special species of long yam, which may be 8 to 10 feet long and is used in ceremonial exchange, described later in this chapter. Its cultivation involves special techniques, such as mounding the soil to create a plant bed and erecting trellises for vines. Soil around the growing point may be carefully loosened as the tuber grows. Abelam villages are more or less permanent and much larger than those of the Tor.

The most complex forms of horticulture in New Guinea are found in the mountains of the central highlands. There, people like the Enga use a variety of labor-intensive techniques. The gardens represent a great deal of labor and may be used for a generation or more. Each garden is made of a regular series of mounds separated by ditches. The mounds are formed from soil and mulch and are used only for sweet potato cultivation. These single-crop gardens are separated from mixed gardens in which most other crops are grown. The yields from the mounded gardens of the Enga are considerably greater than the yields from the two types of horticulture described above. Enga society numbers over 150,000, so there is considerable pressure for land, and Enga clans may even fight one another for land. The complex exchange system of the Enga, which will be described below, is linked to their great productivity. The horticultural systems just described depend upon rainfall for water. However, root crop cultivation can involve water control. The Dani of the Grand Valley in western New Guinea have used dams, ditches, and drainage systems to turn a natural swamp into a productive cultivation area.

Just as hunting and gathering peoples have intimate knowledge of the plant and animal species that they exploit, horticulturalists display an extensive knowledge of soils, food plants, and cultivation techniques. This practical know-how is frequently combined with magical practices performed during the process of production.

The simplest kind of swidden horticulture is practiced by sparse populations, living in widely separated villages that control access to land. As horticultural techniques become more intensified, gardens become more permanent and population density increases. Land becomes the property of kin groups, such as clans. There is increased competition for good land, and warfare is frequently waged by one clan to drive another from its land, as noted above for the Enga. Today, in Papua New Guinea, these subsistence horticultural practices are supplemented by the cash-crop production of coffee in the New Guinea highlands and by coconut production in the lowlands and the Bismarck Archipelago.

Grain Agriculture

Grain is the focus of swidden agriculture in the more temperate areas of several continents of the world—maize in the New World, millet and sorghum in Africa, and rice in Asia. The same technique of cutting down trees and burning off brush is used in preparing fields for growing grain as for growing tubers in swidden horticulture.

There is also a long fallow period after several plantings, as in the swidden cultivation of root crops. The source of water is rainfall.

Throughout much of Europe and Asia, agricultural societies depend upon a technology involving the use of the plow drawn by draft animals and of animal manure as fertilizer. With this type of agriculture, fields become more or less permanent; grains such as wheat, rye, and barley are the predominant crops; and there is a dependence upon rainfall for water. The same fields may be used every year if there is crop rotation and the use of fertilizer. Sometimes a system is employed whereby fields are divided, so that some are used while others lie fallow for a year. The use of draft animals and plows requires raising crops such as hay to feed the animals.

A form of grain agriculture even more productive per unit of land is dependent upon elaborate irrigation systems. These irrigation systems are much more extensive than the type of water control practiced by the Dani, mentioned above. This type of agriculture requires an enormous input of labor to create the necessary artificial environment of lakes, ponds, dikes, and terraces. From the Yellow River in China to the Tigris-Euphrates in Mesopotamia, and in the Andean highlands of Peru, the advent of irrigation systems was associated with urban civilizations and the development of states.

Increased productivity per acre of land, the basis for increasing cultural complexity, depends on a number of factors. These include various techniques to improve the fertility of the soil, some of which, such as building mounds, require a good deal of labor. The degree to which water for agricultural purposes is controlled is another factor. Establishing elaborate irrigation systems initially requires great outputs of labor; maintaining them also requires a certain amount of labor. The crops on which people subsist also vary in terms of their storage potential. This affects how crop surplus will be utilized for social purposes (discussed more fully in the section on distribution). Of course, the nature of the technology utilized is also an important factor. Steel axes and machetes are more efficient than stone axes. Animal labor is more efficient than human labor, except in places of high population density, like China. Machines and the mechanization of agriculture, as has occurred in the United States, represent a quantum jump in efficiency and therefore in productivity.

The intensification of agricultural production in the world has also had unforeseen consequences. Sometimes populations grew beyond the point at which agricultural production could sustain them, resulting in famine. Greater population density resulted in the more rapid spread of infectious diseases. Each technological advance produced its own set of problems. Mechanized agriculture, for example, has resulted in overproduction and the need to store vast agricultural surpluses; the use of chemical pesticides has led to widespread pollution of soil and water. In the United States, fewer farmers grow more and more food, and the family farm has become a corporation and may even be listed on the stock exchange.

Animal Domestication

The domestication of plants, which brought such a significant transformation in the mode of production, was in most areas accompanied soon after by the domestication of animals. In the Old World, including Asia, Africa, and Europe, a wide variety of animal species were domesticated. Most of these animals furnished meat and milk, and together with domesticated plants, provided subsistence. Some animals, such as the horse, donkey, bullock, and buffalo, were also used for transportation. The hair of others, such as sheep and goats, was woven into cloth. In the New World the only significant animal domesticates were the camelids, such as the llama and alpaca. In addition to variations in the uses to which domesticated animals were put, there was also variation in the nature of animal care. Some domesticated animals foraged in the bush for their food but returned to places of human settlement at night; other domesticated animals were kept in pens and depended on humans for their entire care and feeding. The mithan, a type of domesticated ox found in Southeast Asia among the Nagas and Chin of Burma, was allowed to roam freely, depending completely upon forage for food. Only its meat was used, and then only on ceremonial occasions. In contrast, in Europe, the dairy cow, a relative of the mithan, was kept in a stall or on ranges in an enclosed pasture and was milked daily. The dairy cow and the ox were part of the mixed farming complex in Europe and North America.

In New Guinea, the pig is the only domesticated food animal and was introduced there in its domesticated form, since the native fauna includes only marsupials. However, the nature of care varies from society to society. The Tor capture wild piglets, which are tamed and then allowed to forage freely though they are individually owned. They are slaughtered to provide food for feasts. At the other end of the continuum are the Enga, whose pigs are hardly allowed to forage at all. The Enga breed their pigs and completely control pig reproduction, care, and feeding.

The productive system of some societies is completely or almost completely dependent upon their domesticated animals, with little or no cultivation of plants. Such societies are referred to as *nomadic pastoralists*. This is a specialized mode of subsistence that developed from an earlier economy that included domesticated plants and animals. Nomadic pastoral societies, with one or two exceptions, were found on the great landmass of the Old World, particularly in arid zones. Sheep, goats, camels, horses, cattle, yaks, water buffalo, and reindeer constituted the basic herd animals for these societies. All these animals are social, not solitary, in their habits. In most cases one or two types of animals formed the basis for herds.

The animal species upon which particular nomadic pastoral societies depend is related to the nature of the environment that is exploited. Some species, such as camels, are best adapted to arid desert areas and others, such as horses, to well-watered grassy plains. Some can withstand extremes of temperature, while others cannot. Some, such as goats, do best in steeper mountain environments, while others, such as water buffalo, can live only on flat, swampy lowlands. The way of life of nomadic pastoralists involves seasonal movement or migration in a regular pattern from one place to another. The community and its herds may move from summer to winter pasturage or from wet to dry locations. In their seasonal movements, pastoral nomads resemble hunters and gatherers, particularly those who hunt large herds of migratory animals, such as the caribou. However, there is a crucial difference in that hunters followed the migratory herd wherever the herd went in its natural migration, whereas the herds that belong to the nomadic pastoralists follow the people who herd them.

The process of domestication involves a shift in the biological characteristics of the animal species, since the animals are selectively bred to enhance those characteristics that make the animal more controllable and more useful to humans and to eliminate characteristics such as intractability. In a sense, humans have shaped these animals through the process of domestication. At the same time, pastoral societies adapted to the needs of their animals, particularly in the migration cycle followed. Nomadic pastoralists depended upon their herd animals for a range of products. Daily yields of milk and the products made from milk were central to the diet. The wool and hair were also important for making cloth. Nomadic pastoralists were never solely dependent on their pastoral products. Live animals, wool, and milk products were exchanged by the pastoralists for essentials, such as tea, sugar, and flour, with sedentary peoples. Since wealth was measured in numbers of animals in the herd, pastoralists were loath to kill animals for their meat alone; therefore this was done only on special occasions.

Nomadic pastoralists herd different species utilizing a range of environments. The Marsh Arabs of Iraq, who inhabit the swampy area at the confluence of the Tigris and Euphrates rivers, rely completely on their herds of water buffalo. Since they depend solely on the buffalo, they must trade the dairy products produced from the milk of their buffalo for grain and other foodstuffs from sedentary peoples, who are culturally the same except for mode of subsistence. The watery environment of the Marsh Arabs is a sharp contrast to the desert zone of the Arabian plateau inhabited by another Arabic-speaking group, the Rwala Bedouin (studied by Alois Musil in the 1920s). They are mainly herders of camels, but they also have some sheep, goats, and Arabian horses. The camels are herded by men and boys, often at some distance from the nomadic camp. The products of the camel include milk and hair, but even more importantly, the animal is a mode of transportation. The Rwala breed camels for sale to sedentary oasis dwellers and to transporters who need the animals for long-distance caravan trade. The seasonal cycle of the Rwala involves moving into the desert in the spring, when available water has allowed grass cover to grow. As the year progresses, the climate gets drier, and the Rwala move closer to the desert oasis sources of water. Since goats and sheep as well as camels are herded, the Rwala must be mindful of the water requirements of all these animal species.

In the savanna grasslands of West Africa, between the Sahara and the tropical forest area to the south, the Fulani practice still another form of nomadic pastoralism, one that is dependent solely on herds of cattle. The cattle are a long-horned variety of zebu with a humped back. The migration pattern is from the desert fringes in the wet season to the well-watered borders of the tropical forest in the dry season. The availability of grassland is not the only determining factor in the migratory pattern; another consideration is the distribution of the tsetse fly, which is a carrier of sleeping sickness and whose territory they avoid. The Fulani are dependent primarily upon the milk from their herds and milk products such as clarified butter. They migrate within an area containing villages of sedentary grain-growing agriculturalists with whom they trade their milk products for grain in the marketplace.

In the grasslands of Central Asia, nomadic pastoralists such as the Kazak, before the Russian Revolution of 1917, had herds of horses along with sheep, goats, and

A camp of Pushtun nomadic pastoralists in central Afghanistan in the summer of 1971.

two-humped camels. The mares were milked, and the milk was made into a fermented drink called *kumis,* a luxury item. The Kazak spent the winter in protected valley areas and migrated to the steppes in summer. Riding horses and the products of the herds were traded to sedentary people in the market towns.

The most widespread form of pastoral nomadism involves the herding of sheep and goats. Excellent examples are the Basseri, Bakhtiari, and Qashqai, pastoral nomads in Iran. Their migration cycle takes them from winter pasturage in the southern lowlands, roughly at sea level, to summer pasturage in the Zagros Mountains, at an altitude of 10,000 feet. The sheep herded by the Basseri are so adapted to the migratory cycle that they can survive neither the cold winters of the mountains nor the torrid summers of the lowlands. In addition to sheep and goats, the Bakhtiari have in their herds a species of cow that is small and agile and can make the arduous migration. Though most societies have nomadic pastoralism as their dominant mode of production, combinations are frequently found. For example, the Bakhtiari practice some agriculture and hunting and gathering in addition to nomadic pastoralism.

A series of economic factors have brought about significant transformations in the way of life of nomadic pastoralists. Sheep and goat herders in Iran and in Syria no longer migrate with their herds, but rather, move their animals and their belongings by truck from one pasture site to another. They need not even set up camp near a water source, since tank trucks can bring water to wherever they set up camp, which may even be next to a highway. The Rwala no longer raise camels, since trucks have replaced the camel as the principal means of transportation in the desert.

Many nomadic pastoral societies have undergone great changes under political pressure from the governments of their nations and as a result of other contemporary events, such as wars, revolutions, and famines; thus their way of life is no longer as we have described it above. The homeland of the Marsh Arabs became a major battleground of the Iran-Iraq war in the 1980s and was a center of military activity during the Gulf War. The long period of drought in the Sahel seriously affected the economy of the Fulani and has forced them to sell their herds. The Kazaks in the former Soviet Union were collectivized in the 1930s. Since the breakup of the Soviet Union, Kazakstan has been an independent country. Kazaks living in the People's Republic of China first underwent an earlier period of collectivization but now, under a more relaxed political regime, they again have their own herds of horses. The nomadic groups of Iran were forcibly sedentarized by Reza Shah in the 1920s to exercise political control over them, resulting in the loss of their herds and livelihood. Migration was resumed after the abdication of Reza Shah in 1941. Sedentarization was attempted again by Mohammad Shah, Reza's son, in the 1960s, with the same disastrous results. How the nomadic tribes of Iran have fared since the Khomeini revolution is not clear. Since nomadic pastoral peoples usually occupy marginal lands that are not suitable for agriculture, when they are forced to sedentarize, usually for political reasons, we often find them returning to nomadic pastoralism when political pressure is relaxed.

Sometimes, people pursue a mix of different forms of production. The Dolgan and Ngansan, two indigenous groups who live in the North Central forest tundra area of Siberia east of the Yenesei River in the former Soviet Union, had a prerevolutionary economy that was an interesting mix of reindeer herding, hunting, fur trapping, subsistence hunting and gathering, and trade (Zicker, 1998). After the revolution, they were gradually collectivized, forming fewer, larger reindeer collectives over time. At that time the reindeer were being used for transport. In 1970, the two groups were sedentarized into the community of Ust Avam, as reindeer herding had become less viable as a way of life. Men still hunted caribou, fished in the lakes and rivers, and trapped animals for their pelts, primarily for subsistence. There were still 50 to 60 professional hunters who lived in state housing and maintained a high standard of living. The state provided them with the necessary tools, and each hunter had to provide the state with a certain number of caribou, Arctic fox pelts, and fish each season, which was destined for a larger market; the hunters received a salary in exchange (Zicker, 1998: 196). The women would work at a state sewing facility producing beaded sections to be made into caribou fur boots.

During the present transitional period, there is uncertainty as to what will eventually happen to this state enterprise. Severe budget cuts, nonreplacement of tools, and gasoline shortages, as well as the cessation of many rural enterprises have resulted in a real reduction in the standard of living for most people in Ust Avam. There is now a much heavier reliance on the products of local subsistence hunting and fishing. Meat and fish beyond subsistence needs are shared with consanguineal and affinal relatives, since many in the community are related to one another. Friends, neighbors, and those who may be in need may also receive meat. In 1992, President Yeltsin signed a decree that enabled the establishment of family/clan holdings for the "aboriginal people of Siberia." Only a few families have legal control of their ancestral lands. These individuals, interestingly, had holdings near industrial cities, enabling them to become involved "with external sources of capital and energy in recent years" (Zicker, 1998: 230). Even these families, though they have become oriented toward money making, still participate in the sharing of the products of the hunt with the other members of the community.

The Organization of Work

The productive tasks performed by males and females are culturally determined, as noted in the previous chapter. In hunting and gathering societies, for example, there was a division between the female domain of gathering and collecting and the male domain of hunting. Often the gathering activities of women provided the greatest part of the food on which the group subsisted. Nevertheless, the products of the hunt brought back by the men represented the most desirable food, and hunting was a more prestigious activity than gathering, reflecting the relative valuation of male and female roles in the society. As we observed in the previous chapter, the productive tasks assigned to men in one society may be assigned to women in another. In some New Guinea societies, such as the Tor, women cut down the sago palm to get its pith, while in other societies, such as the Abelam, men do this.

In both male and female domains, some work tasks are done individually and others in cooperative groups. The hunting of herd animals, such as caribou by the Nunamiut Eskimo and wild peccary by the Mundurucu of Brazil, was carried out communally. Similarly, organized hunting with nets by the Mbuti Pygmies involved group activity. These were cooperative endeavors carried out communally by all the men of the band or village, in the case of the Mundurucu. However, for species in which the animals tend to move individually, for example, most of the animal species of the eastern United States, such as the moose, beaver, and porcupine, hunting was done on an individual basis. Gathering and collecting by women also tended to be done on an individual basis. Though on the Northwest Coast of Canada, groups of women may have gone to berrying territories as a group, the berry picking was done individually. The preparation of sago from pith was done in many New Guinea societies on a cooperative basis by women.

In societies whose mode of subsistence involves the cultivation of crops, men tend to be concerned with the preparation of the land for growing, that is, the preparation of the garden plot or field, and also with water-control systems if these are present. Both men and women may be involved in planting, weeding, and harvesting. In some New Guinea societies a clear distinction is made between certain crops, such as bananas and sugar cane, that are grown by men, and other crops, such as sweet potatoes, that are grown by women. When plows and mechanized agricultural implements are introduced, the whole range of agricultural tasks usually becomes the province of men, and women are limited to growing vegetables in gardens, if they are involved in agricultural tasks at all. In nomadic pastoral societies, the task of herding and moving the camp is in the male realm, while women milk the animals and manufacture milk products.

The organization of work in a society relates to the nature of postmarital residence and the formation of kinship groups in that society. Cooperative endeavors in which people work communally serve to reinforce the social solidarity of the group. When the most important subsistence tasks for a society are performed by men acting cooperatively, the residence pattern after marriage tends to be virilocal, whereas when the tasks are performed by women working together, the postmarital residence pattern tends to be uxorilocal. As we shall see in Chapter 9, on political organization, the way that work is organized is often also part of the political system. Chiefs, in societies where they are found, are frequently instrumental in organizing certain kinds of production. For example, Trobriand chiefs organize the activities of their clan members in building a canoe, and Kwakiutl chiefs organize the members of their *numaym* when they build a new house.

The organization of work in contemporary societies has also become the subject of investigation. In many societies over the world, more and more women are leaving their homes for full- or part-time work. In our discussion of gender we saw the way in which Yoruba women dominated the marketplace; this is also true in other parts of the world. Javanese market culture, for example, seems to be gendered, in that women play a substantial role in the more localized small-scale trading that occurs while men are more frequently the "wholesalers" (Alexander, 1998).

Distribution

If production is that part of economic organization concerned with how societies utilize labor and technology to convert environmental resources into cultural products, then *distribution* is the manner in which such cultural products circulate through societies. What is of concern in discussing systems of distribution or exchange is who gives what to whom, when, where, and how. In every society, the system of distribution can be described in terms of cultural rules. There will be categories of rules concerning the relationship between giver and receiver; the obligations of the giver to the receiver; the occasions or settings when goods are to be given or exchanged; the types of goods that are to be given to one category of persons and not to another category; the rules for the behavior involving the giving or the exchange; and the location where this takes place. People use these rules as guides for behavior, interpreting the rules in their own way. Thus the manner in which goods move in a society is determined both by the operation of cultural rules and by the way in which individuals in the system interpret them. Even where distribution of goods is carried out in markets, supply and demand are culturally construed.

Market exchange is different from other forms of exchange and operates according to its own principles. Certain general principles apply universally to other systems of exchange. Exchange may be broken down into three components: giving, receiving, and returning. The offer of a material object initiates a process. It may be accepted or declined. Both the offer and its acceptance or refusal have particular consequences. If the object is accepted, then its equivalent must at some point be returned. The acceptance creates a relationship through time, at least until the return is made. The refusal to accept something offered creates a relationship of a negative sort, diametrically opposite to the relationship created by acceptance. This simple model of exchange has certain consequences. Giving, receiving, and returning constitute a process over time. From the initial offer until the return, two individuals or two groups are linked to each other in a relationship. The acceptance of something offered constitutes the assumption of an obligation to return—recipients place themselves in debt to the givers. If such indebtedness continues for a long period of time or if goods go repeatedly in the same direction and are not returned, then, through this process, the recipients become inferior and the givers superior. The recipients are inferior in the eyes of others as well as in their own eyes. Giving, receiving, and returning create links, since exchange may be the basis for seeking assistance, recruiting allies, and creating alliances. But there is also an aggressive component, in that giving, receiving, and returning usually involve competition. Recipients who are in an inferior position and cannot return may even perceive the initial offer as an aggressive act designed to shame them in the eyes of others. Though exchange, or the distribution of economic goods, may be perceived primarily as an economic phenomenon, in fact, it is frequently linked to the political structure and differences in rank, hence the utility of viewing these conjointly as political economy.

Barter is a type of distribution that conforms in part to principles of exchange but goes off in another direction. Barter involves direct, immediate exchange, always of different objects. As a consequence, barter does not create ongoing relationships. It usually involves goods and commodities that each party does not have in its own environment. Occurring within a context governed by cultural rules, it includes haggling and bargaining (Humphrey and Hugh-Jones, 1992). These characteristics make barter much more like monetary exchange.

Distribution in Egalitarian Societies

Several types of exchange systems characterize egalitarian societies, in which rank differences are absent. The simplest type of exchange system involves two sides, of equal status, in continuing exchange with each other. The two sides can be two parts of a village, two clans, or two moieties. This type is referred to as *reciprocal exchange* (see Figure 1). It is identical to the exchange of women in marriage referred to as direct reciprocal exchange (see pages 112–113).

Reciprocal exchange characterizes the exchange system of the Abelam of New Guinea, whose mode of production has already been described in this chapter (Kaberry, 1940). Their reciprocal exchange system involves only the exchange of goods between moieties, since they do not have direct sister exchange or bilateral

Figure 1.   Reciprocal exchange.

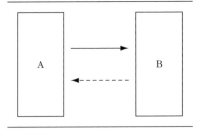

cross-cousin marriage. The moieties are not named, but are referred to as "us" and "them." The Abelam live in patrilineal clan-hamlets that are paired with one another. Men in one clan-hamlet have *tshambura,* or partners, in another clan-hamlet, with whom they exchange. In our discussion of the cultivation practices of the Abelam, we talked about the special gardens in which men alone grow long yams solely for purposes of exchange. These yams are of a different species than the yams grown by the women, which are used for subsistence and are selected and bred for their great length. The head of the clan uses his special magical knowledge to make the yams grow very long. He himself must abstain from sexual intercourse for the whole growing period of the yams, since sexual contact with women will prevent the yams from growing long. The strength, prowess, and magical power of the group is measured by the length of their yams. Under the supervision of the leader of the group, the yams are carefully harvested and individually decorated with flowers, feathers, and masks. They are then displayed at the ceremony, from which all women are barred, where they will be distributed to the exchange partners of the group. All the important men from surrounding hamlets are present as witnesses to the exchange, and they partake of the feast that accompanies it. The giver of the yam keeps a record of the length and circumference of that yam. This is because the yam given in return must be the equivalent of what has been given. The return is not immediate. It is delayed until sometime in the future, when the group that has received is ready to give. Exchange partners also exchange pigs and perform important services for one another in connection with the initiation of their respective sons (Rubel and Rosman, 1978). Reciprocal exchange systems such as that of the Abelam exhibit the following characteristics: They involve two sides that are equal in status. Though they may compete to outdo one another in their continuing exchanges, the rule of equivalence in exchange keeps that sort of competition in check. Each side needs the other, since they perform important services for each other.

When there are alterations in the rules of exchange, more complex systems of economic distribution develop. For example, if more than two groups are involved in an exchange system, the pattern becomes significantly different from that of reciprocal exchange described above. Delays in the exchange also operate in these kinds of systems, but in a somewhat different way. The Maring of the New Guinea highlands have a system of economic distribution or exchange that involves one host group distributing

Long yams dressed as men, painted and decorated with feathers and shells, are exchanged at the Abelam yam ceremony.

simultaneously to a number of other groups (Rappaport, 1984). These groups are equal in status. The distributive system is part of a religious ceremony referred to as the *kaiko,* which extends over many months. A group of closely related patrilineal clans serve as hosts of the *kaiko.* The guests at the *kaiko* come in groups from the surrounding territories (see Figure 2). The host group intermarries with these neighboring groups and is allied with them in times of war. Guests come brandishing their weapons and singing war songs. The dancing performed by both guests and hosts involves an aggressive display. The aggressiveness occurs despite the fact that guests and hosts intermarry, are allied to one another, and distribute food and valuable goods to one another. A great number of pigs are killed by the hosts, and cooked pork is distributed at the final *kaiko* event. Production is directed toward amassing pigs for the *kaiko* distribution. Each of the guest groups, who come from a wide area, will in the future hold its own *kaiko,* at which it will fulfill its obligations to make a return. The Maring distribution system involves not two groups, as in reciprocal exchange, but rather one group giving to many groups at the same time. The host group is invited in turn to the *kaiko* that each guest group will hold in the future.

Still more complex systems of exchange link groups in chains so that goods move from group to group and serve to tie together an entire region. This is an example of *generalized exchange,* and it is identical to the concept of generalized exchange in

Figure 2. *Kaiko* exchange.

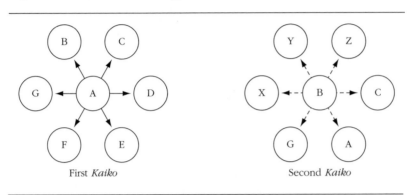

First *Kaiko*   Second *Kaiko*

Figure 3. Enga *Te* exchange.

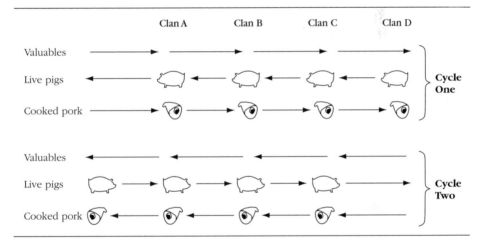

marriage. The *Te* distribution system of the Enga, whose system of production we have already described, is of this type (Meggitt, 1974). Enga patrilineal clans, occupying contiguous areas, fight with their neighbors but also exchange women and goods with them. People who are affines may also become exchange partners, or *Te* partners, to one another. Instead of giving to all one's *Te* partners in many clans at the same ceremony, as is the case for the Maring, an Enga man will have two groups of *Te* partners, one set in clans to the east of his clan and a second in clans to the west of his clan. He transmits goods he has received from his eastern partners at their *Te* ceremonies to his western partners at the *Te* ceremony that his clan hosts, and vice versa (see Figure 3). The Enga therefore have two different kinds of partners to whom they give and from whom they receive, whereas the Abelam and Maring have only one kind of partner. The Enga have a system of delayed exchange in which goods

Sides of cooked pork are displayed on an enormous platform, 90 feet long, before they are distributed at an Enga Te ceremony held in the summer of 1974.

move from one group to the next until they reach the end of the chain, when they must reverse and go down the line in the opposite direction. People who were givers of valuables such as stone axes, shells, plumes, and small pigs in the first stage become receivers of live pigs in the second stage. Live pigs move down the chain as they are distributed at successive *Te* distributions held in turn by each clan. At the end of the chain, there is a second reversal, when the last receiver of live pigs becomes the first distributor of cooked pork. The distribution of cooked pork completes one cycle of the *Te*. It will begin again when initiatory gifts go in the direction opposite to the pork. Built into the rules of the *Te* is the delay in the return, since goods must go down the entire length of the chain through successive *Te* ceremonies before the *Te* partner to whom clan A has given live pigs gives pork back to clan A.

Giving and receiving in the *Te* exemplifies the ambivalence seen in exchange in general. Clans who are neighbors, though potential enemies to one another, are dependent upon one another to pass on the objects of the *Te*. If warfare does break out in the middle of a *Te* cycle, the *Te* is disrupted. It is in the interest of *Te* partners in other clans to make peace between the combatants so that goods can continue to move along the *Te* chains. The Enga production system, as has been shown above, is based upon the intensive cultivation of sweet potatoes, used to feed the large numbers of pigs in the *Te* as well as people. The Enga value their pigs greatly; yet their distribution system sends out the pigs that they raise along a line of exchange partners until the pigs eventually come back as roast pork (Rubel and Rosman, 1978). The value they place on their pigs is what the pigs will bring in reknown when they are distributed to one's exchange partners.

The ceremonial distributions that we have described—the Abelam yam exchange, the Maring *kaiko,* and the Enga *Te*—involve the exchange of highly valued goods toward which much productive energy is directed. Other kinds of distributions of goods are also present in these societies. In all of them, valuable goods must be distributed to affinal relatives, particularly at various rite-of-passage ceremonies. For example, among the Abelam, shell rings are presented as bridewealth by the groom and his family to the family of the bride (see illustration in Chapter 6). The long yams exchanged by *tshambura* have the cultural meaning of competition between equals, in contrast to shell rings, which mean peace and harmony.

Despite significant changes in the economic organization of Papua New Guinea societies—including the introduction of cash-cropping of coffee, the production of cattle for market, and the purchase of Western food and other goods—the Abelam and Maring continue to hold their ceremonial distributions. It seems that the Enga no longer hold the *Te.*

Systems of Exchange in Societies with Flexible Rank

In our general discussion of the principles of exchange, we noted that continued indebtedness on the part of the receiver could lead to status differences, with the giver becoming superior and the receiver, who is unable to repay the debt, placed in an inferior position. The kinds of exchange systems in the societies we have discussed so far stressed the equivalence in status of groups that constitute givers and receivers. There are, however, societies in which rank differences, which are an integral part of the political structure, play a significant role in the exchanges. The Kwakiutl wedding potlatch described in Chapter 2 is a kind of distribution in which rank and rank differences are central to the exchanges. The Kwakiutl have cognatic descent groups, the *numayms.* Theoretically, every person in Kwakiutl society holds an inherited rank position, associated with a name owned by his or her *numaym,* which can be raised through potlatching. The Kwakiutl use a number of rite-of-passage events as occasions for potlatches, ceremonies at which large amounts of food and property are distributed to assembled guests. Great quantities of food and goods must be accumulated in preparation for a potlatch. In the past, this meant gathering and storing smoked salmon, olachen grease (oil from the candlefish), berries, and other food, and accumulating blankets and other valuables such as jewelry, masks, and even canoes, referred to as "trifles." Potlatches may be hosted by one *numaym* or by a group of *numayms* or tribes. At each potlatch, the person whose rite of passage is being celebrated receives a new name. A succession of potlatches was held for a great chief's son as he grew older; at each one he got increasingly more important titles until at the most important potlatch he assumed the name that entitled him to the position of chief.

The guests who come to a potlatch serve as witnesses to the event, for example, the succession to chiefly power, and receive goods for this service. The guests, affines of the hosts, are seated according to their rank and receive goods in that order. The guest *numayms* must at some future time reciprocate by making a return potlatch. Kwakiutl potlatches were sometimes described as if the motivation for them was competition and the desire to shame one's rivals. But all exchange involves some form of competition. Since guests at a Kwakiutl potlatch are also affines, the Kwakiutl pot-latch is no more competitive than some other examples of affinal exchanges. Even when valuable coppers were "destroyed" by being cut by the giver who is the host, as described in Chapter 2, the receiving chief, who is challenged by this act, thanks his host for doing this. One must hold a potlatch in order to raise one's rank, but one needs equally high-ranking competitors to challenge. Once again, as in all exchange systems, the givers and receivers are dependent upon one another at the same time they are competing with one another. In addition, the potlatch provides a mechanism for redistributing the productive resources of Kwakiutl society.

By the end of the nineteenth century, the time period for the wedding potlatch described in Chapter 2, the Kwakiutl were involved in the Canadian cash economy. The goods distributed at potlatch ceremonies came to include, in addition to Hud-son Bay blankets, power boats, sewing machines, tea cups and saucers, and other goods from the Euro-Canadian economy purchased with wages from work in fish canneries, logging, and other kinds of employment. During this period, the potlatch was outlawed by the Canadian government because such large-scale distributions and the destruction of property that sometimes occurred were seen as going against the Protestant ethic, which supported the modern Canadian capitalist economy and which missionaries and government officials thought the native population should emulate. However, potlatches continued to be held in secret. The prohibition against holding the potlatch ceremony ended in Canada in 1951, and since then, large-scale potlatches have been held by many Kwakiutl groups.

The potlatch as a form of ceremonial exchange was found in other Native American societies on the Pacific coast of Canada and Alaska, and took a somewhat different form depending on the nature of the kinship system of the society. This can be seen by a brief look at the potlatch system of the Tlingit, whose economy also enabled them to produce a surplus. However, while the Kwakiutl have cognatic descent and *numayms*—cognatic kin groups—the Tlingit have a social structure based on matrilineal descent, matrimoi-eties, matrilineal clans, avunculocal residence, and a preference for marriage with father's sister's daughter. This means that each Tlingit clan intermarries with two other matrilin-eal clans, both of them in the opposite moiety (see Chapter 6, Figure 11).

While the Kwakiutl held potlaches on the numerous occasions marking the growth and increased achievement of a person, the Tlingit had basically only one occasion for a potlatch. This was when a chief died and his heir, his sister's son, sponsored the var-ious rites of the funeral and had a mortuary totem pole erected (see the totem pole pic-tured in Chapter 5). At this potlatch, the new chief assumed the title, name, and political position of his mother's brother. Immediately after the death of the chief, his heir, with the help of his entire clan, began to accumulate large amounts of goods and property in preparation for the potlatch. In the past, special food, such as olachen grease, pre-served berries, and dried fish, was gathered and stored. The two other matrilineal clans who intermarried with the host clan came as guests to the potlatch since they had per-formed important services for the host clan. One clan built a new house for the heir, and the other clan buried the dead chief and erected the totem pole in his honor.

The Tlingit and Kwakiutl potlatches are both systems in which large amounts of goods are accumulated by chiefs with the help of their kin groups specifically for the

Chiefs in ceremonial garb wearing their crests at a Tlingit potlatch in Sitka, Alaska, held at the turn of the twentieth century.

purposes of ceremonial distribution to other groups. However, potlatches take place on occasions which relate to the different ways in which groups are organized and intermarry in cognatic and matrilineal societies. The potlatch system of economic distribution operates through the kinship system, which provides the links through which the flow of goods is channeled.

The Trobriand Islanders, whose system of production is very different from that of the Tlingit, hold *sagali,* or large-scale ceremonial distributions of yams and other foodstuffs. The distributions are structurally identical to the potlatches of the Tlingit, because, like the Tlingit, the Trobrianders have matrilineal clans, avunculocal residence, and father's sister's daughter marriage (see Chapter 6, Figure 11). An important part of Trobriand funerary rites is the mortuary *sagali,* a distribution to the clan of the wife of the dead chief in exchange for all the funerary services provided by clan members. This is the same pattern as the Tlingit potlatch. Contenders for the chiefly position that is now open compete to be the organizer of the funerary *sagali.* The Trobrianders also hold a *sagali* when the chief's sister becomes pregnant. The chief's sister is important since it is her son who will succeed to the position of chief in this matrilineal society. The guests at a pregnancy *sagali* are the father's lineage of the chief and his sister, who have performed various services for the chief's sister during her pregnancy and are receiving the ceremonial distribution of food, yams, areca nuts, and bananas in exchange. Among the Trobrianders, the two clans that intermarry with the host clan are guests at two separate *sagali,* a funeral *sagali* and a pregnancy *sagali,* whereas in the

Figure 4.   *Urigubu* payments.

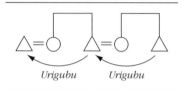

Urigubu   *Urigubu*

Tlingit potlatch these two groups of guests are present at the same time but are seated on opposite sides of the house (see Chapter 6, Figure 11).

As is the case for most societies, the Trobrianders have several types of exchanges. In addition to *sagali,* there is a distribution of yams called *urigubu,* which occurs after every harvest. Marriage initiates this annual payment of yams, the *urigubu,* by a man to his sister's husband (see Figure 4). The Trobrianders have three kinds of gardens: the mixed garden and the taro garden for their own subsistence, and the main yam garden to produce the *urigubu* that goes to the sister's husband. At harvest time, gardeners in sundry Trobriand villages are accumulating piles of yams, which they will display in their own villages. Then these heaps of yams are ceremonially carried to the house of the sister's husband and presented to him to be stored in his yam house. Meanwhile, the giver of yams will in return be receiving yams from his wife's brother. Though yams are the staple crop, great care and productive effort are given to these particular yams, which will eventually be given away. Yams for *urigubu* represent the prestige of the giver as a gardener and as a kinsman fulfilling an obligation. A great deal of effort is devoted to the display and transportation of yams to be consumed by households other than that of the producer. The most rational, economically efficient system would be for everyone to grow and then eat his own yams. The distribution system of the Trobrianders makes sense only in terms of their social system. The *urigubu* is paid to the husbands and fathers of the matrilineal lineage for carrying out the important social role, not the biological role, of father, since in the past Trobrianders did not believe that fathers played a role in conception. Malinowski referred to *urigubu* as economic tribute, and for chiefs, it is indeed tribute (Malinowski, 1935). A chief takes many wives, up to 20 or more, who are given to him by all the village headmen in his district. The headmen's payments of *urigubu* to the chief are used by the chief to make *sagali.* With so many brothers-in-law, the chief accumulates many yams after each harvest, which he then redistributes as rewards to his followers on the various occasions for feasts.

In addition, at harvest time, there are competitive yam feasts between villages called *kayasa.* The game of cricket played by the Trobrianders, discussed in Chapter 5, is part of the competitive *kayasa* being held between villages.

Kula exchange is still another important form of Trobriand exchange. The *kula* exchange system links the Trobriand Islands with a circle of other islands that are different culturally and linguistically and that the Trobrianders considered dangerous places because warfare and cannibalism were endemic in precolonial times. The exchange system organizes the islands in the Massim area into an enormous circle (Figure 5). The

Figure 5.   The *Kula* ring.

Armshell valuables, which have been brought from the island of Kitava, are to be given to kula *exchange partners on Trobriand Island. Photographed by Malinowski during his 1914-1918 fieldwork.*

goods exchanged in the *kula* are two kinds of shell valuables—red shell necklaces, which are exchanged from island to island so that they move clockwise around the circle, and white armshells, which move counterclockwise. Men sailed their small native crafts to the islands of their *kula* partner, which might be some distance across the seas. Nowadays they use motorboats. According to the rules of the *kula,* those who are to receive in the exchange always undertake the voyage to the givers' island. To receive armshells, the Trobrianders would sail in a clockwise direction, east, to the island of Kitava. To receive red shell necklaces, they would sail in a counterclockwise direction, south, to the island of Dobu. Thus, *kula* partners are always exchanging red shell necklaces for armshells, and vice versa, but never armshells for armshells or necklaces for necklaces. *Kula* exchange is identical in structure to generalized exchange, that is, the structure of matrilateral cross-cousin marriage described in Chapter 6.

The exchange of shell valuables in the *kula* creates alliances between groups living in potentially hostile areas. While the *kula* exchange, with its elaborate ceremony, is being carried out, direct barter of food, pottery, and other manufactured utilitarian objects is also taking place between the *kula* visitors and their hosts. Barter, as noted earlier in this chapter, involves the exchange of items that are scarce or absent in one place but not another. For example, when the Trobrianders go for *kula* objects to the Amphlett Islands, they bring food, plentiful on their island, to exchange for the pottery made there. The rules of *kula* exchange require a great deal of ceremonial behavior, while the accompanying barter is just the opposite. *Kula* exchange is delayed, and barter is immediate; *kula* does not involve bargaining, while barter involves trying to get the best deal for oneself, as occurs in market exchanges. Barter is never conducted with one's *kula* partners, but rather, with others on the island that one visits. Over the past decade the results of ethnographic field research with the Trobrianders and others in the *kula* area, as well as ethnohistorical research, seem to point to the following conclusion: Since the Massim area before extensive contact with Europeans was an area of chronic warfare, the precontact *kula* exchange system alternated with warfare and the *kula* system described by Malinowski operated as it did because of European pacification (Keesing, 1990: 152). This relationship between *kula* exchange and warfare appears to parallel that between warfare and the Enga *Te* exchange described earlier.

The different kinds of exchange systems among the Trobrianders—*sagali, urigubu, kayasa,* and *kula*—involve somewhat different ranges of goods. The social structure serves as the matrix for the exchange systems, in that chiefs are the focal points of all three kinds of distributions. All married men give *urigubu,* but chiefs receive many times more than the ordinary person. Many adult men are involved in *kula* exchange, but chiefs own the canoes used, have more *kula* partners, and have in their temporary possession the most valuable objects.

These exchange systems, though somewhat modified, continue to operate among the Trobrianders today, though they are now citizens of Papua New Guinea (Schiefenhovel and Bell-Krannhals, 1996). A recent description of *kayasa* on Kaileuna (not the island where Malinowski or Weiner did fieldwork) indicates that it is now a contest among men of a village to see who can grow the most yams (Schiefenhovel and Bell-Krannhals, 1996). One man will offer prizes for the winners. The *kayasa* organizer uses this as a means of increasing his prestige. Chiefdomship is still a matter of ascribed status, but success in competitive events like the *kayasa* is also an important element (Schiefenhovel and Bell-Krannhals, 1996: 249). Visitors come to the final stages of the ceremony as witnesses. *Urigubu* is also a matter of competition, since men gain prestige from giving large amounts of *urigubu.* Two men may also compete in the growing of special long yams called *kuvi,* whose tubers have enormous dimensions. This kind of competition in the growing of *kuvi* may also be the means of settling quarrels. Though Trobrianders today travel in fiberglass boats and are Christians, "in many respects the Trobrianders of today seem to have stepped from the pages of their famous ethnography" (Schiefenhovel and Bell-Krannhals, 1996: 236).

Though the horticultural mode of production of the Trobrianders is markedly different from the fishing, hunting, and gathering mode of the Tlingit and Kwakiutl, all three have rank systems. This means that there are titles and positions of importance that are inherited from one generation to the next. All three societies produce economic surpluses, despite the differences in mode of production. In these societies, distribution of goods at potlatches and at *sagali* serves to enhance one's rank and prestige. Goods are given to chiefs by their followers in their kin groups as a kind of tribute; the chiefs accumulate these goods and redistribute them on ceremonial occasions. When the chief serves as a host at such a ceremonial redistribution, he thereby validates his claim to high rank. The acceptance of the redistributed goods by the guests means they recognize his claim to high rank. Rank in these societies is flexible, in that the more one distributes, the higher one's rank becomes.

Systems of Exchange Where Rank Is Fixed

The nature of exchanges is significantly altered when there are permanent rank differences. In such systems, aristocrats are separate from commoners, lords from vassals, patrons from clients, and high castes from low castes. These groups differ not only in rank and prestige but also in the economic resources that they control. These societies also have economic specialization and a fixed division of labor. The systems of economic distribution and the exchanges found in societies with ranked strata always emphasize the inferiority of vassal, client, commoner, and low-caste individual, and the superiority of aristocrat, lord, patron, and high-caste individual. When superiors give to inferiors, the act is seen as generosity or largess. When inferiors give to superiors, it is seen as tribute. No matter how much tribute the inferiors give, it does not raise their status; it merely further enhances the prestige of their superiors. At the same time, the greater generosity and continual distributions of the superiors also enhance their status, not that of the inferiors. These cultural formulations are not contrary to the general principles of exchange that have been discussed (although it may seem so); rather, it is a demonstration of the way in which the social structure and political organization determine the meanings of the exchanges. If, in a culture, the lord is defined as superior, his superiority is demonstrated both when he gives and when he receives. Objects given as tribute and objects that are the largesse of aristocrats are usually different types of objects. They derive their cultural meanings solely from the status of the giver, whether the goods move up to a higher-ranked individual or down to a lower-ranked individual.

In precolonial times, the Bunyoro of western Uganda had a fixed system of rank with its concomitant system of economic distribution. Among the Bunyoro, the king granted rights over land and over those who cultivated it to chiefs as a reward for service (Beattie, 1960). Chiefs visited the king to give him tribute, which consisted of cattle, beer, and grain. The king, on his part, gave frequent feasts. For special services, the king might also give cattle to particular individuals. The chiefs stood in the same relationship to their commoners as the king stood to the chiefs. Commoners brought tribute to the chief, and the chief gave feasts. The Bunyoro also illustrate an interesting general point about the cultural meaning of things exchanged—tribute always seemed to be paid in the form of food in its uncooked form, raw or on the hoof, while the generosity of superiors took the form of feasts or cooked food.

In India, castes are endogamous, highly specialized occupational groups. In any particular place, all the castes form a caste system in which members of the various castes perform their services for one another under the supervision and control of the landholders. The castes are hierarchically ordered, from the Brahmans, who are priests, at the top, to the untouchables, who are tanners, washers, and sweepers who carry away human excrement. Though Indian castes are relatively fixed in rank, individual castes may disagree on their placement within the system and today often attempt to change it with respect to other groups.

Where rank differences in the social system are fixed, we find economically specialized occupational groups that are tied together in an interdependent system of economic exchanges. Economic subsistence in these societies, in contrast to those discussed earlier, is completely dependent upon exchange. As noted, distributions in egalitarian societies serve to create and maintain ongoing social relations between groups that are equal in status. In contrast, in societies with flexible rank, distributions allow different groups to improve their rank. Distributions in societies with fixed rank maintain the status of some groups over others. The different types of exchange systems we have discussed are all related to particular types of political organization. This is why many anthropologists prefer to talk about political economy, reflecting the interrelationship between the two.

The Market System

The term *market* has two meanings. The first refers to the location or site where food commodities and craft items are bought and sold. The second meaning characterizes an entire economic system based upon the determination of prices by the market, that is, in terms of supply and demand. This is the exchange system with which Americans are most familiar. Its characteristics are different in many respects from those of the exchange systems we have discussed so far. Perhaps the most distinctive feature of market exchange is that the buyer need have no other social relationship with the seller. While one may deal with the same grocer, butcher, or supermarket over many years, one may shift overnight and carry out the same transactions with another store. The relationship between buyer and seller is not dependent upon any other relationship but has its basis solely in the fact that the seller has something that the buyer wants or needs and is willing to pay for. The relationship can even consist of a single purchase, never to be repeated. This feature is in sharp contrast to all the distribution systems described earlier. The basic premise of a market system is to make a profit, and the essence of profit is to buy cheap and sell for more than you have paid. Transactions in a market system are governed by bargaining or haggling over price rather than determined by social relationships. In haggling, a buyer tries to buy something as cheaply as possible. This is in contrast to a Kwakiutl potlatch, where the more that is given, the greater the prestige of the giver. The receiver of goods who cannot reciprocate gets the worst of the deal. In the market system, the buyer gives as little as the seller will accept.

A market system depends on the existence of money. Societies that did not have market systems did not have money in the usual sense of that term. Money serves a

A busy local market in Rissane, Morocco.

number of purposes. It can be used as a standard of value, because any commodity, service, or labor can be expressed in terms of its monetary worth. Money can be used as a store of value, because it can be hoarded and used later to obtain commodities or services. But most importantly, money can serve as a medium of exchange, whereby one commodity can be transferred for money and then that money can be used to exchange for any other kind of goods or services. The money used in our society is considered all-purpose money, because it can be exchanged for anything in the society, as noted at the beginning of this chapter, and serves all the above uses and others as well. The valuables discussed in connection with ceremonial distribution, like the armshells and necklaces in the *kula,* are objects that have value but can be used only for particular ceremonies, such as the *kula.* There are many other societies within which such special-purpose valuables are found. The restricted uses to which such valuables are put is in sharp contrast to the many purposes that money serves.

When cities arose 5000 years ago, the rural populations became peasants, tied to the city by the sale of surplus grain and foodstuffs and the purchase there of specialized crafts and manufactured goods that the peasants did not produce themselves. Markets served to articulate peasant communities with the economy of the city. There are different kinds of market structures. One kind of market structure links a number of different peasant communities to a central market town. In addition to its subsistence activities, each of these communities specializes in a different craft activity, such as weaving, manufacture of pottery, or manufacture of tiles. People from each of these communities periodically come into the market to sell their wares and to buy the goods that they require but do not make for themselves. Such markets are frequently held once a week. In some places markets are held in different villages and towns on successive days of the week. In northern Nigeria, a village may sometimes be labeled with the day of the week on which its market is held, as in the village called Saturday. Itinerant traders go from market to market with their goods. These kinds of marketing structures, where goods from industrial societies, as well as local products, are sold, define a region.

Whereas in nonmarket economic systems, the economy is embedded in a larger cultural matrix, the growth of a market economy in an industrialized capitalist society marks the development of an economic institution that is separate from other institutions but nevertheless must be seen and understood in terms of the cultural matrix with which it is associated. The Japanese and Americans both manufacture cars within capitalist market systems, but there are differences in these two cultures in factors such as the social organization of factories and the relationships between managers and workers. In our country, the capitalist mode of the economy sets the tone and the values for other institutions. The economy influences morality. The axiom "What's good for business is good for the country" illustrates this point. Some people even believe that if a few bribes or kickbacks are necessary to conduct business, then bribery is not immoral, especially if the bribes are given to individuals outside the United States. At first, social scientists assumed that market economies operated rationally and were not influenced by cultural factors. However, now they recognize that the economy is "embedded" and "Japanese capitalism may be quite different from Chinese, and both in turn from American" (Hefner, 1998: 11). Business as it is conducted by overseas Chinese in Southeast Asia, for example, is based on particularistic relationships in which family as well as the reciprocal relationships known as *guanxi*, discussed earlier, are significant in the conduct of business. The traditional family firm as a basis for conducting business has given the Chinese in Southeast Asia the edge over the less commercially oriented Thai, Javanese, Malay, Burmese, or Vietnamese (Mackie, 1998: 129). The small- and medium-sized Chinese family businesses in Taiwan underlie Taiwan's dynamic form of capitalism (Hamilton, 1998).

In a market economy, all economic behavior is evaluated in market terms, with individuals making decisions in order to cut the best deal for themselves. Anthropologists have been interested in the factors that determine how decisions are made and whether these decisions are based exclusively on expectations of economic gain or loss. Such studies often assume that individuals make rational choices for themselves and that their purpose is always to maximize their own position. In a market economy, labor also operates according to the laws of supply and demand. Workers go to places where employment is available. If a factory closes, its workers are expected to move freely to other places where work is available. In Europe, this sometimes means moving to another country. If an industry like that of manufacturing TV sets in the United States loses out to foreign competition, the workers in that industry are expected to retrain themselves for positions in other industries.

Much of the world today operates as a single market. However, what is good for workers manufacturing sewing machines in the modernized economies of Taipei or Hong Kong creates hardships for workers who have lost their jobs as a result of the closing of a plant manufacturing sewing machines in Elizabeth, New Jersey. The world system of money and markets has penetrated even the most remote societies. In some of them, it coexists with reciprocal exchange and redistributive economic systems.

The market principle, which is based upon the law of supply and demand, assumes that nothing exists within our society that cannot be purchased with money. However, in our society other kinds of exchanges continue to coexist with the market system. We have cultural rules about reciprocal gift exchange. People who give gifts expect to be reciprocated with gifts that are roughly equivalent. Our rules do not require the recipient to return like for like, as the Abelam do. People often bring gifts when invited for dinner. It is appropriate to bring wine or flowers but not considered appropriate to bring a pound of ground sirloin or to give the hostess a $10 bill.

Consumption

In its most general sense, consumption means the utilization of goods, and as with other aspects of culture, consumption is determined by cultural rules. Furthermore, there is a relationship between the consumption of goods and the nature of the social system as well as the system of cultural meanings. In the small-scale societies anthropologists used to study, food and other material goods were consumed in relation to subsistence and in the context of ritual. In many instances these goods were grown or manufactured within the local community, but we also saw how yams as *urigubu* were ceremonially moved from one Trobriand community to another. Frequently, the ritual context was the setting for the distribution of goods that were to go outside the community, as seen so clearly in the discussion of *kaiko* and potlatch distribution. In these examples, goods manufactured in one place were ceremonially distributed and then taken to be utilized someplace else. Hence, in these cases, the aim of production was distribution or exchange. In complex societies, as we shall see below, consumption often stimulates production of more of the same; that is, people's demands for a product stimulate production.

With the development of complex modern industrial society came the notion of the consumer and a narrower definition of consumption. By and large, individuals no longer harvested or made the material goods they utilized; rather, they used goods manufactured by someone else, which are referred to as commodities. Consumption, in this sense, is defined as an increasing reliance on commodities produced by others, rather than the wider definition presented above. Commodities utilized were sometimes further subdivided into goods required for subsistence and luxury items whose acquisition was usually related to high rank or elite status. The anthropological focus shifted to the way such commodity consumption was mediated by the global capitalism that had produced the commodities in various places all over the world and how such objects become incorporated into the local scene.

Sometimes religious beliefs dictate the nature of product consumption. A visit to Lancaster, Pennsylvania, or Shipshewana, Indiana, the location of Amish communities, will immediately demonstrate the way in which their religious beliefs have dictated the use of horse and buggy rather than car and pickup truck, and the wearing of very modest clothing blue or black in color, rather than the latest fashion. They still farm and depend on the products of their fields and herds and carefully control the commodities that enter their world. Their religious beliefs dictate what enters and is incorporated into their community. Their sphere of social relations has resisted "commodification." One can find examples of this process in many other parts of the world.

The sale of religious objects in Cairo, Egypt, represents the reverse process, the manner in which "sacred" objects have been turned into commodities (Starrett, 1995). Religious objects are mass-produced in factories, sometimes even in other countries, like Japan, for sale to devout Muslims. Such objects include a wide variety of items, such as copies of the Qur'an in velvet boxes, which are commonly displayed in the back windows of automobiles or taxis. These objects are displayed in order to obtain God's blessing and protection, to ward off the evil eye, and to signal the owner's Muslim identity. There are real differences of opinion about such objects, and their religious meanings are contested. Educated Muslims feel that employing such manufactured commodities in this way reduces religion itself to the level of mass consumption. This use of sacred objects, which is very widespread, has produced a backlash among more scholarly Egyptian Muslims, who claim such a use of sacred objects is really resorting to magical charms and is counter to Islamic values.

Sometimes commodification of a particular product can result in significant changes in a people's way of life. The lives of the Otavalo, indigenous Quecha-speaking people with their distinctive dress and customs, have been significantly transformed as a consequence of their success in the weaving trade (Meisch, 1998). They were weavers and traveling merchants even before the Inca of Peru incorporated the area of Ecuador into their empire. The Spanish created *encomendias,* estates of land and inhabitants granted to Spanish colonists, and made traditional textiles part of the tribute owed to them. In the mid-twentieth century the Spanish loom was introduced and the weaving of casimir or woolen tweeds was introduced; the latter became a significant Otavalo product. When mass tourism worldwide began in the 1960s and the extension of the Pan-American Highway to Quito made Otavalo accessible, Indian products, such as scarves, ponchos, shawls, belts, and other clothing (and later, daypacks and duffel bags), became popular tourist items. Population growth and land shortages in the 1970s and 1980s sent many Otavalos to towns and cities in other parts of Latin America, Spain, and the United States. Weaving workshops and stores were set up, ties being maintained with the home community. All Otavalos are textile producers, though many still plant crops for their own consumption. To the town, tourism meant expansion not only of the marketplace but of restaurants, folk music clubs, and other businesses, from which the indigenous people profited sufficiently to buy property in increasing numbers. Besides sales to tourists "and other Ecuadorians at local markets and in stores throughout the country . . . sales to foreign exporters constitute another large market" (Meisch, 1998: 20).

As a consequence of this prosperity, the indigenous population, now half the population of the town, has transformed the ethnic and power relations in the valley. Wealth always gives the possessor power in a capitalist society, and the financial success of the Otavalos has significantly altered their position in society. They buy the goods of a capitalist society—refrigerators, cars, trucks, stereos—and send their children to universities to be lawyers and doctors (Meisch, 1998: 24–25). Another consequence of this now transnational textile industry has been the increase in the elaborateness of *compadrazgo* fiestas, including the introduction of new dishes and an increase in the number of *compadres* honored (Colloredo-Mansfield, 1998: 57).

In Western capitalist society, consumption has often been associated with gender; the useful and important activities were conducted outside the home by men, while the home was seen as a place of leisure and consumption rather than of productive activities. Income creation is accorded higher value than the transformation of that income into goods and services important to the maintenance of elite status in society; the realm of production is valorized and the realm of consumption denigrated (Beal, 1998: 158–160). Women and their world are devalued and the activity of shopping is seen as an insignificant female endeavor. Among Jordanian elites, shopping is seen as a critical aspect of the female gender role by both men and women; it is associated with women and is essentially women's work. Even though it is evident from their homes that possession of consumer goods in great number is a significant aspect of social life, the activity of shopping is nevertheless seen as essentially trivial by both men and women. Even the shopping activities of professional women who earn their own income is denigrated, while the hunting, yachting, drinking activities of men, though income-depleting, are not. Since shopping alone, seen as a leisure activity for women, and not the leisure activities of men, is disparaged, it would seem that it is the gendered identity of the shopper rather than the shopping per se that is *the* factor for Jordanian elites (Beal, 1998: 160). Professional women who work in the business world outside the home may denigrate shopping because they are expected to conform to the male idea of what constitutes proper behavior. Jordanian men, though they talk disparagingly about shopping, are consumers themselves, often insisting on choosing the furniture that will decorate the formal, public rooms of the house. The cultural valuation of shopping depends upon the gender of the shopper. Shopping is clearly part of the construction of gender idealogy among the Jordanian elites, and it becomes a means by which female activity and agency can be subordinated and denigrated in contrast to the valorized sphere of male activity (Beal, 1998: 160). This relationship between consumerism, shopping, and gender ideology is interesting to explore cross-culturally. Among Americans, all sectors of society, male and female, seem to engage in shopping and there would no longer seem to be a specific connection with gender ideology.

The suitcase traders of Barbados, young women in their late twenties and early thirties, who work in manufacturing or data entry, go with their suitcases to Puerto Rico to buy cosmetics, jewelry, fabrics, hair care products, clothing, and small electrical appliances at discount stores and shopping malls. These goods will be resold at home at a high markup (Quinones, 1998). This represents an expansion of the earlier role that women played in petty trading. The items purchased are not available in their own country. These suitcase traders must make choices about what to buy in the ever-growing cornucopia of products. Through their businesses, suitcase traders acquire "a sophisticated knowledge of how to manage consumption in a global world of constantly shifting fashions and styles" (Quinones, 1998: 179). These young women, part of a worldwide globalizing trend by virtue of the products they sell, become the trendsetters and innovators for their customers at home, shaping the nature of their consumption.

Often objects are accepted and recontextualized. Until the beginning of the twentieth century, when a Kalmyk Mongol bride married, the Lamaist Buddhist priest would determine the color of the horse upon which she would ride when she moved from her parents' nomadic encampment to that of her husband. When the Kalmyk Mongol bride of today in America moves from the home of her parents to that of her husband, the Lamaist Buddhist priest determines the color of the car in which she will be riding. Kanuri dreams about horses represented fantasies about sex. Today, Kanuri dream about cars, and the meaning—fantasies about sex—is the same.

Earlier studies of modernization and modernity assumed that when Third and Fourth World people adopted the use of money and began to purchase jeans, transistor radios, canned food, and other items of Western manufacture, the result would be either incorporation and a global homogenization of material culture or some form of mass resistance to Western culture. These goods often came to stand for becoming modern, and people could, by the use or nonuse of such objects, signify Americanization and Westernization, or a conscious rejection of such an identification. Sometimes, as on the island of Tanga in Papua New Guinea, modernization and its attendant goods become a separate category, in opposition to *Kastom,* that is, those practices continued from the past (Foster, 1992). Frequently, what has happened has been an acceptance and recontextualization of material items. Sometimes objects used in the past have come to stand for a nostalgia for that past and a continuity of identity. The Japanese tea ceremony performs that function for modern Japanese today. The passion many Americans have for collecting toy trains, metal lunch boxes from the 1950s, and antique baseball cards derives from that same sense of nostalgia for the past, loss of youth, and remembrance of a more tranquil period in the nation's history. There is a market for such items, and they have become commodities.

As noted above, consumption has often had consequences for production. Mintz's study of sugar and political power (1986) illustrates the way the increasing consumption of sugar in Europe was the direct impetus for the development of sugar plantations; agribusinesses organized in the Caribbean beginning in the eighteenth century and had consequences for the emergence of an industrialized Europe.

Economic organization has always played a pivotal role in anthropological theorizing. The evolutionist Lewis Henry Morgan used technology as the basis for defining the stages of human cultural development, and Marxist anthropologists see the economy, defined as the mode of production, as strongly influencing other aspects of culture. Each of the theories of culture discussed in Chapter 1 has a particular perspective on or approach to the economic organization or economic aspect of society. Some stress the function of economic activities, others stress the structure of groups engaged in economic activities, and still others emphasize the role of the individual as an entrepreneur in the economic sphere. The economy as a system of symbolic meanings is the focus of some theories, while the economy as the means by which society adapts to the environment is the major concern of others.

Economic organization deals with the way a society provisions itself in order to enable it to reproduce itself. There are a variety of modes of production, including hunting and gathering, agriculture, and animal husbandry. Technology plays an important role in all these productive modes. In every society a division of labor is based on gender and age. More complex modes of production produce storable surpluses, which are used to support full-time specialists and social hierarchies. There are also a variety of modes of distribution, which vary depending on the presence or absence of ranking or stratification. In egalitarian societies, the system of distributions expresses the equal relationships between groups. In societies with flexible rank, distributions are the means by which the ranking of groups is raised or lowered. In stratified societies with fixed rank, based on caste or class hierarchies, the system of distributions expresses and reinforces the hierarchy. Market economies, originally thought to be based upon rationality, are in effect, culturally determined. The nature of consumption in various societies is also culturally determined, following cultural rules.

Chapter Nine

Governing Society: Politics, Government, Law, and Conflict

What is politics? Does politics always involve the use of power? What does it mean "to get an offer you can't refuse"? In American society, that phrase represents the exercise of power in a variety of contexts. It may be a way of getting a competitor to remove herself from the competition, or a way of forcing someone to do something he doesn't want to do. How does this idea, or other ideas about power and politics, operate in different societies? A Trobriand man aspiring to chiefly office might seize the opportunity of his mother's brother's death to organize the latter's funeral *sagali*. Thus, a Trobriand funeral *sagali* is a political event. So too are the funeral of a Mafia boss and the funeral of a dictator in a totalitarian state. In these examples, though the successor comes from a small circle of eligible individuals, there is no fixed rule regarding succession. The politics of power is an important aspect of the tapestry of culture.

Questions about politics and power may be addressed first by comparing the processes of political organization in two contrasting small-scale societies, whose classic ethnographies are well known to most anthropologists. Durkheim long ago pointed out that one or two detailed examples were useful explanatory devices. Trobriand political organization involves the division of the main island of Kiriwina into a number of districts, each of which contains several villages. Members of the four matrilineal clans are dispersed throughout the districts, though subclans are localized. Within a particular district, one subclan will rank higher than all the others, and its chief will be the paramount chief of the district. The other villages in the district will have headmen who are subordinate to the chief and give their sisters to him as wives, as pointed out in the previous chapter. Each year they furnish him with yams—*urigubu*—as tribute. Since there is no rule of succession like primogeniture, when a chief dies, his real or classificatory sisters' sons compete with one another to succeed to the position. Before the man who succeeds to the position can make the funerary *sagali* for his predecessor, he must demonstrate that he has many followers who will support him as the new chief and assist him at the *sagali*. The chief controls resources as well as labor and is the titular owner of all the land in the district, although the garden magician and actual users of the land also have some rights to it. The chief decides when the time is propitious to declare a *kayasa,* a period of feasting and competitive games, such as cricket, between his own village and another to be held at harvest time. As a result of the chief's decision, all the people of the village are bound to work their hardest so the *kayasa* will be a success.

Malinowski mentions that the chief had "special henchmen" to punish people who did not obey him. They might even inflict capital punishment. Frequently, people obeyed the chief because they were afraid that he might command that evil magic be used against them. Several political symbols are associated with Trobriand chieftainship. Special signs of deference are shown to the chief. No man's head may be higher than that of the chief, so either the chief sits on a high platform or people bend when they walk past him. The chief's large, elaborately decorated yam house, displaying the *urigubu* yams given him as tribute, is another symbol of his political authority. Only the members of the chief's subclan may wear a certain kind of ornament, red spondylus shell disks, on their foreheads. The food taboos that must be observed by people of rank are also symbols of political authority.

Yanomamo political organization provides a clear contrast (Chagnon 1992). Every Yanomamo man is his own boss; no other Yanomamo can give him orders. Each Yanomamo village is a completely independent unit. One village will entertain and feast another village in order to win its support as an ally. Villages that are enemies of one another will raid each other to capture women. Every Yanomamo village has a headman, an individual who has demonstrated leadership qualities. These include fearlessness in war, as well as wisdom and judgment in planning the course of action for the village—in making alliances with other villages, in planning attacks on other villages, and in moving the village to another area when gardens are depleted. The position of headman is not hereditary. Consensus among the men of the village must be obtained by the headman before any course of action is adopted. The headman does not direct individuals to do things; first he does them himself, setting an example for the others to follow. Headmen are constantly challenged by others who aspire to the position. A man is headman only as long as the villagers have confidence in his judgment. Another individual with supporters can begin to oppose the headman in his decisions. As this opposition grows, the headman, if the people lose confidence in him, may be supplanted by his rival, or the headman may inspire his villagers to use force to drive out the opposing leader and his followers to form their own village. Since there is no fixed rule of succession, the younger brother or son of a headman is no more likely to succeed as headman than any other adult man in the village. No one performs labor for the headman; he works his own garden. The headman has no special magical knowledge. Since there are no rank differences among the Yanomamo—all adult males are equal—there are no outward signs of rank, no special deference, and no special food customs to differentiate aristocrats from commoners or those with power from those without it. The equal status of all adult Yanomamo males is consonant with the egalitarian relationship they have in exchange (see Chapters 6 and 8). Today, the Trobriand and Yanomamo political structures that we have just described are both encompassed within nation-states, with attendant consequences.

Concepts in Political Anthropology

These examples provide us with a framework within which to examine concepts employed to analyze political systems found in human societies, including our own. Power is the key concept used in defining political organization. *Power* is the ability to command others to do certain things and to get compliance from them. On this point, one can immediately see the contrast between the Yanomamo and Trobrianders. The Yanomamo headman does not have the power to compel villagers to act in a particular way, whereas the Trobriand chief demonstrates his power in a whole range of activities. Power must be distinguished from *authority*. When power becomes institutionalized, we say it has been transformed into *authority*. This means that there is a recognized position or *office,* the occupant of which can issue commands that must be obeyed. It is apparent that the Trobriand chief has authority as well as power, which derives from his chiefly office, and his commands are always obeyed. What about the Yanomamo headman? Does he have any authority? The headman among the Yanomamo holds a recognized position or office, but since the headman has no power to compel people to obey him, he has no authority. Nevertheless, he is a leader, since others will follow him if he has influence with them. *Influence* is the ability to persuade others to follow one's lead. They will continue to follow him and he will have influence over them as long as they have confidence in his leadership ability. Some kind of leadership is found in all human groups. When leadership is not vested in a formal institutionalized position and is based solely on influence, as is the case of the Yanomamo headman, loss of confidence means loss of followers and loss of leadership position.

A distinction is also made between *government* and *politics. Government* refers to the decisions made by those in office on behalf of the entire group in carrying out common goals. This may involve going to war to maintain the defense of the group, and dealing with the day-to-day matters of law and order. Thus, the Trobriand chief carries out important governmental functions. For example, when he decides to hold a competitive *kayasa* with another village, as we have described in Chapter 8, he organizes the production of those under him. The chief initiates the overseas *kula* exchange we have described previously and is the owner of the canoe used. *Kula* deals with overseas relations between Trobrianders and other peoples, in effect, foreign affairs. Today, Trobriand chiefs are sometimes members of the Papua New Guinea Parliament, continuing this chiefly control over external affairs. In contrast, among the Yanomamo, the consensus of the whole group is what is important, even though they have a headman as their leader.

Politics is concerned with an entirely different aspect of political organization. Whereas government involves the carrying out of shared goals, politics involves people's competing for power. Politics concentrates on the manipulation of people and resources, the maneuvers intended to enhance power, the rise of factions that compete for power, and the development of political parties with differing points of view. Politics emphasizes opposing points of view and conflict, divergent rather than common goals. Of course, in our own society as well as others, those vying for power in the political arena usually claim that they are operating for the common good and not just for their own personal aggrandizement. They may actually believe this to be true.

Politics operates among both the Trobriand Islanders and the Yanomamo. When a Trobriand chief dies, the choice of a new chief is open to political maneuvering and competition among the individuals in the group of people eligible to succeed. These candidates must demonstrate their political abilities to followers who are their fellow subclansmen. At this point, potential claimants to the chiefly office make promises and point to their demonstrated skills in organizational leadership and their wealth. The man who is recognized as the new chief now has the authority to govern and assumes the appropriate Trobriand symbols of political authority.

Politics is constantly present among the Yanomamo, since Yanomamo headmen regularly face the potential opposition of those who also aspire to leadership in their village. Even the decision to hold a feast may be the basis for political maneuvering. A rival for the position of headman may himself try to organize a feast. He tries to convince others in the village that this is a wise decision politically. If he succeeds in enlisting the support of the majority of the villagers, then he has in effect become the new headman. If he can mobilize only partial support, he will come to lead his own faction in the village, and he may try again in the future. He may also fail to get any support, in which case he retires to the sidelines and sulks.

Forms of Political Organization

In all human societies some form of authority and leadership has always existed. Though the forms of political organization that we will describe characterize societies that are now parts of nation-states, their description will provide us with a picture of how successively more complex political structures developed.

In the simplest form of political organization, leadership was manifested intermittently. This type of organization may be called *situational leadership*. The Iglulingmiut, an Inuit (Eskimo) group of eastern Canada, illustrate this form of political organization. The name given to the group means the people (*miut*) of Iglulik, who were all those living in that area. There were no fixed political offices, and a number of men, but never women, exerted leadership in certain situations. There were winter villages along the coast where a number of families related through various kinds of kin ties, though not the same families every year, came together to spend the winter, exploiting the resources of the ocean. The men of influence who exercised leadership in the winter village were the "boat owners," the senior males of the kin units that owned the boats, which were used to hunt seals. Leadership was also exhibited in connection with the inland summer hunting of caribou, at which time numbers of families came together. The hunting of caribou was conducted under the leadership of a man with hunting expertise. At the end of the hunt, the families scattered, and the leader was no longer a leader. Leadership operated only through influence, and different men exercised their influence in those areas where they had special knowledge or ability. These temporary leaders did not have the power to compel people to obey them. This kind of political organization was found only among peoples whose subsistence was based exclusively upon hunting and gathering.

Band Organization

Some hunting and gathering societies had a more complex form of political organization known as *band organization*. Bands had a more fixed membership that came together annually to carry out joint ritual and economic activities. The Ojibwa—hunters and gatherers in the forests of the eastern Canadian subarctic—had this type of political organization. During most of the year, small groups of related families moved from one hunting area to another. In the summertime, the whole band frequently came together on the shores of a lake and remained as a unit for the summer. The men with influence were leaders of the group.

The Yanomamo structurally have band organization, though dependent on horticulture, a completely different mode of subsistence. Each village has a delimited membership and a headman, who has influence over his fellow villagers. In Ojibwa and Yanomamo societies, the band had more cohesiveness than societies with only situational leadership. The band acts as a unit under recognized leadership, though that leadership is based on influence, not on authority.

Big Man Structure

A still more complex political organization is the *Big Man structure*. There is usually a term for the Big Man position, and frequently, it literally means "big man." The Big Man structure represents a greater delineation of the leadership position, in comparison with that of band organization. As leadership becomes more clearly defined, so does the group of followers. In Melanesia, the Big Man takes the initiative in exchanges with other groups. In contrast, ordinary men fulfill their obligations in exchanges with affines and kin and contribute to what is accumulated by the Big Man of their group, as described in the depiction of Abelam and Enga exchange ceremonies in Chapter 8. The followers of a Big Man also include rubbish men, unmarried men who do not fulfill any of their obligations with regard to exchange. The Big Men organize their group's production and are the nodes in the exchange system. The Big Man derives his power from his direction of the ceremonial distribution of the goods accumulated by his group and the decisions he makes in the redistribution of goods within his own group. The Abelam Big Man depicted here wears the emblem of his office around his neck.

The Big Man also directs a range of other activities. As noted in the previous chapter, not only does the Abelam Big Man organize the labor involved in the production of long yams, but he also acts as the ritual expert, since he alone knows the magical spells that make the yams grow so long. On behalf of his entire group, he maintains sexual abstinence for the whole growing period. Artistic ability as a carver or painter of designs is also a desirable characteristic in an Abelam Big Man, but the most important characteristic is his ability to produce the long yams on which the prestige of the entire group depends. Throughout New Guinea, the oratorical skills of the Big Man are essential, since he must deliver speeches at ceremonial distributions as the representative of his group. The Big Man should also show prowess in warfare, though his involvement is usually in

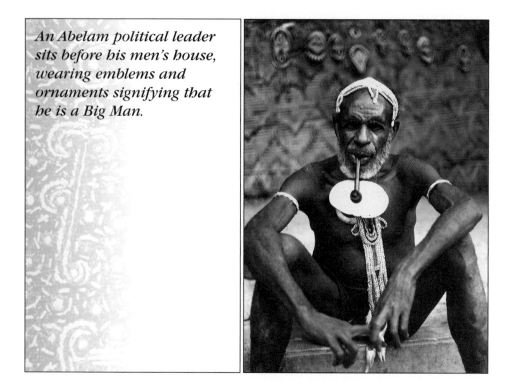

An Abelam political leader sits before his men's house, wearing emblems and ornaments signifying that he is a Big Man.

the organizational area. Since women cannot be near any phase of the growing or exchange of long yams among the Abelam, they cannot be Big Men.

The position of Big Man is dependent on personal qualifications and individual ability. Anthropologists refer to this position as an *achieved status,* in contrast to an *ascribed status,* which is a position one inherits. As he ages, a Big Man may no longer be able to carry out all the activities necessary to maintain his influence in his group. In that case, his leadership position may be challenged by other aspiring Big Men. Competition between challengers involves political skills and maneuvering. Though in a patrilineal society the Big Man's son may have an initial advantage, he will not be able to become a Big Man himself if he lacks the necessary abilities. A man who has leadership qualities, although he may be from another family in the clan, may surpass the Big Man's son in gaining followers and, in time, be recognized as the new Big Man.

Though women have influence and play an important role in exchange in many matrilineal societies of Melanesia, they rarely occupy the Big Man position. The women of the island of Vanatinai in the Coral Sea, one of the islands in the *kula* ring, are an exception. The term *giagia,* which literally means "giver," is a gender-neutral term that refers to Big Men and Big Women (Lepowsky, 1990). These Big Women are central nodes in the exchange of goods and valuables. They lead *kula* expeditions, organize mortuary feasts, and orate at ceremonies, just like Big Men do.

Big Man political structure is associated with reciprocal exchange systems, like that of the Abelam, and also with more complex exchange systems, like the *Te* of the Enga.

Chieftainship

The introduction of fixed positions of rank and some method of succession leads to a fourth type of political organization—*chieftainship*. In chieftainships, individuals as well as kin groups of the descent system are ranked with respect to one another. The Trobriand case, with which we began this chapter, exemplifies this type of organization. As shown earlier, the chief does not merely exert influence over others but has real authority, which means that he has the power to enforce his decisions. Power and authority are vested in the office, and whoever occupies that office exercises this authority and has power. In the Big Man structure, any man can become a Big Man if he has the ability and works hard. In chiefdoms, which are ranked societies, the chiefly position is restricted to certain high-ranking individuals. Among the Kwakiutl, who have chiefs, the oldest child, regardless of sex, inherits the chiefly position through primogeniture. This position is represented by the highest-ranking name in the *numaym,* or kin group. Though a Kwakiutl female may inherit the name, a male kinsman usually carries out the duties of the office.

In chieftainships, there is a hierarchy of other political positions. These are ranked with regard to one another. Whereas the Big Man has influence over a group of people—his followers, who are members of his kin group or clan or even others not of that clan—in the chieftainship, the chief exercises control over an area and the kin groups contained within that area. For example, the Trobriand chief heads a district with villages whose headmen pay tribute to the chief in the form of *urigubu.* These village headmen are not of the chiefly subclan but of other subclans lower in rank than the chief's.

The political economy of chieftainships is a more complex redistributive system than that associated with the Big Man structure. In a chieftainship, because there are more levels of political organization, villagers give to their village headmen, who in turn give to the chief. This is exactly what happens at a Trobriand *kayasa,* when two villages compete with one another. Yams are presented to the chief by the heads of the two villages. The chief later redistributes what he has received in feasts to reward the villages in his district for various services. Chieftainship is also associated with potlatch-type exchange systems like those of the Kwakiutl and Tlingit.

Transformation from Big Man to Chieftainship and Back Again

The Kachin, a hill people of northern Burma, provide an example of the transformation from Big Man structure to chieftainship. Segmentary lineage structures, such as those described in Chapter 6, can be found in combination with either the Big Man type of political organization or with chieftainship. Big Men operate at each of the levels of the segmentary lineage structure. Minor Big Men head lineages, and important Big Men head clans composed of several lineages, all equal in rank. Edmund Leach, in his analysis of the political system (1954), which is a patrilineal lineage structure, shows how the Kachin Big Man structure can develop into the chieftainship and how chieftainship may collapse into the Big Man structure. In its Big Man form, which the Kachin call *gumlao,* a number of Kachin villages, all equal in rank, are tied together by a patrilineal genealogy. Each village has a headman, who can come from any lineage in the village. Each lineage is headed by its eldest male, and there is a council of elders (from each lineage) for every village. At village ceremonies and festivals, the heads of lineages separately sacrifice to a variety of spirits. The Kachin marriage rule favoring marriage with mother's brother's daughter separates lineages who take women (wife-takers) and those who give women (wife-givers) (Chapter 6, Figure 10). Among those Kachin with the *gumlao* structure, there are no differences in rank between wife-givers and wife-takers, bride wealth payments are low, and a number of lineages in the same village tend to marry in a circle in such a way that lineage A gives wives to lineage B, which gives wives to lineage C, which returns wives to lineage A.

If one lineage in a village grows wealthier or stronger than the others, it may try to raise its status by offering to pay a higher bride wealth and by seeking wives from high-ranking lineages in other villages. If successful, it can transform itself into a chiefly lineage that will dominate the other lineages in its own village, sponsoring village feasts, which will further raise its prestige. The head of this lineage becomes the village headman, since his lineage is deemed to be the highest-ranking lineage of the village. Succession to this position becomes ascribed rather than achieved. The rule of succession is *ultimogeniture,* which means that the new chief is the youngest son. His line is superior to the line of descendants of other sons. If the aristocratic lineage of a village succeeds in gaining control of other villages, the newly formed domain is subordinate to the chiefly lineage. At this point, the Kachin would say that the political form is of the *gumsa* type. It has become a chieftainship.

In the *gumsa* form, the chief, called *duwa,* holds both a political and ritual position. Though there is still a council of lineage heads, only the chief makes sacrifices on behalf of the domain to his ancestral lineage spirit, which is now taken to represent the ancestral spirit of all the lineages in the domain. Since the chief is entitled to receive a hind leg of all animals killed either in hunting or for sacrifice from everyone in his domain except his own lineage, he is referred to as the "thigh-eating chief." This right to the hind leg is one of several symbolic manifestations of chiefly authority, including the erection of a special kind of house post. The chief also has the right to have the people in his domain build his house and work on his agricultural land. In addition, in some cases, he exacts a portion of the rice harvest from each household in his domain every year. Whereas under the *gumlao* system, all lineages were equal in rank and married in a circle, in the *gumsa* form, there is a ranked series of lineages, and a lineage that gives women to another lineage is superior to it. There are also gradations in bride wealth to match the ranking of lineages. Since women move down the ranking order, the men of the chiefly lineage must get their wives from the aristocratic lineages of other domains.

Not only can the unranked *gumlao* turn into the *gumsa* chieftainship, but the reverse process can also occur, among the Kachin. When the *gumsa* structure places great economic strains upon the people, there is a revolt and the egalitarian *gumlao* system is reestablished. Thus the process can go in either direction, from *gumlao* to *gumsa* and back again to *gumlao*. It appears that the Kachin marriage pattern has the potential for the development of rank differences from a state in which lineage groupings exchanging women are equal.

The State

The last type of political organization that we will discuss is that of the *state*. Archaeologists have been interested in the conditions that produced the earliest states in Egypt, Mesopotamia, the Indus Valley, China, Mexico, and Peru. Cultural anthropologists focused upon still-functioning indigenous states that existed as a consequence of the colonial policy of indirect rule. Many of the well-studied examples are to be found in Africa and Southeast Asia.

The state differs from the other types of political organization in a number of significant ways, the most important of which is a difference in scale. Though some states may be quite small, the state has the potential for encompassing within its orbit millions of people. It is organized on a territorial basis, made up of villages and districts, rather than on the basis of kinship and clanship. Though in the chieftainship there was often a differentiation between the chiefly lineage, which controlled power and wealth, and other lineages made up of commoners, the system was still tied together by kinship. In contrast, in the state we find social stratification—rulers, aristocrats, commoners, and various low-status groups. All those under the control of the state are its citizens or its subjects. Frequently today, states contain not only small-scale societies like the Yanomamo but also multiethnic populations, who speak different languages and are culturally different from one another.

The state is governed by a ruler whose legitimate right to govern and command others is acknowledged by those in the state. Many of the early states were theocracies; that is, the ruler was head of both the religious hierarchy and the state. The same symbols were used for the merged religious and political structure. In many indigenous states, the ruler is not only the political but also the religious symbol of the whole society. This was particularly true in East African states, where the ruler's state of health and ritual purity affected the welfare of the entire kingdom, as was the case among the Aluund of southwestern Zaire, whom we discussed in Chapter 5. In the symbolism of the Aluund, the paramount chief is the lord of the soil and must not show disease, decay, or old age, since the productivity of crops depends on the state of his health.

The administrative functions of the state are carried out by a bureaucracy, which is delegated authority by the ruler and which grows in size and complexity as the state expands. Customary law becomes formalized into a legal code. The adjudication of disputes by the leader grows into a court system, which enforces its decisions through the police. The tribute given to the chief is transformed into taxes paid to the state, which support the growing bureaucracy. The state expands by conquering neighboring peoples, who become culturally distinct subject peoples, and whose territories are incorporated within the state. The ruler maintains an army, mobilized from the subjects to protect the state from attack by external invaders as well as to expand it by conquest.

The way in which an indigenous state functioned in the twentieth century can be seen from a description of the empire of Bornu, the Kanuri state on the borders of Lake Chad in northern Nigeria. This state was studied in 1956 when it was still under British colonial rule, by Abraham Rosman, one of the authors of this book. When the British entered the area at the turn of the century, they resurrected the partially collapsed indigenous state and governed through the Shehu of Bornu, the head of state.

Mounted retainers of a Kanuri district head in northern Nigeria demonstrate their allegiance to their leader. This photo was taken in 1956, when Nigeria was a British colony.

The highly stratified society included, besides the royal family, aristocratic families; commoners, including village farmers and different kinds of traders and crafters; and slaves. Only the Shehu could grant aristocrats titles, which sometimes came with land, including entire villages. The slaves were war captives and their descendents, who became the personal property of the Shehu. They could become titled aristocrats, though they remained the Shehu's slaves.

Prior to the arrival of the British, there was an empire of Bornu, which was located at the southern end of a strategic caravan route that led from the Mediterranean Sea across the Sahara to the populous states of West Africa. Caravans brought manufactured goods from Libya, and returned there with slaves, ivory, and other raw materials. The government of Bornu did not issue its own currency. Maria Theresa silver dollars from Austria, brought in by the caravan trade, served as a medium of exchange. Muskets, which had been introduced through the caravan trade, were monopolized by the state. The army of Bornu was completely controlled by the Shehu. Its generals, who bore high titles, were slaves of the Shehu. Besides conquest and the raiding of neighboring tribes for slaves, the army also defended the borders of Bornu from incursions by other states, particularly Bornu's enemies, the Hausa states to the west. As a result of conquest, non-Kanuri people, such as the Babur and some Bagirmi, permanently became part of the empire of Bornu.

In the fourteenth century, Islam spread to Bornu, following the same path as the caravan routes, and as happened with Christianity and the Roman Empire, Islam was adopted when the ruler of Bornu converted. The entire population rapidly followed suit. The Islamic legal code, as practiced in North Africa, was adopted, and judges trained in the Qur'an and in Islamic law were appointed by the Shehu to hear criminal cases. The Shehu and his appointed district heads heard and arbitrated personal and family disputes. The Kanuri believed that persons in authority at every administrative level up to the Shehu must be available every day to hear the disputes and complaints of their people.

The administrative structure of the state was centered in the capital city, from which the Shehu and his personal court governed. There were also districts, with their capitals, in which district heads, who were titled aristocrats, resided. Titles, positions, and their associated districts tended to be inherited along family lines, but these appointments were ultimately at the discretion of the Shehu, who could also depose the titleholders. Districts included many villages, with village headmen appointed by the district head. Though the village headship tended to be inherited along family lines, the officeholder had to demonstrate loyalty to the district head, who could appoint or depose him. Members of the district head's retinue, freemen or slaves, were assigned to collect taxes from villages and nomadic pastoral peoples in the district. These pastoral peoples, who were Fulani, not Kanuri, paid their taxes by patrilineage, according to the number of cattle that they owned.

Though the Bornu government was a hierarchical structure with the Shehu at the apex, politics operated with regard to succession to that position. Only the son of a man who had been Shehu could himself become Shehu. But the Shehu had many wives, including slave wives, so there were always many contenders. After the death of a Shehu, the eligible contenders vied for support among the members of the council of aristocrats, who made the final decision, and politics was rife until a successor was chosen. When a new Shehu came to power, the district heads had to shift their loyalty to him or else lose their positions. On the other hand, the new Shehu would appoint as many of his own supporters to district head positions as he wished. In the same way, a reshuffling of power at the district level led to the appointment of new village heads.

Under British colonial rule, Kanuri officials of the indigenous state structure, including the Shehu, carried out the actual administration of districts, applied native law, and collected the taxes. They were supervised by British officials under a lieutenant governor who resided in the provincial capital. Real authority was in the hands of the colonial masters. Under British pacification, the Kanuri army had been disbanded. After gaining independence in 1960, Bornu became a province within the new state. Nigeria had a democratic government for a brief time, but since 1966 it has been ruled by military governments, although democratic elections have taken place and a civilian government is currently in control.

Law and Social Control

At various points in this chapter, we have touched upon the subject of law. Anthropologists have been interested in the way disputes have been settled in the societies they have studied. In the absence of any written legal codes or formal courts before which lawyers argued cases, anthropologists in the field would listen to and record the manner in which disputes were aired and conflicts resolved. By doing this, they

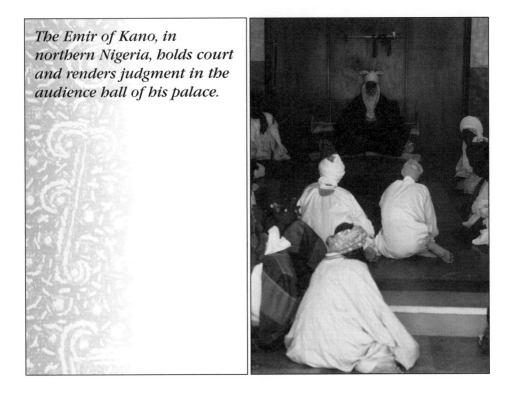

The Emir of Kano, in northern Nigeria, holds court and renders judgment in the audience hall of his palace.

tried to get at the rules, what constitutes proper behavior in light of those rules, what is the acceptable range of deviation from the rules, and what is unacceptable behavior and how it is dealt with and punished. The legal principles or bases upon which disputes are resolved were frequently not explicitly verbalized by the people. They emerge only through the analysis of cases, from which anthropologists have abstracted the legal principles that are the basis for decision making. As with other aspects of culture, law is a cultural system of meanings that the anthropologist must interpret (Fuller, 1994: 11).

Anthropologists have come to realize that "classic" studies in legal anthropology written in the decades between the 1930s and 1960s were studies of legal systems that had already been transformed as a consequence of European contact and encapsulation within colonial empires. As Fuller notes about one of the South African societies whose legal system had been intensively studied, "Tswana 'law and custom,' in other words, became more law-like as the indigenous normative order was reconstituted within the new colonial environment, in which Christianity and trade were at least as crucial as the colonial legal system itself" (1994: 10).

The broadest anthropological approach to law considers that whenever conflicts or disputes arise and a cultural mechanism for resolving them exists, or behavioral infractions occur that are punished in some way, we are dealing with law. There are also anthropologists who argue that law should be more strictly defined and recognize it as being present only when it exists as a codified system with courts, judges, and a penal system. Societies without written legal codes had a variety of ways to settle conflicts or disputes, which some might consider fundamentally law. Sometimes the two parties thrashed it out themselves; the solution might be a fair one, or the stronger party would force the weaker to capitulate. Sometimes each side mobilized support from people with whom they had economic relationships (as among the Ndendeuli of southern Tanzania). Song contests might be held in which an audience decided the winner (as among both the Inuit and the Tiv of Nigeria), or the disputants might simply disperse (which is what the Hadza of Tanzania did).

Some societies have an authority who, as a third party, acts to resolve disputes and either decides the case on its merits or plays the role of a mediator. Such authorities may be political leaders or judges who have the power or influence to force the disputants to accept their decisions or recommendations. The legal principle applied in a particular case becomes the legal principle for future cases. This idea of universal application is what makes it a principle of law, rather than simply the political decision of someone in authority. When a legal decision is made after a violation of the law, some sort of sanction must be applied, possibly the use of force. A punishment just as severe may result if the community avoids someone or shames a person by public flogging. Other methods of social control in addition to the law include gossip and accusations of witchcraft, a topic to be discussed in greater detail in Chapter 10.

In complex societies, a distinction is made between civil, or private, law and criminal, or public, law. Civil law deals with private disputes between individuals, in which society acts as an arbitrator. For example, if a car stops short on a highway and your car plows into it, the owner of the car will take you to civil court and sue you for damages to his car. Criminal law deals with crimes, such as theft, assault, and murder, that are considered offenses against society as a whole. The wronged party against whom a crime has been committed is not allowed to punish the offender himself; the accused perpetrator is tried in criminal court. Since private disputes in small-scale societies rend the fabric of the social structure, they are dealt with as actions against society as a whole and no distinction is made between civil and criminal law.

Law is also associated with morality and value systems. When viewed as a series of statements of what constitutes proper behavior, the law differentiates right from wrong, good from bad. In our own legal system, some of our laws represent, in effect, the continuation of ancient religious commandments, such as "Thou shall not steal." For most members of the society, laws of this sort have been internalized. That is, most people do not break such laws, not because they are afraid of being punished but because if they did break such laws, they would feel guilty. The enforcer of the law is the person's own conscience.

Postcolonial nation-states, like the Sudan and Papua New Guinea, have been very interested in anthropological studies of customary law. They have sought to take into account the various forms of customary law found within their borders in creating legal codes for their nations, rather than simply adopting Western-oriented legal systems.

The concept of legal pluralism, which refers to the relationship between indigenous forms of law and the originally foreign (European or American) law that developed in colonial and postcolonial societies, may also be used to describe the situation that develops when people migrate from postcolonial states to European countries. This has occurred in France when Muslim people from Algeria and other parts of North Africa migrate there with their Islamic culture and Islamic legal ideas (Botiveau, 1992-1993). There are two possibilities—either the Islamic migrants completely submit to the hegemony of the French legal system or the French legal system takes into account the Islamic legal system. During the colonial period, Islamic law had already been codified in accordance with the French legal system in both Egypt and Algeria, so migrants were familiar with more modern procedures. For example, the modern legal systems in Arab states such as Syria, Jordan, and Morocco require that civil marriages or the civil registration of a marriage takes place before the Muslim religious ceremony.

At present, with regard to matrimonial matters, foreign Muslims in France to some extent may choose the law that they wish to be applied. French mayors cannot celebrate polygamous marriages, but a Muslim man can choose to have a consular marriage, though this marriage has no legal status in France. When polygamous marriages have taken place prior to emigration, the French courts have recognized the husband's obligation to support each wife. Nor could the second wife of a polygamous North African migrant be denied entry into France. However, if a North African man first marries a French woman and then a North African woman, the latter's right to inherit is barred by the French courts. With regard to child custody in mixed French-Algerian marriages, particularly when the mother is French, the results sometimes have to be negotiated directly by the two governments because a judicial solution cannot be reached. Islamic revivalism has developed today in France, and Islamic law is accepted by the French if there is no contradiction "with public order." When Muslims become French citizens, the definition of equality of rights is at stake and "Islamic positive law" is becoming a part of French legal culture (Botiveau, 1992-1993: 96).

In recent years, Native Americans have more and more frequently been engaged in legal battles with federal and state governments as well as with non-Native Americans, asserting their hunting and fishing rights, or their rights over land promised them in treaties, or the freedom to pursue their own religious practices, or their rights to tribal cultural objects now in the hands of various museums. These cases represent the clash between Native American cultural practice and state-instituted legal practice. This confrontation can be seen, for example, in cases involving the use of Native American sacred sites. In the past, tribal people have been discouraged from using the courts to protect their freedom of religious expression because legal doctrines often categorize such customary religious expression with fringe nonindigenous religions, which mainstream Americans regard with great skepticism (Carillo, 1998: 277). In 1978, Congress passed the American Indian Religious Freedom Act, which was supposed to protect Native American religious expression. Though this act was supported in principle, only sometimes did the courts uphold Native American claims. In others, such as *Lyng* v. *Northwest Indian Cemetery Protective Association,* in which a road construction project was to invade sacred sites that were significant in the belief systems of native people of Northwest California, the Native American litigants lost their case (Carillo, 1998: 7).

In another case, Earl Platt was unsuccessful when he tried to prevent the Zuni from crossing his land when they made their regular quadrennial summer solstice pilgrimage from their reservation to the mountain area they called Kohlu/wala:wa in northeastern Arizona (*U.S. on Behalf of the Zuni Tribe* v. *Platt,* 7300 F. Supp. 318 1990, in Carillo, 1998). In this case, the United States government acted on behalf of the Zuni when in 1985, Platt, one of the largest landowners in Arizona, challenged the right of the Zuni to cross his land and sought to interfere with their pilgrimage. Evidence was presented indicating that the pilgrimage had been taking place at the time of the Spanish conquest of the area and until recently had been largely uncontested. The area is believed by the Zuni to be their place of origin and the home of their dead. The trek, which takes four days and is 110 miles long, has been consistently the same. The Zuni had lost control over the ancestral land, which the pilgrimage traversed, after 1876. To the Zuni, the pilgrimage was the fulfillment of a religious obligation (Meshorer, 1998: 318). One of the problems encountered during the trial, which has characterized other court cases regarding Native American religious practice, was the need to present evidence to support the case while at the same time trying to avoid revealing ritual place-names and esoteric information that normally remains secret. Since Zuni witnesses were reluctant to testify, archaeological, ethnohistorical, and contemporary information from non-Indian local inhabitants was provided to demonstrate that the Zuni pilgrimage continued to be held. In its decision, the court deemed that the defendant, Platt, was aware that the pilgrimage had been taking place and went across his property, that such usage was "actual, open and notorious, continuous and uninterrupted," that "such use was known to the surrounding community," and that the Zuni believed that their crossing was a matter of right (*Zuni Tribe* v. *Platt,* in Carillo, 1998: 318). The court then ordered that the Zuni be granted an easement over Earl Platt's land for 25 feet in either direction of the route of their pilgrimage for a 2-day period every four years during the summer solstice, without rights to use Platt's water, or light fires on this pathway, and with the necessity to notify Platt at least 14 days before the pilgrimage.

Not only Native American religious practices, but the religious practices of ethnic minorities are also challenged in the courts despite the fact that the United States has had a long tradition of accommodating cultural differences. Especially in the area of religious practices, one would expect a wide degree of tolerance in a nation whose earliest settlers came here seeking freedom from religious persecution. However, the Supreme Court case *Church of the Lukumi* v. *City of Hialeah, South Florida* (Palmie, 1996) reminds us that the American majority, if permitted, will suppress religious practices that it finds offensive. Hialeah is part of greater Miami, and its politics are dominated by Cuban Americans who escaped from Cuba during the Cuban Revolution. These Cuban-American political leaders are successful middle-class people who, though proud of their Cuban heritage, seek to distance themselves from the waves of lower-class Cubans who came here during the Mariel "invasion." The Church of the Lukumi Babalu Aye, of the Afro-Cuban religion known as Santeria, which had its origins in Cuba in the 1930s, moved into Hialeah in 1987. One of its religious practices is the sacrifice of live animals to "feed the gods." This brought about an impassioned debate within the Hialeah City Council. Anglos saw sacrifice as a form of devil worship, and even the Cuban Americans on the city council sought to distance themselves from Santeria. As the Hispanic chaplain to the police department testified, "Nations that are controlled by this system of religion are in darkness, and the Bible says that these things are an abomination to the Lord" (Palmie, 1996: 188–189). In 1987, the mayor of Hialeah approved a bill outlawing the sacrifice, and the possession for sacrificial purposes, of animals in the city of Hialeah (Palmie, 1996: 193). Within two weeks, Ernesto Prichard, a Santeria practitioner and leader of the Lukumi Church, filed suit against the mayor and the city council. Though two lower courts upheld the ordinances, in June, 1993, the United States Supreme Court ruled that these ordinances unlawfully suppressed rights guaranteed by the First Amendment. Justice Kennedy, in his opinion, wrote: "Although the practice of animal sacrifice may seem abhorrent to some, religious beliefs need not be acceptable, logical or comprehensible to others in order to merit First Amendment protection" (Palmie, 1996: 185). As we will see in our discussion of American multiculturalism in a later chapter, tension continually exists in American society between the desires of the (white Christian) majority to assert themselves and the rights of minorities to express religious beliefs that differ from those of the majority.

War and Peace

If crimes and disputes represent conflict within a social group, warfare represents conflict between groups. Decisions about going to war are among the most important decisions made by those in positions of authority. Warfare, feuds, and revenge seeking are resorted to when no lawful, mutually acceptable means of peaceful resolution of conflicts between social groups exists. Under such conditions, one group will make the decision to take hostile action against the other group to force it to submit. Anthropologists have defined *feuding* as hostile action between members of the same group and *warfare* as hostile action between different groups. Feuds, conducted according to rules, involve collective, not personal, responsibility, so revenge can be taken against any member of the group. In a segmentary lineage system, such as that found among the Enga, discussed earlier, it is hard to tell the difference between feuding and warfare, because subclans within the same clan may fight each other on one occasion but come together as a single clan when fighting another clan. It is then hard to say which is feud and which is war.

Contrary to the belief that warfare is a no-holds-barred action aimed at exterminating one's foe, it operates according to cultural rules, like all other forms of cultural behavior. Peacemaking, the opposite of warfare, is also governed by cultural rules, as we shall see below. Anthropologists have attempted to comprehend warfare in small-scale societies to try to understand it in today's complex societies. Unfortunately, by the time most anthropologists went to do field research, those small-scale societies that they studied had been conquered and pacified and were under colonial rule or were parts of nation-states. It is only from field descriptions of societies in Amazonia and New Guinea, where warfare continued despite contact with Europeans and colonial rule, that we have some understanding of indigenous ideas about warfare, its causes, and how it was conducted. There is also ethnohistorical data on how warfare was conducted by Native Americans during the early period of European colonization.

One of the fullest accounts of warfare practiced by a small-scale society is that of the Yanomamo in Amazonia (Chagnon, 1992). There are several levels of hostility among the Yanomamo, each of them representing a distinct phase in the escalation of conflict, but hostilities can terminate at any level. The chest-pounding duel is the most innocuous form of fighting, halfway between a sporting contest and a fight. It can take place between two individuals of the same village or, on the occasion of a feast, between the men of two different villages. In a chest-pounding duel, men are paired and take turns striking each other on the pectoral muscle of the chest with a bare fist. Chest-pounding duels arise from accusations of cowardice, stinginess with food, or gossip. The next, more-intensive level is the side-slapping contest, in which the blow is administered with a hand to the side of the body between the ribs and the pelvis. The provocations are the same as for the chest-pounding duel. The third level is the club fight, which can also take place within or between villages. Two men attack one another with wooden clubs 8 to 10 feet long and attempt to hit each other on the skull. Such fights typically arise as a result of arguments over women. These contests end when one opponent withdraws. The most intensive kind of hostility is the raid, conducted by one village against another, which one could define as warfare. Villages that have a history of being enemies raid one another to take revenge for past killings. However, even when there is no immediate history of enmity between villages, hostile relations can build from a club fight to raiding if one or another individual has been seriously injured or killed. Though raiding may be precipitated by motives of revenge, women are frequently captured in the course of a raid, and this becomes another reason to continue to raid.

Periods of warfare alternate with periods of peace for the Yanomamo as for all other peoples. According to Chagnon, the Yanomamo are both warriors and peacemakers, in that "peacemaking often requires the threat or actual use of force" (1992: 7). The Yanomamo ceremonial dialogue, or *wayamou,* is a ritual that takes place as a way of making peace when relations between villages that normally have close ties are deteriorating or when people from more distant, potentially hostile villages come to visit. The venting of grievances prevents violence from breaking out, and the ceremonial dialogue strengthens existing connections. Pairs of individuals from both sides speak in succession in a reciprocal exchange of words. Stylized body movements, rapid speech, and particular rhetorical features, such as metaphors, metonyms, repetition, and incomplete sentences, are utilized. The subject matter of the dialogue may include warfare, gender relations, hunting, magic, and witchcraft. Goods are often requested, which will be returned when the present hosts of the feast are invited to a feast at some future time.

Once gold was discovered in the Yanamamo area of Northwest Brazil, the Yanomamo became the victims of raids by gun-toting Brazilian gold miners, who successfully took over their land. In this conflict, Yanomamo rules of warfare and peacemaking no longer applied.

Anthropologists have been very concerned with offering explanations for warfare. Most find unsatisfactory the explanation, frequently offered, that warfare is due to instinctive human aggressiveness. Warfare is prevalent at certain times and not others, and under certain conditions and not others. The task of the anthropologist is to

The side-slapping duel among the Yanomamo represents a low level of conflict, but one that can escalate.

explain why warfare occurs when and where it does. Proposing a universal human aggressive instinct cannot explain this variability. The Yanomamo themselves say that they go to war to avenge a previous killing and as a result of conflicts over women. But anthropological explanations for warfare must be distinguished from those of the combatants. Lizot (1994), who has also done fieldwork with the Yanomamo, likewise sees warfare and peace as related, or as transformations of one another that relate to the social structure of reciprocity in which sisters are exchanged, as well as goods at feasts (see Chapter 6). Revenge and warfare are also governed by reciprocity; when a killing occurs, it must be avenged by a return killing. Lizot's explanation of Yanomamo warfare is a structural one—warfare is the exchange of blow for blow and blood for blood, while peace is the exchange of sister for sister, feast for feast, and goods for goods. Earlier, Chagnon argued that the Yanomamo went to war in order to maintain their political autonomy (1983). More recently, he has adopted a sociobiological approach, noting that successful warriors known as *unokais* (men who have killed) have more wives and over three times as many children than do other men (Chagnon, 1997: 205). He concludes that the cause of warfare is ultimately biological or reproductive success. Harris has offered a competing cultural materialist explanation, indicating that

Yanomamo villages need large forest areas for hunting, and warfare results when villages are in competition for hunting territory to ensure their supply of protein (1984). Chagnon disagrees, arguing that the Yanomamo have more than an adequate supply of protein and are not competing over hunting territory. In a more recent reanalysis of all the historical and ethnographic data on the different Yanomamo groups in both Venezuela and in Brazil, Ferguson argues "that the actual practice of war among the Yanomami is explainable largely as a result of antagonisms related to scarce, coveted and unequally distributed Western manufactured goods" (1995: 8). He claims that before Western contact, warfare was limited or absent among the Yanomamo (Ferguson, 1995: 75). When Western goods were introduced, access was unequal, leading to conflict between Yanomamo groups and increased warfare. Koch offers another kind of explanation for warfare in small-scale societies based on his research among the Jale in New Guinea. He claims that warfare breaks out when no third party exists to settle disputes. In his view, war is just another means of dispute settlement.

Many of the points made about warfare in small-scale societies are also applicable to complex societies. The motives of those who carry out the war, both the soldiers and the planners, are different from the causes of war as seen by analysts. For example, the United States declared war on Japan after Pearl Harbor was bombed. We, as natives, explain the war as a result of Japan's aggressive act. A disinterested analyst might explain the war as a result of the fact that Japan, an increasingly more powerful and industrializing state, needed to expand its sphere of influence to obtain more raw materials, such as oil from Indonesia (then the Dutch East Indies), and thereby impinged on the U.S. sphere of influence in the Pacific.

Like the wars fought by the Yanomamo, our wars are also conducted according to rules. After World War I, the use of poison gas in warfare was outlawed by international agreement. The Korean War was conducted as a limited war—limited in that nuclear weapons were not used. When certain unspoken agreements about the geographical extent of the war were violated and the United States moved its troops north of the Yalu River, the People's Republic of China entered the war and the level of conflict escalated.

Materialist or ecological explanations of warfare seem to be as applicable to modern complex societies as they are to small-scale societies. The desire to obtain more land or other important strategic resources, such as mineral wealth or oil, has often caused warfare in modern times. Sometimes modern states carry out preemptive strikes, that is, attacks on the enemy when they believe that the enemy is about to launch an attack. This corresponds to Chagnon's explanation of Yanomamo warfare as being conducted to maintain the political autonomy of a group. In a sense, this same explanation operates for ethnic groups today who are trying to maintain their autonomy within a larger nation-state. Sometimes, as in the Kosovo crisis, Albanians used warfare to try to gain their independence from Yugoslavia.

◼ Politics in the Contemporary Nation-State

Many political anthropologists are interested in the modern nation-state. It is necessary at this point to distinguish between state and nation or nation-state. As noted earlier, the state is a type of political organization. It may be culturally homogeneous or, more likely, include members of several different cultural or ethnic groups. The idea of *nation* or *nation-state* developed in Europe with the rise of nationalism, which assumed that a people who had a culture and a language should constitute a separate nation or nation-state. The concept of nation-state links an ethnic ideology with a state organization. *Ethnonationalism* refers to the desire on the part of a minority ethnic group in a multiethnic state to have its own nation-state. In many of the states that succeeded colonial empires in Africa and Asia, attempts were made to develop a new national culture, and as we shall see below, the results have been highly variable. In Chapter 14 we will discuss in greater detail the ways minority ethnic groups in states in which other ethnic groups are dominant are today seeking their autonomy or independence.

Anthropologists interested in contemporary politics have found the distinction between social structure and social organization, referred to in Chapter 1, particularly useful. Though they agree that political structure is important, they have focused primarily upon the organizational dimension—how individuals go about making choices and decisions in the political arena and the factors involved in such choices. Choosing to support one leader over another or one faction over another is a decision that will determine who will have power. The person who gains power makes administrative decisions, rewards supporters, and punishes the opposition.

One of the recurring themes in the study of local-level politics has been factionalism. Many of the earlier studies of peasant communities in the Old and New Worlds explored the operation of political factionalism as it related to the way national politics was played out on the local level. Leaders of factions vying for power may build their followings in a number of different ways, depending upon the structure of the village community. The faction consisting of the leader and his followers is much like the Big Man and his followers. Like the Big Man, the leader of a faction is in opposition to other faction leaders. The faction leader vies with other leaders to attract followers, as does the Big Man. There is an exchange relationship between the faction leader and his followers, as there is between the Big Man and his followers, and both types of leaders need to continue supporting and rewarding followers in order to hold onto them. When the leader in either case loses power or dies, the faction or group of followers dissolves. In this aspect, factions contrast with political parties, which continue to exist though individual leaders may come and go. However, within political parties in the United States, factions may be found on a local level as party leaders and their supporters compete for control of the party apparatus at that level. In nation-states, factionalism may be based on differences in ethnic background. In such situations factionalism may be transformed into ethnic conflict.

The *patron-client relationship* discussed in connection with *compadrazgo* in Chapter 6 also has important political dimensions. Patrons, frequently landowners, play roles as intermediaries between the peasants of a village and the provincial or national government. Problems with tax collectors and the court system bring clients to their patrons, who are always of a higher class, for assistance. The patrons can help clients because of their wide social contacts with their social equals in the towns and cities. The social contacts of clients, in contrast, are usually entirely within their own villages. Though there are no links of actual kinship between patrons and clients, the *compadrazgo* ties between the families of patron and clients may be perpetuated over generations. Patrons as landlords and clients as tenants are distinguished by their differential access to land and by their class differences as gentry and peasants. These social and economic differences are the basis for a difference in political power. Patron-client relationships may be superseded when opposition between socioeconomic classes serves to separate and oppose them.

A form of patron-client relationship continues to be important in the political economy of Bangladesh. At first a homeland for Bengali Muslims and a province of the Islamic republic of Pakistan, Bangladesh became an independent nation in 1971 after a bloody civil war. Earlier, it was basically a peasant society composed of a great number of small landholders and tenants at the bottom, overlaid by a small group of landlords and rent collectors, all of whom formed the mass of commoners, with an upper-class nobility of urban Bengal who had little in common with the rest. This dichotomy, present until the late nineteenth century, has been replaced by a system based on landownership, wealth, education, and power, in which a hierarchical network of interpersonal patron-client relationships dominates (Kochanek, 1993: 44). In the countryside, this system is reinforced by economic forces, such as scarcity of credit, land, tenancy contracts, and employment opportunities, along with political factors, such as the need for protection. The concept of *daya,* meaning "grace" or "blessing," constitutes the intellectual underpinning of the reciprocal patron-client relationship. Individuals feel that they have the moral right to demand food and subsistence from those "well placed," and the well-placed individuals, who acquire their prosperity from a higher moral authority, are expected to give generously to their clients. The patrons who distribute are expected to be authoritarian and to be feared and obeyed (Kochanek, 1993: 45).

This pattern of patron-client relationship has extended beyond the rural area and has come to dominate not only the whole of the Bangladesh political process but the business community as well. Though Bangladesh has formal legal, constitutional, and administrative governmental structures, these have come to be monopolized by a "traditional pattern of patron-client relationships based on *tadbir,* a process of personal lobbying" (Kochanek, 1993: 251). Policy making and implementation always require personal connections. For example, the entire governmental structure of General Erhsad from 1982, when he came to power as a result of a military coup, to 1990 was based on the patron-client pattern. He traveled through the countryside "like a ward boss distributing benefits in exchange for support" (Kochanek, 1993: 265). The business community, which is in its early stages of development and modernization, is characterized by the same pattern, with primary emphasis on personal relationships. Businessmen often obtain exemptions from rules and other kinds of business benefits by manipulating the regulatory system and the administration of policy, using their personal connections. Patron-client relationships from the countryside to the capital are a way of life in Bangladesh.

Patron-client relations have been seen as characterizing the Mafia in the United States and in Sicily. The patron-client relationship is characteristic of the Sicilian rural scene from which the American Mafia emigrated. As we all know, the American Mafia don serves as godfather to the children of his followers. A study of the Mafia in Sicily and in Detroit explicitly likens the don to a Big Man (Louwe, 1986). The Big Man in the Mafia family provides for a source of income for his "family" and protection against the risks of making money illegally; in return, family members pay him respect, grant him complete obedience, and give him a share of their profits from the criminal enterprise. His status is achieved through the demonstration of his ability. The don maintains his influence by manipulating his connections with the police, politicians, and judges. Loyalty of followers to him is paramount. The greatest threat to the family is the member who is turned into an informer by the police. A son may succeed his father as don and continue as patron to his father's clients. However, more in keeping with the Big Man structure, the clients whose patron has died may move to become followers of another don.

Within the past decade, the media have begun to refer to the Russian Mafia in the United States. Not much is known about the organization of crime among Russians, many of them Jewish, who began to emigrate in large numbers in the late 1970s and who settled in that part of Brooklyn known as Brighton Beach, now often referred to as "Odessa by the Sea." In a recent study, *Russian Mafia in America,* there was disagreement regarding whether Soviet émigré criminal groups operated like La Cosa Nostra or were less organizationally complex and hierarchical. However, particular leaders have been identified as "capo di tutti capi" (Finckenhauer and Waring, 1998: 164). Many Brighton Beach residents, in discussing crime in their area, used the term *Russian Mafia* and saw the Italian Mafia and Soviet émigré crime groups as being very similar in their mode of organization. Others saw Russian crime groups as less well organized, resembling, perhaps, the first stage of the development of the Italian Mafia, with leadership and followership not yet fully distinct (Finckenhauer and Waring, 1998: 224–226). The film *Shanghai Triad* shows the organization of a Chinese crime organization with its boss in complete control. His henchmen or followers came from the same rural area as did the boss and all had the same family name of Tang, indicating they were related and were members of the same clan. Like the Mafia, the Chinese triad uses the ties of kinship to ensure loyalty.

Colonialism and the emergence of new nation-states in Africa and Asia have brought about great political changes. Traditional forms of leadership and politics were transformed as they were integrated into the state systems of these new nations. Modern methods of social control were also introduced to deal with detection and prevention of crime. However, as has happened in many parts of the world, the new modern Western forms did not completely replace the older indigenous forms, but existed side by side with them. In Ghana, a police force was established soon after conquest by the British (Abotchie, 1997). The British colonial government curtailed the authority and jurisdiction of the indigenous political leadership. The jurisdiction over all criminal and civil cases was vested in a Supreme Court, with colonial district commissioners dealing with lesser offences. Postindependence governments modernized the police force and expanded the court system to include magistrate's, district, and circuit courts when the level of crime rose.

Social change and the impact of formal education and Christianity have wrought many changes in the lives of the southern Ewe of Ghana. However, Abotchie describes in detail the way in which despite "the prohibition under the Criminal Code of some of the traditional modes of crime control such as trial by ordeal, the 'patronage' of these techniques has persisted side by side with modern methods of crime control" (1997: 7). Many people, though nominally Christian (Abotchie calls them "Christians of little faith"), still believe in the traditional deities and express fear of them. As a consequence, traditional forces serve as a greater deterrent to criminal activity than do modern police methods and the fear of imprisonment (Abotchie, 1997: 116–119). The Ghanaian police are seen as corruptible. They may be bought, and one may escape from them. Prison is not viewed as a reforming experience, and police activity is seen as retarding justice. Supernatural forces, however, are inescapable, and their penalties are more severe. Those involved with the deities who accept bribes will suffer their wrath, or instant death. Though lineage leaders and chiefs have lost their politico-legal authority, their "religious functions, and [the] sanctions of the lineage head and the chief, however, remain effective . . .: besides, both rulers still hold themselves accountable to the supernatural forces" (Abotchie, 1997:128). Ceremonies and rituals serve to reinforce the traditional system of values and norms. Though female puberty rites and marriage rituals have been transformed, participation in the "outdooring" of the newborn—during which the child is named and is symbolically socialized into society and introduced to the notion of good and evil—and mortuary rites are still performed.

Western Samoa is now an independent country. Its chiefly system, which had been its political organization before contact with Europeans 200 years ago, has undergone an interesting transformation under the effects of urbanization, modernization, economic transformation, and the emigration of a large number of Samoans to the city and to other nations (Yamamoto, 1994). Earlier, each 'aiga—cognatic kin group—had its own housing plots, farmland, and chiefly title names—or matai—each with certain prestige, privileges, and role. The matai titleholders of each 'aiga attended ritualized council meetings and governed the villages, which were autonomous. As the system was transformed by Western contact, the higher titles and forms of authority fell into disuse, leaving only the matai holders at the village level. The matai had an important role to play in ceremonial exchange, although those ceremonial exchanges were formerly only for high chiefs and their families. They have now come to be practiced by every matai, as titles became equalized, more goods became available, and the number of ceremonies increased. The criteria for matai selection has changed, including not only connection to the 'aiga through male or female descent, since even spouses of members have succeeded to titles. The increase of "title splitting" has permitted the proliferation of titleholders and also made possible the bestowal of titles on many nonresidents.

Earlier, titleholders were required to reside with the 'aiga and assume chiefly duties, attend all functions, and care for the 'aiga. However, as people have moved away, even to New Zealand and the United States, they have continued to maintain contact and send cash remittances, which are important for ceremonial exchanges and house building. As a consequence, these expatriates have become nonresident matai. Even those who do not plan to return, along with second-generation émigrés, hold on to titles in order to maintain connections. Their monetary contributions are important to enable the 'aiga to maintain its prestige. Giving titles to well-known or important members of the 'aiga not only recognizes their accomplishments but connects the 'aiga to a conspicuous individual to the 'aiga's benefit. In this way, the matai system has expanded and functions to tie overseas Samoans to their homeland, to the benefit of all parties.

Today's nation-states contain culturally diverse populations. The newly emerged states of Africa and Asia were successors to colonies that were arbitrarily carved out by the colonial powers. These colonies brought together as a single political entity tribal groups that often were very diverse culturally. Lewis has recently made the point that precolonial states in Africa, such as the kingdom of Ethiopia and Zulu, Bemba, and Ganda states, were also multiethnic in their composition (1999: 58 ff.). This was also true of other conquest states, like the empire of Bornu, described earlier in this chapter, which included non-Kanuri peoples like the Bagirmi. After independence was gained, tribalism was seen as a problem to be overcome in forging a new national identity. However, tribalism does not die; rather, it is transformed and then maintained as ethnic difference. Though the ideology of ethnicity is new, the members of an ethnic group have returned to a conceptualization of themselves as all related by bonds of kinship. When the state developed, the kinship links tying a community together disappeared, only to return as an ideal when ethnicity becomes important.

Ethnic differences become the basis of political competition in the new nation-states. The drive to establish a national culture may be (or is often seen as) an attempt by the dominant and most powerful group or the numerically superior ethnic group to establish its culture as the national culture. This was the case with the Javanese, who dominate Indonesia. In the former Soviet Union there had been efforts to develop a "communist" culture, but this became, by and large, an attempt to Russify the distinctly different Central Asian and Caucasian peoples. This policy was met with opposition but little overt conflict because of Soviet suppression. Under the policy of glasnost, which opened up Soviet society, ethnicity and nationalism reasserted themselves, and many republics, such as the Baltic states, Moldavia, the Ukraine, Tadjikistan, Kazakstan, Kyrgyzstan, and Uzbekistan, became politically independent. For the non-Russian republics, this meant moving out from under the domination of Russian culture. These independent states now have the problems of defining themselves as nations and dealing with their own internal ethnic minorities. In Sri Lanka ethnic conflict has exploded into prolonged warfare between the dominant Sinhalese and the Tamil ethnic minority, which is demanding independence, or at least cultural autonomy. The attempt on the part of the Indian government to submerge the Sikh ethnic and religious minority has resulted in guerrilla warfare and a demand for Sikh autonomy. The Kurdish ethnic minority, which straddles the borders between Turkey, Syria, Iran, and Iraq, has been fighting an unending war of independence in order to establish its own state.

Even after hundreds of years of existence as independent nation-states, tribalism and ethnic differences continue to be manifested periodically. The southern area of Belgium, Walloonia, where French is spoken, is in conflict with the northern area, where Flemish, a Dutch dialect, is spoken. The conflict concerns not only language but also control over economic resources. Each of these areas of Belgium now has its own legislature and regional executives, and the central government includes a fixed proportion of ministers from each group. The topic of ethnic conflict, why and when it arises, and its relationship to class conflict will be considered in greater detail in Chapter 14.

At the beginning of this chapter we talked about power as the ability to command others and authority as the institutionalization of power. Over the past decade, a new term, *empowerment,* has become a buzzword in many political contexts. It has been used variously to refer to actions by the people to get what they want, populist action, revolt from below to subvert those in authority, and the devolution of power to place it in the hands of the have-nots. Using the ideas of Foucault about the way in which power is vested in discourse, one can say that with empowerment, the have-nots gain a voice. When successive African states gained their independence, empowerment of the African populace was a primary policy. In Zimbabwe, for example, when independence was gained in 1980, there was a presidential directive on Africanization of the Zimbabwean civil service. Its goal was the indigenization of the civil service and the empowerment of the African population. Though the public sector and various types of funds are now managed by indigenous Zimbabweans, most Zimbabweans continue to participate in the economy as unskilled, seasonal, and unpaid domestic and agricultural laborers. The policy of indigenization and empowerment of the black population has been articulated by the male, black, self-employed business lobby. The rest of the black population, however, was convinced that black politicians and leading bureaucrats were interested only in empowering themselves (Gaidzanwa, 1999: 118–119). Those Zimbabwean groups lobbying for empowerment, such as the Indigenous Business Development Council, a black business lobby; the Affirmative Action Group, which included the War Veterans' Association; and the Indigenous Businesswomen's Organization, themselves were still involved in patronage politics, by and large. Even the businesswomen's group, which was organized to combat the problems women encountered in venturing into business in a male-dominated world, and which explicitly supports the economic empowerment of black women, supported Robert Mugabe in the 1996 election and relies on the patronage of his ruling party. There have been no plans for the democratization of landholding, from which women are barred, though they are the sources of labor and management. The emphasis has been on acquiring land from white farmers. It is clear that the term *empowerment* serves as an effective political slogan; in Zimbabwe the policy of indigenization and empowerment, in practical terms, has meant the empowerment of a limited, predominantly male, political circle.

The concepts we have discussed in this chapter can be applied to our own society. The operation of leadership in terms of power and exchange, the politics of empowerment, bureaucracy and administration, the emergence of leaders through political maneuvering, factionalism, and patron-client relationships are as relevant to political situations in our own society as they were in the situations in which they were described. For example, in the past, the ward boss in big American cities was like a New Guinea Big Man in redistributing patronage in the form of material benefits among the "ward heelers." Factions representing different political positions and coalitions operate at every level of our political system. They may coalesce around individuals or around an issue, such as abortion, equal rights for women, or affirmative action for minorities. Ethnic politics are as active today in American cities as they are in any nation-state in Asia or Africa. Elections pit Poles against African Americans in Chicago, Hispanics against Anglos in Texas and California, and Cubans against African Americans in Miami.

Political Economy

At the beginning of this chapter we again noted that political organization and economics are intimately interwoven and that this interrelationship is referred to as political economy. As shown throughout this chapter, the various types of political organization are associated with different forms of distribution and often different forms of production. For example, chieftainship is interwoven with redistribution systems, described in Chapter 8, where surplus goods funnel into the central political position, that of the chief, and are distributed on ceremonial occasions to other chiefs, who in turn redistribute to their followers. The chief maintains political authority by controlling and disbursing economic goods, while the economic system is dependent upon the establishment of fixed positions of authority. The only kind of political structures with which markets are associated are state structures. The state as a political system, as we have pointed out, operates on a territorial basis beyond the level of kinship and clanship, and the less personal relationships of a market are in accord with this type of system.

Ortner's discussion of political economy as a framework of analysis points out its advantages (1984). She notes that an approach in terms of political economy is very open to symbolic analysis. Throughout this chapter, we have indicated how symbols are used to express rank and authority—as, for example, among the Trobrianders. Among the Kachin, who oscillate between two forms of political structure, the Big Man of the *gumlao* type and the chieftainship of the *gumsa,* symbols are used in different ways to express these opposing structures. In the context of the modern nation-state, symbols become a powerful means of constructing ethnic identity, and they are employed to express ethnic conflicts as well as class struggles.

As opposed to an emphasis on particular societies as isolates, political economy tends to promote a regional perspective. As we pointed out, systems of ceremonial exchange such as the *kula* demonstrate how societies with differing political systems are joined in a regional system of ceremonial exchange and barter. An emphasis on political economy can show how societies have been drawn into a world system, a topic to be explored in greater detail in Chapter 13.

The discussion of political organization in anthropology involves the use of a number of concepts, such as the distinction between power and authority, and that between government and politics. There are various forms of political organization differing in degree of complexity, the nature of leadership, and the centralization of power. These include situational leadership, band organization, Big Man structure, chieftainship, and the state. Though formerly anthropologists were concerned with the nature of dispute settlement in the societies they studied, today legal pluralism and how it functions in complex nation-states is a focus of concern. There are cultural rules for conducting warfare as well as for making peace, in small-scale and in complex societies. When anthropologists turn their attention to political topics in contemporary nation-states, they focus on factionalism, ethnic politics, internal conflict, and the microanalysis of the political process.

Chapter Ten
Religion and the Supernatural

Many people in the world believe in an order of existence beyond the observable universe, that is, in the supernatural. For example, the Trobriand Islanders believe that when a person dies, his or her spirit splits in two. One part goes to live on the island of Tuma in the village of the dead, to remain there until it is reincarnated in the spirit of a newborn child. The other part of the spirit haunts the favorite places of the deceased, and its presence is frightening to the villagers still alive. They are even more afraid of sorcerers, especially flying witches, who are thought to have caused the death in the first place.

Beliefs in sorcery, spirits, and witchcraft are not limited to societies like that of the Trobriand Islanders. One can ride along a country road in England and see a billboard announcing an impending meeting of a local witches' coven to be held the following week. Meetings of American witches' covens are announced in the newspaper. There are people in England and America today who believe in witchcraft as a religion. To them, the witchcraft trials in seventeenth-century Salem, Massachusetts, were an example of religious persecution. Can witchcraft and Christianity coexist as sets of religious beliefs in a society like our own? Believers in witchcraft, like the believers of many other faiths in America today, are protected by the fundamental right to religious freedom. Is the modern belief in witches, or Wiccan, the same as the belief in witchcraft described in classic ethnographies?

Although our country is founded on freedom of worship and belief, one periodically finds accounts of religious communities that run afoul of the law in the practice of their religious rites. In the course of their religious rituals, Snake Handlers hold up venomous snakes. Believers, while in an ecstatic state, pick up large rattlesnakes, a practice based on the belief that if they are free of sin, worshipers will not be bitten by the snakes. This belief derives from the Scriptures, in which it is stated that "they shall speak with new tongues; they shall take up serpents" (the Bible). Members of this religious community, like many other fundamentalist Christian groups, take the Bible literally. Some people who are bitten during the ritual subsequently die. The worshipers believe that those who die in this way are being punished for their sins.

A contemporary witches' coven in Salem, Massachusetts, site of the seventeenth-century witch trials.

The snake, in this instance, is seen as acting as an agent of God. Whether a person is pure or sinful determines if the snake will bite that individual. This is a matter of belief, not an empirical explanation of why rattlesnakes bite. The cause of this phenomenon is understood to be supernatural. Though their beliefs may be considered extreme by some Americans, the Snake Handlers are part of the larger Christian community. Despite beliefs that seem aberrant to some, the sect is a historical offshoot of the Christian tradition, in which one aspect has been developed to an extreme.

The Trobriand belief in the power of sorcerers and the Snake Handlers' belief that, because of the purity of their character, God will protect them from the snake's bite go beyond the observable universe. Such explanations rely on phenomena that fall into the domain of the supernatural. From the Western point of view, empirical explanations of the observable world are scientific. Further, explanations that do not depend on empirical evidence, but instead rely on strongly held beliefs in nonempirical or supernatural forces, are categorized as religious. However, people in other societies, like the Trobrianders, consider their spiritual culture heroes and the ghosts of their ancestors absolutely real, no less real than the physical world around them. Culture heroes and ghosts are as real and natural as wind, rain, and thunder. In our society, scientific explanations that involve the forces of nature are distinct from religious beliefs and ideas about the supernatural.

How can we distinguish between religion as a belief in the supernatural and the other parts of culture? This is a question similar to the one encountered in the discussion of economics and political organization. Religious phenomena involve the use of symbols that evoke powerful emotional responses. One has merely to consider

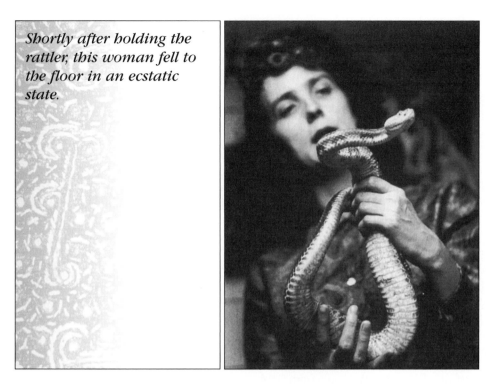

Shortly after holding the rattler, this woman fell to the floor in an ecstatic state.

the difference between water and holy water and the emotional response evoked only by the latter to realize this. Water is transformed into holy water by the blessing of a priest. However, symbols that evoke strong feelings are to be found in parts of culture not labeled religious. Political symbols, such as the flag and the national anthem, produce emotions. Sometimes the emotion evoked by secular symbols and secular rituals is as strong as a religious response.

Religion is defined as the cultural means by which humans deal with the supernatural, but humans also believe that the reverse is true—that the supernatural deals with humans. In this interaction, the supernatural is usually seen as powerful and human beings as weak. Another definition of religion has recently been proposed. Saler (1993) defines religion in terms of a pool of elements that tend to cluster together. They include a belief in God, gods, or "spiritual beings" with whom humans can have spiritual contact; a moral code believed to emanate from extrahuman sources; belief in a human ability to go beyond human suffering; and rituals that involve humans with the extrahuman (Saler, 1993: 219). The "spiritual beings" and the extrahuman of Saler's definition can be equated with what we call "the supernatural."

If religion involves the interaction of humans with the supernatural, then it is necessary to pose the question, Why do human beings believe in the existence of the supernatural in the first place? What is it about human life and the world in which that life is lived that seems to compel human beings to propose that the world is governed by forces beyond their empirical observations? Many theorists over the years have attempted to answer this question. Max Weber (1930) has argued that since life is made up of pain and suffering, human beings have developed religion to explain why they were put on earth to suffer. Sigmund Freud (1928) proposed that religious institutions represent society's way of dealing with childish needs of dependency on the part of individuals. What would otherwise be a neurotic trait thereby finds expression in the form of all-powerful gods and deities who control the individual's destiny. Melford Spiro (1966) has attempted to deal with the issue of religion by suggesting three kinds of needs that religion fulfills. The first is called the cognitive need, that is, the need to understand. This is the need for explanations, the need for meanings. The second is the substantive need—to bring about specific goals, such as rain, good crops, and health, by carrying out religious acts. The third is the psychological need to reduce fear and anxiety in situations in which these are provoked. Émile Durkheim (1915) and others who have followed Durkheim's approach saw religion as the means by which society inculcated values and sentiments necessary to the promotion of social solidarity and the society's ultimate survival.

From these different considerations of why religion exists, we can suggest some tentative answers to the questions we have posed. Human beings are part of a social world as well as a natural world. They are dependent upon the actions of other humans, as well as upon the forces of nature. Some of these actions and forces can be controlled through their own behavior. However, they are helpless in the face of other actions and forces. Humans attempt to understand and at least influence or control what is otherwise uncontrollable and unexplainable through a belief in the supernatural. As Spiro (1966) suggests, by doing this, they alleviate their anxieties about their helplessness in the situation. The organization of the supernatural world that is constructed by human beings reflects the society in which they live (Durkheim, 1915). The sentiments and emotions generated by the supernatural are an important force in the enhancement of social solidarity.

Religion, Science, and Magic

There is a distinction between the explainable parts of the universe and those aspects that are unexplainable. Today, we would say that many aspects of the natural world, which were formerly explained by religion, are now accounted for by means of science. In the seventeenth century, the Catholic Church insisted that the Earth was at the center of the solar system, and persecuted Galileo for his scientific research, which demonstrated that Copernicus' earlier research was correct and that the Sun, not the Earth, was at the center of our solar system. Despite conclusive evidence supporting this scientific view of the solar system, it took the Catholic Church hundreds of years to admit its error. The theory of evolution is another example of this shift from a religious explanation to a scientific explanation. Judeo-Christian belief states that humans, along with all the other species, were created by God. The seventeenth-century clergyman Bishop Ussher determined for Christians that creation occurred in the year

4004 B.C. Until the late nineteenth century, this was the Western belief about creation. Darwin proposed his theory of evolution based upon scientific evidence from comparative anatomy, geology, and paleontology in the mid-nineteenth century. This scientific theory proposed an alternative explanation for the development of all the species in the world and the appearance of human life. For a time, both religious and scientific explanations of creation competed with one another.

Today, many people accept the scientific theory of evolution. Some see it as incorporated into a divine plan. However, in America many people (perhaps 48 percent of the population) believe in what is called creationism. This belief that each of the species on Earth was created and placed here by God is spelled out in the Bible. Some religious groups, such as the Jewish Hassidim, even deny that dinosaurs existed 60 million years ago. Fundamentalists in the United States have attempted to transform creationism into a scientific theory, which they would like given equal status with evolutionism in school curricula. United States courts have ruled that creationism is a religious belief, while evolutionism is qualitatively different and, as a field of study, open to question and thus teachable in U.S. public schools. Recently, however, creationists gained the upper hand in Kansas when the Kansas Board of Education voted in August 1999 to delete any mention of evolution from the science curriculum of the state's schools. Though teachers are not forbidden to teach about evolution, the examination of students will no longer include evolution, discouraging school districts from spending students' time on evolution (*New York Times,* August 12, 1999). For those who accept Darwin's theory of evolution, religion has not ceased to be important. However, religion is no longer used to explain how humans came to be on Earth, because the creation of humans is no longer in the realm of the unexplainable.

Observations of the world are the basis for scientific knowledge for people in less complex societies as well as for those in the Western world. The Trobrianders used their empirical knowledge, about the displacement of objects in the water and about wind currents, in the construction of their outrigger canoes. Since they had no scientific explanation based on empirical evidence for why the wind blows or why storms come up, they resorted to supernatural explanations. They tried to control the wind through the use of wind magic. In our own society, some people also resort to nonscientific explanations. Scientific knowledge cannot at present determine why some children contract leukemia while others do not. If such a disease strikes a child in a family, the family may search for nonscientific cures through faith healing or religious mysticism.

Science and religion, which includes magic, are all ways of understanding and influencing the natural world. Magic and religion differ from science in that what is unexplained by science in the natural world is explained in magic and religion by recourse to the concept of the supernatural. Magic and science are similar in that the aims of both are specific, and both are based upon the belief that if one performs a set of specific actions, one will achieve the desired result. Magic and science differ in that they are based on different theories of knowledge—magic (which is part of religion) is based on the belief that if spells or rituals are performed correctly, the supernatural will act in such a way that the desired end within the natural world will result.

Magic is based on the idea that there is a link between the supernatural and the natural world such that the natural world can be compelled to act in the desired way if the spell is performed as it should be. Science, on the other hand, is based on empirically determined logical connections between aspects of the natural world. Its hypotheses concerning these logical connections are subject to change if new empirical data suggest better hypotheses. Science is based on empirical knowledge obtained through the five senses, whereas the defining feature of religion is the supernatural, a belief in a reality that "transcends the reality amenable to the five senses" (Lett, 1997: 104).

Magic differs from other aspects of religion in that people attempt to manipulate the supernatural through magic. If the right magical formula is used, success is inevitable because magic is seen as being able to bend the supernatural to the will of the practitioner. Other religious practices, on the other hand, are not as specific in their aims. Religious rites emphasize the degree of human beings' powerlessness and do not compel direct results in the way that magic does. Religious rites involve people making appeals to the gods, which the all-powerful gods may or may not choose to grant. Magic is therefore manipulative and religion is supplicative. Magical knowledge manipulates on behalf of individuals, whereas religion is the belief system and ritual practice of a community.

Conceptions of the Supernatural

People see the supernatural world as inhabited by a variety of superhuman creatures, agents, and forces whose actions will bring about good fortune or misfortune, rain or drought, famine or fertility, health or disease, and so forth. Since these superhuman creatures are the cultural creation of human minds, the real world serves as a model, though not an exact one, for people's conceptualizations of the supernatural. It would be too simplistic to say that the supernatural world is simply a mirror image of people's life on earth. Nevertheless, there is a direct relationship between the social structure of a society and the way in which its supernatural world is organized. Similarly, the power relationships in the supernatural world are related to the kind of political organization found in the society.

The kinds of spirits that populate the supernatural realm may be grouped into types using English terms that analysts have developed to describe them. Several different categories of spirits of the dead are recognized. These usually include the ghosts of the recent dead; the ghosts of the more remote dead of previous generations, who are considered ancestor spirits; and the ancestral spirits of the ancient past, who were founders of the group in mythological times. In societies with totemic clans, as described in Chapter 5, founding ancestors may be represented as animal spirits, not human spirits. This belief in totemic animal spirits as ancestors of human groups links humans with the natural animal world.

In addition to totemic animal ancestor spirits, some people believe that all animal and plant species have both physical and spiritual components. The natural world is then seen as having its spiritual counterpart. Inanimate forces such as rain, thunder, lightning, wind, and tide may also be seen as spirits themselves, or as motivated by spiritual beings, or controlled by deities or gods. If the spirit is directly perceived as having human characteristics as well as supernatural power, then it is referred to as a god or deity and not a spirit. The population of gods and deities recognized by a society is referred to as a *pantheon*. The relationships between the gods of a pantheon are frequently conceived of in human terms. The gods show jealousy, have sexual intercourse, fight, and live much like human beings. Human characteristics of this sort are also attributed to ghosts and ancestral spirits in many societies. The origins and activities of supernatural beings are depicted in myths, a topic we will discuss in the next chapter.

In some societies, individuals go out alone to seek a vision of an animal spirit, who then becomes their protector and *guardian spirit* throughout life. There is also a widespread notion that particular individuals acquire special supernatural powers that enable them to perform evil deeds. Finally, there is the belief in an impersonal supernatural force or power that is inherent in people or things, to which the Polynesian term *mana* is applied.

Ideas about ghosts and spirits are part of a larger category of beliefs about the spiritual or noncorporeal counterparts of human beings. Tylor (1874), the nineteenth-century evolutionist, termed this *animism*. He saw this idea as the seed from which all other forms of religion grew. He hypothesized that primitive people saw all living things, including the forces of nature, as composed of a corporeal, or bodily, form and a spiritual aspect. This was an extension of the idea that each person has a body and a separable other self or soul. This other self was seen in the person's shadow, or in the reflection in a pool, and it traveled far and wide in the person's dreams. Tylor saw this belief in a separable spirit projected onto the natural world. Tylor's ideas about animism were the cornerstone for the development of his evolutionary theory of religion, in which animism evolved into a pantheon of deities and finally into monotheism.

Any particular combination of different kinds of spiritual entities may be found in a given society. The supernatural world conforms to its own logic. This will become apparent as we examine the supernatural worlds of several different societies. Often people believe in a monotheistic god, such as occurs in Judaism, Christianity, and Islam, and still maintain beliefs in ghosts, witches, and spirits of nature as parallel systems. Indeed, as we have observed, this occurs in our own society.

The religious synthesis that is the belief system of the people of Wogeo, an island off New Guinea, represents a particular combination of spiritual entities (Hogbin, 1996). To the Wogeo, the supernatural world is just as real as the natural and cultural world around them. Their traditional supernatural world is made up of three kinds of beings. The first is called *nanarang*, or culture heroes. These culture heroes are the founders of the Wogeo natural world and the givers of all cultural inventions. The Wogeo believe that the earth is a huge platter under an upturned bowl, which is the sky. The island of Wogeo, seen as the home of humankind as well as of the culture heroes, is at the center, and radiating out are other islands, the moon, and the stars. Myths provide the stories of how the culture heroes formulated all the customs of Wogeo society. Those culture heroes who disappeared left behind black basalt columns as reminders of their deeds, while the remaining culture heroes still

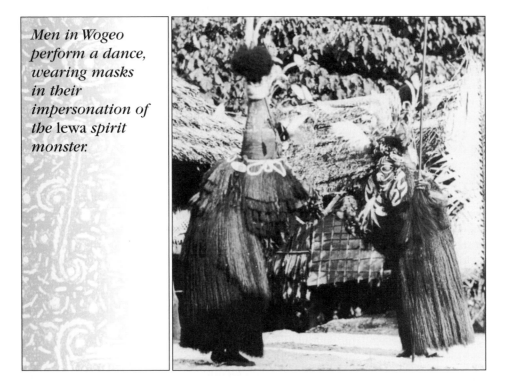

Men in Wogeo perform a dance, wearing masks in their impersonation of the lewa *spirit monster.*

dwell in certain sacred places, which they guard against intruders. Present-day magic rites are directed toward them to bring about what is desired.

A second category of supernatural beings is the ghosts of the dead. Only the spirits of men killed in a raid or women who have died in childbirth are harmful. They may try to steal the spirit of a living person. Persons who have lost part of their spirit become unconscious or delirious. They are deemed to be in a cold state and are fed hot curry so their spirit will return. When the soul of a dead person appears in a dream, it may try to take the soul of that person to the land of the dead.

In addition, there are two types of spirit monsters: one represented by flutes, called *nibek*, and the other by masks, called *lewa*. Prior to ceremonial distributions, people are not allowed to collect certain crops so that large quantities will grow, and they are not allowed to kill pigs so that a sufficient number of them will mature. Men put on masks to impersonate the *lewa* spirit and blow the flute to impersonate the *nibek* spirit. As a consequence, men are in a dangerous ritual state. The *lewa* are said to be cold and are offered hot curry to warm themselves. The *nibek* spirits are said to have "eaten" the pigs distributed at the ceremony before they are sent back to the spirit world.

These three kinds of Wogeo spirits do different kinds of things and deal with different kinds of problems. Accounts of culture heroes, who are the creators of the natural and cultural world, form the basis for mythologies, as do such supernatural individuals found in other societies. The spirit monsters are that part of the supernatural and the sacred which is involved in large-scale ceremonial distributions that have political and economic aims. These monsters are called forth to lend their sacred presence to the ceremonial to promote the well-being of the society and are given offerings of food and pigs. Lastly, there are the Wogeo ghosts, who connect people to their ancestors. Christianity, in its Roman Catholic form, was introduced to the people of Wogeo in 1934. By and large, the traditional belief system continues, in a synthesis with the belief system of Christianity and the Roman Catholic church structure.

A somewhat different conceptualization of the supernatural is found among the Kachin, discussed in both Chapters 6 and 9. Kachin social organization consists of a patrilineal segmentary lineage structure with mother's brother's daughter marriage, so there is a division between wife-givers and wife-takers (Chapter 6). The Kachin supernatural world is made up of spirits called *nats*, who are hierarchically ordered like the hierarchical *gumsa* world of Kachin political organization. Shadip, the chief of the *nats* and the reincarnation of the creator of everything, is responsible for good fortune and fertility. Beneath him are his children, the sky spirits. Since the Kachin have a rule of succession of ultimogeniture, the senior-most sky spirit is Madai, the youngest of the sky spirits. *Nats,* like people, belong to lineages. Madai's daughter is said to have married a human being who was the first ancestor of all Kachin chiefs. The Madai *nat* gave a woman to the first Kachin chief and is therefore wife-giver to the most senior Kachin line of chiefs. This links the world of the supernatural to human beings through marriage alliance. The sky spirits are superior to humans because they are wife-givers to humans. Below the sky spirits are the ancestor *nats,* the spirits of the ancestors of the various Kachin lineages. The sky *nats* are approached by making offerings to one's ancestor *nat,* who acts as an intermediary. Only the senior chief can make offerings to Madai directly, because his ancestor was wife-taker to Madai.

Another category of *nats* is seen as inferior to humans because they are the offspring of a human girl and an animal. These inferior spirits are said to cause all kinds of misfortunes to humans, such as death in childbirth and fatal accidents. Witches, who are human beings, also have a relationship to the supernatural. Witchcraft is inherited in a particular lineage, and the people in the lineage themselves are unaware that they possess this attribute. They unknowingly cause misfortune and illness to people who are their affines, those to whom they give wives.

It is apparent that the Kachin picture of the supernatural world is an extension of and directly correlated with their own social organization. The relationships among the spirits and between the spirits and human beings are the same as the relationships between individuals and social groups on the human level. Like human beings, the spirits are also organized into lineages, with wife-takers always lower in rank than wife-givers. The Kachin example supports Durkheim's idea that the supernatural world mirrors the organization of human society and that human propitiation of the supernatural world through prayers and sacrifices has the function of reinforcing the human society and reinforcing social solidarity. Human worship of the supernatural was, in effect, the worship of a projection of society. The relationship between the social structure and the organization of the world of the supernatural is often not such a simple one-to-one relationship. For example, the Kaguru of East Africa believe that witches, unlike humans, walk upside down, on their hands. In this case, the supernatural world is an inversion of the real world.

▚ Ritual—Approaching the Supernatural

Generally speaking, human beings approach the supernatural by carrying out ritual acts, usually involving a combination of speech and patterned behavior that alters the emotional states of the participants. *Hortatory rituals* consist of exhortations to the supernatural to perform some act (Firth, 1951). Just before a shipwreck, the captain of a Trobriand canoe will exhort the supernatural powers to send the marvelous fish to guide the drowning victims to a friendly shore. The Trobrianders have a native term for this category of exhortation. The term means "by the mouth only." *Prayer,* involving words only, differs from hortatory ritual in its method of approach and intent. Prayer emphasizes people's inferior position to the gods since they beseech the gods to act on their behalf.

Sometimes, the gods can be approached only by going into a self-induced or drug-induced trance. The Yanomamo blow the hallucinogenic substance *ebene* up their noses to induce a trance and enable contact with the spirit world. In the trancelike state produced by the drug, individuals may hallucinate that they are flying to the spirit world. Sometimes trances may be induced without the use of any drugs. Many North American Indian societies have the *vision quest,* in which a man, through starvation, deprivation, and sometimes even bodily mutilation, attempts to induce a trance in which a supernatural being will visit him and thenceforth become his guardian spirit and protector. Among the Crow of Montana, an adolescent boy would go out into the wilderness and fast and thirst for days in order to induce a vision. He might even mutilate himself by cutting off a joint of a finger on his left hand if the vision was not forthcoming. The vision usually came on the fourth night, since for the Crow the number 4 has magical significance. Supernatural visitors came most frequently in the form of animals, sometimes powerful ones like buffalo and eagles, at other times animals like dogs or rabbits. The Crow believed that the supernatural spirit adopted the individual who saw him, and thereafter the spirit acted as a protector, teaching its protégé a sacred song, instructing him in special medicines, and imposing special dietary restrictions. The man wore tokens of his vision and accumulated a medicine bundle consisting of sacred objects connected to the first and subsequent visions of his spirit protector. Part of the man's power could be used to protect others whom he adopted for this purpose, as his spirit protector had adopted him.

Still another way of approaching the supernatural is by making sacrifices. The Kachin attempt to intercede with the *nats* or spirits when they cause sickness or misfortune by making sacrificial offerings. There is a relationship between the size and value of the sacrificial offering and the importance of the spirit to which it is offered. The inferior *nats* are offered rats, dogs, pigs, and chickens, but never cattle. Household ancestral spirits are offered only chickens. The village headman's ancestral *nats* are given offerings of pigs. Sky *nats* are given offerings of pigs and buffalo. Shadip, the creator, is given a sacrifice of a whole pig, which is not eaten but is buried. In all other cases, the essence of the sacrificial animals is given to the *nats,* while the meat is consumed by the human participants. Sacrifices are made on ritual occasions to ensure the supernatural protection of crops and their fertility. The *nats* must be remembered or they will cause misfortunes. The sacrifice consists of giving up something of value in an exchange with the spirits. Eating the meat from sacrificial animals is eating sacred food, which brings humans into contact with the gods.

W. Robertson Smith (1889), another nineteenth-century theorist on religion, saw the sacrifice as the eating together of god and man, which signified the bond of kinship between them, just as eating together among men symbolically signifies kinship, as noted in Chapter 5. The widespread sacrifices and offerings of live animals, food, vegetables, incense, and even money are a way of approaching the supernatural by bearing gifts. Since the relationship between humans and the supernatural emphasizes the subordination of the humans, people can only hope for supernatural support in fighting wars; in warding off misfortune, sickness, and death; and in providing fertility in exchange for their gift. The sacrifice of live animals is the sacrifice of life itself.

Rites of Passage

Two broad categories of ritual have been identified by anthropologists: *rites of passage* and *rites of intensification*. *Rites of passage* are communal ceremonies held to publicly mark the changes in status an individual goes through as he or she progresses through the life cycle. The beginning of life—birth—and the end of life—death—are always marked by some kind of ritual. In addition, one or more points between life and death at which one's status changes, such as a girl's first menstruation or marriage, as described in Chapter 2, may be marked with a ceremony. In Chapter 7 we discussed the cultural construction of gender as expressed in such rituals. Cultures may emphasize a biological change in their rites of passage, or the changes may be culturally determined, such as the first catch of a fish or a child's first haircut. The cultural determination of such rites is demonstrated in the variation in the age at which a male child is circumcised in societies over the world.

Van Gennep (1960), in his analysis of rites of passage, pointed out that all such rites involve three stages. The first stage marks the separation of the individual from the category or status previously occupied. Next is a period of transition in which the individual is in a kind of limbo. During this period, the individual is frequently secluded from the rest of the society. Victor Turner (1967) has characterized this period as a particularly sacred one, a *liminal period* in which the individual is literally "in between," no longer in one status and not yet in another. The last stage is one of reincorporation, in which the individual is ceremonially reintegrated into society, but this time in the new status. Frequently, this three-stage process is represented by means of the metaphor of death and rebirth. The individual in the former category "dies" and is "reborn" into the new category. In the third stage of the ceremony, the person is often given a new name and puts on a different type of clothing, marking the birth of a new person.

The Arapesh of New Guinea celebrate several different kinds of rites of passage. Though the Arapesh have a patrilineal rule of descent, as noted in Chapter 5, they believe their blood comes from the mother while the father contributes the semen. When one's blood is spilled, the mother's group must be recompensed by the payment of shell valuables. This principle underlies all rites-of-passage ceremonies, as well as other aspects of Arapesh culture. After the birth of a child, the child's father "pays for the blood" by giving shell rings to the mother's brother of the child. Through this act the child now belongs to the father's group, though the mother's lineage is still said to "own" the child's blood. Ear and nose piercing are minor rites of passage that take place during childhood and are performed by the mother and the mother's sister.

At puberty, several boys are initiated at the same time to make them into men. The rites involve isolation from females, with whom the boy has spent most of his time, the observance of a series of taboos, and the incision of the boy's penis. He is also introduced to the Tamberan Cult, the secret cult of men. He learns that the Tamberan spirit is really only the sounds of the drums and the flute secretly played by the adult men. This information is kept from women and children. During initiation, the boy also goes through an ordeal in which his mother's brother beats him. The boy's penis is incised by a man designated the Cassowary, representing the spirit of the large flightless bird found in New Guinea, who acts on behalf of all the men to remove the "female" blood. The initiate then drinks blood that has been contributed by all the old men of the group and is thereby reborn as a man. At the end, the initiate is bathed, puts on new clothing, and is reincorporated into society as a man at a feast made by his father to honor the boy's mother's brother, who must be paid for the shedding of the boy's blood. Finally, the boy, now a man, goes on a trip and meets all his father's trading partners, signifying his new status.

The Arapesh have child betrothal, and a girl, while still a child, frequently goes to live with the parents of her future husband. Her first menstruation is marked by a rite of passage, during which she is secluded and does not eat. After this period of seclusion and fasting, she is scarified on the shoulder and buttocks by her mother's brother. This represents the initiation of a girl into the status of an adult woman. She is ceremonially fed by her new husband. He then hunts for meat, which is used to make a feast for the girl's mother's brother, since her blood was shed by the scarification process.

The final Arapesh rite of passage occurs at death. Once again, the mother's lineage of the deceased is paid in shell rings in compensation for the death. The same kind of ceremonial payment that marked all the other Arapesh rites of passage marks the death.

Several rites of passage characterize American culture. These include the Jewish circumcision rite, Christian baptism, bar mitzvah, confirmation, the wedding (described in Chapter 2), (in a sense), the retirement party, and the funeral. The same stages of separation, transition, and reincorporation can be seen in these rites of passage as in those of other cultures. Jewish male circumcision and Christian christening or baptism are both similar in that they perform the same function. When a child is born, he or she is not a member of society at that point. Just as the Arapesh payment of shell rings marks the entry of the child into his or her father's patrilineal group, circumcision and baptism perform the same function. At birth the child moves from being a neonate into a liminal state, not yet part of society. On the occasion of the Jewish circumcision, the cutting of the foreskin by the *mohel* marks the male child as a Jewish male. The recently introduced naming ceremony for Jewish girls

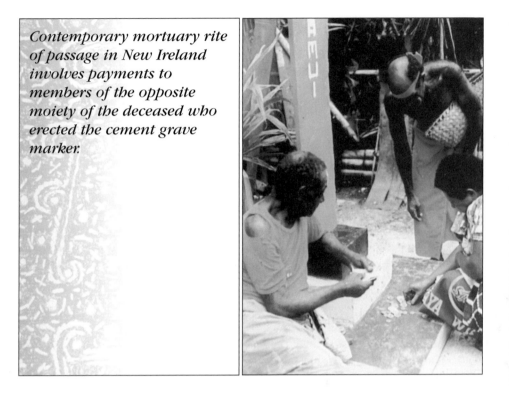

Contemporary mortuary rite of passage in New Ireland involves payments to members of the opposite moiety of the deceased who erected the cement grave marker.

soon after birth performs the same function. At the christening, the priest or minister dabs the child's forehead with water and names the child, thereby marking its entry into Christian society.

The funeral is the final American rite of passage. We will describe, in general, how American funerals are carried out by Christians. This may vary in some details from that of funerals among other religious groups in America. Death, which moves the person from life into a liminal state, may occur at home or, much more often, in a hospital. Immediately after death, the body is taken to a funeral parlor or a funeral home. The body is prepared for the funeral by a full-time specialist, a funeral director, formerly known as an undertaker, and a casket is chosen by a member of the family. In earlier times, when people died at home, members of the family prepared the body and made the casket. A member of the clergy is selected to carry out the religious rites, and a cemetery plot is arranged for. Neighbors, friends, and relatives as well as organizations to which the deceased belonged are notified of the death. The funeral is a reflection of the social status of the family. While the deceased is in a liminal state, there is the viewing of the body, sometimes called the wake, which may last for several days. In former times, the wake was held at home and friends, acquaintances, and distant relatives came to pay their respects to the deceased. Visitors view the corpse and comment on how well the deceased looks. To say that the corpse looks good is a direct denial of death.

The body in the casket is in a liminal state—no longer part of our living world, but not yet in the afterlife. There is no organized ritual or leadership at the wake, which is predominantly an occasion of social intercourse. There are variations in the range of behavior at wakes, reflecting ethnic differences. Some groups allow joking and ribaldry, but the somberness of funeral parlors usually inhibits such rowdy behavior. Some groups bring in food and drink, but this may not be permitted by many funeral parlors.

The funeral service, usually a religious rite, begins the movement of the deceased out of the liminal stage. It may be held either at the church or at the funeral parlor. The casket is placed in front of the group, with the closest relatives nearest to it. More distant relatives and friends sit farther back. The minister conducts the religious service. The interment of the body at the cemetery marks the incorporation of the deceased into a new category. The deceased is dead, but he or she is once again alive—with God. The casket and mourners are transported to the cemetery. At the cemetery, the minister officiates in a brief religious rite. Though the rite is short, the finality of the event is brought out by the power of the religious formula recited—"Ashes to ashes . . . ."

Rites of Intensification

The other major category of ritual—*rites of intensification*—is celebrated communally either at various points in the yearly cycle, such as spring, fall, or the winter and summer solstices, or at times when the society is exposed to some kind of threat. Societies may hold rites of intensification to mark planting, in hope for a good crop, or to mark the harvest, in thanks for what has been given. The Kachin ceremonial sacrifices known as *manau,* which are carried out by the chief on behalf of the whole community, are rites of intensification. One such occasion occurs during the growing period when there is anxiety about whether the crop will be satisfactory. The sacrifices to the whole series of *nat* spirits, which are part of the ceremony, serve to reiterate the social structure. The major sacrifice made by the chief serves to reinforce the solidarity of the group.

When an event of importance to the whole community on Wogeo takes place, such as appointing the official heir to the chief, a rite of intensification, known as a *warabwa,* is held. The *nibek* spirit monsters are summoned. The community as a whole sponsors the *warabwa* and is host to many other villages. The climax of the ceremony is a great distribution of food and pork. One of the occurrences at a Wogeo *warabwa* takes place the day before. At this time, there is a free-for-all at which the rules regarding the respect relationship between certain categories of relatives are suspended, and they may insult and humiliate each other. The suspension of rules in this case serves, in a negative fashion, to emphasize the rules of the group. The rites allow the expression or release of tension in a ritual context that could not be permitted in the everyday course of events. A similar reversal of everyday behavior occurs at Mardi Gras, just before Ash Wednesday, which marks the beginning of the 40-day period of penance leading to Easter. Mardi Gras rites, marked by great exuberance and extravagant behavior, contrast with the restraint and somberness of Lent that follows.

Thanksgiving, the "giving of thanks," is an American rite of intensification. It has a historical basis in the Pilgrims' celebration, when they gave thanks to God for their survival during their first year in the New World. Today, most Americans participate in a Thanksgiving meal and, by their participation, give thanks in a way that is completely secular. The religious aspect, if present, involves saying grace at the start of the meal. This rite of intensification demands that particular foods be eaten to symbolize Thanksgiving. It is turkey, not lamb chops or meatballs, that symbolizes this celebration. Though Native Americans, who were conquered by European immigrants, are said to have contributed to the first Thanksgiving, today most do not celebrate Thanksgiving as a rite of intensification. They feel they have no reason to do so.

Ritual does not simply mirror society and culture, but helps shape its defining features. Ritual can also challenge the existing order, as Gluckman pointed out in his work on rituals of rebellion in Africa. Today, rituals are seen as dynamic and flowing, ever responsive to the changing aspects of modern and postmodern life. Experimentation and the development of new rituals, such as the Wiccan rituals we will discuss below, have become important foci of anthropological research. Anthropologists study the performative aspects of ritual and are interested in how participants "constitute themselves through their actions." They are interested in the way in which "ritual's capacity to shape and shape anew is rooted in its capacity to create experiences of self, society, the world and cosmos that reinforce tradition or generate new views and ways of living" (Alexander, 1997: 140). However, there is a tension or dialectic between the traditional rules of ritual and innovation or experimentation in actual performances. The meaning of the ritual for the participants, its subjective aspects as encompassed in the "native point of view," is in line with the postmodern perspective.

Religious Specialists

The supernatural is often approached indirectly, through intermediaries, who have access to it because they possess some special gift, have been through some training, or have inherited esoteric knowledge or ability. Religious specialization is found in small-scale societies and in complex, hierarchically organized societies. Religious specialists often have a primary function, such as curing illness or predicting the future. The English labels for these specialists—diviner, oracle, magician—usually refer to that function. Beyond these primary functions, the specialists may have additional functions, which overlap with those of other specialists. Religious specialists operate on a full- or part-time basis.

Shamans

In small-scale societies, the *shaman* was usually the only religious specialist. Though these part-time specialists used their powers primarily to diagnose illness, cure illness, and sometimes cause illness as well, they also had other functions, such as divining the future. Early travelers referred to these individuals as witch doctors, to highlight their curing functions. The term *shaman* comes from the Tungus of Siberia.

Shamans were found throughout Asia and among a great many indigenous societies of North and South America.

The activities and functions of the Kwakiutl shaman typify shamanic activities elsewhere. Kwakiutl shamans are classified on the basis of the level of their expertise or power. The least powerful are those who are able only to diagnose and locate the disease, that is, determine the place in the body where the object causing the disease is lodged. But the most powerful can not only cure diseases but can also cause illness in others. Both Kwakiutl men and women can become shamans. One becomes a shaman as a result of an initiation by a supernatural spirit, the most common being wolf, killer whale, and toad, that comes to the person while he or she is sick. The spirit teaches the novice songs and dances and gives the shaman a new name, which is always used by the shaman when acting in that capacity. The shaman wears certain paraphernalia—a neck ring of shredded red cedar bark to which is attached a pouch bearing small objects, which represent the diseases the shaman can cause—and uses a special rattle and a ring of hemlock branches for purifying patients.

The curing of a patient takes place at a public ceremony. Diagnosis is made by the shaman through contact with the supernatural spirit. If the cause of the disease is loss of the soul, the shaman uses the purification ring to call back the soul. If the cause is the intrusion of some foreign object, the supposition is that it has entered by accident or been "thrown" by another shaman acting on behalf of an enemy of the patient. The shaman removes it by sucking or squeezing it out of the patient's body. The shaman resorts to a variety of tricks to produce the removed object. He might conceal bird down (tiny bird feathers) in his upper lip and then bite his lip and spit out the bloodied bird down as if it were some wormlike object. In keeping with the ranked social structure of the Kwakiutl, great chiefs "own their shamans," who protect them by throwing disease into their enemies.

In a nonranked society like the Inuit, shamanistic activity was not limited to curing or causing disease. The Inuit shaman intervened with the supernatural in attempting to control the forces of the environment that directly affected the life of the community. When game was unavailable, shamans were asked to call on their spirits to divine where animals were located. Shamans were also said to control thunder and stop snowstorms and the cracking of the ice. Shamans were called in to protect the community against malevolent spirits and monsters. The Inuit believed that sickness was caused by the sufferer's loss of his or her soul or by evil ghosts and spirits who were usually angered by the breach of some taboo. The shaman, who was called to act in either case, invoked the supernatural spirits with which he was in contact. An Inuit boy became a shaman by joining the household of an elderly shaman as a novice, where he observed special taboos, had visions, and was taught special shamanistic techniques. The novice also had to refrain from sexual relations.

Shamanism was widespread in Siberia. It was and is still found among the Buddhists of the Buryat Republic, and in Tuva, an autonomous, Turkic-speaking republic in the geographical center of Asia, both of which are part of the Russian federation. Tuvan shamans are healers dealing with various diseases and with the

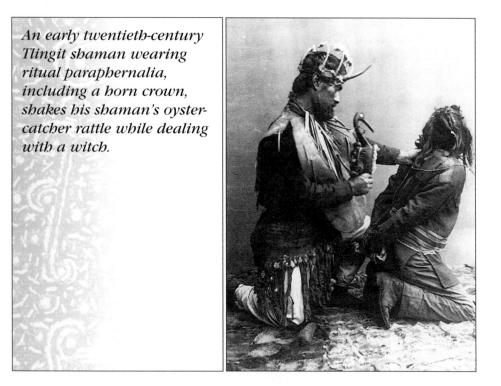

An early twentieth-century Tlingit shaman wearing ritual paraphernalia, including a horn crown, shakes his shaman's oyster-catcher rattle while dealing with a witch.

loss of the soul. They treat the sick by holding seances, which begin at nightfall and last until dawn, during which time the shaman contacts the spirits and "voyages" to the three worlds—the subterranean, the celestial, and the middle world of humans (Kenin-Lopsan, 1997: 110). The shaman employs spirit-helpers, animals ranging in size and power from bears to moths, and these spirit-helpers are artistically portrayed on wands, which the shaman employs in the ceremony. In addition, the Tuvan shaman wears a decorated coat and boots, and uses a drum and a rattle.

The Tuvan shaman may also be called in to divine the location of game for a hunter, or a childless couple may seek help from the shaman to "summon the soul" of an unborn infant to their home, a felt yurt (Kenin-Lopsan, 1997: 127). Kenin-Lopsan, a Tuvan ethnographer who collected many poetic chants or songs performed by Tuvan shamans, pointed out that these songs were a major form of Tuvan artistic expression, and served to keep the Tuvan language alive. Tuvan shamans in their shamanic performance employed the "throat singing" for which Tuva is famous. In this special kind of singing, they imitated the languages of their animal spirit-helpers (Kenin-Lopsan, 1997: 132–133). Tuvan shamans may be female or male. Kenin-Lopsan's maternal grandmother was a famous shaman imprisoned several times by Stalin. She died in prison in the mid-1940s. The renewal of Tuvan shamanism in the post-Soviet era is demonstrated by the fact that in 1992 a Society of Tuva Shamans was formed and was subsequently recognized by the Tuvan Ministry of Justice (Kenin-Lopsan 1997b: 132). Tuvan shamanism continues to be an integral part of Tuvan culture, and today, in particular, is part of their ethnic identity.

These examples of shamanic practice reveal some of the basic characteristics of shamanism. Shamans enter the spirit world in order to benefit members of their communities in the material world, rather than themselves. Through a variety of means they go into an altered state of consciousness, or a trance, during which they have direct contact with the spirit world. They also have the ability to travel in the spirit world or use spirit-helpers for that purpose; they can call spirits to be present during their seances (Townsend, 1997: 431–432).

Diviners

Diviners are part-time religious specialists who use the supernatural to enable people to make decisions concerning how they should act in order to have success. The Chinese, in general, have always placed great emphasis upon omens. Archaeological information has revealed that the Chinese interpreted the cracks in tortoise shells to foretell the future. They also used geomancy—the interpretations of the future from cracks in dried mud—and fortune-telling. Diviners use other methods to gain their information. Sometimes chickens or other animals are killed and their entrails inspected to determine what action to take in the future. Roman diviners, or augurs, inspected the entrails of sacrificial animals for good or bad omens. Julius Caesar was advised not to venture forth on the Ides of March because the animal sacrificed had no heart. Calendrical divination was used in Mesoamerica before the arrival of Columbus.

In our own society, many people seek help to divine what their future holds for them. Gypsy fortune-tellers in storefronts in many cities, large and small, as well as at rural fairs are paid to read palms, tea leaves, and Tarot cards, and to look into crystal balls to foretell the future. The services of astrologers, who foretell the future from the positions of the stars, were even sought by a president to help him make decisions affecting the entire nation.

As part of his functions, in addition to curing, the Inuit shaman would also tell hunters where they would find animals. They took the shoulder blade, or scapula, of an animal such as a reindeer, a moose, an elk, an otter, or a seal and placed it on a fire until cracks appeared, which formed a pattern. This practice is called *scapulimancy*. The pattern of cracks was then interpreted to locate the place where animals were to be found. Scapulimancy is similar to the Chinese use of tortoise shells, just described. Omar Moore (1957), a sociologist, has pointed out that since the cracks appear in a random fashion, the hunter following the omens will pursue game in a random fashion, avoiding overhunting in one area. Similar techniques of divination were used in the past by hunters in northern North America and Siberia.

Sorcerers and Witches

Sorcerers and witches, as religious specialists, concentrate upon doing evil things, causing illness and death rather than curing. Since there is a logical connection between curing illness and causing it, in many societies the same specialist, the shaman, sometimes performs both functions. Sorcery is defined by anthropology as something that is learned, whereas witchcraft is something people are born with a propensity toward. As pointed out in the discussion of the Kachin, Kachin witches are unaware that they have this power. *Witchcraft* and sorcery involve the use of supernatural means to cause bad things to happen to one's enemies, or to the enemies of individuals who engage the services of a sorcerer. These enemies may be persons outside one's own group or persons within one's own group with whom one is in opposition. Kwakiutl shamans could use sorcery against enemy groups. Among the Trobrianders, as noted in Chapter 9, the people of a district fear that their chief will use sorcery against them if they go against his commands. Sorcery here, as in other societies, is being used as a means of social control.

In many societies, when a person in the prime of life becomes sick or dies, it is necessary to ascertain what caused the illness or death. This means going beyond the immediate cause of, say, a death, such as the tree that fell or the lightning that struck, to the more important underlying reason this particular person died. There is often a belief in such societies that the illness was caused by witchcraft or sorcery. British social anthropologists working in Africa, especially E. E. Evans-Pritchard and Max Gluckman, adopted an approach in which they saw such sorcery and witchcraft accusations as the product of tensions and conflict within the community. When a person in the prime of life dies, investigators try to divine through supernatural means who caused the death. Like the detective in a "whodunit" in our own society, the diviner asks who has the most to gain to determine who is the most likely suspect.

Claims of witchcraft are usually made in such a way that they reveal the cleavages in a society. According to Douglas, who analyzed witchcraft accusations, such as the witch trials of sixteenth-century England and the accusations of witchcraft among Yao villagers from Malawi in the 1950s, the witch is someone on the opposite side of a power conflict, accused of antisocial behavior or libeled by his or her accuser (1991). Accusations of antisocial behavior may involve eating food that is repellent to the accuser, even human bodies; aberrant sexual behavior, such as sex with the devil; or the murder of children for occult ritual purpose.

Magicians

Magic is another kind of religious specialization, as noted above. Magic, witchcraft, and sorcery all involve the manipulation of the supernatural. Magic is directed toward a positive goal—to help individuals or the whole community. In parts of Melanesia one frequently finds societies in which there are several part-time religious specialists who carry out magical rites to bring rain, promote fertility in the gardens, and ensure successful fishing. The garden magician among the Trobrianders is one of the most important people in the village. He recites his magical spells and performs his rituals at every stage of the process of growing yams, and what he does is seen as being as essential to the growth and maturation of crops as weeding and hoeing. He officiates at a large-scale ceremony involving all the men of the village that takes place before any gardening begins. He carries out specific rites at the planting and weeding and in assisting the plants to sprout, bud, grow, climb, and produce the yams. Since the garden magician must perform his rites before each stage of production, through his spells he acts, in effect, to coordinate and regulate the stages of work throughout the entire village (Malinowski, 1935). Each village has its own special system of garden magic, which is passed on by matrilineal inheritance, so a sister's son succeeds his mother's brother as garden magician.

Magical practices have always coexisted with universal religions such as Christianity, Islam, and Judaism in many Old World societies. The institution of the evil eye operates in the same way as witchcraft. If misfortune occurs, it is assumed to have happened because of the use of the evil eye by some enemy. People believe that it is dangerous to praise a child as beautiful, strong, or healthy, since this will create jealousy on the part of others and cause them to invoke the evil eye. Various kinds of magic, including protective devices and verbal ritual formulas, are used to ward off the evil eye. Among the Basseri, a nomadic pastoral society of Iran, a mirror is placed on the back of the horse on which the bride is taken to her groom, since a joyous occasion like a wedding is likely to promote envy on the part of some onlookers. The mirror is used to reflect the evil eye back to its sender. Communities of believers from Cairo to New York City recite magical spells to ward off the evil eye, wear charms and religious medals to bring good fortune, and nail religious symbols to walls and doorways to protect households. These are all forms of magic practiced today. The religious objects whose commodification and sale in Cairo we discussed in Chapter 8 all represent magical ideas set within the context of Islam (Starrett, 1995). The refracting vinyl stickers of raised hands and unopened copies of the Qur'an displayed in automobiles are intended to ward off the evil eye. Islamic religious leaders consider these practices as running counter to the basic teachings of Islam, for the Qur'an is to be read, not to be used as a charm for protection.

Priests

With the evolution of more complex forms of society, in earlier and later states, religion became more elaborated and more differentiated as a separate institution. In contrast to the shaman and the magician, who operate as individual practitioners and part-time specialists, priests function in concert, carrying out a more codified and elaborated series of rituals, and their activities are associated with a shrine or temple. The body of ritual knowledge, which is the priest's method of contacting the supernatural, must be learned over a lengthy period of time. Archaeological data on Mesopotamia reveal that in societies that were the forerunners of full-fledged states, there was a single figure who was both the political and religious head of the community, and there was a priestly class. Subsequently, as the state evolved, there was a separation of political and religious positions. In Chapter 9, we noted that formal legal codes evolved out of religious codes in early states. These religious codes comprised moral statements that have remained an integral part of the universal religions. The class of religious specialists was but one of a number of stratified classes in an increasingly more hierarchically organized society.

Priests were intimately associated with development and control of the calendar in the early civilizations of the Maya and the Aztecs, and in Egypt and Mesopotamia.

It is not known whether priests invented the calendar, but it was used for determining when communal religious rites should take place. In these early civilizations the priesthood seems also to have been associated with scientific observations of the heavens. In ancient Egypt, the flooding of the Nile was absolutely regular; its onset could be dated 365 days from the last onset. The development of a solar calendar, in place of the more widespread lunar calendar, enabled the flooding to be predicted. The development of this solar calendar depended on a certain amount of astronomical knowledge. The ability to predict natural phenomena, such as the yearly flooding, was connected, in the eyes of the people, to priestly proximity to the supernatural. This in turn gave the leader of the theocracy—the priest-king—great power over the ordinary agriculturalists.

Old Religions in New Guises

The imposition of colonialism and subsequent independence has transformed the nature of sorcery in many places. For example, among the Kaliai of West New Britain there has been a syncretism of traditional Kaliai forms of sorcery with European culture (Lattas, 1993). The term *syncretism* refers to the integration of older cultural traits into newly adopted cultural practices. Men who have traveled widely while working for Europeans and serving in the constabulary have the reputation of being sorcerers. Their great power derives from their connection to Europeans and from the sorcery knowledge they have had the opportunity to acquire while working in other areas. In fact, the nation-state, conceptualized as a white institution, is itself seen as imbued with the powers of sorcery.

Shamanism has taken on a modern appearance in Westernizing societies in Asia. Before Korea began its rapid industrialization 30 years ago, shamanic rituals were held in response to life-threatening illnesses and to promote the health, harmony, and prosperity of the small farming families. These families were primarily rural in outlook, though they were tied to commercial markets (Kendall, 1996: 522). Today these same shamanic rituals, or *kut,* have spread from the rural farmers to a new class of small-businesspeople and entrepreneurs living in the cities, who are holding *kut* ceremonies to ensure success in their business enterprises as well as to cure their illnesses. For those engaged in high-risk enterprises, business is precarious and success or failure seems arbitrary and beyond their control. Thus, "doing well by the spirits" is important. Since financial distress and worry can often lead to illness, it is understandable that the *kut* ceremony has dual functions (Kendall, 1996: 516–518).

In the United States, we have also had a period of religious transformation and innovation which began in the 1970s following the demise of the counterculture movements of the "flower children" of the 1960s (Bromley, 1998: 328). At first, the development of these alternative religious movements, sometimes referred to as New Age movements or New Religious movements, was paralleled by an erosion of the "major" religions—Judaism, Catholicism, Protestantism. However, in the most recent past, the growth of Christian Fundamentalism and the resurgence of

Orthodox Judaism have marked a turnaround for these dominant faiths. Nontraditional religious movements have a long history in the United States. Some of these groups, for example, the Shakers, are only minimally present today, while others, the Mormons (Church of Jesus Christ of Latter-day Saints), for example, continue stronger than ever. In recent years, the immigration of many non-Westerners, Buddhists, Muslims, Hindus, and others into our now multicultural, pluralistic society have introduced still other religion belief systems into the mix. Many of the New Religious movements are cultural transplants representing groups of Asian origin, such as the Hare Krishna movement (International Society for Krishna Consciousness). These New Religious Movements are seen as "different responses to the failure of mainline religious traditions to provide a meaningful moral context for everyday life" (Bromley, 1998: 330).

For the same reasons that New Religious movements have become popular, shamanism has also grown in importance in America and Europe. Spurred by an interest in the writings of Carlos Casteneda and the work of Michael Harner, an anthropologist who is an authority on shamanism, Westerners disillusioned with their own religious institutions have turned to "neoshamanism." As Atkinson notes: "It [shamanism] presents in the 1980s and 1990s what Buddhism and Hinduism provided in the preceding decades, namely a spiritual alternative for Westerners estranged from Western religious traditions" (1992: 322). Harner holds seminars in shamanism. Participants attend these seminars, which are in reality shamanic rituals, either to be cured of illness, the traditional function of the shamanic ritual, or to enable them to make the journey into another world simply to undergo the shamanic experience (Drury, 1989: 93 ff). Neoshamanism is nonhierarchical in comparison with traditional Western religions, emphasizes self-help, and links participants to nature. Consequently, it is appealing to seekers of alternative religious experiences.

Witchcraft has existed in America, in one form or another, from the seventeenth century on (Melton, 1982). There have been periodic infusions from Europe, as its popularity waxed and waned. Douglas, as noted earlier, sees basic similarities between Malawi witchcraft and sixteenth-century witchcraft. In both instances, accusations of witchcraft reflect cleavages within the community and are, in effect, methods of social control. However, though witches today see themselves as the reborn victims of witch-hunts in past centuries, in fact, there have been no accusations of witchcraft paralleling those in sixteenth-century England and seventeenth-century Salem (Orion, 1995: 52). The flowering of what has come to be known as the Neopagan religion, or Wicca, began in the 1960s. In 1954, shortly after the repeal of antiwitchcraft laws in Britain, Gerald Gardner published an account of witchcraft that stimulated its revival. While in Gardner's version of Wicca, covens, the minimal religious unit, were characterized by levels of initiation, a hierarchical organization, and a more codified set of traditions and rituals, Wicca in America is democratized, individualized, highly creative, and inventive. Its major focus has been to disown, by lifestyle, word, and philosophy, the religious and political ideas that dominate the rest of American society. Christian conservatives and fundamentalists understandably see this opposition to American society and to Christianity as a direct threat. Interestingly, those who identify themselves as members of Wicca come primarily from Protestant and Catholic backgrounds

(Orion, 1995: 63). Wicca is therefore a pointed rejection of Christianity—it is both pre-Christian and the object of Christian persecution.

The Wiccan belief system is widely diverse in the interpretation of fundamental beliefs; there is great variation in organization and practice and constant creativity in the development of the ritual structure. However, there are certain ideas that are held in common. Wicca and Neopaganism partake of a new vision of the witch as the healer, the champion of alternative therapies, such as massage therapy, spiritual healing, crystal healing, and homeopathy, distrusting of and in opposition to the omnipotent physicians in the prevailing medical establishment. They also support midwifery and the use of herbs in healing. Their approach to their own health care usually involves healers and medical doctors as supplements to rather than substitutes for one another (Orion, 1995: 165).

People also look to Wicca as a way of regaining control over their lives. Nature and human beings are seen as one, and worship of nature is important. Human action and sacred forces are counterparts of one another and can influence one another; hence ritual action involves using human action to enlist the assistance of the sacred. The world is seen as constantly in motion, vibrating with energy as a life force intrinsic to all things, infusing, creating, and sustaining humans and all other life. Energy is thereby empowering, and most rituals have been created to concentrate and channel energy to where it can do the most good, whether healing an individual or supporting those who oppose the despoiling of the environment by the building of a nuclear power plant (Orion, 1995: 111).

Wiccan rituals usually involve the sacred circle, formed of individuals whose constant circular movement generates a cone of energy directed to specific tasks to better the earth. This is also seen as a form of therapeutic "healing magic," releasing and dissipating "maladaptive emotional states" for the individual as well as for the earth by creative energy. Wiccan celebrations mark the solstices, equinoxes, and key occasions of the agricultural year, as well as biweekly sabbaths. They also have come to include rite-of-passage ceremonies; such as Wiccaning—the blessing and presenting of infants to the pagan spirits; girls' and boys' puberty rites or initiation; handfasting, the tying together of the hands of the couple at a ceremony to signify trial or permanent marriage, heterosexual or homosexual; and ritual preparation for death. The *New York Times* even included a description of a Wiccan ceremony of handfasting in its wedding section of June 30, 1996, in which the bride's and groom's hands were bound together with ribbon by all the guests. A high priestess, licensed by the state, pronounced them man and wife, and the June wedding ended in the traditional Wiccan way, with the couple jumping over a broomstick.

The Wiccan pantheon has the Mother Goddess, giver of life and incarnate love; the Sun; and the Moon at the core. In addition, magical beliefs from ancient Egypt, Greece, Babylonia, and the Jewish Kabbalah, as well as Celtic, Druid, Norse, and Welsh pagan beliefs, have been eclectically included (Melton, 1982). Women enjoy a special status, and the person of the high priestess is venerated.

Wicca in America has all the organizational characteristics of a religion. In fact, a federal appeals court in 1986 ruled that Wicca was a religion protected by the Constitution. As a consequence, believers in Wicca are today trying to change the public view of their belief system. Its practitioners feel that Wicca should be protected by the same laws that protect the practice of other religions against the attacks of Christian fundamentalists. In an article in the *New York Times* on October 31, 1999, entitled "Witches Cast as the Neo-Pagans Next Door," Wicca worshipers were quoted as saying, "We will change the future through tolerance, education and through love" and "I'm probably going to have a sign that says, 'I'm Wiccan and I vote [on the Nebraska Capital steps].' " In addition, some Wiccan rituals are advertised as "open rituals," which the public can attend. Pagan Pride Days have been organized by witches in various cities. Fundamentalist Christians, however, still associate witches and Wicca with satanism. When some soldiers at Fort Hood, Texas, conducted Wiccan rituals near the base, local ministers and Representative Bob Barr of Georgia objected to these "sinister rites." In the same manner, the opponents of Santeria in Hialeah, Florida, discussed in the last chapter, objected to the practice of animal sacrifice, characterizing it as "devil worship."

Politics and Religion

In today's world, religion seems to play an extremely important role in politics. In a sense, we have come full circle. When states and civilization began in the Middle East, they were theocracies, and politics and religion were intertwined. This connection between politics and religion has been widespread throughout history and in different societies. For example, today, political parties in Europe often have religious labels, such as the Christian Democratic party in Germany.

In the past 20 years, Islamic fundamentalism has become a very significant dimension in Middle Eastern and Central Asian politics. Throughout their history, Islamic peoples have responded to the call of religious leaders like the Mahdi, "the rightly guided one," who, in the Sudan in the late nineteenth century, called for a renunciation of corruption and a return to the true moral values of Islam. Present-day fundamentalists are merely following these earlier examples. Reza Shah Pahlevi, the Shah of Iran, had embarked on a program of Westernization and modernization after World War II. Women were no longer required to wear veils and were encouraged to attend schools and colleges. Western clothing, Western music, and Western ideas were emphasized. In the late 1970s, the Ayatollah Khomeini, with his fundamentalist ideas involving a strict interpretation of Shi'ite Islam, succeeded in overthrowing the Shah. This Shi'ite fundamentalism of Iran has been influential in many parts of the Muslim world, reverberating as far as northern Nigeria, where Shi'ite and Sunni Muslims have, very recently, been fighting one another. This contrasts with the long-standing conflict between the Muslims in the north and the Yoruba and Ibo Christians of the south. The Muslim Brothers, a Shi'ite movement centered in the Hausa city of Zaria, are calling for an Iranian-style Islamic revolution in Nigeria. This call has resonated with unemployed angry young men, who see little hope for the future under a corrupt and repressive military dictatorship.

In widely separated Muslim countries like Algeria, Egypt, and Turkey, fundamentalist groups have launched political movements, attempting to take over the governments of these countries and govern strictly according to the Qur'an. Afghanistan, a monarchy attempting to modernize, turned Communist in 1978 under Soviet pressure, resulting in a civil war. The Taliban movement controls most of the country and has proclaimed an Islamic fundamentalist government in Afghanistan. The movement was originally formed by students from rural areas, studying in Islamic religious schools (*madrassah*), in the Kandahar region of Afghanistan. Their number was swelled by young men eager to end the factionalism and fighting. The Taliban have instituted decrees banning women from attending school or working and permitting them to leave their houses only when completely veiled. Men must give up wearing Western clothing and must wear full beards, and children must abandon music, dancing, kite flying, and playing marbles. Islamic fundamentalism has expanded from Afghanistan, to threaten Turkmenistan, Uzbekistan, Tajikistan, and Kyrgyzstan, now independent republics, formerly part of the Soviet Union. Armed fighters, presumably supported by the Taliban, seek to undermine the governments of these republics by taking hostages and conducting guerrilla warfare. Though the population of these countries is almost exclusively Muslim, they are not doctrinaire like the Taliban. But living standards have plummeted since the collapse of the Soviet Union, making people easy targets for radical fundamentalism. The fighting in Dagestan and Chechnya, republics farther to the west, and also Muslim has also been stirred up by Muslim fundamentalists (*New York Times,* October 31, 1999).

In an interesting way, Islamic fundamentalists have their parallel in Christian fundamentalists in America today, who are calling for a return to Christian values and politically mobilizing their followers to help bring this about at the ballot box. Many of these Christian fundamentalists were formerly mainline Protestants who joined evangelical denominations, which were practicing an unambiguous, stricter morality and a close adherence to biblical text. Members of such religious groups may teach their children at home instead of sending them to school, thereby controlling the content of their education and fostering ideas about creationism discussed earlier in this chapter. They seek to keep the interactions of the members of their families within their own religious community. They listen to their own kind of music on Christian radio stations, read books written for Christians and purchased in Christian bookstores, and watch Christian television. As members of the new Christian Right political movement, they have tried to shape elections from local school boards to presidential politics by being active in the Christian Coalition.

■ Why Religion?

Much of religious behavior has an instrumental goal; that is, the individual has some particular goal in mind when the religious ritual is performed. Those who carry out the rites and perform the spells desire to produce results, such as stopping a storm, bringing rain, or ensuring fertility for their crops. The Inuit shaman contacts his spirits to find out where the hunter should go to find his prey. The Trobriand garden magician recites the particular spells that will make the yams grow. The Kachin sacrifice to the *nats* to ensure that their crops will successfully grow to maturity. In many cultures, women perform religious rites to help them become pregnant. For example, in Poland, Catholic women go to the tombs of Catholic saints and Jewish rabbis to recite prayers to enable them to become pregnant. Orthodox Jewish women in Israel go to the tomb of Rachael, in Hebron, with the same goal. The motives and goals in all these cases are to bring about quite specific results to make natural forces and natural processes respond to human need.

Some religious behavior is directed toward guiding human action and enabling people to make decisions about how to act. Oracles and fortune-tellers are consulted to determine which course of action to take when faced with a choice. Whenever individuals are uncertain about what they should do, what course of action to take now or in the future, they may enlist the assistance of the supernatural to enable them to make a decision. What are the motives of the individual in doing this? When filled with doubts about making the right decision, one is provided with a reassuring means for obtaining an answer.

In many societies religious behavior is directed toward curing illness. In shamanic societies, the cause of the illness must be ascertained from the supernatural. Illness is often seen to be the result of the manipulation of the supernatural by evil people for evil purposes. The cure, of necessity, will also involve supernatural means. In our own society, believers in Christian Science (members of the Church of Christ, Scientist) believe that prayer alone will cure illness and refuse to accept medical care for themselves and their children.

Sometimes, worshipers and religious practitioners may say that the purposes of the religious rite are to emphasize communal values and to inculcate these values in the young. At this point the conscious purposes are close to the latent functions of reinforcing the communal bonds of society. Rites of passage specifically have this purpose. Such rituals serve not only to teach those involved the specifications of their new roles, but also to reinforce the structure of the society, as people are moved from one social position to another. Rites of intensification tied to the yearly calendar also provide order, structure, and meaning for the organization of society as well as for the life of each individual. Religious ritual is a dramatization that acts to reinforce and standardize a world view among the members of a congregation.

Sometimes religious action has particular effects that the individual may not be aware of. These are different from the conscious goals and purposes of the participants themselves. When the Trobrianders were on the hazardous open sea, where their small canoes might be smashed against the barrier reefs, they relied on magical formulas to protect them. Being in such a dangerous situation produces anxiety. Malinowski argued that reciting magical formulas reduced their anxiety and gave them confidence. American baseball players use magic rituals and formulas in areas of the game most fraught with uncertainty—hitting and pitching (Gmelch, 1971). Reducing anxiety for the pitcher or the hitter and giving the individual a sense of confidence, even if it is false confidence, improves performance. Anxiety is reduced for the Korean businessman after he goes through the performance of a shamanic ritual. He feels more confident as a consequence.

One could argue that anxiety itself has important functions in dangerous situations. Under such circumstances adrenaline should be flowing and all one's senses should be alerted to potential danger. In terms of this argument, performing magical rites just before such situations produces anxiety, which is advantageous, since it makes people alert. To resolve these two seemingly irreconcilable positions, one could say that excessive anxiety may be paralyzing, but overconfidence may also lead to bad performance. When a person is faced with uncertainty in possibly dangerous situations, alertness to the real dangers and confidence in one's ability to cope with the situation is the most desirable mix and can be brought about by performing some magical or religious ritual.

Religious Syncretism

At the beginning of this chapter, we noted the existence of witchcraft side by side with Christianity in England and the United States. In these same societies, people still wear amulets to ward off the evil eye, seek advice from fortune-tellers, and go to faith healers to be cured by the laying on of hands. Various pagan beliefs and local spirits were incorporated into Christianity as it spread through Europe and into Islam as it moved through the Middle East and parts of Africa. The same process occurred when Christian missionaries carried Christianity throughout the world. This missionary activity, which continues today, did not result in the eradication of earlier traditional beliefs and activities. Instead, Christianity has combined with local belief systems in many different parts of the world. This same process has also occurred with Islam. We will discuss this in greater detail in Chapter 13.

We have pointed out that religious institutions respond to changing conditions and are influenced by other belief systems. In America, this process has produced new forms of Christianity and Islam, for example, Mormonism (Church of Jesus Christ of Latter-Day Saints), Christian Science (Church of Christ, Scientist), and the Nation of Islam. Sometimes entirely new religions, such as Scientology, emerge. These religious groups represent responses to the distinctly American scene. Although the forms of religious expression may change, the functions they fulfill remain constant.

Religion fulfills certain universal functions, such as the allaying of anxiety; explanatory functions, which answer such questions as why humans came to be on earth and the meaning of life, and expiatory function, which individuals are assisted in dealing with guilt and misfortune. The forms that religious practices take vary from society to society. In terms of its explanatory function, religion is to be distinguished from science, in that the latter is based on empirical observations and the former on belief. Societies have a variety of ways of conceiving of the supernatural. These conceptualizations are directly related to the ways in which their societies are organized. A variety of techniques are used to approach the supernatural, such as prayer, sacrifice, and different kinds of rituals, including rites of passage and of intensification. Religious specialists, with special abilities that connect them to the supernatural, exist in all societies to assist members of their societies in approaching the supernatural. Frequently, older religious ideas, such as shamanism and Wiccan, are resurrected in new guises. The adoption of new religious ideas frequently involves political considerations, and religion sometimes becomes a potent political force. This has been the case historically and is still true today.

Chapter Eleven

Myths, Legends, and Folktales

People attempt to explain the unknowable by constructing a supernatural world; they also talk about that world. They tell folktales about supernatural creatures. They relate legends about the distant past of unrecorded history in which knights slew dragons. They tell myths about the origins of the world and of people and their social groups. They tell the myths of how God gave them the very land on which they dwell. They tell stories about the exploits of supernatural animals that talk; about big bad wolves that swallow grandmothers; about the brother of the wolf, the coyote, who acts as a trickster. They tell stories about fairies, elves, and the Little People. These different types of stories all deal with certain universal themes, such as birth, growing up, male-female relations, and death.

Myths, legends, and folktales represent a continuum. These categories derive from our own culture, but they provide a useful framework for organizing this material. Myths deal with the remote past, often with the time of the origin of things both natural and cultural—how the world and its people were created, how fire was discovered, and how crops were domesticated. As the time period becomes less remote, myths fade into legends, which are sometimes thought to have a basis in historical fact. Folktales deal with an indeterminate time, which, in European folktales, is indicated by the standard opening, "Once upon a time. . . " To the tellers of these stories, they constitute accounts of real people and real events.

Myths

The people of Wogeo, whose cosmology was described in the preceding chapter, have a myth that tells how the flutes that represent the *nibek* spirits came to be. As is typical, this myth takes place in the distant past when the culture heroes who created everything in the world lived. Two female heroes dreamed the idea of making flutes. They cut two sticks of bamboo and bored a hole in each, forming flutes that immediately began to play. They were overjoyed with the self-playing flutes. When

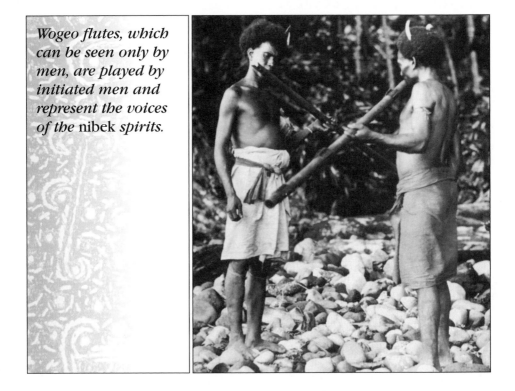

Wogeo flutes, which can be seen only by men, are played by initiated men and represent the voices of the nibek *spirits.*

they went to work in the gardens, they stoppered the holes to make the flutes stop playing. An adolescent boy stole the flutes from the two women and tried to blow them, causing the women to return. On seeing that the boy had stolen the flutes, the women told him that the flutes would never again play by themselves. Though the flutes were intended for everybody, since a male had stolen them, no female could ever look at the flutes again. The women told him that it would be hard to learn to blow the flutes, but if boys did not make the effort, they would never grow up to be men. The two women then set off, leaving the island of Wogeo in disgust. The two islands where they eventually settled, Kadovar and Blupblup, and the mainland of New Guinea, where they passed some time, are the only places where bamboo for flutes can currently be found.

Anthropological approaches to the interpretation of myths are directly related to various theoretical frameworks. One approach interprets myths as literal history. People who use this approach view the myths about great floods that inundated the world as the retelling of stories about actual floods. Myths about the disappearance of the lost continent of Atlantis are seen as based upon the actual disappearance of a real civilization located on an island. In such an approach, the Wogeo myth would be interpreted as signifying an earlier period of matriarchy, when women controlled those aspects of society men now control. Nineteenth-century evolutionists, such as Lewis Henry Morgan and Johann Jakob Bachofen, would have interpreted this myth as demonstrating an earlier stage of matrilineal social organization and matriarchy. They hypothesized that all societies went through such a stage as they developed. This stage was followed by patrilineal social organization and patriarchy. This method of interpreting myths as literal history was discredited by anthropologists, along with the unilineal theory of the evolution of societies through a fixed succession of stages.

Twentieth-century approaches to the interpretation of myths include, among others, the Freudian approach, which has been adopted by people interested in psychoanalysis, including anthropologist Alan Dundes. The Wogeo myth lends itself readily to a Freudian interpretation. The flutes are masculine objects, associated only with males, and are obvious phallic symbols. What happens to the flutes in the myth seems to involve penis envy on the part of the women and anxiety about castration on the part of the men. Just as individuals express unconscious fears and anxieties in symbolic form through dreams, myths are seen as reflecting the collective anxieties of a society. Myths in this approach give cultural expression to these anxieties. Freud considered certain repressed anxieties and frustrations to be universal—that is, connected to panspecies characteristics related to growth and development.

Another approach to myths was provided by Malinowski, who was antievolutionist and anti-Freudian. He insisted on the necessity of analyzing a myth in relation to its social and cultural context. Myth to Malinowski was a charter for how and what people should believe, act, and feel. Just as our Declaration of Independence states that "all men are created equal," a body of myths lays out the ideals that members of a culture use to guide their behavior. Myths may also be charters for social groupings like clans, containing statements about their rights to land and other clan possessions, their relations to totemic ancestors, and their relative rank and relations to other social groups. The Malinowski approach to myth as charter requires that the Wogeo myth be examined in the context of Wogeo culture. To interpret the myth from this point of view, one needs the following additional cultural facts. There is a men's cult that revolves around the men's house where the sacred flutes are kept. At adolescence, boys go through a rite of passage and are initiated into this cult. The initiation involves scarification of the tongue so that the boys can be rid of the effects of their mother's milk. Only after this is done can they learn to play the flutes. Boys are also taught to incise their penises at the same time. They stand knee-deep in the ocean, and each makes an incision in his penis with a sharpened clamshell so that the blood flows into the ocean and not on his body, which would be dangerous and polluting to him. Men do this periodically to rid themselves of the pollution resulting from sexual intercourse with women. Both men and women are seen as polluted by sexual intercourse. Women get rid of this pollution through menstruation, but men have to be taught to incise their penises to accomplish the same end. Women are kept away from the men's house and are never allowed to see the sacred flutes. When the *nibek* spirits appear prior to the large ceremonial distribution, their voices are the flutes. The people of Wogeo say, "Men play flutes, women bear infants." When the men play the flutes, they are in a ritual state that is considered dangerous, and they must abstain from sexual intercourse. Malinowski's approach to myth would interpret the Wogeo myth as providing the justification and rationale for men's performing certain ritual and ceremonial roles from which women are excluded.

The American anthropologist Clyde Kluckhohn stressed the interdependence of myth and ritual. This approach has its antecedents in the nineteenth-century work of William Robertson Smith who saw the two connected, with ritual antedating myth, which is an explanation of it (Segal, 1999: 37 ff.). In many instances, according to Kluckhohn, myths provide statements about the origins of rituals as well as details of how they are to be performed. However, Kluckhohn saw ritual and myth as fulfilling the same societal needs. The same kinds of emotional feelings are aroused in the telling of the myth and in the performing of the ritual. He also saw myth and ritual as serving the psychological function of alleviating various forms of anxiety. There is a direct connection between the myth and the ritual in Wogeo. The flutes have a central role in ritual activity, being the voices of the *nibek* spirits. The initiation ritual of boys, which involves their learning how to play the flutes, is directly connected to the mythic statement about a boy's not growing up until he learns to play the flute.

Lévi-Strauss has pursued a large-scale, detailed analysis of myths from North and South American Indian societies (Lévi-Strauss, 1963, 1971). According to Lévi-Strauss, myths provide explanations for contradictions that are present in a culture and that cannot be resolved. The Wogeo myth emphasizes the separation of women from men, after men obtained possession of the flutes. In Lévi-Strauss's terms, the myth attempts to resolve the contradiction between the ideal of keeping males and females apart and the need for them to come together in order to reproduce society. Like all other myths, this myth, too, fails to provide a permanent solution to this contradiction.

The theoretical approaches to myth are not inconsistent with one another, with the exception of the explanation of myth as literal history, which has been completely discredited. Each approach examines myths from a different point of view. Analysis of the Wogeo myth shows that the sexual symbolism that Freud emphasized is present there, the myth as charter for male-female relations that Malinowski stressed is also evident, as well as the close connection between the myth and rituals of male initiation that Kluckhohn pointed out. Finally, the myth deals with an irreconcilable contradiction, which is the focus of Lévi-Strauss's concern.

Myths must always be understood in connection with other cultural facts. In Wogeo, the aphorism "men play flutes, women bear infants" is very important. Male and female are seen as separate but complementary. Women bear children as part of a natural biological process. Flutes are cultural objects manufactured by men. During the difficult process of initiation, men must be taught how to play the flutes. Women are therefore associated with natural things and men with cultural things. When men play the flutes, they are associating with the *nibek* spirits, whose voices are the flutes, and they must practice sexual abstinence. Since the people of Wogeo believe that when men and women have sexual intercourse, they become polluted, both men and women must be ritually cleansed. Women do this in a natural way, through menstruation. But men must do this through culturally learned behavior—the incising of their penises. Once again, women are associated with nature and men with culture. In Wogeo, symbolic barriers are erected to keep men and women apart. Ideally, each sex should lead its life separately, but in order for women to bear children, as the aphorism says they should, the sexes must come together. This is the only way that society can reproduce itself.

Boys' initiation consists of a series of ceremonies during which the boys are symbolically separated from women and turned into men. When very young boys have their ears pierced, they are told that the *nibek* monsters, the "big things," have bitten them and will come back later and eat them up. When the boys are 10 years old, a ceremony is held during which they are admitted to the men's house. The boys are symbolically swallowed by the *nibek* monster, pass through his bowels, and are "reborn," not from women, but from the anus of the *nibek*, which is associated with men. Several years later each boy's tongue is scarified. This is to allow the pollution resulting from drinking mother's milk to flow away and to make the tongue more pliable, permitting him to play the flute. Initiation is therefore a process through which boys, who are associated with women, are separated from them and are re-born from the *nibek* spirits as men.

The myth deals with a time when women dream and then make the flutes, which play by themselves. No cultural learning is involved. At this time men and women are not separate. After the boy steals the flutes, men must learn to play them, because the flutes will no longer play by themselves. At this point, men separate themselves from women. The same pattern is repeated in the aphorism "men play flutes, women bear infants," in the initiation ceremonies and in the myth. That is, men, representing culture, are separated from women, representing nature. Boys, who are associated with their mothers and have not yet learned the secrets of their culture, learn those secrets at initiation and acquire culture in the process. But the myth says more than that. It says that, at one time, women were superior to men. They bore the children and had the flutes as well. The present domination of men rests upon their having stolen what was once women's. Women by nature are superior because they can bear children, because they can cleanse themselves naturally through menstruation, and because for them, the flutes played by themselves. Men have to do everything the hard way—by means of cultural practices that must be learned. But their control of culture enables them to dominate women. Ultimately, the myth is about the origins of culture and the tension inherent in male-female relations.

This theme of the tension in male-female relations is universal in human societies and, as such, is often expressed in their mythologies. On the other side of the world, the Mundurucu of the Amazon forest of Brazil have a myth that is strikingly similar to the Wogeo myth (Murphy and Murphy, 1985). The Mundurucu have sacred trumpets that are kept from the women. In the myth, the trumpets were discovered by the women, who then owned them. At that time, men performed all the women's tasks, such as getting firewood and water and making manioc cakes, and women were dominant over them. The trumpets had to be fed meat, which only the men could provide through hunting. Finally, the men took over the trumpets, as well as control of the men's house. The women were no longer allowed to see the trumpets, were no longer permitted into the men's house, and were henceforth subordinate to the men. Like the Wogeo myth, the Mundurucu myth is a justification for male domination over females. As in Wogeo, the myth begins with a reversal of roles and the attribution of superiority to females in mythic times. Tension in the relationship between males and females in Mundurucu and in Wogeo, and male insecurity about domination over females, leads to the common occurrence of such a myth.

In ancient Greek mythology, which is an integral part of our Western civilization, there are echoes of the same theme. In his introduction to the Greek myths, Robert Graves (1955) linked the myths to what he believed to have been an earlier matriarchal stage in the development of European society. Both the Amazons, superhuman women who controlled their society, and the Fates, women who, through their weaving, determined the destiny of all humanity, are supposedly evidence in the myths for this matriarchal stage of society. But the Greek myths cannot be taken as evidence of literal history any more than the Wogeo or Mundurucu myths can. These Greek myths tell us about contradictions and tensions in ancient Greek society. As we can see, the universal theme of male-female relations is handled in similar ways in very different societies.

Legends

Myths treat the ancient past and the origins of things, while legends deal with the less remote past, just beyond the fringe of history. Frequently, legends are about heroes who overcome obstacles, slay dragons, and defeat conquering armies to establish the independence of their homelands. Such legends are retold to justify the claim of a people to their land and their integrity as a people. The traditions of Polynesian societies, as they have been retold over the generations, illustrate the way myths fade into legends. For example, the Maori, the Polynesian population that first settled New Zealand, have a myth of how Maui fished up the island of New Zealand from the ocean depths and later became a culture hero who obtained fire. Kupe, another culture hero, subsequently rediscovered the island while chasing a supernatural octopus and reported back to the other Maori living in their legendary homeland. The first settlers set sail and reached the island now called New Zealand by following Kupe's directions. Maori genealogies are remembered and repeated down through the generations. These genealogies, which go back as far as 40 generations, link the present population to the first settlers and to Kupe. The legends of the Maori are concerned with the several migrations to New Zealand and the manner in which each tribe and kin group successively occupied its land. Maori legends, which were recorded by English missionaries and scholars in the nineteenth century, are now being used in various political contexts in which the Maori, as the indigenous people of New Zealand, are not only asserting their ethnic identity but demanding restitution for lost land.

The traditions of the native Hawaiians, who are also Polynesian speakers, are similar to those of the Maori. Like the Maori, the Hawaiians are great genealogists, with a tradition of migrations by canoe from Tahiti to the islands of Hawaii. The genealogy of the Hawaiian royal family, the Kumulipo, is a prayer chant that traces descent directly back to the gods. The gods appear to be like men in their form and actions, and it is hard to separate them from chiefs who lived and were later deified. Thus the world of myth imperceptibly becomes the world of legend and finally, the known world of history.

Folktales

Folktales are set within a timeless framework. They are concerned with imparting moral values and usually take the form of demonstrating what happens to individuals who violate the moral code of the society. Often animals freely interact with humans as heroes or villains; at other times tales may be about animals who talk, act, and think like human beings. Fairy tales are also included within the category of folktales.

One of the most common folktale motifs is that of the trickster. Among many North American Indian societies, the trickster takes the form of the coyote, though among the Kwakiutl, the trickster is a raven. There are many sides to the character of Coyote. Sometimes he is depicted as being very cunning—he feigns death in order to catch game; he cheats at races and wins. At other times he is singularly stupid. In some tales he is a glutton, and in others he is involved in amorous and ribald adventures.

Typical of the Coyote tales is "Coyote and Bullhead," which was told by the Wintu of northern California (Pitkin, 1977). Coyote, while traveling north, encounters a swarm of small, black bullhead fishes and is able to roast and eat all but one by tricking them into swarming onto hot stones over a fire. Subsequently, he meets a rotten tree stump creaking in the wind who refuses to respond to him. Thinking himself teased, Coyote punches at the stump until he is stuck fast. Some people come along and free him. Later, Coyote again encounters the sole surviving bullhead, whom he provokes, insulting him by implying that his relatives are all dead, until the fish eats Coyote. The fish then rolls into the water under a big rock. The people come looking for Coyote and see the fish. They spear the fish after they get a magical sky-spear, slit open its belly, and out pops Coyote. On emerging, he pretends that he has dozed off and does not know how he came to be in the fish's belly. The people then sew up the bullhead and return him to the water.

In this Wintu tale about Coyote, he is revealed as a strange combination—the clever deceiver and teaser, as well as the dupe and victim of his own actions. The people refer to him as "uncle," though he is really more like a child. He must be extricated from his difficulties by the grown-ups—the people in the story, who lecture him not to behave in this way anymore. Like a mischievous child, he of course does the same thing again. This sequence of events has a twofold function—it amuses the listeners while at the same time imparting the moral that insulting, provoking, and teasing are wrong.

A structural analysis of this Coyote tale will enable us to understand its message more clearly. It can be broken down into three distinct episodes: (A) Coyote eats the little bullheads, (B) Coyote fights with the stump, and (C) the last bullhead eats

Coyote. Arranging the three episodes in columns allows us to see the relationships among the episodes more clearly:

Episode	I	II	III
A	Coyote tricks bullheads.	Coyote eats bullheads.	One bullhead escapes.
B	Coyote is provoked by the stump.	Coyote is stuck to the stump.	Coyote escapes with the people's help.
C	Coyote teases the last bullhead.	Bullhead eats Coyote.	Coyote escapes with the people's help.

When lined up in this way, the three episodes are seen to be very similar. However, episode B is diametrically opposed to episode A. In A, Coyote successfully tricks the bullheads, while in B he himself is tricked as a result of his own stupidity. In A, he wins and eats all but one of the bullheads; in B, he loses and is trapped, though he ultimately escapes. Episode C reconciles and unites the seemingly unrelated episodes A and B into a single story. Episode C refers back to episode A in that the bullhead has his revenge on Coyote for eating his relatives. Episode C is a reversal of episode A, since the bullhead eats Coyote in C, while Coyote eats the bullheads in A. Episode C is very similar to episode B in that Coyote's teasing leads to his entrapment in both episodes.

What is the meaning of this Coyote story? What message does it convey? The structural analysis reveals the message of the tale. In Wintu culture Coyote represents the child. This story is an attempt to teach Coyote the rules of the society, though Coyote will never really learn. Though Coyote succeeds as a trickster in the first episode, he fails in the second and third episodes and must be extricated by the people, the larger community. The message conveyed is that, though a trickster may seem at first to be successful, one must ultimately conform to the rules in order to be a successful member of the group. The Wintu rules that Coyote violates are striking out on one's own, teasing, and insultingly referring to the dead. The gathering of food was a communal activity; striking out on one's own, as Coyote did, violated this. Teasing and allowing oneself to be provoked by teasing were not considered proper adult behavior by the Wintu. But worst of all, Coyote broke the Wintu taboo against referring to the dead by teasing the last surviving bullhead. The message to the listeners was that if you violate these rules, you will end up like Coyote, a child who can survive only if he is constantly rescued by adults from dilemmas. In the Wintu tale, humor and teasing are emphasized. In contrast, among the Okanagan of the Plateau, Coyote is portrayed as a culture hero who named the tribes and taught them the essential cultural practices, though he also played tricks and did many foolish things (Teit, in Baillargeon and Tepper, 1998: 74). As John Fire Lame Deer, a traditional Sioux holy man was quoted as saying, "Coyote, Iktomi, and all their kind [Tricksters] are sacred. A people that have so much to weep about as we Indians need their laughter to survive" (quoted in Erdoes and Ortiz, 1998: xxi).

The trickster figure seems to be a universal folklore figure that represents the incongruous combination of monster, loutish liar, braggart, creator and destroyer, and duper, as well as the one who is always duped himself (Goldman, 1998). According to Peck, "European immigrants brought to North America tales in which a *human* trickster outwits other people, and such stories have never waned in popularity" (1998: 203). In European tales, the trickster is almost always a human male, while in Native American tales he is usually personified as an animal, though he may sometimes assume a human shape (Erdoes and Ortiz, 1998: xiii). Goldman identifies two main strands of "trickster scholarship," those who have studied the trickster motif. In the first, the trickster enables breaches of the accepted order to occur within the realm of the imagination, allowing adults and children to be amused by behavior categorized as antisocial while at the same time being socialized. The Wintu tale about Coyote does this. The second deals with the marginal, liminal status of the trickster who is a mediating being, resolving dilemmas of human existence. It is a way of talking about ourselves in a satiric, ironic, and comedic fashion (Goldman, 1998: 90).

Just as Coyote tales taught morality to children, fairy tales, according to Bruno Bettelheim, teach children about what it means to grow up. While myths are about extraordinary, superhuman heroes or gods, the characters in fairy tales are ordinary mortals. "Whatever strange events the fairy tale hero experiences, they do not make him superhuman, as is true for the mythical hero. This real humanity suggests to the child that, whatever the content of the fairy tale it is but fanciful elaborations and exaggerations of the tasks he has to meet, and of his hopes and fears" (Bettelheim, 1977: 40).

Performance

Originally, myths, legends, and folktales were transmitted orally, and each telling was a performance. They were retold from generation to generation, to the awe and amusement of successive audiences. Each time a story was retold, it came out slightly differently. Variations were introduced, different episodes were included, and eventually, different versions of the same story developed. Stories usually spread from one society to another over a wide area, and in each of these societies a somewhat different version of the story could be found. Anthropologists collect as many versions of a single story told in a particular society as they can. By comparing these different versions, they are better able to ascertain the meaning of the story. In similar fashion, the same and related stories in different societies over a wide area are collected and compared by anthropologists. Lévi-Strauss analyzed different versions of the same myth and related myths in different South American Indian societies (Lévi-Strauss, 1971). His analysis revealed the presence of the same themes and contradictions in mythologies throughout this large area.

When we shift to an examination of the performance aspects of myths, legends, and tales—which are, in effect, oral narratives—the factor of creativity enters the picture. Huntsman points out that the different presentations of the same story move from a veneration of "tradition" to a celebration of "creativity" (1995: 124). Tokelau tales, or *kakai,* which are fictitious tales told as entertainment, must contain the episodes, chants, songs, and key phrases that the audience expects. But the tellers of these tales have a wide latitude to elaborate and embellish a story as long as they include what their listeners expect (Huntsman, 1995: 125). In contrast, Tokelau *tala,* which are myths, legends, historical narratives, or accounts of the pre-Christian past, have as their primary purpose to inform, though they may also be entertaining. Specific geographic place-names " 'ground' the narrative as an account of events that happened at known, named places" (Huntsman, 1995: 154). These place-names must be narrated accurately. Huntsman also makes the point, made by many others, that storytellers and raconteurs "tailor" their narrative performances to their audiences (Huntsman, 1995: 154). It should be noted that tellers of stories and tales also vary in their storytelling abilities.

Consideration of the performance aspects of oral narratives places them within a temporal framework, which brings up the question of the continuities and changes of such accounts. The ghost narratives of the Cook Islands, or *tupapaku,* recount stories about spirits in animal form, which are deeply rooted in Polynesian history. Recently, they have come to include stories about cows, pigs, dogs, goats, horses, and cats—introduced domesticates—as spirit vehicles. As Clerk notes, *tupapaku* accounts "have never been separated from the life of the community as a whole. They have adapted consistently to new circumstances, incorporating new experience, yet maintaining a continuity with traditions of great antiquity" (Clerk, 1995: 173). Continuity and change also characterize other aspects of culture. As we noted for the potlatch in previous chapters, although people now give away power boats and Hudson Bay blankets instead of elk skins, the organization of the potlatch remains the same. The contents of myths, tales, and potlatches may change, but their structure remains the same.

When myths, folktales, and legends are written down, an oral narrative becomes written literature. The stories may form the basis for the literary tradition of the society. The legends of King Arthur and the Knights of the Round Table ceased to be stories told by bards, or professional storytellers, and became English literature. The fact that the story is now written down does not mean that it will not continue to change. The story may be rewritten by poor writers or by good writers and may change with each retelling. The characters, motifs, and central themes of these stories may often be used by poets, novelists, and dramatists in their own works. For example, in Mary McCarthy's novel *The Group* (1963), the knights have been transformed into female students at Vassar in the 1950s. The American musical *Camelot* also retells the legend of King Arthur and the Knights of the Round Table.

█ Legends and Folklore in American Culture

One may pose the question, Does our culture have myths, legends, or folklore? Myths deal with the remote past and with superhumans who created the world, the people in it, and all their material objects and cultural institutions. American culture does not include these kinds of myths. However, stories about how American culture was forged, and its origins, are our American myths. Legendary figures abound. Some were real people, such as Billy the Kid, Davy Crockett, Daniel Boone, Kit Carson, Annie Oakley, and Buffalo Bill. Stories about their lives became legends, but other legends about them had no basis in fact. Other heroes, such as Pecos Bill, John Henry, and Paul Bunyan, probably never lived. The setting for all these legends was the expanding American frontier. The stories demonstrated how these people conquered natural obstacles and made the frontier livable. They were scouts who led the wagon trains across the dangerous and endless Plains. They were rivermen who opened up the rivers to settlement and commerce. They were railroad builders who laid the steel track across an expanding nation. They were the sheriffs and marshals who made the frontier safe. In American legends, the theme is a characteristically American one—the conquest of the frontier and the settlement of the land. As occurs in legends in general, American heroes, by their bravery, their ingenuity, and their labor, assert the claim of a people to their land. This, of course, totally ignored the claim of the Native American population who were on the land first.

Sometimes the heroes of the legends assumed superhuman proportions. Paul Bunyan was a legendary lumberjack and logger. As the lumber industry moved across America from Maine to Michigan and Minnesota, and then later to Washington and Oregon, the Bunyan stories moved with it, and Paul Bunyan, at first a regional hero, became a national hero. The Paul Bunyan stories all have a distinctive character. Bunyan, his ax, and his blue ox Babe are of enormous and superhuman size. Bunyan's feats are distinctive because of both his cleverness and his great strength, and many of the stories are humorous (Peck, 1998: 131 ff.). In some of the stories he creates natural landmarks, like Puget Sound. Many stories demonstrate his ability to conquer nature. In one story he makes a river run backward in order to break up a log jam. Paul Bunyan stories are also told in the oil fields of Texas and Oklahoma. Here, Bunyan is an oil man who is even given credit for inventing the tools and methods of drilling for oil. The Bunyan stories began in the tales told in the lumber camps of northeastern Michigan and reached a maximum popularity and audience when they became the subject of newspaper columns and advertising copy in the second decade of the twentieth century. At this point they were no longer folktales; they had become popular literature.

While the legends of Paul Bunyan and other tall tales are indigenously American, many folktales and fairy tales told in America are largely derivative, having come with immigrants from other countries. Fairy tales like "Cinderella," "Little Red Riding Hood," and "Jack and the Beanstalk" were part of a body of European tales written down by the Brothers Grimm in the nineteenth century. These stories continue to be told in America today to amuse children while at the same time conveying moral lessons. Joel Chandler Harris recorded a series of stories from African Americans living on former plantations in the American South in the latter part of the nineteenth century. These stories, revolving around the characters of Uncle Remus and Br'er Rabbit, were also derivative, having been brought primarily from West Africa to America by African slaves. This area is particularly known for its animal tales, such as the stories of Ananse the Spider, a trickster figure similar to Coyote. The theme of the rabbit as a trickster also appears in the tales of the Creek, Natchez, and other southeastern Native American groups. Scholarly analysis has shown that the tales were borrowed by them from slaves.

The character of Uncle Remus was modeled after Remus Banks. The boy in the picture is the grandson of author Joel Chandler Harris, who recorded the stories.

Legends and tales are rarely told by storytellers in present-day America and are infrequently read in books—except by parents to small children and, perhaps, in required courses in literature. The major themes of such stories, however, continue to be repeated, but now in the media of mass communications. It is in films and television that these same themes from legends and tales reappear. One has only to think of the Western film to understand this point, since Westerns have become inextricably linked to the American identity. The hero of the classic Western, like the heroes of American legends, is a rugged individualist who tames the frontier. But Americans have an ambivalent attitude about taming the frontier. They look back with fondness to the time when the frontier represented escape from the constraints of society—a time when individuals took the law into their own hands. The cattlemen who used the open range for cattle grazing represent the beginning of law and order. But they fought the farmers who wanted to fence in the range and who represent a further step in the process of control over nature. In the classic film *The Man Who Shot Liberty Valence,* director John Ford captures the ambivalence between the wilderness of the frontier, represented by the outlaw Liberty Valence; civilization, represented by Senator Ransom Stoddard; and Donovan, the real hero, who straddles both worlds. The story of the killing of Valence, the villain, is told in a series of flashbacks from a civilized present time to an earlier frontier time. But a sense of loss and nostalgia for that earlier period pervades the film. Despite the changes in emphasis of

The only known photograph of Billy the Kid, whose life became an American legend.

the 1960s and 1970s, "the Western's overall thrust sanctified territorial expansion, justified dispossession of the Indians, fueled nostalgia for a largely mythicized past, exalted self-reliance and posited violence as the main solution to personal and societal problems" (Coyne, 1997: 3). However, the usual representation of American identity in the Western was white and male. This picture was to some extent transformed in the late 1970s, when the TV miniseries *Centennial,* based on a novel by James Michener, presented the history of a Colorado town, emphasizing the multicultural composition of the frontier and condemning the butchery of the Indians by a racist army officer (Coyne, 1997: 184). More recently, *Dances With Wolves,* which many might not call a Western, clearly presents a different picture of Native Americans than do classic Westerns such as *Stagecoach*.

The legend of Billy the Kid has been told and retold in films, plays, novels, and ballets. How did Billy the Kid, who was a real person, turn into a legend, and what are the characteristics that differentiate the legendary Billy from the real Billy? Billy the Kid was shot and killed by Pat Garrett (himself a legendary figure), the sheriff of Lincoln County, New Mexico, in July 1881. He had been arrested for murder and sentenced to hang seven months earlier, but shot and killed his two guards and escaped from prison. Garrett and his posse tracked him down to Fort Sumner, an abandoned army fort, where they killed him. Shortly thereafter, Garrett, with the help of a former newspaperman, wrote the book *The Authentic Life of Billy the Kid,* and the myth was launched. Since so many false stories were being told about Billy at that time, Garrett wanted to set the record straight. According to Garrett, Billy committed his first murder at the age of 12 to defend his mother's honor. Billy carried out later murders in Lincoln County after the execution of his friend John Tunstall, becoming an avenging angel until Sheriff Garrett, with a heavy heart, ended his life. Much of the information in Garrett's account was either mistaken (including Billy's real name) or invented.

Years later, a researcher collecting folklore as part of an oral-history project in New Mexico interviewed a Hispanic member of Sheriff Pat Garrett's posse. The Billy that he recalled was very generous, spoke fluent Spanish, and wore moccasins. "Everybody liked Billy the Kid." He claimed that Garrett's account of Billy's death was all wrong and that Billy was much too smart to be caught in the room where Garrett said he shot him. Though for two weeks the posse surrounded the house where the shooting took place, they never caught sight of Billy or recovered his body.

Each teller of the Billy the Kid story expands a different aspect of the "myth." What do we know about the real person who was Billy the Kid? On page 247 is the one photograph extant of the man who was known as Billy the Kid. He was born Henry McCarty, probably in New York City, of Irish Catholic ancestry. While he was still young, his mother took him and his brother out West, ending up in Silver City, New Mexico. Before he came to Lincoln County, New Mexico, Henry McCarty, at the age of 18, seems to have killed a man in a gunfight in Arizona in 1877. After that, he assumed the name William Bonney. The Lincoln County "war" into which Henry McCarty was drawn was, in reality, a battle between two factions for political control. One faction consisted of a group of Irish Catholics. The other faction consisted of Protestants led by John Tunstall, an Englishman who was killed. The Lincoln County war has been interpreted as a continuation of the ethnic-religious conflict that took place in Northern Ireland (O'Toole, 1999). McCarty, born a Catholic, was on the opposite side of the Irish-Catholic faction in this war. Since Henry's mother remarried when he was 13 to a Scotch-Irish Protestant man, it appears that Henry and his mother converted. Therefore Henry, now Billy, became a member of a group of gunfighters for the Protestant faction, which ended in his capture and trial for murder and his killing by Pat Garrett after he escaped from jail.

What are the elements in the myth of Billy the Kid that resonate and touch the emotions of so many Americans? From the very beginning, even in Pat Garrett's story, which has as its primary purpose to glorify Garrett, the sheriff, we see the figure of Billy as the avenging angel and the fighter for justice. Though an outlaw, he is no wanton killer. Garrett sees the first murder that Billy committed as justified, because he was defending his mother's honor. Billy was driven to commit this crime. He is an outsider, yet he understands and obeys a code of honor. He honors friendship and loyalty. He is generous to the poor, and consequently, they help him escape from the authorities, who are evil. Like the wind, Billy cannot be captured. He lives on somewhere. The characteristics attributed to Billy were those of legendary outlaws and heroes such as Jessie James and Robin Hood. Finally, Billy the Kid is only 21 when he is killed. His youth itself is an important part of the myth. These features may not, in fact, describe Henry McCarty, but they are all characteristics of the myth of Billy the Kid. They explain why his story has been and will continue to be retold in films, with Paul Newman, Val Kilmer, Kris Kristofferson, or some un-known young actor playing the role of Billy.

In addition to seeing Western films as contemporary versions of American leg-ends, some analysts have examined American films as myths whose meanings en-code somewhat different symbolic patterns characterizing American society. Nathanson, for example, has analyzed the film *The Wizard of Oz* in terms of the way its specific mythic properties relate to the important problems of human existence. This film has become a classic. As Nathanson notes, "*The Wizard of Oz* may be called a 'secular myth' because, though not overtly religious, it functions in a modern os-tensibly secular society, to some extent, the way myths function in traditional and religious societies" (Nathanson, 1991: 312). The use of fantastic imagery, the inclu-sion of supernatural forces and beings, and the fact that it relates to basic human questions, such as where we have come from, where we are going, where we be-long, and who we are in relation to others, situate *The Wizard of Oz* in the realm of myth. *The Wizard of Oz* is about coming of age and building new relationships and also about going home. Though the Wizard himself initially appears to be a fraud, he is the source of important folk wisdom: The qualities Dorothy and her compan-ions are searching for—a heart for the Tin Man, courage for the Cowardly Lion, a brain for the Scarecrow, and the capacity to be grown-up for Dorothy—are to be found within oneself. The heroine, Dorothy, comes of age in the Emerald City where she is transformed from a child into an adult, after which she is transported back to Kansas. The film was made during the Depression, a very unsettled time, and films from this period often depict explicitly going home and implicitly growing up. Var-ious American symbolic landscapes can be identified in the film, including Munchkin City—a small Midwestern city; the Emerald City—the Eastern metropolis; the Haunted Forest—the wilderness, threatening and hostile untamed nature; the Yellow Brick Road—a path that pierces the wilderness and represents the unification of America, as well as the freedom and hope of the open highway; and, finally, the Frontier Farm—home, order, and civilization. The Wizard also communicates the no-tion of the progressive urban setting as set against the traditional rural countryside of the populist world view, the ultimate resolution of the two being technological agriculture in a bucolic paradise (Nathanson, 1991: 173). Kansas is the beginning, the paradise, Oz is the world in which Dorothy searches for order in chaos (the Haunted Forest). At the end of the film, she finally returns home, having grown up. The film gives mythic expression to what are seen as the deepest feelings of the American people, a nostalgia for the past combined with a hope for the future.

The *Star Wars* trilogy, to which a fourth film has recently been added, has been said to represent "one of the great myths of our time," combining the theme of a heroic journey with that of the eternal battle between good and evil (Henderson, 1997: 3). As noted above, Westerns as a film genre popular from the end of World War I to the early 1970s were no longer very significant in either films or television after that point. However, in the *Star Wars* series, George Lucas, the filmmaker, recy-cled some Western themes, which resonate with more general American conceptual-izations. At the beginning of the first film, *Star Wars: Episode IV, A New Hope,* Luke Skywalker is living with his foster parents on the remote desert planet Tatooine, the frontier of civilization, which is also occupied by the Sand People, the equivalent of the Native Americans, as the uncivilized Other. Luke starts on his heroic journey of revenge after his foster parents are killed and his home destroyed. This parallels the destruction by Native Americans of frontier settlements established on Indian territory by American pioneers, who saw the area as a wilderness to be occupied and tamed, and the survivors who sought revenge. Some of the characters in the film recapitulate proto-typical figures from Westerns, for example, Han Solo (the loner), the quick-on-the-draw gunfighter, and Greedo, the bounty hunter. This first film in the series is climaxed by a classic Western-style shoot-out with Death Star, with the evil Empire as the O.K. Corral (Henderson, 1997: 129). In *Return of the Jedi,* Luke, representing the force for good, returns to his home planet, now overrun by a powerful criminal and his gang, and turns out the villains. This theme in *Return of the Jedi* is a recapitulation of the themes of *Dodge City* and *My Darling Clementine.*

Since the beginning of the twentieth century, Americans have been captivated by technology and its great potential; this is a also a significant theme in the *Star Wars* series. Science and technology transformed our lives and held out the potential for exploring space and the world under the sea, areas heretofore unknown and foreign to humans, as well as for unlocking nature's secrets. To Americans, science not only has the potential to solve the world's problems but also can eventually provide knowledge about all aspects of nature. Science fiction, in the form of literature, comic books, and film were the settings in which this category of themes was explored. In the *Star Wars* films, intergalactic travel is an everyday occurrence, and the level of technological development is accelerated to a degree far beyond what today's humans experience or can even imagine. American faith in the future of technology began to be undermined, to some extent beginning in the 1970s, when Rachel Carson in *Silent Spring* and Charles Reich in *The Greening of America,* among others, depicted how technology run wild was despoiling our environment and threatening the future of the earth as a place habitable for human beings as well as all the other creatures of nature. How should we solve the "dilemma of how humans . . . maintain their humanity in relationship to technology" (Henderson, 1997: 152)? Both sides of this dilemma are depicted in *Star Wars.* In the Empire, technology is in complete control of human beings. The goal is to make technology supreme and to turn human beings into machinelike servants to technology, suppressing their humanity. The Empire becomes a dystopia, the opposite of a utopia, a place where totalitarian power and violence reign supreme (Henderson, 1997: 152–153). Luke Skywalker must use his interior strength and fortitude to fight the system, not to oppose machines as the Luddites of the last century did, but to put humans and their feelings and emotions in control of the machines, instead of having the machines control humans. In this battle between good and evil, Luke takes on heroic characteristics. In the recent Republican primary contest, John McCain referred to himself as Luke Skywalker because, like Skywalker, he fought against the system.

Two other themes important in post–World War II America are recapitulated in the *Star Wars* films. The first is the fear of danger from the Evil Empire, a term taken from Apocalypse, the last book of the New Testament. To us, this term meant the Communist world; for the Rebel Alliance of the *Star Wars* world, it referred to the

Empire. The fear of aliens is still another theme that has periodically surfaced in America, whether *aliens* meant immigrants from unfamiliar places or creatures from Mars, or the alien doctrine of Communism. Besides *Star Wars,* this theme has characterized such films as *Invasion of the Body Snatchers* and *Invaders from Mars.*

Film as myth also deals with gender and often reflects the changes that have occurred in pre- and postfeminist conceptions of masculinity and feminity. In the 1970s many women moved into the workforce, challenging men "in their own backyards." Women sought equality in many other spheres of life as well. This is reflected in some recent films where " 'uppity women' (read: economically independent and sexually pro-active) are [seen as] dangerous and must be tamed or destroyed" (Tollefson, 1998: 109). Such women are frequently portrayed as "the other woman" who tries to lure men away from their wives and into a different world of exciting sex, secrecy, and often, violence. Tollefson likens this type of character to Lilith, first wife of Adam, who was his equal and who was banished from the Garden of Eden to be replaced by the more compliant Eve (1998: 109). Alex, in *Fatal Attraction,* whose otherness is emphasized by her blond hair, her seductive nature, her smoking, and her professional work as an editor, contrasts with Beth, the wife of Dan, the hero. Beth, a brunette, is merely a submissive housewife. Mythically, the Good Woman wins out and the Other Woman goes off in disgrace, though in *Fatal Attraction,* the other woman, Alex, tries to kill Beth and is in turn killed by her lover, Dan. More recently, some films have emphasized the bond of love and friendship between two women, at the expense of ties between men and women. For example, in *Thelma and Louise,* the two women run away from uninteresting jobs and a meaningless marriage. Thelma is robbed by two cowboys and raped by one of them, whom Louise then kills. The sheriff tries to entice them to return, but they speed off into the sunrise, ending by plunging off a cliff. Interestingly, in this film, women who bond become outlaws, living outside the law.

Today, the mass communication version of folklore is a product of an ongoing process, having all the characteristics of folklore, namely, social relevance and tradition as applied to current needs (Degh, 1994: 1). Basic human ideas recur in new interpretations, as they are adjusted to new vehicles of communication, reaching ever wider audiences. These ideas employ the attitudes and meanings of modern industrial society. Degh analyzes television commercials, showing how giants like the Jolly Green Giant, elves like those that bake Keebler's cookies, the anthropomorphic bugs killed by Raid bug spray, and even the use of "once upon at time" represent the employment of traditional tale motifs to enlighten our view about the value of certain commodities (Degh, 1994: 35–38).

Fine analyzes the "Kentucky Fried Rat" stories, whose basic theme involves rat meat being served as chicken at Kentucky Fried Chicken fast-food stores (1992). He shows how this and other similar "food legends," which had earlier involved Italian and Chinese restaurants, represent fear of outsiders—in one case, foreigners; in the other, giant multinational corporations, both outside the community. Food earlier came from family, church, and community, constituting nourishment from known individuals. Now food is provided by unknown persons in corporations, whose only reason for existing is to make a profit. Though the public has eagerly accepted fast foods as part of a transforming environment with its increased emphasis on leisure time and the changing roles of women, it is not completely reconciled to the structural changes entailed. In this as well as other cases, new values continue to exist with and often in contradiction to the traditional values (Fine, 1992: 132–133). The "Kentucky Fried Rat" story is told and retold as the tellers themselves stop at the nearest fast-food chain for burgers. This story belongs to the folklore category known as urban legends (Brunvand, 1998). It is similar to the story about the mouse tail found in a soda bottle. Such stories are recounted as true stories, though witnesses to the event can never be found. You may have heard the tale that Brunvand calls "The Elevator Incident," in which a large man, who "happens to be black," enters an elevator occupied by three elderly ladies, with his Doberman pinscher dog. The man says, "Sit, Lady," and the three women slowly drop to the elevator floor. Urban legends like this are told over and over, with slight variations. The mass media often play a key role in their dissemination, which lends a further aura of truth to the story. Brunvand points out that "the stories do tell one kind of truth. They are a unique, unselfconscious reflection of major concerns of individuals in the societies in which the [urban] legends circulate" (1998: 146). In this sense, urban legends in our culture are no different from the myths we discussed earlier, which also deal with such major concerns. Besides these urban legends, folklore in our culture also includes other genres, such as jokes and riddles.

Narratives with universal themes, embodied in myths, legends, folktales, and contemporary forms of mass communication, are found in all societies, including our own. Myths, dealing with the remote past and the origin of things; legends, thought to have a basis in historical fact; and folktales, which deal with indeterminate time, form a continuum. They all reflect the problems and contradictions with which all cultures wrestle. They embody the values of the culture and point out what has significant meaning in that culture. The performance aspect of such storytelling involves creativity and provides a window on the changes that take place. In America today, myths, legends, and folktales are carried by the mass media. American concern with the encroachment of technology, the power of multinational corporations, and decreasing control over our lives are reflected in our myths and legends. What we as Americans see in film and watch on television, as well as how we respond to it—whether we love it or hate it, accept it or reject it—is revealing about the nature of our culture.

Chapter Twelve
The Artistic Dimension

Every culture, universally, produces what we of the Western world label art. Objects are not only shaped and formed to meet utilitarian needs, but also frequently embellished and decorated. Such embellished objects are referred to in the West as the decorative arts. Other objects have no utilitarian purpose, but are created solely for aesthetic reasons. Everyday language communicates information, thought, and emotion. However, poetry and song are heightened and more expressive, embellished ways of communicating the same things.

Like language, art is a mode of communication. It conveys messages. Anthropologists like Anthony Forge and Nancy Munn see art as a system of visual communication. Forge (1973) also includes dance and gesture, along with painting, sculpture, and architecture, as part of this system of visual communication. Munn (1973) has analyzed the art of the Walbiri of Australia in terms of the fundamental graphic elements of which it is composed. Each element has a range of meanings, and the elements combine in regular ways according to rules. In this approach, art has rules of combination, similar to rules of grammar in language. The artistic products of the Walbiri, such as sand drawings or decorated objects used in ceremonials, contain representations of totemic myths, known as dreamings. These are stories about the mythical totemic ancestors of the Walbiri and their travels.

On the Northwest Coast, masks, totem poles, sculpted house posts, painted house fronts, decorated ceremonial bowls, and other utilitarian objects include designs that represent particular clans. (Such a totem pole is illustrated in Chapter 5.) These designs depict the mythological ancestors of the clan, such as the wolf, the grizzly bear, the sea bear, the raven, the eagle, and the killer whale. The message conveyed here is that the art object represents the kin group. The kin group and its representation are conceptually one. Art objects may be used at rituals, as are, for example, the masks worn by individual chiefs at the Kwakiutl wedding potlatch (described in Chapter 2). During such rituals, myths recounting the adventures of the mythological ancestor will be told, or the dance or song associated with that myth will be performed. Forge (1973) points out that in Arnhem Land, in Australia, art, myth, and ritual are completely interlocked and interdependent. They are three different ways of expressing the same thing—in words, in actions, and in visual form. The interconnection among art, myth, and ritual on the Northwest Coast illustrates the same point.

Art also communicates emotion. The emotion may be awe, as is the case when statues represent powerful supernatural spirits. It may be terror, as when the Poro masks, which we will discuss later in this chapter, are invoked. It may be mirth and pleasure, as when masked dancers carry out their antics or when satirical art caricatures pomposity.

Is it possible to talk about a universal aesthetic impulse? Are masterpieces of art produced in one culture recognized as such by people in all cultures? Or does the aesthetic appreciation of art objects extend only to the members of the society within which they are made? Each society has particular standards by which it judges its art. However, there are masterpieces that are appreciated aesthetically by people of very different cultures. In some instances, the emotional impact of the object appeals to some universal sense and does not require particular cultural knowledge in order to be appreciated. In an experiment carried out by Irvin Child, a psychologist, and Leon Siroto, an anthropologist (1965), photographs of BaKwele masks from Central Africa were shown to BaKwele elders, including carvers, all of whom were knowledgeable about masks. These men ranked the masks in terms of their aesthetic value, from the best mask to the worst. The same photographs of the masks were then shown to a group of art history students at Yale University, and they too ranked the masks according to their opinions of the aesthetic value of each mask. There was significant agreement between the two groups of judges. Though the American students knew nothing about the masks or about BaKwele culture, they tended to agree with the BaKwele experts about which masks were aesthetically superior and which masks were mediocre. This is an area in which investigation is just beginning. However, research seems to indicate that there is some universal aesthetic sense manifested in all cultures in what we call the arts.

Beyond this universal aesthetic impulse, which enables us to identify cross-culturally a category called art, cultures differ from one another with regard to the form of their artistic expression. The Tikopia stress poetry but have little in the way of visual arts. The Chimbu of Highland Papua New Guinea decorate their bodies, while the Kwakiutl decorate their houses. This kind of concentration on one or another of the arts is also found in many societies in the Western world if one examines them over a long span of time. In German culture, the highest achievement among all the arts is to be found in music; English culture excels in literature; painting finds its highest expression in Holland and in Italy. Still others seem to stress each of the arts equally. The reasons a culture emphasizes one art and not another are unclear.

The interpretation of the meaning of a work of art in a culture can be made only in terms of its symbolic system. Witherspoon, in his work on the Navajo, shows the nature of the relationship among the categories of the beautiful, the good, and the evil, and the ways these are reflected in Navajo rug design and sandpainting. However, as we noted in our discussion of the BaKwele experiment, people from other cultures can appreciate a work of art in terms of its aesthetic qualities, without understanding its meaning in the culture that produced it. Art embodies the style with which a particular culture expresses its symbols. Each culture has its own distinctive style, in the same way that a tapestry does.

Only in the Western world is art produced for art's sake, to be hung in museums, galleries, and homes or to be performed in concerts before large audiences. In the kinds of small-scale societies that anthropologists first studied, art was embedded in the culture. Ritual performances employed art, and the meanings that the art communicated related to the meaning of the ritual and the mythology associated with it.

In our own culture, much of what is labeled art is created solely to give aesthetic pleasure, to be admired. This point has so influenced the definition of art in our society that we make a distinction between that which is useful or utilitarian and that which is art and has no practical use. Utilitarian objects are often recognized as art at a later time, when they are valued for their aesthetic beauty and referred to as decorative arts. Furniture and other objects made by the Shakers and quilts made by the Amish are examples of this type of art. Today, the term *decorative arts* has come to include objects in current use that are admired for their aesthetic qualities. In small-scale societies there was no such thing as pure art; therefore, in those societies this distinction has no relevance.

The Visual Arts

The visual arts include such modes of representation as painting, sculpture, body decoration, and house decoration. Masks are a special kind of sculpture, found in a number of societies around the world, but certainly not universally. We have chosen to examine masks as an exemplification of art in culture because they have certain intrinsic features, yet their meaning and use differ from one culture to the next. The two stone masks pictured here have been acclaimed as works of art. What makes them works of art? What do we know about their place in the culture that made them? These two masks were collected from the Tsimshian of British Columbia in the late nineteenth century. They were found in two different locales by two different individuals and ended up in two different museums, one in Ottawa and the other in Paris. An anthropologist, Wilson Duff, thought they matched. In 1975 he brought them together for an exhibit at Victoria, British Columbia, and found that the sighted mask fit snugly into the back of the unsighted one, the two forming a single entity. The inner mask had holes drilled in it for the wooden harness with which it was attached to a human head. We know, therefore, that they were used as masks, but this is the only direct information that we have on their use. The two masks form a set, and their meaning must be interpreted in that light. The alternation of sighted and unsighted has a particular meaning for us, but what did the masks mean in Tsimshian culture?

Masks

We do know a good deal about the meaning of masks and how and when they were used in ritual and ceremonial life among the Kwakiutl, southern neighbors of the Tsimshian. Using these data, in addition to what we know about Tsimshian culture, we gain some insights into their uses among the Tsimshian. In the Kwakiutl wedding potlatch, described in Chapter 2, chiefs wear masks and costumes that depict the supernatural ancestors who are the mythological founders of their *numayms*. Each chief makes a speech in which he relates how his privileges, including the right

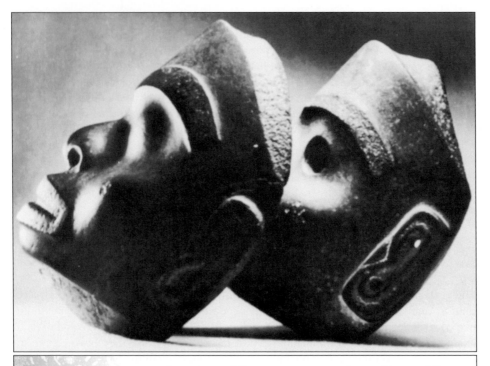

Tsimshian stone masks, one with eyes open and another with eyes closed, fit together as a set.

to wear a particular mask, have descended to him from mythological times. Two different masks are described in Chapter 2. One is called The Devourer of Tribes and represents a sea bear, a mythological monster combining characteristics of the bear and the killer whale. The father of the bride is able to call forth this supernatural creature because his *numaym* is descended from it, and only that *numaym* has the right to make a mask representation of it and personify it in a ritual. Similarly, another chief, Made-to-Be-Tied, wears the great wolf mask of Walking-Body, the chief of the wolves. The chief is descended from the original mythological owner of the wolf mask and the great wolf ceremonial. The Kwakiutl masks, which now hang inertly on museum walls, were used in ritual performances to enact the myths of the spirits they represented.

The Tsimshian, carvers of the twin stone masks, used masks in a way similar to that among the Kwakiutl. Tsimshian masks represent supernatural spirits. They were used at potlatches and at supernatural dance society rituals. Contact with supernatural spirits operated along lineage lines, and at initiation, power from the supernatural spirits, associated with a boy's own lineage, was "thrown" into him. Somewhat later he was initiated into a secret society. He then had the right to sing the song of his spirit and wear its mask at ceremonies. When a chief wore his mask, the supernatural spirit was in him. Its presence was also indicated by the sound of a whistle, which represented the voice of the spirit. Among the Tsimshian, carvers of masks, artists, song composers, and dramatists were all men who had received supernatural power. Returning to the stone masks, we can imagine these masks, now in museum cases, being used in a Tsimshian ceremony. It is dead of winter in a village on the Skeena River, and the *halaïit,* the sacred dance of the Tsimshian, is being held. Whistles announce the approaching spirit, and before the entranced audience the chief appears with the face of the sightless stone mask. As he slowly dances, the stone mask miraculously opens its eyes. The great power of the spirit residing in the chief has caused this miracle.

The two stone masks represent a single face, which opens and closes its eyes. What does this mean? Wilson Duff (1975) suggests that the sighted/sightless states represent looking outward and looking inward or self-recognition, sight and memory, seeing and imagining, looking ahead and seeing the past.

Let us now look at the use of masks in another part of the world, West Africa, an area where masks also play a central role in the art of societies. These masks, one of which is pictured on page 256, are associated with the Poro, the secret society found among a group of tribes in Liberia and adjacent Sierra Leone. George Harley, a missionary doctor, amassed a great deal of information on the *Poro Society* among the Mano of Liberia to enable him to better understand the significance of the masks he collected during the many years of his medical practice there.

All the Poro Society masks represent some kind of spirit. In fact, the same word, *ge,* is used for both "spirit" and "mask" in Mano. When a person dons a mask, the spirit is said to be present in him. Among the Mano, as among the Tsimshian, whistles and horns symbolize the voice of the spirit. As we noted in the previous chapter, the people of Wogeo believed that the flutes were the voices of the *nibek* spirits. Mano women and uninitiated boys are not permitted to see masks or anything else associated with the Poro Society spirits, except for special masked dancers who perform on stilts and entertain a general audience at certain occasions. There are basically two kinds of masks. The first are portrait masks, the repositories for the spirits of important deceased leaders and more ancient tribal heroes, who are also ancestor spirits. The spirit of the mythical founder of the Poro Society is also embodied in a sacred portrait mask. The other kind of mask is a grotesque half-animal, half-human associated with the spirits of nature and other spiritual beings, such as the god of the dance, the god of fertility, and the god of war. Ritual sacrifices of chickens or sheep were made to the masks on a regular basis in order to enable them to sustain their power. The masks were smeared with the blood of the sacrificed animal.

The Poro Society, with which these masks were associated, was a secret male cult with several initiatory grades. Men wishing to gain access to the higher grades had to pay large sums of money in order to go through the rites that earned them these high positions. At the top of the hierarchy were the old men who, through a combination of inheritance and payments to the Poro Society, achieved the right to wear the most powerful masks. Among the activities of the Poro Society was the ritual for determining whether an individual accused of a crime was innocent or guilty. After discussion by

A Poro Society mask from the Gio of Sierra Leone.

the powerful elders, the masks were said to make the judgment. Since the wearer of the mask assumed its spirit when he put it on, the Mano would say that the mask punished or even executed someone when the wearer carried out the mask's decision. The masks and their wearers also stopped village quarrels, controlled fighting warriors, promoted fertility of the fields, presided at various public functions and life crisis rituals, and taught young initiates the proper ways to behave in the bush schools of the Poro. People conformed to societal rules because they feared the power of the spirits, which were contained in the wooden masks of the Poro Society. Here spirits, which are physically represented by artistic means in masks, were used as a means of social control.

For the Mano people, how the masks came to exist poses an interesting problem in view of their role in the Poro Society. Warren d'Azevedo (1973) has studied woodcarvers among the Gola and Vai peoples, neighbors of the Mano in Liberia who also have the Poro Society. In these societies, the link between the carvers and the masks that they manufacture is denied. Young children are punished if they ask who made a particular mask. Adults, if questioned, simply say that the masks must have been made long ago and were passed on by the ancestors. But there are always carvers who continue to make masks. D'Azevedo found that parents try to dissuade their children from becoming wood-carvers. Carvers, like professional singers, dancers, and musicians, as we shall note below, are regarded by the community as irresponsible and concerned more with their own creativity than with communal well-being. Boys intent on becoming carvers frequently run away and apprentice themselves to master carvers. Many carvers have a direct relationship with a particular spirit, and inspiration for masks comes to them from that spirit through dreams.

Since they carve masks for the Sande Society, the secret women's society, as well as for the Poro Society, carvers are the only younger men who have direct contact with women in the Sande and know the secrets of their society. Because he is a man with access to women's secrets, the carver is in an ambiguous position. In his negotiations with the Sande Society, the carver shows reluctance to take on the task, and the women try to induce him to make the mask by offering him sexual favors. The carver of the mask and the women of the Sande Society, who own the mask, never fully terminate their relationship. He has special access to the group, and they jokingly use the term meaning "lovers" for one another. The carver in these West African societies is someone who, through his creativity and artistic skill, produces an object with supernatural power. But the relationship between the carver and his artwork is not even formally recognized. Like his work—the mask, which is a combination of the natural and the supernatural—the artist who creates this thing is himself somewhat outside society. Artists in a great many societies, including our own, are frequently considered marginal people who are not bound by the norms of usual behavior.

Masks have some special characteristics that differentiate them from other forms of art. A mask is worn by a person and is always a face. It can represent the face of a human being, the face of an animal, or the face of an imaginary creature, such as a monster or a supernatural being, in which human and animal features are combined in the face portrayed on the mask. In Bali, Indonesia, the face itself is considered a mask. While the Balinese do wear masks in ritual performances, donning a mask and leaving the face bare are symbolically equivalent. The masks in Kwakiutl, Tsimshian,

A Kwakiutl Dzonokwa mask (left) and a Kwakiutl Xwexwe mask (right).

and Mano societies represent statements about the nature of the individual in each of these societies. Each society has a particular view of the individual—what his or her relation is to others in the society, where he or she came from, how he or she came to be, what his or her place is in the natural world. Thus, Tsimshian clan masks make a statement about the connection between the individual human wearer and the mythical clan ancestor, often an animal, that the mask portrays.

Lévi-Strauss has pointed out that the Kwakiutl Dzonokwa and Xwexwe masks used in the Winter Ceremonial are stylistically reversals of one another (1979). The eyes in both are emphasized. In the Dzonokwa mask they either are deeply recessed or are deep holes, while in the Xwexwe they protrude extraordinarily, as can be seen in the illustrations. This emphasis on eyes runs throughout Kwakiutl art, as well as through the art of other societies of the Northwest Coast, including the Tsimshian. Lévi-Strauss has suggested that the protruding eyes of Xwexwe indicate extraordinary visual abilities, such as clairvoyance—the ability to see the future. The sighted stone mask has normal vision; the Xwexwe mask has the capacity to see the future; the sightless stone mask has the capacity to see the past. In these societies, eyes as a recurrent theme in the art seem to relate to the great importance placed on shaming. When an important man trips and falls or accidentally overturns his canoe, he is shamed and must give a potlatch in order to wipe out the shame. Thus it may be said that eyes are constantly watching and observing everyone's behavior. Kwakiutl individuals believe that their behavior is always in public view, and they must avoid actions that will shame them. The theme of eyes in the art, especially in the masks, reflects this view of the individual. If an American painter constantly used eyes in his or her art, we would say that the paintings reflect a slight paranoia.

On the top are the masks of wolf and eagle worn during secular potlatches. The eagle is a transformation mask that opens up to reveal another mask, representing the face of a man (middle). These masks contrast in style with the wolf and Crooked Beak (eagle) of the sacred Winter Ceremonial (bottom).

Among the Kwakiutl, summer and winter were clearly separated as the secular and sacred periods, and the art objects employed in the different rituals in summer and winter contrasted in style (Rosman and Rubel, 1990). Summer was the time for potlatching, such as the wedding potlatch discussed earlier in this chapter, and on these occasions claims to rank were demonstrated. Chiefs wore masks illustrating their mythological ancestors, such as the wolf mask of Walking-Body, the chief of the wolves, in order to show their ancestry and high rank. The wolf in this mask, as shown in the illustrations on page 261, is portrayed in the secular art style. Between the secular world of summer and the sacred world of winter, there was a ritual period of transition when the spirits came into the village and the Winter Ceremonial was held. The Kwakiutl Winter Ceremonial dances, which lasted several months, parallel the *halaīt,* the sacred dance of the Tsimshian discussed earlier. Young people who were seized and devoured by the spirits were initiated into secret societies and then subsequently emerged during a ceremony. The spirits were portrayed by individuals wearing masks that represented particular spirits. The initiated members of the secret society were considered shamans, since they crossed the border from the natural world into that of the supernatural and became dangerous cannibal spirits. The art style used in these Winter Ceremonial masks was an exaggerated and distorted style, in contrast to that used in the masks of secular summer rituals. It was a style appropriate to the supernatural world of the shaman. As can be seen in the illustrations, the strongly curved beak of the eagle in the secular potlatch mask becomes the greatly distorted beak of the Crooked Beak of Heaven. The pronounced snout of the wolf in the secular potlatch mask becomes the exaggerated mask worn in the Winter Ceremonial.

Masks are embedded in culture and play a significant role in the performance of religious rituals. The masks along with the dances and songs performed by the wearer usually symbolize central ideas in the culture and convey important information relevant to kinship and political activities, as in the Kwakiutl Winter Ceremonial. In contrast, once they are removed from the society and displayed as inert objects in museums, they assume a completely different character.

New Ireland Malanggans, Yesterday and Today

Malanggan mortuary sculptures from northern New Ireland, now part of Papua New Guinea, were striking examples of visual art. European explorers of the early nineteenth century, who spent only a short time on the island, were sufficiently captivated by them to bring back examples to Europe and America. The carvings were used in the religious ritual held to commemorate the deaths of several individuals of a single clan and simultaneously to initiate the boys of that clan. When missionaries brought Christianity to the people of New Ireland in the late nineteenth century, they tried to suppress the *malanggan* ceremony and the carvings associated with it, since these represented earlier pagan beliefs. However, the *malanggan* ceremony continues to be celebrated today. The Catholic Church no longer sees a conflict between the *malanggan* rite and Catholicism and has even incorporated *malanggan* sculpture into church architecture.

The designs for *malanggans* are still owned and sold by one clan to another. When a *malanggan* sculpture is ordered, the owner of the design tells the carver the myth embodying the design and what the carving should look like. The carver then translates the words into a visual image. Sometimes the process of translation for the carver involves dreaming the image, which he will then carve. Like the carver of masks for the Poro Society, the carver of a *malanggan* works within a set of constraints such that the design can immediately be recognized as a member of a particular named category of images. Further, the owner of the design must be able to recognize it as his particular design. Since the carver does not use a sculpture from a previous *malanggan* ceremony as a model, a degree of artistic creativity is also involved. Carvers are evaluated in terms of how well they express the design, and several have islandwide reputations.

Earlier, after the *malanggans* were used in a ceremony, they were burned or left to rot. After European colonization, *malanggans,* since they were no longer valued after the ceremony, were given or sold to Europeans, and many wound up in museums all over the world. Today, after they are used in ceremonies, *malanggans* may sometimes be sold to tourists and collectors. One contemporary carver has carved a *malanggan* on a post for the National Museum in Port Moresby. Modern carvers use steel chisels and commercial paints. When shown pictures of *malanggan* carvings 100 years old and now in the Australian Museum, they admired the workmanship of the earlier carvers, particularly since the earlier carvers had only stone tools to use. However, the present-day carvers felt their own carvings were superior. The three-dimensional *malanggan* art of New Ireland has provided the inspiration for the New Ireland printmaker David Lasisi.

Toraja Art and Ethnic Identity

The architecturally based carvings of the Toraja have graced museum walls over the world for a hundred years. Heretofore, art has been treated as a minor and passive aspect of ethnic identity marking, but it can be "an active ingredient in identity politics . . . as well as a critique of established ethnic, colonial, or political hierarchies" (Adams, 1998: 328–329). The Sa'dan Toraja of highland Sulawesi, a province of Indonesia, have been marginalized in the multiethnic Indonesian state not only by their small numbers and geographic isolation, but also because they are Christians in a predominantly Muslim country. The Toraja area has recently become a mecca for international tourists who travel seven hours by bus to see the interesting architecture and elaborate carving of the houses and the slaughter of bulls that accompanies what seems to be a never-ending series of funeral rituals. The carving on the Toraja house, or *tongkonan,* is the visual embodiment of the ancestry and elite rank of the family that occupies it. It is a key symbol of an individual's identity. The motifs represent mythic designs, emblems of the status and solidarity of the family, and the activities of peasants and slaves, toward whom the "nobles" had a range of responsibilities. Nowadays, nonnoble Toraja tourist guides often introduce newer explanations of motifs, such as the cross motif used long before Toraja conversion, which is said to represent "evidence of their ancestors' intuitive proximity to Christianity" (Adams, 1998: 333). A few carvings include sequences, which represent the ambivalent Toraja relationship with the Dutch, their former colonial masters. For example, a soldier is seen beating a Toraja child who flees to his mother's arms. The postindependence period of upheaval is represented on one carved panel by troops of the Darul Islam movement of lowland Sulawesi, which sought to establish a separate Muslim state, shooting a Toraja man. In the 1960s, the Indonesian government and the Protestant Toraja church encouraged the abandonment of this type of house because it represented a visible sign of Toraja "backwardness," and the Toraja were encouraged to move into houses built of cinder block (Adams, 1998: 337).

However, in the 1970s and 1980s, both the government, which began to celebrate regional diversity as a cornerstone of Indonesian national identity, and the church, where Dutch clergy moved out of positions of power, reversed their positions. Churches began to be embellished with Toraja motifs, and new churches were built that resembled *tongkonans* in their architecture. Tourism had become more and more important, and the house architecture that had formerly represented elite power now came to represent Toraja ethnic identity. *Tongkonan* images began to be seen decorating pubs and intersections in Rantepo, the Toraja capital, on T-shirts, as model houses, and on silver jewelry. More recently, Toraja carvers have begun to produce finely carved wall plaques, or carved paintings, which the carvers themselves see not as ornaments or handicrafts but as art (Adams, 1998: 341). This new medium of expression is frequently used to portray the symbols of political dissent. Toraja carvings and motifs have also begun to appear in Ujung Pandang, the South Sulewesi port city occupied by Bugis and Makassarese, rival ethnic groups. The growth of tourism has led to the increase in the use of this type of "exotic" motif. As a consequence, there have been changes in ethnic conceptualizations and relationships. Whereas formerly, the Toraja were seen as the victims of Bugis-Makassarese raiders, the relationship is being renegotiated. The Toraja see this use of their traditional motifs and house architecture as a minor ethnic triumph, while the Bugis and Mukassarese have misgivings about this and feel vague ethnic malaise. Even the Indonesian government has co-opted the image of the *tongkonan,* featuring it on the 5000 rupia banknote.

Decorating the Body

A rather special kind of visual art involves the decoration of the human body. People all over the world "use the skin as a surface for artistic expression and embellish themselves with decorations which carry a wide variety of meanings" (Reichel-Dolmatoff, 1998: 12). The messages conveyed by body decoration range from statements about social, economic, or political status or class; or the different phases of a life; to ones referring to the sacred and profane. Body decorations must always be examined within a particular context in order to decode their meanings. Of course, the nature of body decoration often changes as the culture changes. For example, Maori tattooing, performed with a chisel-like implement by a revered and highly paid expert over a period of years, was a very significant aspect of Maori culture up to the nineteenth century. Today, Maoris use the same tattoo designs for ceremonial purposes, but they are applied with pigment. Now, body decoration usually reflects the heterogeneity and multiplex nature of most societies.

Among the peoples of the central highlands of New Guinea, body decoration is the most important type of art, since these people do little carving, painting, or mask making. The decorations people wear and the painting of the body at ritual performances and exchange ceremonies, like the *kaiko* of the Maring (discussed in Chapter 8), convey messages about the social and religious values of the people

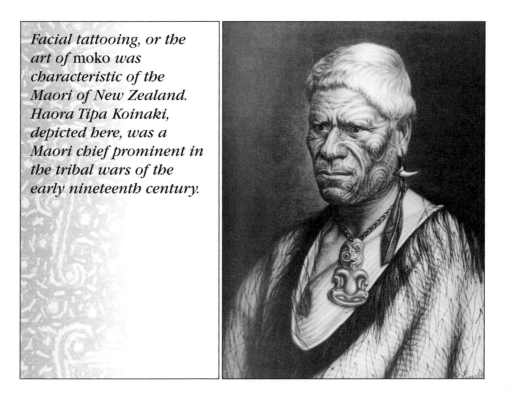

Facial tattooing, or the art of moko *was characteristic of the Maori of New Zealand. Haora Tipa Koinaki, depicted here, was a Maori chief prominent in the tribal wars of the early nineteenth century.*

and also demonstrate the relationship of the people to their clan ancestral spirits. Certain ideals and emotions are evoked for audience and participants by the wearing of the decorations. The use of particular colors in body painting and certain combinations of colors in feathers, shells, and beads, taken together, convey abstract qualities like health and vitality among the Melpa of highland New Guinea (Strathern and Strathern, 1971). Similarly, darkness and brightness relate to the opposition between men and women. The Wahgi of highland New Guinea, who live not very far from the Melpa, also express their aesthetic impulses entirely through the decoration and adornment of the human body. These displays of feather adornments and painting of the face and body during dances carried out at the Wahgi pig festivals serve to communicate the strength and health of the clan hosting the festival. But the most important part of the message conveyed is the moral strength of the host group. This derives from the absence of sorcery accusations or of friction within the group and from its sense of security in having fully fulfilled its obligations to others. The moral strength or weakness of the host group directly affects the brightness and quality of their adornment and the success of their performance during the ceremony (O'Hanlon, 1989).

Body decoration, or body modification as it is sometimes called, also occurs in modern American society. Tattooing and piercing are popular ways of embellishing the body. Hewitt sees a parallel between the transformation of the body and religious conversion since such self-alterations are, in effect, acts of self-transformation, ways of creating a new identity, or expressing one's individuality or affiliation with a particular alternative subcultural group (1997: 3, 4). For example, the punk look, which was developed first in England in the late 1970s as a reaction to the conservative Thatcher regime and then spread to America, is a distinctive, provocative demonstration of a counterculture (Groning, 1998: 234–235). The spiked, brightly colored hair; the black, metal-studded leather clothing; and the face piercing and makeup clearly set this group apart, representing their rejection of middle-class subculture.

Body tattooing with a hot needle, originally associated with the exoticism of the circus in America, became popular with lower-class and blue-collar workers at the beginning of the twentieth century (Hewitt, 1997: 71). In the 1950s, there was a tattoo renaissance as a new, safer technology was introduced and the new interest in Asian cultures, which revere tattooing, made it into "more of a fine art" (Hewitt, 1997: 71,73). Clients with more income and better education often design their own tattoos, making the tattoo into an aspect of self-expression and self-identification. Various types of body piercing have also recently become popular, especially among Generation X females. Piercing has moved from a countercultural sign of identity to become a trend and a fashion, represented in mainstream magazines. Americans have transformed a marginal practice into a trendy one (Hewitt, 1997: 84).

Style

Art can be examined in terms of style, beyond its communicative function. If the function of art is the role it plays in society, its use in rituals, and the information and the aesthetic pleasure that it communicates, then its structure is the component parts. *Style* refers to a consideration of the component elements of art and how the elements are put together. For example, the art of the Northwest Coast is characterized by a particular style, as is apparent from previous illustrations. What are the characteristics of that style that make it easy to identify art from that area? The art of the Northwest Coast area is primarily three-dimensional carving in wood. This undoubtedly relates to the fact that the societies of the Northwest Coast are located in the northern coastal rain forest, where massive trees like cedar and spruce provided excellent raw material for the carver. The colors used in Northwest Coast art were predominantly yellow, black, red, and green-blue, with the unpainted natural wood as a background color. The pigments used were made from natural materials—fungus, berries, ochre, moss, charcoal. The distinctive green-blue used was produced by allowing native copper to corrode in urine.

Because of the emphasis on sculpture, round, oblong, oval, circular, and curvilinear forms predominate, even on flat surfaces. The interlocking of animal and sometimes human forms, such as that found on totem poles, is typical. Franz Boas noted that the depiction of animals in Northwest Coast art is characterized by the emphasis of certain features—eyes, mouths, ears, fins, feathers, and tails. Each animal species, from killer whale to dragonfly, can be identified by the representation of the features unique to that species. Thus, as pointed out earlier, the curved beak is the distinctive feature of the eagle, and the snout, the distinctive feature of the wolf. The same tech-

*Painting from a Tsimshian house front
representing a bear.*

niques for carving wood were adapted for use in other media, such as stone, bone, and metal. Besides carving in the round, Northwest Coast artists also worked on two-dimensional surfaces. The change from three dimensions to two dimensions required a transformation of design. The technique adopted on the Northwest Coast for two-dimensional designs is called split representation. The painting on a Tsimshian house front above illustrates this technique. The bear has been sliced in half and the two sides placed next to each other to make up the house front. This represents a bear—the two sides in profile—but together they form a bear looking frontward.

Two other features of Northwest Coast art style are also important. Design elements cover an entire surface, leaving no blank spaces, and eyelike shapes are used as fillers and in place of joints. Earlier, we discussed the significance of the portrayal of eyes in masks and indicated the great importance of eyes in Northwest Coast society. All these features, taken together, form the distinctive style of the art of the Northwest Coast.

There is a hierarchical aspect to the concept of style. One can speak of the style of the individual artist, that is, the features that are characteristic of the work of a particular artist. Sometimes the art style of a village can be identified. It is more frequent to refer to the art style of a single society, such as Kwakiutl. Certain general features delineate the art style of a larger area, made up of a number of societies, as we have shown above for the Northwest Coast. Contemporary Northwest Coast artists, such as the remarkable Haida carver Bill Reid, use the traditional content and the distinctive style of Northwest Coast art but add their own individual quality to it. The style of each artist is therefore different, as is the case for European and American contemporary artists. The sculpture in bronze, patinated to look like argillite, by Bill Reid (page 268), entitled "The Spirit of Haida Gwaii" ("The Spirit of the Haida Islands"), exemplifies the combination of traditional themes from Haida mythology and the genius of a creative artist. The same hierarchical concept of style applies to the art of complex societies. One can speak of the style of Renaissance art, of the Italian Renaissance in particular, of the schools of Venice or of Florence, and of the particular style of Raphael. The concept of style is applicable at each level.

Detail from sculpture by Haida artist Bill Reid, which stands in front of the Canadia Embassy in Washington, D.C.

The Artist

In an earlier period, scholars questioned whether one could speak of the style of the individual artist in small-scale societies, as comparable to the style of Raphael in terms of its uniqueness. As we have noted, art in such societies was embedded in social, ritual, and ceremonial contexts, and therefore it had to be produced within a set of constraints, since it had to convey certain messages. The artist who carves a Poro Society mask operates under such a set of constraints, but beyond that he can show some degree of inspiration and individualism. After all, he does not merely copy a previously existing mask. He carves a representation of a known spirit in terms of his conceptualization of that spirit. He gets his inspiration in dreams. Accounts from other societies indicate that there, too, inspirations are said to come from dreams. As noted above in our discussion of *malanggan* carvers on New Ireland, the carver dreams the image he will carve. Dreams are the sources of individual creativity since each person's dreams differ. William Davenport (1968) reports that wood-carvers in the Solomon Islands receive their inspiration from the supernatural, which comes to them in dreams. Creativity or genius in some people and not in others is a difficult phenomenon to explain, and people the world over resort to external factors, such as divine inspiration from the supernatural or the Muses, to account

A contemporary malanggan *carver from New Ireland, holding his carving adze, beside an unfinished carving.*

for it. In addition to inspiration, the artist must also have the technical skills to translate a vision or a dream into a work of art. Thus craftsmanship is also a part of creativity. Not all carvers and artists are the same. Some are better than others and some are worse. People in all societies distinguish between good and bad art. They do this by applying a set of aesthetic standards.

Seeing the art of small-scale society as the product of an anonymous artist working within a communal tradition and the art of our society as the product of the creativity of the individual artist is an erroneous construct of Western society (Price, 1989). Within the cultural context and in the community in which the art is produced, the creativity of the individual artist in small-scale societies is recognized and rewarded, and the names of superior artists are known far and wide. Such art is made anonymous when it is extracted from its original cultural context by Westerners and transformed into objects in their museums representing "other" or "primitive" art.

The fame of Yoruba artists and carvers was known well beyond the towns in which they lived (see Walker, in Abiodun et al., 1994: 91). However, when King Tezifon of the Yoruba kingdom of Alada sent a carved divination board to King Felipe IV of Spain in 1659, the carver's name was not included. Like almost all examples of art from small-scale societies that wound up in European museums, the artist who carved it became "Anonymous." The carved divination board now resides in a German museum. In response to this gift, Felipe IV sent 12 Capuchin missionaries bringing with them a translation of Christian doctrine into the language of Alada. We can therefore assume that the Alada divination tray was, in a sense, equal to the text on Christian doctrine brought by the missionaries. As Yai, a Yoruba scholar explains it today, "the king of Alada, in an attempt to establish an equal cultural and political exchange must have thought of sending to European kings a divination tray that he perceived as a perfect equivalent of the text European missionaries carried with them along the West African coast. . . . It was a carved text par excellence. Tezifon was therefore engaging the contemporary European elite in a cultural dialogue, an exchange of texts or discourses" (1994: 111). The tray was used by an oracle or diviner and was meant to hold the blood of sacrifices. As Bassani points out, the carving on

Contemporary malanggan *carvings, which utilize traditional designs, displayed at mortuary rites held at Tabar Island, off Ireland.*

the tray portrays the Yoruba cosmos that the diviner employs in his ritual perform-ances (1994: 81–82). The Yoruba artist's task is to translate this cosmos or text into another form—into artistic, visual expression. Like the New Ireland carver, who translates a myth into a *malanggan,* the Yoruba carver translates one medium into another; he translates words into visual art. How well he does this is a measure of his creativity. Though the identity of the carver of this divination tray can probably never be recovered, anthropologists today attempt to find out who the artists were who carved many of the masterpieces to be found in museums. They are very often successful, as in the case of Olowe, a carver who died in 1938, considered by many the most important Yoruba artist of the twentieth century. Although he was famous in Nigeria, ethnographers of the time paid no attention to the identity of this out-standing carver (Walker, 1994: 91).

Collecting "Artificial Curiosities"

The removal of artifacts from exotic places began with the Age of Exploration. Cap-tain Cook brought back many specimens that people in Europe saw as represen-tative of the way of life of the people he encountered. He also brought back a living specimen—Omai, the Tahitian—"Artificial curiosities" as well as "natural cu-riosities" such as fossils, rocks, and shells. These found homes in the collectors' cabinets of royalty and the aristocracy. Such collections were the nuclei around which museums like the British Museum were later formed during the nineteenth century. In the heyday of colonialism, the latter part of the nineteenth century, large quantities of such objects were taken by traders, missionaries, and govern-ment officials from small-scale societies that had become parts of colonial empires and sent to museums in all the capitals of Europe, as well as to America. In the course of this process, the ethnographic objects that now hang on museum walls were removed from the cultural context in which they were created and used, and their creators were reduced to anonymity.

    At the turn of the twentieth century, European artists such as Vlaminck, Matisse, and Picasso began to appreciate and to collect what Westerners then called "primitive" art. These artists, who created what is called modern art, were seeking new ways to depict the world about them, in particular, the human form. Much of the art they collected came from the French colonies in Africa. In these carvings and sculptures, the Western artists saw what was for them a completely new way of conceiving of and depicting the human figure, and they used these conceptualizations in their own sculpture and paintings.

Just as Western artists borrowed artistic ideas from the peoples of colonized areas, so did the artists of colonized areas borrow from Western societies, this time of content but not of style. Numerous examples from all over the world showing how the art of subject peoples reflected their views of their colonial masters were provided in Julius Lips's book *The Savage Hits Back* (1937). This art makes pointed political comments and is both humorous and satirical in nature.

Art Markets Today

The translation of a sculptural style into modern graphics has occurred not only on New Ireland, but on the Northwest Coast as well. For example, the Kwakiutl artist Tony Hunt is a printmaker as well as a sculptor. Traditional styles of what were small-scale societies like those of New Ireland and the Northwest Coast continue today, vibrant and alive, translated into new media. In these new forms, the art has become part of a commercial art market, exhibited in elegant galleries and sold to buyers from all over the world. Northwest Coast designs have also been incorporated into glassmaking, another medium not traditional for this area, by Preston Singletary (*Native Peoples,* 1999).

When tourism develops in an area, simplified versions of traditional art objects and objects embodying traditional motifs in new media frequently begin to be manufactured as *tourist art*. In the mid-nineteenth century, the Haida of British Columbia began to carve miniature totem poles, platters, and boxes out of argillite, a soft, black, easily carved form of coal, using traditional designs. This is a medium that the Haida had not used before European contact. These items were all carved for sale to tourists. Some argillite carvings portrayed Europeans, such as ship captains and their wives. What has been called airport art, can be found from Nairobi to Port Moresby. When style and content are dictated by what tourists buy, and Navajos make crosses and Stars of David out of silver and turquoise to be sold in Albuquerque, then it is impossible for a traditional art style to completely retain its characteristics. Silver jewelry is itself an introduced art form. Sometimes, the designs of tourist art become so popular that miniature ivory totem poles, symbols of the Northwest Coast, are made in Japan and sold in Vancouver, and Navajo silver and turquoise jewelry, mass-produced in Hong Kong, is sold in Santa Fe. This tourist art is clearly distinct from creative translations of traditional forms by artists like Reid, Singletary, and Lasisi.

The Art World

When cultural anthropology began to investigate modern urban society, it turned its gaze upon new kinds of communities. The New York art world is the core of one such community, composed of commercial, communicative, and social networks that spread from there all over the world (Sullivan, 1995). This art world includes the artists, dealers, art critics and theorists, collectors, curators of corporate collections, curators and directors of museums, and auction house personnel who decide what will be the important images to be illustrated in international art magazines and shown at museum shows, and who formulate what will become the posterity of Western art. The community is defined not only in terms of a shared identity, common interests, and a network of social relations, but also in terms of politics and economics.

Sullivan focuses on this community and the changes that have transformed it over the past 30 years (1995). At the beginning of the 1960s, a communications explosion took place, which changed the way people encountered art by expanding the number and the types of settings—studios, new museums, and public collections—within which such an encounter could take place. There was also a concomitant growth in the number of art publications devoted to reviewing and critiquing contemporary art. Artists perceived themselves as increasingly alienated from their art and losing control over it. They felt that they were not benefiting sufficiently from their art and demanded legal agreements from purchasers to ensure some remuneration to them in resales, which were becoming increasingly frequent. Art was being treated as a commodity, especially by artists, to be purchased and resold, most often at auction. The 1970s found many artists, whose works were increasing in value, becoming economically successful and entering the leisure class, with more affinities to middle- and upper-class collectors and dealers. This was in contrast to the peripheral position artists had earlier held in American society and in other societies as well, as we have noted above.

Curators' decisions on what to exhibit and critics' decisions whether or not to praise the art determined the aesthetic value of the artwork. Their decisions crucially determined who was creating art and who was not. Art dealers and gallery owners were in a parallel position, deciding whose work to include in a show and whose work to advise collectors to purchase. At the apex of this structure were the world-famous artists, collectors and dealers, and museum directors. In the 1970s this world began to change as contemporary art moved into the auction galleries and price was determined publicly rather than by means of the backroom negotiations that dealers and clients had formerly engaged in. Collectors began to shop at auctions, paying astronomical prices for works by world-famous artists. New money was entering the scene, and financiers of many nationalities, interested in art as an investment, were bidding up prices. Van Gogh's painting *Irises* sold for $53 million in 1987, and his portrait of Dr. Gachet sold in 1990 for $82.5 million, the highest price ever paid for a painting. Even museums moved into the auction market to reconstitute their collections, de-accessioning works "not of museum quality" in favor of what their directors thought represented important trends, to broaden their collections. Museum directors learned "the art of the deal" in sales as well as exchanges. This process also occurred in the area of ethnographic art. Sotheby's auctioned off a Maori house post, whose sale price was over a million dollars, and Navajo blankets, which sold for hundreds of thousands of dollars.

By focusing on the art "community," which represents the type of unit anthropologists have always studied, one can see the ways in which the roles and positions of people in the art world have changed. Art, like the religious artifacts in Cairo discussed in Chapters 8 and 10, on economics and religion, has become a commodity, purchased by the wealthy as an investment and to show their good taste. Both the art market and the meanings of the art have been transformed in the process.

Music and Dance

Like painting and sculpture, music and dance are considered arts because they evoke emotion and can be evaluated in terms of aesthetic qualities. However, music and dance differ from painting and sculpture in a number of ways. Music and dance are like spoken language in several important respects. All three unfold through time. Every sentence, every musical composition, every dance has a beginning, a middle, and an end. This is not true of a painting or a carving, which has no beginning or ending and for which the dimension of time is irrelevant. Once made, it continues to exist. Musical compositions and dances are ephemeral. They find expression in performances, but once the performance is over, they no longer exist. The musical instrument upon which the composition was performed is still there, and an idea of how the piece should be performed persists; however, the performance of the piece dies away, unless it has been recorded on tape or film, a modern phenomenon. Like the tale or legend told by a bard, the musical piece exists as a concept in people's minds, and each performance is a slightly different manifestation of that idea. In this conceptualization of a piece of music, it is like the mental template a potter uses to make and decorate a certain kind of pot. Only in complex societies were musical compositions written down, using some form of musical notation. Until recently, dances were performed and only memory guided the next performance. Now there are systems of dance notation, which are analogous to written language. Ethnomusicologists and anthropologists, when they studied music and dance in small-scale societies, were studying a tradition, transmitted orally and by performance. In these societies, music and dance, like oral literature and folktales, were taught and learned without benefit of written notational systems.

The anthropological emphasis has always been on the relationship between music and dance and other aspects of culture. In our discussion of the visual arts in small-scale societies, we saw that art was not produced simply to be admired but was integrated with other aspects of culture. The same is true of music and dance. In fact, when anthropologists first began to study dance, they were more interested in the cultural context of the dance than in the dance itself. There is a great range of ritual and ceremonial settings in which music and dance play important roles. Birth, initiation, weddings, and funerals are typically occasions for music and dance. The Kwakiutl and American weddings described in Chapter 2 both included music and dancing. These two examples illustrate the contrasting ways in which music and dance function in the two societies. The dances and songs performed at the

Kwakiutl wedding were owned by the *numayms* of the chiefs who performed them, as were the crests on the masks worn by the performers in contrast to the dance music played at the American wedding by a hired band. The ancestral myths recount how the mythical ancestor spirit gave these songs and dances to the ancestor of the *numaym* to be transmitted down through the generations. In Kwakiutl culture, music and dance are forms of communication that convey messages. In addition to the message of ownership, the songs and dances of the groom's side convey the power, based on supernatural contacts, that is intended to move the bride. We must also consider who has the right to perform a piece of music or dance and who owns it. There is a great range of variation regarding the degree of specialization involved in the performance of music and dance, even within societies. Sometimes, as is the case among the Kwakiutl, songs and dances are privately owned and may be performed only by their owners. There are dances that may be performed only at a particular stage in life, such as dances for a male initiation. Within all societies, there are always some songs or dances that everyone, regardless of age or sex, may perform.

Ethnomusicologists and anthropologists also investigate music in complex societies, from Iran, Japan, and Bali to the urban barrios of New York and Los Angeles. Adelaida Reyes (1999) has analyzed the way certain aspects of the music and dance of recent Vietnamese immigrants to New Jersey persist, while new elements from the American scene have been introduced. The maintenance of ethnic identity by the New Jersey Vietnamese centers on the celebration of Tet, the Vietnamese New Year. At the event that Reyes describes, a piece by a well-known émigré Vietnamese composer was performed, which incorporated many regional Vietnamese folk songs within an overall symbolic theme of Vietnamese unity. In the social dancing that followed, the dance forms were Western (tango, rumba, bebop, and twist), while the lyrics were sung in Vietnamese and the music was considered Vietnamese. The performance of music and dance is a sensitive indicator of the dialectic between continuity and the adaptation of immigrant groups in America. The Vietnamese are only one of many immigrant groups whose music and dance demonstrate this dialectic.

Music

While the function of music and dance is similar to that of the visual arts, each is characterized by a different kind of structure. The elements of music are sounds and their characteristics, such as pitch and duration. Sounds produced consecutively form what is called a melody. Sounds produced simultaneously form harmony. Melody, harmony, and rhythm, which is a steady succession of beats marked by regular accents, represent the basic concepts for analyzing the structure of music. The music of different cultures varies in terms of its structure. For example, most of the music of our society is based upon a system of 8 tones, an octave—usually taught as do, re, mi, fa, sol, la, ti, do. However, from time to time, other structures have also been used, such as Debussy's use of a whole-tone scale and Schoenberg's use of a 12-tone scale. Many other societies in the world base their music on a scale in which there are only 5 tones. This is called a pentatonic scale, and in fact, it is

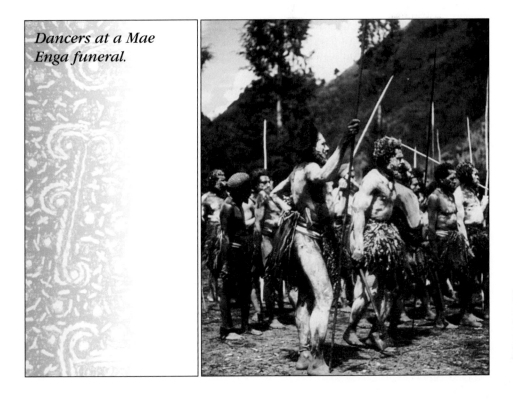

Dancers at a Mae Enga funeral.

more common in the world than our octave, or 8-tone scale. Rhythm is also subject to cultural variation. In our own society, each musical composition is usually characterized by a single, regular rhythmic impulse. A waltz has one kind of rhythm, and a march another kind of rhythm. Recent music in Western culture may shift rhythms throughout the piece. This is in contrast with other societies, such as those in Zaire in Africa, where a single musical composition can have two different rhythms carried on simultaneously. These and other marked variations make the music of other cultures sometimes sound strange to our ears. In addition, the instruments created to produce musical sounds are enormously varied.

Music is a form of communication. The music at an American wedding conveys a message. When the organ plays as the bride, dressed in white, marches down the aisle, the audience silently repeats the words, "Here comes the bride, all dressed in white." The message conveyed is the ideal of the purity and virginity of the bride. This message is carried by the whiteness of the bride's gown, by the words of the song, and even by the melody of the music. Music also plays a role in funerals. In this instance, music can convey the emotions of grief and sadness better perhaps than any other medium.

Because music is a powerful vehicle for expressing emotions as well as ideas, it can be a central mechanism for symbolizing culture and cultural differences. Vietnamese music is a means for maintaining ethnic distinctiveness. The style of playing panpipes (a group of pipes bound together, each one emitting a differ-ent note) among the Aymara, the indigenous people of highland Peru, was equally distinctive of their culture. From the 1920s on, it has had an interesting diffusion, which reveals the nature of asymmetrical power relations in Peru (Turino, 1991). This musical style among the Aymara, who were the clients of mestizo patrons living in the town of Conima, was characterized by ad hoc mu-sical ensembles organized in an egalitarian fashion playing music in several dif-ferent traditions at various kinds of fiestas. This was in keeping with the emphasis on equality and on group solidarity in Aymara communities. Any man could play in an Aymara panpipe ensemble. The mestizo rural elites held the Aymara in dis-dain until the 1920s, when a movement, *indigenismo,* made people begin to take an interest in the local indigenous culture. Aspects of Aymara culture, such as the panpipe tradition, began to be selected as symbols to stand for Peruvian national identity. In this process, however, the panpipe tradition of the Aymara was trans-formed into one with fixed membership, regular rehearsals, the maintenance of performance quality, and change in the nature of the harmony. This transforma-tion took place in the town of Conima, and the changed musical form was later brought to Lima and other cities when the newly organized group traveled there to perform. During the 1970s, by which time Lima was swollen with rural mi-grants from the highlands, the panpipe tradition from Conima began to be per-formed by migrants who had heretofore been ashamed to perform their music in the city because of social prejudice against Aymara culture. Radicalized middle-class students in the city also began to perform the panpipe music and subse-quently brought it back to the rural towns from which these students came. Young Aymara people in the villages, increasingly influenced by national culture, now ignore the majority of indigenous musical instruments and community tra-ditions in favor of the urban panpipe movement. This example illustrates the way in which an indigenous musical tradition is altered in form and comes to sym-bolize Peruvian national culture, and then is brought back to the countryside where it displaces earlier musical forms.

In many societies, men and women have two rather differentiated spheres of ex-pressive activity. Concurrent with the increased interest in gender roles, researchers have begun to more systematically explore women's musical practices (Koskoff, 1987). Since a woman's identity is believed to be embedded in her sexuality, women's role in music frequently expresses this. Musical performance is seen as en-hancing sexuality, and female court musicians in the past in India, Indonesia, and Tunisia were associated with sexuality and profane pleasures. In many societies, the genre or type of music performed, the style of the performance, and the location of the performance are different for males and for females.

As societies become more complex, musicians as well as dancers often become full-time specialists. For example, Kanuri musicians are a highly trained and spe-cialized group who occupy a particular position in the social structure. The per-formers play as a group, which includes a vocalist, drummers, and a player of an oboelike reed instrument. The musicians are male, but the vocalist may be female. They are referred to as praise-singers. They frequently are attached to a patron, an

An ensemble of Kanuri praise-singers and musicians in Geidam, Nigeria.

aristocrat, who supports them in exchange for singing his praises on ceremonial occasions. They can also travel and perform as a group, living on the money they receive from their audiences. They are generally considered to be of low status by the rest of the Kanuri populace, since the way they earn their living is considered to be begging by the Kanuri. Nevertheless, virtuoso performers are greatly admired by everyone. Though the performers are aware of what other people think of them, they consider themselves artists. They value their own talents and thrive on the admiration of the audience. Thus the musician in Kanuri society is ambiguous in a way similar to that of the carver in Mano society. In general, artists are in a vague and enigmatic position in most societies, including our own. Artists' talents are admired; yet the creativity that makes them different from other people also makes them suspect. The Kanuri musician wears an earring in one ear, unlike ordinary Kanuri males.

The praise-singers of Mali, called *jeli* but also known by the French term *griots,* were, like Kanuri praise-singers, a separate, endogamous group in the social structure. However, their position has undergone a transformation (Schulz, 1998). In the past, praise-singers were attached to freeborn upper-class families in a patron-client relationship. In exchange for citing the illustrious genealogies and extolling the virtues of their patrons, praise-singers were provided with food and housing for life. With increasing modernization and urbanization, praise-singers began to appear who were not *jeli,* and who would sing anyone's praises for money. A still further transformation of praise-singers was brought about when radio and television came to Mali in 1958 and 1985, respectively. Praise-singers became media stars, but they were considered "inauthentic" because they performed for financial payments. They would sing the praises of the ancestors of people they didn't even know, those newly rich people who gloried in these praises. Praise-singing had become a commodity, to be bought and sold. Nevertheless, praise-singers on TV were thought to be carrying on an important tradition of the culture. These new "media stars" on TV and in urban theaters would sing about the evil and corrupting effect of money, and people would rush to the stage to shower them with money.

Sometimes performers are of a different ethnic group from the rest of the people in the society. Gypsies of Afghanistan and Pakistan are traveling performers and musicians who differ from the rest of the population and are considered a low-status group, completely outside the existing social structure. The Gypsies of Romania, distant relatives of those in Afghanistan, are also professional musicians who play the Gypsy violin, which is so closely associated with Romania.

Dance

Dance has been defined as those cultural practices that "formalize human movement into structured systems in much the same way that poetry formalizes language" (Kaeppler, 1985: 92). There may or may not be an indigenous conceptualization that translates into the category of dance. Kaeppler has proposed that the anthropological consideration of dance focus upon the movement dimensions of particular cultural activities and the messages such movements are conveying, to develop a cultural conceptualization of dance for a particular society (Kaeppler, 1985). The basic elements used to analyze the structure of dance are body movements. A formal description of dance would include the steps, spatial patterns, relationships to music, and postural positioning. Beyond the description, the focus of an anthropological analysis of dance is on its cultural setting and its meaning. Dances, like all other forms of art, encode particular cultural messages. They may be visual manifestations of social relations, as we shall see in examples below, or they may be part of a visual aesthetic system. Westerners frequently isolated the formal movement aspects of rituals and ceremonials as dance, neglecting the role such movements played in the total social phenomena within which they were performed. In doing this, they were utilizing a Western categorization, since in our society, dance, for the most part, has become entertainment, disassociated from ritual and ceremonial.

The culture of the Swahili, a Muslim people living in East Africa, represents a syncretism of Islamic cultural codes and indigenous Swahili culture. The Swahili have a category, *ngoma,* that means "drum," or "dance," or "music," illustrating the interrelationship, indeed in Swahili, the inextricable connection, between music and dance. Among the Swahili, *waungwana,* or high status, was marked by the possession of tall white-washed stone houses with enclosed courtyards, within which women were completely secluded, in keeping with the custom of *purdah.* They were the settings for rituals and ceremonials, poetry and dance competitions, held in the public rooms and the courtyard (Franken, 1992). Two *ngoma* performed in these houses were exclusive to the Swahili high-status class. One was the *ngoma la hazua,* a men's dance performed in spotlessly white prayer robes and richly embroidered prayer caps at weddings and circumcisions. It was a line dance performed with music and accompanied by a singer recounting the heroic deeds and distinguished ancestors of the family. The men held swords, moving them as they moved their bodies. Today this dance is held outdoors at weddings during the week celebrating the birth of the Prophet. The *lelemama* was performed by married women as a rite of passage. It was also a line dance in which the dancers wore special costumes and finger cymbals and danced to the accompaniment of music and poetry.

The movements in the *ngoma* or dances of lower-class Swahili contrasted with the dance movements of the high class *waungwana*. Lower-class people are the recent arrivals to town, economically poor, lacking important ancestors, and not very religiously observant. The men's dance, the *uta,* or the "coconut-cutters' dance," is held outdoors, during the birthday week of the Prophet on a sandlot between houses (Franken, 1992: 206). The dancers, wearing typical Swahili men's work clothing and leg rattles, dance in a circle, leaning on canes and stamping their feet in unison to the rhythm of *uta.* The second lower-class dance, the *mwaribe,* used to be performed together by men and women to a drum accompaniment. It is also performed outdoors during the week of the Prophet's birthday. The participants, wearing Western street clothes, invite partners to dance, then hop forward and backward in unison to the music. Today, this dance is performed by young men. Its lower-class character was demonstrated by the fact that it brought men and women together in violation of the rules of *purdah,* or female seclusion, and because it was also associated with non-Muslim believers. It is clear that the movements in these dances communicate contrasts about status. But they also demonstrate the inextricable connection between music and dance.

Art is a mode of communication, communicating ideas as well as emotions. Art is more than communication since it involves an aesthetic impulse—what constitutes beauty. There seems to be a universal aesthetic impulse, though cultures may express aesthetics in many different ways using different art forms. One culture may emphasize visual arts like carving while another places greater emphasis on music and dance. Masks, which are to be found in a variety of societies, illustrate the range of meanings that can be attached to what is a single form of art. Masks also make statements about a culture's view of the self. Art can be analyzed structurally in terms of what is known as art style. Style characterizes the art of all societies and can also be used to characterize the art of an individual or a particular historical period. Various forms of art may be used to express ethnic identity, as illustrated by Toraja carving and Vietnamese dance and music. The various arts we have discussed in this chapter usually operate within a set of traditional constraints. Yet every carver, painter, musician, and dancer adds his or her individual conceptualization, his or her own interpretation to the final product. It is in this aspect of art that creativity is to be found, and this creativity forms the basis for the audience's judgment of the aesthetic worth of the art produced. In the nineteenth century, the collecting of the artifacts of the small-scale societies that anthropologists were to later study was referred to as the collection of "artificial curiosities." Global tourism has resulted in the production of tourist art, the manufacture of objects by local artists to meet the demands of consumers, that is, tourists, who want a remembrance of the places they visited. The art world has become a community of buyers and sellers as a consequence of the commodification of art and the development of a worldwide auction market.

Chapter Thirteen

The Colonial and Postcolonial Periods: Globalization, Migration, Diasporas, and Transnationalism

In the past, anthropologists, for the purposes of analysis, looked at cultures as if they were static, unchanging entities. Malinowski, who carried out several years of fieldwork among the Trobriand Islanders, recorded his observations without paying attention to the changes taking place before his very eyes. In reality, cultures are constantly undergoing change, sometimes at a barely perceptible rate, but in today's world at a very rapid rate. If we conceptualize cultures as having an overall design as a tapestry does, then in situations of change we see either a part of the design beginning to unravel or sometimes a transformation taking place in the overall design itself. Under extreme or traumatic circumstances the tapestry of culture survives only in shreds.

In the 1930s, American anthropologists, recognizing that the American Indian cultures they were studying had been and were continuing to be drastically transformed, turned their analytical attention to this topic of culture change under the pressure of external forces. A memo was published in the *American Anthropologist* outlining the topics that were important to consider under what was then being called "acculturation." They were particularly concerned with the drastic effects that the American government's policy toward Indians had had on their lives over the centuries. British social anthropologists, including Malinowski, also began to be concerned with the effects of culture contact and the colonial administration on the small-scale societies they were studying.

Migration and contact between different cultures did not begin with the appearance of travelers or explorers from the West, but goes far back beyond recorded history. Migration of people from one territory to another has been a characteristic of our human species from the very beginning. It was the means by which humans came to occupy the various parts of the world. Conquest and colonization also resulted in the movement of large populations. Below we will discuss such migrations, or diasporas, as they are now called, their causes and consequences. Contact between cultures, in the form of long-distance trade networks, existed in many parts of the world over a long period of time, as demonstrated by the similarity of prehistoric tool types over broad areas. Resources not found in one place, like shells and obsidian for making stone points, were traded to areas far from their points of origin. For example, obsidian from the Admiralty Island, in the Pacific, has been found in archaeological sites farther out in the Pacific, in New Britain and New Ireland. Early visitors commented on the presence of long-distance indigenous trade networks like *kula* exchange in the Massim area (which includes the Trobriands) east of New Guinea. Sometimes cultural innovations from the West reached tribal peoples even before the first physical contacts with agents of the Western world. The horses brought to Arizona and New Mexico in the 1500s by the Spanish explorers had spread to the tribes of the Plains, for instance, the Blackfoot of Montana, by the 1700s, before sustained contact with the West took place. This radically changed the subsistence pattern, the residential pattern, and concepts of wealth and status. The effects of the introduction of the horse were so great that horticultural societies like the Omaha and the Hidatsa, who lived in the river valleys of the Missouri and its tributaries, became equestrian nomads for part of the year.

The forces for change in the world today are numerous and powerful. Colonialism, which was one of the strongest forces for change, is all but gone, and in its place is a series of new nation-states based on the geography of colonial empires rather than on sameness of culture. These new nations form a large part of what is known as the Third World. Within most of these Third World nations are the tribal people, who constitute the *Fourth World peoples.* Fourth World peoples are brought to public attention when they put up heroic struggles to preserve their autonomy and culture, such as the Kurds of Turkey, Iran, and Iraq and the Nagas of India did and are still doing. These new postcolonial nation-states are building national cultures that attempt to supplant and suppress the various indigenous cultures, in the same way that in the past the nation-states of Europe attempted to forge national cultures with varying degrees of success. However, despite political independence, the continued economic reliance of one-time colonies on their former colonial masters, in many places, constitutes neocolonialism. Over several centuries, changes have greatly altered earlier economic institutions. These changes include the introduction of cash crops, the desire for modern manufactured goods, foreign exploitation of native resources, and the need for labor. The enormous expansion of cities in these new nations presented economic and cultural inducements, which attracted many migrants from the rural areas. When they returned to their villages, they brought urban culture with them, introducing changes into village culture. Even those remaining in remote villages are now familiar with urban ideas as a consequence of mass communications. Transistor radios, tapes, and video bring new images, sounds, and ideas to the countryside. The Fourth World peoples mentioned above are the people with whom anthropologists have always been concerned. At the present time, it is the anthropologists who are studying the effects of economic expansion and transformation, mass communication, rural-urban migration, and the other consequences of globalization upon the lives of Fourth World peoples.

Colonialism and postcolonialism can be examined at several different levels. The unit that anthropologists usually isolate for study in the field is at the microanalytic level. However, they do not study it alone, but in relation to like units and to the more inclusive political levels. The next more inclusive level of analysis is that of the nation-state, where the focus of the anthropologist has been on the construction of a national culture and the creation of national identity. Since nation-states operate as independent, politically autonomous units, political decisions and economic planning take place at this level. Consequently, the unit of analysis of economic development is also the nation-state.

At a still higher, more inclusive level of analysis is the world system. This concept, developed by Immanuel Wallerstein (1974), refers to the historic emergence of the economic interrelationship of most of the world in a single market system, in which the concept of the division of labor, usually seen as operative in a single society, is projected onto the world. Wallerstein sees the system developing after the breakdown of feudalism and the rise of capitalism and entrepreneurship and the succeeding Industrial Revolution. During and after the Age of Exploration, Europeans vastly expanded their search for sources of raw materials and mineral resources, as well as for markets for their manufactured goods. These European countries formed the core of a world system, and the colonies and protectorates that they dominated formed the periphery. The world system operates according to capitalist market principles, with profits constantly reverting to the investors of capital, who are located in the core. In general, the gap between core and periphery was constantly widening, but, on the other hand, the system was constantly expanding in the search for new markets. Anthropologists have been particularly concerned with the effects of the penetration of the world system on tribal peoples all over the world and their active responses to this penetration. Eric Wolf (1982), in *Europe and the People without History,* has explored this topic, focusing, for example, on how the Kwakiutl and other native people of North America responded to the fur trade network set up by the Hudson's Bay Company in the eighteenth century.

Within recent years, another concept, *globalization,* has come to the fore. World systems theory focused primarily on the existence of structures, like core and periphery, with anthropological research directed toward the examination of the dynamics of the relationship between the smaller, local parts of the system in the periphery and the larger parts of the core. In contrast, globalization is a process that has been marked by rapid transformations in the lives of people in most parts of the world (Orlove, 1999: 195–196). Globalization has been brought about by the development of a worldwide network of finance and capital. This has occurred on a greater scale than ever before, and at an increasingly rapid rate as a result of enormous advances in telecommunications and computer technology. International institutions like the World Bank, the World Trade Organization, and the International Monetary Fund represent attempts to integrate states into a global economy. At the World Trade Organization meeting held in late 1999, American citizens demonstrated their dissatisfaction with what this organization stands for. Some demonstrators were concerned about ecological devastation and global environmental threats. Labor unionists were dissatisfied with changes in tariffs, which in turn would threaten workers' jobs. Others expressed a general unhappiness that Americans may no longer have complete control of their economy. The latter speaks to the issue that nation-states no longer have the ability to make fundamental decisions regarding exchange rates, tariffs, taxation, and the like, having lost this power to global institutions.

As transnational or multinational corporations expand and "globalize," they move beyond the scope of nation-states, and the latter lose the power to regulate and control them. These corporations have also expanded into the former Communist countries, participating in the privatization of state enterprises. Within various parts of the industrializing world, globalization has resulted in great economic successes, for example, in South Korea and Malaysia, while other parts of the world, like the Central American countries, have fallen behind, no longer being seen as targets of global investment.

Transnational migration, which we will discuss in detail later, has been brought about by the disappearance of the kinds of jobs people formerly had. New positions become available as a consequence of the new global economy, but they are positions for which these people do not have the skills. Though globalization seems to be similar to and represent historical continuities with colonialism and the neocolonialism of the latter part of the twentieth century, in reality it represents a quantum leap in the reach, penetration, and power of global capitalism (Loker, 1999: 13–14). Capital, goods, communications, pollutants, knowledge, images, cultural information, fashions, belief systems, crime, and drugs all flow very freely across national borders. The anthropologist's role in the study of the phenomena of globalization is to focus as they always have on the people in particular communities, in order to "put human faces on what would otherwise would be anonymous, impersonal statistics" (Orlove, 1999: 196). They pose questions such as; How have local institutions adapted to the challenge of manufacturing new products and exploring different markets? What has been the consequence of the establishment of a factory by the Nike corporation in a Malaysian urban area? In Chapter 8 we documented economic changes of this type. Clearly, globalization affects economic institutions and political organization. Ideologies and value systems are being changed, and these changes have also been the focus of anthropological research. Let us now go back in time to examine the colonial period, where one might say that globalization had its beginnings.

The Colonial Period

Colonialism over the course of history has taken many forms, with different effects on the peoples colonized. It is important to grasp colonial history to understand what is happening today. There were various reasons for the establishment of colonies.

Sometimes it was the search for raw materials and markets. At other times, colonies were established because of the need to protect the boundaries of an empire from marauding peoples or other empires. Sometimes, only colonial administrators and people involved in the extraction of resources lived in the colony. In other instances, many people came to the colony as settlers. The idea of colonies was not invented in sixteenth-century Europe. In ancient times, Persia, Greece, and Rome conquered other lands and established colonies. As a result of Roman conquest and colonization, the people of the Iberian Peninsula and Romania speak Romance languages, which derive from the Latin language spoken by the colonizers. In another example, in the earliest period of conquest, the only contacts that Native American societies had were with explorers and governmental representatives of the British and French colonial empires. Over time, a large and more powerful immigrant population engulfed these societies and often completely destroyed them. This situation soon became one marked by grossly unequal power and coercion.

In Australia, the kinds of changes affecting the indigenous peoples, the Australian Aborigines, were similar to those found in the United States. A small native population was soon overwhelmed by the much larger settler population. In New Zealand, the indigenous Maori population was proportionately larger than its counterparts in Australia and the United States, and the greater political influence of the Maori today is probably a result of this proportional difference. In Kenya and Zimbabwe, the settler population remained a minority in relation to the larger indigenous population, whom the settlers used as a labor force to exploit the natural resources of the area.

In most of Africa, South and Southeast Asia, and Oceania, European colonial empires were established without large numbers of European settlers. Instead of a small indigenous society confronting waves of technologically advanced settlers, as was the case in America, in these colonial situations, usually, a large indigenous population was conquered and placed under the domination of a small colonial administration, backed by armed forces. These colonies endured in some cases from the sixteenth century to the end of World War II.

The initial motivation for the establishment of colonies was economic gain, which frequently took the form of exploiting raw materials as well as providing markets for the goods of the mother country. The Industrial Revolution led to shortages of resources locally and the need to find them farther afield. Often, a single large trading company, such as the British East India Company, the Hudson's Bay Company, or the Dutch East India Company, held a monopoly on trade and was sometimes given political control as well.

There were differences in the ways colonial powers, established after the Industrial Revolution, governed. The British developed the policy of indirect rule, which was then applied throughout the British Empire. This model was first used in India, where a handful of Englishmen controlled a subcontinent of Indians by means of indigenous governments—the princely states. In contrast, the French ruled directly, establishing military garrisons and large administrative staffs throughout their empire. The French had a policy of accepting an educated individual from their colonies, who was then referred to as an *évolue,* as a citizen of France. The British never had such a policy and refused to accept the best-educated Indian, Pakistani, or African as their equal. Though the indigenous population was usually much larger than the foreign population, power and wealth were all in the hands of the representatives of the colonial power. The nature of these contacts was in every respect an unequal one.

Recent writings by anthropologists on colonialism indicate how complex were the dimensions of colonial life (Cooper and Stoler, 1989). The colonizers felt that it was constantly necessary to define the boundary between themselves and the colonized, whose "otherness" was perpetually being redefined. European colonizers had a variety of intentions toward the indigenous populations. Methodist missionaries hoped to turn the tribes of southern Africa into yeoman farmers modeled on the yeomanry of eighteenth-century England (Comaroff and Comaroff, 1986). Other colonizers attempted to transform the existing social organization to provide laborers who would work in the mines. The boundary between the European colonizers and the local population was sometimes eroded by sexual relations between European men and local women, which produced an intermediate population with an ambiguous identity in the European racial system of classification.

It should be clear from the preceding discussion that the complexities of the colonial period are relevant to anthropological research and need to be understood. Each example of Western colonial expansion may appear to be different from any other case. Nevertheless, the establishment of the colony and the course of events that followed can be described in terms of a number of variables. These include land policy, resource exploitation, type of labor recruitment, and intensity and type of missionary activity.

The Nature of Initial Contact

Initial contact and the establishment of Western sovereignty over areas inhabited by tribal peoples occurred in a number of ways. Colonial control was sometimes set up in the form of patrol posts in the native territory. This method was used by the Australian government to achieve control over the tribal peoples of highland New Guinea. The initial response was frequently hostile. But gifts of trade goods such as steel tools and the large number of ritually important shells brought in by the Australians succeeded in reducing overt expressions of hostility. The aims of the colonizers were to eliminate warfare between tribes and between villages and to introduce a police force that would transfer jurisdiction over serious crimes from the native population to the larger government. Wherever the process of government contact, pacification, and control occurred over the world, politically autonomous tribal peoples lost their independence and the ability to determine their own destinies.

First contact was often peaceful, as illustrated in the picture of the mutually beneficial exchange between the Maori of New Zealand and a member of Captain Cook's crew on his first voyage on the *Endeavour* (1768–1771). Military resistance usually occurred later, when people realized that they were losing their independence, autonomy, and cultural distinctiveness. The Maori vigorously resisted the settlement of the English after this initially peaceful exchange, and the fighting culminated in the Treaty of Waitangi in 1840. The Maori were being treated as a sovereign state with which treaties were made. Under the terms of the treaty, the British

An unknown artist's depiction of the first exchange of a crayfish for a piece of cloth between a Maori of New Zealand and a sailor from Captain Cook's crew.

Crown received all rights and powers of sovereignty over Maori territory. The Maori chiefs thought they were giving the British only partial rights, and the British did not correct this mistaken interpretation. Such cession could only occur in societies that were chieftainships or states, like the princely states of India. In societies that were less complex politically, there were no leaders who could legitimately speak on behalf of the group and cede sovereignty. Much later, such treaties became the bases for lawsuits in which indigenous groups sought to regain land taken from them. In 1996, an official report found that an entire province in New Zealand had been illegally taken from the Taranaki Maori tribes by the Treaty of Waitangi. This victory meant that Mount Taranaki and the land surrounding it should be returned to the Maoris or an equivalent financial compensation given to them.

In many situations contact with traders preceded military and political control. When North America was being colonized, fur was in great demand in Europe for men's hats and women's coats. Ambitious traders ranged far and wide, purchasing furs in exchange for cloth, tools, beads, and whiskey. Some of them established trading posts in strategic locations. This was often far in advance of political control of the area by colonial governments. The Hudson's Bay Company, established in the seventeenth century, had a string of trading posts throughout the northern woodland area of North America. The people of this area were dependent upon hunting and gathering for their subsistence. The demand for furs that the traders introduced resulted in a shift from hunting for food to trapping for furs. Band hunting territories exploited for subsistence were often subdivided into individual family hunting territories, as among the Naskapi of eastern Canada, and exploited for furs only by members of that family. This economic change affected the residence pattern and the nature of social relationships, and people slowly became dependent on the trading post to supply them with most of their food.

Land Rights

Land is a basic resource, and how rights over land are handled is a crucial variable in colonial situations. Different colonial empires had somewhat different policies with respect to the rights of native peoples over their land. Furthermore, these native peoples themselves had a variety of different conceptualizations about land rights. In Australia and the United States, a large immigrant population of settlers grew to overwhelm the much smaller indigenous societies. However, their policies toward native land rights were very different. In the Australian case, the government did not recognize that the native people had rights to any of the land. The native Australians were hunters and gatherers who, with their simple technology, exploited the whole of the continent. Though the colonial government understood the native pattern of land utilization and the claims of various Australian bands to ancestral homelands, it chose to ignore them and claim the entire continent as unoccupied wasteland, recognizing neither the land rights nor the sovereignty of the natives. Reserves for the native peoples were later established, but they were set up at the discretion of state governments in the least desirable areas, and not even these areas were for the exclusive use of native peoples.

In America, the government recognized Native Americans' rights to land. Though Peter Minuit's legendary purchase of Manhattan Island for 24 dollars' worth of trinkets may be the shrewdest real estate deal in history, it was a recognition of these rights. The recognition of land rights was also the basis for British policy in the colonial period and was reaffirmed by the fledgling American government in the Ordinance of 1787 for the Government of the Northwest Territory. Treaty relationships were maintained with Native American tribes through the nineteenth century. As the immigrant population of the United States grew and with it the demand for land, the Indian land base began to be reduced by successive treaties that the Indians were forced to conclude with the United States government.

The Cherokee illustrate how an Indian group lost its land to the U.S. government by a succession of treaties. In the latter part of the eighteenth century, while still in Georgia, their ancestral homeland, they were forced to begin ceding land to the government. By 1822, the white population had greatly increased and now demanded all the rich farmland owned by the Cherokee and Creek. These demands were not met; the Cherokee did not wish to cede any more land. Finally, in 1830 President Andrew Jackson's Indian Removal Act was passed by Congress, calling for the removal of all southeastern tribes—namely, the Cherokee, Choctaw, Chickasaw, Creek, and Seminole—to "permanent" Indian country west of the Mississippi. As President Jackson proclaimed, "Beyond the great river Mississippi . . . their father has provided a country large enough for them all, and he advised them to move to it. There their white brothers will not trouble them, and they [their white brothers] will have no claim to the land and they can live upon it, they and all their children, as long as grass grows and waters run." The Florida Seminole resisted relocation and fought a six-year war at a cost to the United States of 1500 soldiers and $20 million. The Cherokee fought the Removal Act up through the Supreme Court, won their case, but nevertheless had to surrender 17 million acres and were forced to go to Oklahoma. Fourteen thousand Cherokee left for the Oklahoma Territory, and four thousand died en route. This relocation is referred to as the Trail of Tears. The deceit of Jackson's promise was revealed when the Cherokee lost much of their land in Oklahoma, which had been promised to them for "as long as grass grows and waters run." They had to surrender it 40 years later after they made the mistake of siding with the South during the Civil War.

From the beginning, individuals within the dominant settler community in the United States agitated against traditional Indian communal use and ownership of land. In the view of the settlers, Indians would never be absorbed into the larger American society until each family lived on and owned its own plot of land in the European fashion. This belief culminated in the Allotment Act of 1887, which authorized the division of tribal lands into plots assigned to individuals. It also bestowed citizenship upon Indians who left their tribes and adopted "the habits of civilized life." These successive changes in the nature of Indian land tenure had far-reaching effects on subsistence and ultimately on all other aspects of Indian culture.

The fight over land continues today, but the positions are reversed. Tribes like the Passamaquoddy of Maine have gone to court to lay claim to their traditional land, on the basis of their contention that the United States government broke treaties made with the tribes in centuries past. The native Australians have also made legal claims to their ancestral lands. In Papua New Guinea and Nigeria, the native land tenure systems were legally recognized by the colonial governments because there were only a few settlers to compete with the indigenous population and drive them off the land.

Resource Exploitation

In some situations, exploitation of resources other than land was critical in defining the nature of the colonial experience. In contrast to land rights, which are appropriately examined on the level of the nation-state, colonial exploitation of resources is better analyzed at the level of the world system. The demand for rubber by the core countries of the world system has had an interesting history. It illustrates the way the economic fates of people on three different continents were linked. The natural stands of rubber trees in the Amazon and Congo river basins were exploited during the wild rubber boom of 1895 to 1910. In both places, tribal peoples provided the source of labor for the tapping of latex from the rubber trees in the tropical forest. People who had formerly been subsistence agriculturalists became full- or part-time rubber tappers. They were drawn into one aspect of the world economy, with effects on their own economic system.

British entrepreneurs took wild rubber plant seedlings and transported them to the British colony of Malaya, where they established rubber plantations to provide a steady source of this raw material. Rubber from these plantations captured the world market, bringing to an end the boom in wild rubber from the Congo and Amazon basins. Subsequently, rubber plantations were developed in Liberia by the Firestone Rubber Company of America, and this rubber also gained a share of the world market. Since rubber was the dominant cash crop, the entire economy of Liberia at that time was controlled by this single foreign company. The shift to synthetic rubber, developed during World War II, signaled the great reduction in importance of plantation-grown rubber.

Exploitation of resources took other forms as well. Extractive industries, such as lumbering, fishing, and mining, were also very important for a world market. The increasing scarcity of lumber led to a rise in price, especially for valuable hardwoods, and to a more intensive search for such hardwoods in out-of-the-way places. In recent years, Malaysia and Japan have been extracting valuable hardwoods from the forests of Borneo, Sumatra, and Papua New Guinea, radically changing the local ecology of the areas and the nature of the subsistence base in the process.

Probably the most valuable natural resources to be found on the lands of tribal peoples are mineral resources—gold, copper, tin, oil, coal, and uranium. Mineral rights are rarely exploited by tribal peoples themselves; however, they do benefit from royalties if minerals are found on their lands. In the United States some reservation lands that had been set aside for tribal peoples were later discovered to have extensive mineral resources. This happened in many western states. For example, the Ute tribe's reservation lands in Utah, though undesirable for agriculture, contain mineral resources, including coal, oil, natural gas, uranium, and oil shale. In fact, 25 to 50 percent of all uranium deposits in the United States are on lands owned by Native Americans. At first the Native American tribal councils gave concessions to private companies to extract the resource in exchange for a fixed royalty, for example, 25 cents per ton of coal. These royalties do not go to individuals, but rather, are paid to the tribal council fund to be used for the benefit of the entire tribe. Some tribes seek expert advice so that they can exploit these resources themselves and get a fairer return. A consortium has been formed of tribes with extensive mineral holdings to share expertise and lobby the U.S. government.

The exploitation of mineral resources was also significant in the African colonial experience. Starting in the 1880s, important discoveries of gold and diamonds were made in South Africa. Cecil Rhodes and other financiers formed the companies that exploited these resources, and with the mines came urbanization and industrialization. Rhodes influenced the British colonial government to expand north into what is now Zimbabwe in order to exploit the mineral resources there. The mineral wealth in gold, diamonds, cobalt, copper, chrome, zinc, and later uranium was highly prized by the colonial powers because of the demand for these resources in the core countries of the world system.

Labor Exploitation

Exploitation of resources in colonial areas and their successor nation-states required labor. This need for labor was met in a variety of ways, which had profound effects on the indigenous peoples, dislocating their economies and their traditional forms of family and social organization in varying degrees. In the earliest period of the colonization of the New World, the demand by the colonizers for a large-scale labor force to exploit resources was satisfied by the enslavement of native tribal peoples. The Portuguese did this with the Tupi-speaking coastal peoples of Brazil, whose population was decimated as a result of disease and the conditions of slavery. The Spanish did the same with the native Arawak-speaking peoples of the Caribbean islands, and they too perished in the same way. From the sixteenth century to the beginning of the nineteenth century, some 8 to 10 million Africans were brought to the New World as slaves to furnish labor for the plantations there. Great dislocations took place in the West African societies from which these people came. As Africans from different cultures speaking different languages were forced to adapt to the new conditions of slavery and to the cultures and languages of their plantation masters, new cultures were forged.

Plantation labor was also obtained by means of indenture. Contracts were signed between the laborers and the plantation owners for a fixed period of time. In Trinidad, the period of indenture for laborers from India was five years. The laborers' passage from their homeland was provided by the owners, and they were not free to leave their employer until the period of indenture was over. Other Indians went as indentured laborers to British Guiana (Guyana), to Fiji in the Pacific, and to South Africa, where they form significant ethnic groups today. Their Indian culture has changed and reflects the differing cultural conditions to which they have had to adapt. They have become important economically and politically in the countries in which they now live. In Fiji, half of the population is Indian in descent, and there has been conflict between Indians and indigenous Fijians for political control of the country.

During the colonial period, when the local population was unwilling to provide its labor, various forms of coercion were sometimes used. King Leopold of Belgium personally owned the Congo from 1884 to 1908. He exploited the rubber resources of the Congo during the wild rubber boom referred to earlier by using local corvée labor, that is, by requiring that each adult male provide a certain amount of labor as payment of tax. Another means of obtaining labor during the latter part of the nineteenth century was through "blackbirding." Unsuspecting tribal men from various islands of Melanesia were tricked or shanghaied aboard ships and taken to the sugar plantations of Queensland, Australia, and Fiji. These kidnapped men were compelled to work for three years on the plantations for low wages, after which they were permitted to return to their tribal homelands, if they survived the experience.

In time, these various coercive means for acquiring cheap labor were either outlawed or reformed. Slavery was abolished, and blackbirding and indentured service were halted. These forms of labor recruitment eventually gave way to contract labor. Contract labor has been very important in meeting the demand for labor to exploit the mineral resources of southern Africa. Men migrate from the tribal areas to the mines for a period of 9 to 18 months. The South African government, in the past, controlled the free flow of workers through the Pass Laws, preventing those without a contract from leaving tribal areas for the towns and cities more than a thousand miles away. Most migrants, who ranged in age from 20 to 40, were men whose wives remained behind. This migration left the tribal areas bereft of men, children without fathers, and wives without husbands. The earlier organization of the family was undercut and weakened, and women alone raised the children. Women bore the burdens of everyday subsistence, and the cycle of economic activities based on the traditional male/female division of labor was no longer possible. During the time they worked in the mines, the men became increasingly familiar with urban life. At first, tribal affiliation and tribal leadership were emphasized; but gradually new associations such as unions developed, and leadership based on skill and on education superseded tribal leadership in most situations.

Missionaries and Culture Change

When a colonial administration was set up in a tribal area, concerted efforts were made to abolish those practices that violated the colonizers' moral code, a product of their own Western European cultures. Missionaries were the most zealous enforcers of these kinds of changes. Who were these missionaries? Where did they come from? Let us examine the missionaries who came to Melanesia. Before 1860, missionary activity in this area was primarily in the hands of Protestants of the London Missionary Society. Their mission was "to convince all men (in whatever state, all equally condemned) of their innate depravity, of their need for a saviour or mediation with God, and finally of belief in the atonement and the consequent salvation of believers" (Gunson, 1987: 27). Missionaries often arrived first, followed by the establishment of a colonial administration. In the early days, the missionaries coming from England to the Pacific were from the lowest classes. Though of humble origins, they were men with a calling. Later, missionaries began to come from the middle class. Wesleyan Methodist missionaries who went to the Bismarck Archipelago tended to come from rural areas and had close connections with Wesleyans in Australia and New Zealand. The motives of those drawn to missionary work in the distant and dangerous Pacific were twofold: the desire to serve God by converting the "savages," enabling the latter to redeem their souls and not descend into hell, combined with a feeling that by doing this, they, the missionaries, were growing spiritually as well as saving their own souls. Missionaries saw themselves as men of destiny, determined to overthrow idolatry and heathenism. The preconceptions of some missionaries regarding the ignoble heathens were modified by their experience and their intellectual curiosity to learn more about the way of life of the people whose lives they had come to change (Langmore, 1989: 10). Such missionaries had a closer relationship to their converts than other paternalistic, authoritarian missionaries. For the Methodists, the goal was to establish churches that would be led by local, indigenous leaders. From the beginning, they trained local men as catechists, who eventually became ministers with their own churches. Much later on, these men became leaders of the church, determining church policy. Catholic missionaries followed a different plan of action. They established mission stations totally staffed by Europeans, and only much later did local Catholics become involved on the lower level in the activities of the church.

Head-hunting and cannibalism, where they occurred, were actively suppressed by the missionaries. Sexual practices that differed from Western custom and that missionaries considered abhorrent were also forbidden. Missionaries had been in the Trobriand Islands for some time when Malinowski arrived to do fieldwork in 1914. Trobriand rules and attitudes about what constituted proper and improper sexual behavior were quite different from Western missionary ideas. Young people were permitted free expression of sexual impulses. Missionaries disapproved of groups of young girls going to a neighboring village to take lovers for the night. A special regulation was instituted to put down this "abominable abuse." On the other hand, the Trobrianders considered sexual intercourse between people of the same subclan, or *dala,* to be incest, and individuals caught in the act were forced to commit suicide. The missionaries defined incest in a different way and put an end to this form of punishment. As a consequence, the Trobrianders saw this as weakening native customs about incest. The missionaries also brought their ethnocentric point of view to bear on other areas of social life involving marriage and the family. Frequently, they forbade child betrothal, bride wealth payments, and polygamy, and enlisted the support of colonial administrators to put into effect edicts to suppress these customs. As noted in Chapter 6, the Trobrianders do not recognize the father as having anything to do with the conception of a child. The missionaries repeatedly attempted to convince them of the importance of physical paternity, to persuade them to accept the doctrine of the Holy Trinity. However, the Trobrianders would not accept the missionaries' arguments.

Sometimes an entire ritual or ceremonial complex was outlawed on the insistence of the missionaries. Anglican and Methodist missionaries among the Haida considered the potlatch a heathen custom, since it was a significant native religious rite that they felt impeded the spread of Christianity among these people. The missionaries also objected to the economics of the potlatch. The amassing of material goods was a good thing, but the practice of inviting guests and giving away the goods to them at a potlatch seemed irrational since it violated Western ideas of capitalist economic behavior. The Protestant ethic of working hard, saving, and investing one's savings conflicted directly with the potlatch ethic of generosity and giving away great amounts of goods to validate one's name and position. The potlatch reinforced the indigenous status system and the entire social structure in these Native American

Missionaries taught Christianity to the people of New Guinea in the early 1900s.

societies. The Canadian administration had to do away with the potlatch to turn these people into useful Canadian wage earners and productive citizens. The Canadian Indian Act of 1876 was passed, prohibiting Northwest Coast peoples such as the Kwakiutl, the Tsimshian, the Haida, and the Tlingit from potlatching or carrying out the winter ceremonials.

Despite this law, the Kwakiutl potlatch continued to flourish through the first two decades of the twentieth century. The Kwakiutl, now in commercial fishing and wage work, were able to accumulate ever larger amounts of goods. However, the potlatch had to be held secretly, away from the government agency and missionary station at Alert Bay. One of the largest potlatches ever given among the Kwakiutl was held in 1921. Thirty thousand blankets were given away. The kinds of goods distributed at this potlatch in addition to blankets reveal the changes that were taking place in the potlatch as it accommodated to changing times. Besides five gas boats and 25 canoes, there were bracelets for women, gaslights, violins, guitars, shirts and sweaters for young people, 300 trunks, two pool tables, sewing machines, gramophones, and furniture. At this potlatch, for the first time, the law was enforced, and the givers of the potlatch were arrested by the Royal Canadian Mounted Police. They were tried and sent to prison, and their carved masks, instruments, and costumes were confiscated and eventually ended up in the National Museum in Ottawa. However, this important ceremonial could not be abolished by fiat. It continued secretly, until finally the Canadian government, in the Revised Indian Act of 1951, no longer prohibited potlatching and winter dances. The potlatch is important today among the peoples of the Northwest Coast, and large-scale potlatches continue to be held. The masks and other ceremonial paraphernalia that had been confiscated in 1921 were returned to the Kwakiutl recently when they built two museums at Alert Bay and at Quadra Island to house this material.

New Ireland: An Example of Increasing Incorporation into the Global System

It is useful to examine the ways in which the variables we have just discussed operate in a particular case, that of New Ireland, now part of the nation-state of Papua New Guinea. New Ireland is located in the Bismarck Archipelago, close to the equator and east of the much larger island of New Guinea. The first Westerner known to have made contact with New Irelanders, in 1619, was the Dutch explorer Schouten. He was searching for trading opportunities in the Pacific outside the geographic area over which the Dutch East India Company had a monopoly. Schouten tried to exchange beads with the New Irelanders for needed supplies, but the exchange could not be transacted because, as one would expect, neither side understood the other. When the New Irelanders attacked the intruders with their slings and clubs, Schouten responded with cannon fire, killing 10 or 12 of them. This initial contact with the West was a violent one, not easily forgotten by the New Irelanders. Over the next two centuries some seven European expeditions sought to replenish their supplies on New Ireland. They offered trade goods, such as beads and cloth, which did not seem to interest the New Irelanders, and consequently they were given little in the way of supplies in return.

During the first decades of the nineteenth century, ships put in more and more frequently at New Ireland. By this time, the New Irelanders knew that the European ships anchoring in their harbors wanted to reprovision with coconuts, tubers, and pigs, and the Europeans had become aware of the New Irelanders' desire for iron. Iron hoops, used to hold casks together, were cut into 3- or 4-inch segments, and given in exchange for supplies. They were greatly prized by the New Irelanders and used to make adzes and axes. The introduction of iron made the men's role in clearing trees for gardening much easier. The process of carving *malanggan* sculptures, mentioned in Chapter 12, became much easier. When whaling became an important activity in the Pacific, English whalers and American whalers from New Bedford and Nantucket put in to the bays of New Ireland for fresh water and supplies, giving hoop iron, along with buttons, bottles, strips of cloth, and later, tobacco in exchange. A number of seamen became castaways on New Ireland at this time. In 1825, Thomas

Manners, an English whaler, asked to be put ashore on New Ireland, where he subsequently lived with the villagers, took wives, and fathered children. The New Irelanders probably learned a great deal about his culture from Manners. As a result of Manners's presence, the Big Man of his village seemed to have had more political power. For men such as Manners, the islands of the Pacific were a romantic escape from the alienation of industrializing society.

During this period, the island was visited by traders seeking tortoise shell to be sent to Europe for the manufacture of combs and other decorative items, which became the rage of fashionable Europe. Bêche-de-mer (sea cucumbers) were also collected and then dried and sold to the Chinese as a food delicacy. By this point, a mutually agreed-upon barter system had been established, and some New Irelanders were able to communicate in Pidgin English. (The descendant of this language is known today as Neo-Melanesian.) The New Irelanders, without being aware of it, had thus become part of the global system of trade.

The first trading post on New Ireland itself was set up in 1880 by the German trader Eduard Hernsheim to purchase coconuts. From his base on Matupi Island in New Britain, Hersheim set up a network of trading stations, including a number on New Ireland. His agents—Englishmen, Scandinavians, and later, mostly Chinese—at these stations bought unhusked coconuts, and later, only the nuts, from the New Ireland villagers in exchange for tobacco, beads, and ironware from Europe. The price the villagers received for coconuts varied, depending on the price of copra on the world market, the price of beads in Europe, and the number of competing traders in the area. These were factors from the world economic system of which villagers on the local level were completely unaware. In the indigenous system of exchange, shell valuables and pigs did not fluctuate in value. Hernsheim transported the dried copra on his own ship to be sold in Hamburg. With capital raised in Hamburg, Hernsheim was able both to run and to expand his business in New Ireland, with the profits being returned to Hamburg. The success of his business enterprise depended on the world price of copra. Hernsheim had competitors in the area, among them some colorful South Sea Island adventurers such as His Majesty O'Keefe, Bully Hayes, and the notorious Queen Emma, the daughter of a Samoan mother and the American consul to Samoa.

Relying on villagers to bring in their coconuts did not produce a steady supply of copra. As Hernsheim notes in his memoirs, "It was impossible to make long-term agreements with these savages; there were no chiefs and no large villages" (1983). Because the New Irelanders had Big Men, rather than chiefs, there was no one in a position of central political authority with whom traders and later political administrators could make binding agreements and sign treaties. There was no single political structure that unified the whole island. The alternative to the unpredictable supply of copra provided through trading stations was the establishment of a plantation system, which began on New Ireland at the beginning of the twentieth century. Land for plantations had to be purchased by Europeans from New Irelanders. Since land on New Ireland was owned by matrilineal clans, unless clan representatives negotiated such sales, land transfers by other individuals, who "sold" land to Europeans, were later disputed by their fellow members.

Labor recruiters began in the 1880s to call at locations in New Ireland to recruit workers for plantations in Fiji, sometimes resorting to "blackbirding," mentioned above. Captain Wawn, one of the first labor recruiters, or blackbirders, in the area, recruiting for the sugar plantations in Queensland, Australia, in 1883, reports that men eagerly scrambled aboard his ship without knowing the pay or the length of service. Within a week, when the opportunity presented itself, 14 of the 143 "recruits" jumped overboard and escaped, having realized what they had committed themselves to. The remainder were forcibly taken to Queensland to work as laborers. When they returned home three years later, the recruits brought back boxes filled with Western goods, which they used to maximize their positions in the political arenas of their own villages, becoming leaders and Big Men. Many came back to New Ireland speaking Pidgin English, and this enabled them to deal more successfully with the European traders on the island. The sugar produced in Queensland and the copra from Fiji and Samoa where the New Irelanders worked were destined for sale on the world market.

Missionary activity began in New Ireland in 1875 when the Methodist Reverend George Brown, an Englishman, stationed two Fijian religious teachers there. There was no colonial administration on New Ireland at that time. Fijian teachers were important to the Methodist missionary enterprise because it was felt that, since they were more like New Irelanders than Europeans, they would more effectively spread the message of Christianity than the English themselves. In the following year, the first Methodist church on New Ireland was opened. The Methodist missionaries voiced their strong opposition to the New Irelanders' wearing no clothing; to ritual dancing, which the missionaries considered lewd; and to cannibalism. The progress of missionizing was impeded, according to the Reverend Brown, by the absence of authoritative leadership and the many languages spoken on the island. When a chief converts, as in Fiji, an entire chiefdom converts with him; Big Men do not have the same kind of authority over their followers. Catholic missionaries visited New Ireland in 1882. The Catholic approach to missionizing represented a point of view toward the New Irelanders different from that of the Reverend Brown. It involved setting up mission stations run by Europeans to which the local people would come for religious instruction and schooling.

There was one attempt at European settlement on New Ireland, sponsored by the Marquis de Ray, a French aristocrat who had never been in the Pacific. It was ultimately a failure. Four ships, with 700 settlers, left Europe for New France, that is, New Ireland, between 1880 and 1882. Unfortunately, the area chosen was the least suitable for the settlement envisioned. Completely unprepared for what they had to face in New Ireland, within two years most of the settlers died of tropical diseases and the survivors were eventually taken off the island to Australia. The Marquis de Ray was later tried in France and found guilty of fraud.

Although traders of several nationalities were operating in the Bismarck Archipelago after 1880, German companies dominated the area economically. Australia, then a British colony, was concerned about German influence on the island of New Guinea and proceeded to annex the southern half of that island. This prompted action on the part of both Germany and Great Britain, and within a year an agreement was signed between them in which Germany took control over northern New Guinea and the Bismarcks and the English were to control the remainder of New Guinea. The German flag was raised over New Ireland in November 1884. While it had already been tied to the rest of the world economically for several decades, New Ireland now politically became part of the German colonial empire.

It was not until 1900 that a government station was established at Kavieng, the present provincial capital, with Franz Boluminski as district commissioner. For the first time in its history, the whole island constituted a single political entity, a district within the colony of German New Guinea, instead of many autonomous villages. Former employees of the large German trading companies began to apply for land to establish plantations in such numbers that shortly thereafter the colonial government had to enact regulations to prevent the New Irelanders from losing all their land. The monument Boluminski left in New Ireland was the coastal road, stretching for over 100 miles from Kavieng, built by means of corvée labor extracted from the villages along its path.

During the German administration, great efforts were made by the colonial government to end the state of perpetual feuding between local communities and to end raiding and looting of European trade stations by the New Irelanders. Beyond the retaliatory raids against offending communities by the local native police organized and led by the Germans, pacification took the form of moving villages to the coast, where they could be more easily supervised. This movement of inland villagers to the coast tore whole communities away from their ancestral clan lands, bringing them into the coastal villages as intruders. This left the interior of New Ireland relatively deserted. Headmen, called *luluais,* not always the traditional leaders, were appointed for each village by the German administration. Sometimes the men who had worked in plantations overseas, learned Pidgin English, and had become Big Men were appointed *luluais.*

In contrast to most of the earlier European traders, like Hernsheim, who went to Australia or returned to Europe after they had made their fortunes, Chinese traders, who came somewhat later, stayed on in New Ireland, intermarried with the local people, and eventually took control of the trade stores. The Chinese, who had come as traders, did not feel the same way as Europeans did about maintaining sharp boundaries between colonizers and colonized.

The Germans were stripped of their colonies, including New Ireland, after they lost World War I, and Australia took over the administration of New Ireland under a mandate from the League of Nations. The Australians expropriated German-owned plantations and sold them at favorable rates to Australian ex-servicemen, who employed local New Irelanders from nearby villages. In other respects, life for the New Irelanders did not change much when colonial control passed from the Germans to the Australians. When the price of copra rose on the world market in the 1920s, Australian plantation owners became quite successful, but when it fell during the Depression, they lost money. Villagers had to sell coconuts from their own trees to raise cash to purchase trade goods and to pay the head tax. Patrol officers encouraged the villagers to cut and dry the meat of the coconut kernels themselves so that they could sell it as processed copra and receive a higher price for it than for the kernels.

The Australians established patrol posts at various locations over the island. Patrol officers periodically visited almost every village to collect the head tax; to adjudicate disputes, particularly over land; to examine health conditions; to see that labor recruitment rules were adhered to; and to conduct censuses. In this way, the colonial masters increasingly penetrated many aspects of the daily life of the New Irelanders. The Australians continued to use the *luluai* system put in place by the Germans. By this time, Pidgin English had developed as the lingua franca for New Ireland, as well as many other areas of the southwest Pacific. In addition to its use by Europeans to communicate with the local people was its use by New Irelanders from different parts of the island, who spoke different languages, to converse across linguistic boundaries.

During World War II, Rabaul, on nearby New Britain, was the main Japanese base in the southwest Pacific, and New Ireland was occupied by the Japanese. For the New Irelanders, the primary hardship arose from Japanese confiscation of pigs and foodstuffs. The expatriate Europeans and Chinese traders were dealt with by the Japanese much more harshly.

The Australians returned after World War II to administer Papua New Guinea as a United Nations Trusteeship Territory, with independence as the eventual aim. The Australian plantation owners reopened their plantations, and the economy continued much as it had before the war, though new crops, such as cocoa, began to be grown alongside the coconut palms. In the 1950s, as a first step toward independence, the Australians introduced a system of elected local government councils, which took over some of the functions that had been carried out by patrol officers. A House of Assembly was established in Port Moresby, with representation from all over Papua New Guinea.

In 1975 the independent nation of Papua New Guinea was established. New Ireland was set up as a province, with its own elected provincial assembly and a provincial government headed by a prime minister. Representatives from New Ireland were also elected to the national parliament. Since independence, Australian expatriates have been withdrawing from the economic system of New Ireland, though they still own many of the plantations. Some of the plantation laborers are New Irelanders, while others have been brought in from the Sepik River area of New Guinea. The world price for copra has been very low in recent years, and many of the plantations are run at a minimal level since the owners do not wish to take a loss. As plantations are abandoned, they revert to the local villages. Villagers still have a subsistence economy, supporting themselves, for the most part, through gardening, raising pigs, and fishing. But in addition, the local villagers have moved into cash cropping, producing copra and cocoa to sell to government marketing boards, which then sell these products on the world market. Sometimes villagers have organized themselves into cooperatives to buy and operate a truck or a boat. In recent years, Malaysian and Japanese companies have been exploiting the timber resources in the interior part of the island. Though fixed royalties are paid to national and provincial governments and to local people, no thought is being given to the replenishing of this resource through reforestation.

The legacy of the Reverend George Brown is the many Methodist congregations all over the island led by indigenous religious leaders. The Catholic mission stations of the island are now run by expatriate American priests of the Order of the Sacred Heart, while the diocese of New Ireland is headed by a German bishop.

The significant unit for most New Irelanders continues to be their village. Villages had been politically independent before New Ireland became a colony. Today, though there are still Big Men and matrilineal clans, every village is part of an electoral district. In contrast to people elsewhere who have become wage laborers or who depend exclusively on cash crops, New Ireland villagers have resisted being completely absorbed into a market economy. Many prefer to sell products only when they need cash. However, for more than a hundred years, New Irelanders have not been able to think of themselves solely in terms of their clan or village membership. They are increasingly forced to view themselves in regional terms, as New Irelanders, and in national terms, as Papuan New Guineans. Changes at the world level affect them economically and politically, and they see themselves as necessarily part of the world system.

The Role of the Anthropologist in Governmentally Instituted Change

During the colonial period, government administrators in colonies all over the world instituted many changes in all aspects of life, as we have documented earlier. They saw these changes as bringing "progress" to peoples, helping make them "modern"—that is, civilized and Westernized. Though many of these changes were not desired by the peoples themselves, their opinions were not sought. In the postcolonial period, national governments may institute sweeping changes, but the tribal peoples in such nation-states who are most affected by such changes are usually not consulted. Once a policy is made introducing changes, anthropologists are frequently consulted regarding the most efficient way to implement them.

There are two areas in which governments make policy decisions to implement culture change. The first is technology and economics; the second is health. The anthropologist rarely makes policy. The decision to build a dam for hydroelectric power and irrigation is made by economic planners in the national government. The lake created by the dam will flood dozens of villages. The anthropologist usually is brought in to help devise ways to resettle the villagers with the least amount of dislocation. Because anthropologists assisted colonial governments to achieve their goals, they were sometimes considered tools of colonialism. During the Vietnam War, governmental policies sealed the fate of tribal Montagnard peoples, and ethical questions were raised when some anthropologists were involved in suggesting the most efficient ways of carrying out these policies. When anthropologists are involved in implementing change, they should ask the following questions: Do the people themselves seek the changes and understand their consequences? Have they been involved in a collaborative effort with the policy makers to plan the changes that will take place?

Within recent years, nongovernmental organizations (NGOs) in many countries have become an important vehicle for development at the local level as a consequence of the failure of "bureaucratically driven inflexible governmental development programs" (Weisgrau, 1997: 1). These programs tend to be small-scale, individually organized programs at the village level, able to reach the rural poor in remote areas. The NGOs try to involve villagers in both planning and execution, addressing locally identified priorities. Their budgets are usually small, often with some money coming from outside organizations. Anthropologists provide a perspective on the activities of NGOs in villages and evaluate their strategies and successes (Weisgrau, 1997; Loizos, 1991).

Among the technological changes that development programs sponsored by the government as well as by NGOs have addressed is the introduction of new crops and improved varieties of older crops. New food crops have been successfully introduced to tribal peoples all over the world. Sometimes an improved variety of an old crop is introduced that has a taste somewhat different from the old one and is not accepted. Sometimes a new method of processing food is introduced as a labor-saving device, but if the taste of the food changes, the new method may be unsuccessful. Traditionally, Kanuri women grind sorghum, the staple crop, by hand between two stones to make the basic food dish of the Kanuri. Mechanization of the grinding process was attempted by setting up a mill to grind the grain, which would have saved enormous amounts of daily labor, but the mill-ground sorghum did not have the gritty taste that the Kanuri liked, and they would not use sorghum ground in that way.

The advances in Western science have been put to practical application in the field of animal husbandry. Nomadic pastoralists like the Bakhtiari in Iran readily worm their herds with pills distributed by the veterinary services of the national government. In general, changes in veterinary practices that the people themselves see as increasing the productivity and fertility of herds are readily accepted. However, proposed long-term changes, such as reduction in the size of herds, are frequently opposed. For example, among the Navajo during the mid-1930s, the United States government introduced a stock-reduction program. The Department of the Interior had made an extensive study of all the rangeland on the Navajo reservation, concluding that overgrazing had caused soil erosion. It was clear that the number of sheep, goats, and horses kept by the Navajo tribe would have to be reduced. This caused great consternation among the Navajo since their livestock represented their wealth and was a source of great prestige. Navajo resentment toward the government simmered for many years after. Attempts to reduce herd size among pastoral cattle-keeping peoples of East Africa have also met with little success because of the cultural importance of their herds.

Another and more drastic form of directed culture change involving nomadic pastoralists was the programs to sedentarize them. Nomadic pastoralists lived in many countries in the Middle East. Since they were highly mobile, it was difficult for national governments to control them. Their emphasis on tribal identity above national loyalties also constituted a political threat. As a result of this, governments throughout the area have attempted to settle the nomadic pastoralists in villages. These plans have invariably been resisted. As noted in Chapter 8, a policy of forced sedentarization of nomadic tribes was instituted by the government of Iran during the period 1925 to 1941. Among the Basseri, for example, most families were prevented from migrating. Since their herds of sheep and goats were adapted to the migratory cycle, large percentages of the herds died because the enforced sedentarization subjected the animals to extremes of temperature to which they were not accustomed. After 1941, most of these nomadic pastoral tribes resumed migration. Attempts at sedentarization or partial sedentarization in other countries, as in the case of the Bedouins of the Israeli Negev, have been more successful.

Earlier in our discussion of law and social control, we pointed out that anthropologists, because of their expertise in customary law, have been called in as consultants by newly established nations who were in the process of developing new legal codes. The Customary Law Project in Papua New Guinea had the task of assembling information on the legal systems of different cultural groups to develop a Papua New Guinea common law that would be in accord with customary law. Legislators and policy makers in the national government are attempting to reconcile the customary form of managing the resolution of conflicts with the demands of modern life. Many of the societies that constitute the nation of Papua New Guinea pay homicide compensation after a killing. The size of the compensation varies with the severity of the act and the magnitude of the dispute, but payment of compensation acknowledges acceptance of responsibility and the termination of conflict. In recent times, demands for homicide compensation have been extended to deaths due to automobile accidents. The Papua New Guinea government is attempting to construct a legal code that will incorporate indigenous ways of resolving conflict (by the payment of compensation), define the limits of applying them, and determine what aspects of homicide compensation will be standardized.

■ Internal Migration, Transmigration, and Diasporas

Internal migration refers to population movements within a nation-state. Such migrations have been taking place in our own country since its settlement almost 500 years ago. The expansion of our country from the original 13 colonies represents a form of internal migration. The nineteenth-century movement of population ever westward to the Pacific Ocean continued this pattern. At the beginning of the twentieth century, large numbers of African Americans, dissatisfied with life in the segregated rural South began their movement to the northern urban cities where they hoped to find work and freedom from the segregated culture of the South. This movement continued for many years. During the twentieth century, migration from rural areas to cities represented another significant movement of population. Whereas in the nineteenth century most of the population of the United States lived in the rural areas of the country, increasingly, in the twentieth century, the urban and suburban populations have come to dominate. The mechanization of farming and farm consolidation forced many farming families to seek their fortunes in the cities of the nation. Labor migration, the movement of people to where jobs are available, is also a form of internal

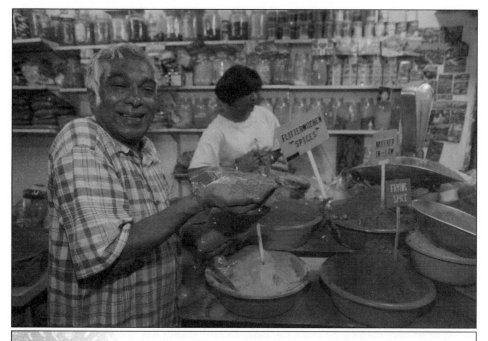

An Indian spice seller living overseas in South Africa. The signs in his shop are in Afrikaans and English.

migration. After World War II, many people sought their fortunes in "sunny California," where they saw new employment opportunities. People have also moved from the urban Northeast to seek employment elsewhere, since the industries of that area were moving to other parts of the country or even overseas. Senior citizens, whose retirement communities we discussed in a previous chapter, move from northern states, with their cold winters, to Florida, California, and the Southwest, where the climate is more to their liking. One might even consider professors as exemplifying internal migration, since, during the course of their careers, they may teach at different colleges and universities in different parts of the country.

Transmigration involves populations' migrating far from their homelands to many different parts of the world. These people may be completely assimilated into the culture of their new country, as occurred for many people who were persecuted in their homelands or who were dissatisfied with their lives in the countries of their birth and sought their fortunes in America. Some migrants to other countries may maintain their ethnic identity for centuries. We have already noted the way Indian populations retained their Indian identity long after their periods of indenture in Fiji. "Overseas Indians" are to be found in other places in the world, including countries in East Africa and Trinidad. "Overseas Chinese" have lived for generations in many countries in Southeast Asia, in Indonesia, in Papua New Guinea, in Cuba, and elsewhere. They are well established in these countries and are frequently very successful economically. Their ethnic identity still remains Chinese or Indian. These "overseas" populations have been studied extensively by anthropologists, who have been concerned with the adaptations that the Chinese and Indians have made in different cultural settings and the means by which they have maintained their ethnic identities.

In recent years, the overseas migration of groups like the Chinese and Indians just described have come to be known as *diasporas*. This term is now applied to populations who have moved to other parts of the world and retained some connection to their homelands. The word "diaspora" was originally a Greek term that meant "dispersion." The term came to be applied to the uprooting of the Jewish people after the destruction of the Second Temple in A.D. 70, their exile from the Holy Land and subsequent dispersion throughout the Old and later, the New World. They kept alive their memories of Jerusalem and of the land of Israel, and a belief in a Messiah who would deliver them. At every Passover ceremony, Jews everywhere express the hope that next year will mark their return to Jerusalem. The term *diaspora* is now applied to diverse migrant groups settled in countries away from their homelands for a whole variety of reasons. Some analysts have argued "that the term should be reserved for groups forced to disperse, and whose members conscientiously strive to keep past memories, maintain their heritage and are involved in a survival struggle" (Tatla, 1999: 3). Such diaspora groups have faced ethnocide—forced cultural integration—or even genocide in the effort to eliminate or exterminate them. Cohen (1997) has suggested a number of specific features that all diasporas have in common. First, they all represent a dispersal from a homeland. Members of the diaspora always maintain a collective memory about their homeland, including its location, history, and achievements, idealizing their ancestral home. They have a collective commitment to its maintenance, restoration, safety, and prosperity, and to its re-creation if it no longer exists as a separate political entity. Frequently, a movement to return to the homeland among members of the diaspora becomes important to the group. Diasporas also sustain strong ethnic group consciousness over a long period of time, based on a sense of distinctiveness, a common history, and the belief in a common fate. They may have a troubled relationship with the host society, which does not accept them, and in such situations there is always the possibility that another calamity, a wave of persecution or perhaps another dispersal, will befall the group. In contrast, in some situations, where the host country constitutes a plural society, members of a diaspora may continue to have a distinctive creative life. Diaspora populations also have a strong sense of empathy and solidarity with co-ethnic members residing in other countries (Cohen, 1997: 26).

The reasons for the dispersal of a diaspora population may vary. Armenians, Africans, and Jews represent "victim diasporas." That is, their movement was a consequence of forced removal, as was the case for the Africans who were brought to the New World, or persecution and threats of death, which forced the Armenians to flee from Turkey and the Jews to flee from the pogroms in Poland and the Ukraine. Sometimes, like the Indians or the Turks, men had to leave families and their homelands, in which employment was scarce, and go in search of work abroad. The Chinese and Lebanese represent the movement of people to other countries in search of trade opportunities (Cohen, 1997). More recently, the process of globalization has had an effect on diasporas. Air transportation has made international migration much easier. People migrate more frequently, and rather than permanently settle in another country, remain in continuous contact with their homelands, to which they often return upon retirement. Cities have become more international, more cosmopolitan in their acceptance of cultural differences. Notions of plural societies and multiculturalism in many places have replaced the idea of a national culture. Complete assimilation and the idea of the "melting pot" no longer characterize not only our country but others as well.

The diaspora population of Germans in Russia, who were known as Volga Germans, retained their ethnic identity over centuries and recently were able to return to their homeland. In the eighteenth century, Germans were invited to settle in Russia to introduce their agricultural and organizational skills to a Russia that had just been opened up to Western ideas. When they first arrived, they lived in an area around the Volga River. Many were moved to Siberia during World War II, ending up in Kazakhstan, still remaining ethnically German. When Kazakhstan recently became independent from Russia, the nationalist hostility against Germans increased, as it did against European Russians. German laws guaranteed ethnic Germans full citizenship and automatic access to the liberal welfare system, while children of Turkish workers who were born in Germany did not have such rights until very recently. More than a million ethnic Germans have moved back to Germany since the end of the Cold War, only to encounter hostility because of the strain on economic resources, the lack of employment for them, and especially, their cultural differences. They have trouble with the German language, which is no longer their native language. Though encouraged by the German government to return, in their former homeland, the Volga Germans now constitute a separate ethnic group.

Transnationalism refers to family members' migrating from their homes to another country, such as the United States, continuing to maintain close contact with those left behind, and forming new kinds of families (Kearney, 1995). Other relatives may follow them, in a pattern of chain migration. These family members now in the United States maintain a kind of dual existence. They live and work in our country, sometimes even in different cities, but remain members of their families back home, sending money, owning property, and even voting. They may become United States citizens and still maintain these close connections. In Chapter 6 we referred to this type of transnational family, which uses the mails, the telephone, and the airlines as ways of maintaining close contact. In a recent Dominican election, individuals living in New York, the "absent Dominicans," were seen as playing an absolutely vital role in terms of not only their votes but also their financing of one candidate or another. Turkish people who migrated to Germany or the Netherlands as "guest workers" (sometimes referred to as "international commuters") also operate in this manner. Often, they may remain for many years, completely separate from the members of the host nations, without the possibility of citizenship. They bring over spouses for their children born in European countries, and they return to their homelands when they are pensioned off. German people have reacted negatively toward the Turkish people who have lived in their country for decades. The Turks are always seen as outsiders. One may expect that second- and third-generation Turks born in the Netherlands and in Germany will have a gradually weakening connection with their homeland. However, they will probably not be assimilated and, like other diaspora populations, will remain Turkish in identity, as have the overseas Indians and Chinese.

Terms such as *internal migration, transmigration, diasporas,* and *transnationalism* represent relatively new concepts in the anthropological vocabulary. However, anthropologists have been studying ways of life of Haitian migrants in New York City, Turkish guest workers in Germany, Kalmyk Mongol immigrants in New Jersey, African Americans in New York and Philadelphia neighborhoods, and Chinese in San Francisco for decades. These new concepts are of assistance analytically, enabling anthropologists and others to have a better understanding of what is happening. For example, they permit us to describe more accurately a new type of family, the transnational family. By using the concept *diaspora populations,* we can more readily recognize the necessity of looking at African Americans, African Cubans, and African Brazilians in terms of what they have in common.

Cultural Identity Reasserted and Transformed

Most tribal people recognize that the introduction of changes from the industrialized world, which is itself constantly undergoing change, has had and will continue to have a profound effect on their cultures. Frequently, people are ready and willing to accept those changes that they perceive as immediately useful, such as steel axes. Sometimes change is forced upon them, and sometimes they forcibly resist change. One form of resistance is to run away, as the Kreen-akore of the tropical forest of Brazil ran from attempts to contact and pacify them. But you can only run so far and for so long, and eventually, even the Kreen-akore stopped running. Other tribal groups retain their identity and uniqueness by conscious efforts to preserve the traditional and customary and to reject the new. As the Menomini man defiantly said to the former Commissioner of Indian Affairs, "You can make the Menomini reservation into Menomini County but you can't make a white man out of me!"

It has been recently pointed out that predictions made in the first half of the twentieth century about what would happen to small-scale tribal societies have turned out to be incorrect (Sahlins, 1999). An earlier generation of anthropologists, typified by Boas and Malinowski, assumed that such societies could not withstand the onslaught of industrialization and Westernization, that they would either become like "us" or would disappear entirely. As Sahlins has observed, this prediction has not come to pass. Throughout the northern areas of the globe, peoples who formerly practiced hunting and gathering have accepted modern technology to carry out the same subsistence practices. They use rifles, snowmobiles, and modern traps. They have transformed their technology without giving up many other aspects of their culture. The distribution of results of the hunt is carried out as it was done in the past. For example, the relationship to animals of the Yup'ik-speaking people of Alaska has continued in the same manner as in the past. As one Yup'ik informant puts it, "When we bring animals into our houses, we treat them as guests" (Hensel, cited in Sahlins, 1999: xvi). Despite their long and intensive interaction with the global market economy, northern hunters like the Yup'ik "have not fundamentally altered their customary organization of production, modes of ownership and resource control, division of labor, or patterns of distribution and consumption; nor have their extended kinship and community bonds been dissolved or the economic and social obligations thereof fallen off; neither have social (cum 'spiritual') relations to nature disappeared; and they have not lost their cultural identities, not even when they live in white folks' towns" (Sahlins, 1999: xvii). The last point is a particularly important one. It is precisely when they live in "white folks' towns" and cities that there is a need to assert their cultural identity as different. The manner in which cultural identity is asserted differs according to the social context, for example, multicultural America versus ethnonationalistic European nations. As Sahlins states it, "I am simply making the point that the Eskimo are still there—and still Eskimo" (1999: vii). So are the Kwakiutl; so are the Trobrianders.

When a national identity is being built, political pressure is applied to suppress cultural differences, as noted in Chapter 9. Frequently, this pressure has the opposite effect from what was intended. In response to such pressure, cultural identity is often reasserted. Malaysia has been dominated by Moslem Malay speakers since it gained its independence. The non-Moslem Iban, who live in Sarawak, that part of Malaysia on the island of Borneo, have recently begun to reassert their cultural identity. In the past, the Iban had been headhunters and pirates in the South China Sea. Today, when Iban boys leave home to go to school, search for work, or join the military or the police, that is seen as symbolically equivalent to the traditional journey into the unknown that an Iban boy made as part of his initiation into manhood. The Iban rite of passage from boyhood to manhood is being maintained, but in a new form. Iban politicians talk about preserving their traditional lifestyle while at the same time fighting for a larger share of civil service and other employment in the Malaysian government for their people.

People develop various ways to assert their continued cultural identity. The ways they separate themselves from the dominant society are known as *boundary maintenance mechanisms*. For example, the Rio Grande Pueblos of New Mexico—Tewa and Keres—who were in contact with the Spanish missionaries and explorers in the seventeenth century, have divided their religious life into two separate domains: the indigenous one with its *katchinas* (religious figurines), priests, and *kivas* (underground religious chambers), which is operated in secret, closed off from the outside world and the eyes of the white man; and the village structure of the Catholic Church, which is part of the outside world. By preserving their language and much of their ritual structure, the Rio Grande Pueblos have been able to maintain their culture and their identity for more than 300 years, despite their nominal conversion to Catholicism and their integration into the U.S. economy. In contrast, the Navajo living in the same general area have been more receptive to changes, from their acceptance of livestock raising, silver working, and rug weaving from the Spaniards, to their acceptance of new ideas brought back by Navajo veterans who served in World War II.

Often, after changes have taken place in significant aspects of their culture, people recognize that they are in the process of being stripped of their own culture but have not been assimilated into the hegemonic culture. The uncertainty of their position makes them ready to follow a religious innovator, who has a more concrete vision of a better future. Out of these conditions, religious cults are born, which have

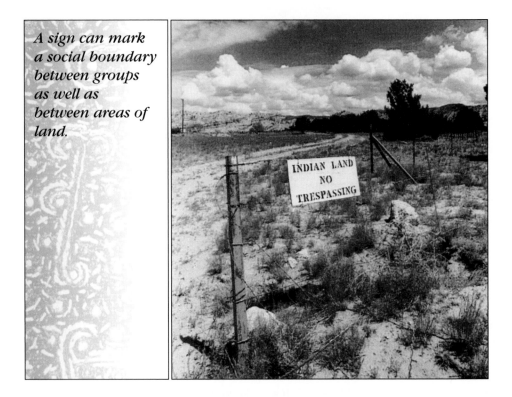

A sign can mark a social boundary between groups as well as between areas of land.

been termed *nativistic movements* or *revitalization movements.* These religious movements synthesize many traditional cultural elements with elements introduced from the dominant society.

An example of such a movement is the Handsome Lake religion of the Seneca, one of the six tribes that constituted the League of the Iroquois. By the end of the American Revolution, the Seneca had suffered partial devastation of their villages, decimation of their population, and the general dislocation of many aspects of their culture. In the 1780s, Handsome Lake, who was a sachem, or tribal leader, of the Seneca, had a series of visions, during which he had contact with the various Iroquois deities and foresaw what the life of the Seneca should be like in the future. What he envisioned was an amalgam of older Iroquois traditions and new ideas derived from the Quakers and other missionaries. The social organization of the Seneca had been based on matrilineal descent and uxorilocal postmarital residence. In contrast, Handsome Lake stressed the importance of the nuclear family and de-emphasized the matrilineage. The Quakers had come as missionaries to the Seneca, and many of their economic values, such as thrift, were adopted by Handsome Lake. At the same time, much traditional Seneca ceremonialism was also maintained. Handsome Lake had many adherents during his lifetime, although there were other political leaders who opposed and competed with him. After his death, his doctrines were written down and formed the Code of Handsome Lake. Though it was revolutionary when it first appeared, over the centuries the Handsome Lake religion, as it came to be called, became a conservative force as more and more changes were accepted by the Seneca. Today the supporters of the Handsome Lake religion are among the more conservative members of the Seneca tribe living on their reservation in upstate New York. What began as a vision of Seneca accommodation to the culture of the white population was transformed over time into a bulwark resisting change.

A particular type of revitalization movement that has occurred repeatedly in Melanesia is the *cargo cult*. Cargo cults made their appearance early in the twentieth century. However, they proliferated after World War II, which was a period of more intensive contact with outsiders, particularly with the American soldiers who drove out the Japanese and used the islands of Melanesia as a staging base. The Melanesians were astonished by the technological might of the Western world, as represented by the American armed forces. Like all revitalization movements, these cargo cults revolved about a charismatic leader or prophet who had a vision. This vision usually involved conversations with the spirits of deceased ancestors, and the prophet foretold that the ancestors would rise from the dead. At that time, black Melanesians would get white skins, and white people either would become black or would be driven into the seas. The ancestors would arrive in a big ship or plane, bringing with them an inexhaustible cargo of steel axes, razor blades, tobacco, tinned beef, rice, and rifles. More recently, the expected cargoes include transistor radios, wristwatches, and motorcycles. People built piers into the sea, erected huge warehouses, and even prepared landing strips when planes were expected. They neglected their gardening and often killed off their pigs, since the expectation was that no one would have to work anymore after the cargo arrived. Sometimes elements of Christianity were included in the visions of the prophet, so that Jesus Christ was expected to arrive along with the cargo.

Like all other revitalization movements, cargo cults are a synthesis of the old and the new. In a situation of culture contact where tribal peoples find themselves helpless and overwhelmed by the power of the dominant society, a prophet appears who preaches turning to the ancestors to seek their help in acquiring the very things that make the dominant society so powerful. The cargo is seen as the secret of the white people's power. Like all forms of religion that attempt to explain the inexplicable, cargo cults attempt to offer a supernatural explanation of what it is that makes white people so powerful. Converts to the cargo cult have faith that the secret of white people's power, the cargo, will come to them as a result of supernatural forces. Cargo cults are religious movements, though many of them are short-lived. At the same time, however, they make statements about power relations; for when the cargo comes, the present situation will be reverse—black will become white, and the powerless will become powerful. Cargo cults exemplify how the force and emotive power of religious belief can add great strength to a political movement. In the past, such religious cults in East and West Africa were dreaded by colonial powers. Nativistic movements, revitalization movements, and cargo cults represent responses to colonialism that combine cultural continuity as well as cultural change. The particular forms they take not only represent responses to colonialism but also reveal a great deal about the cultures in which they are found.

Sometimes, a group loses everything except its sense of its own cultural identity. The Mashantucket Pequot Tribal Nation of Connecticut is such a group. The Pequot were nearly obliterated as a people in the Pequot War of 1637 and stripped of most of their land. However, they were able to demonstrate to the Department of the Interior that their tribal existence never ceased, enabling them to receive recognition as a tribe from the American government on October 18, 1983. The introduction of high-stakes gambling in 1992 has made the tribe wealthy and influential and has enabled members to fund events that are part of a conscious attempt to "re-create" their culture. They have approached the task of cultural building or rebuilding on two different fronts. First, they have sponsored Mashantucket Pequot historical conferences, which bring together scholars to discuss topics such as the history of the Indians of New England and the current state of knowledge about native peoples of New England and their adjustment to the encounter with Euro-Americans. They have established their own museum, which focuses on Native American culture in general and on Pequot culture in particular. Second, they have sponsored a powwow, or *schemitzun,* translated as "Feast of Green Corn and Dance," which brings together American Indian performers from many tribes all over the country. The performers were attracted by the $200,000 purse, the richest purse offered on the competitive powwow circuit. After almost 300 years, the traditions of the Pequot are almost forgotten, along with their language and ceremonial songs and dances. The Pequots are endeavoring to re-create their own culture by borrowing and adapting what they can from other tribes. The process the Pequot are now going through, as they attempt to construct a tribal or cultural identity, is identical to that involved in the fashioning of ethnic identity which is now going on in multicultural America.

Contact and colonialism can produce a process by which a people assert a new ethnic identity. This is known as *ethnogenesis.* William Sturtevant first used the term to refer to the process through which the Seminole historically became differentiated from the Creek. Nancy Hickerson (1996) points out the way the historic record reveals the disappearance, often quite abruptly, of certain peoples (like the Mayan Empire) and the sudden appearance of others (like the Scythians), likening this process to the three-stage sequence that Van Gennup proposed for rites of passage, discussed in Chapter 10. The first phase is separation, the severing of a group's previous loyalties; the second is a liminal phase during which surviving ties wither away and new ones are initiated; the third is the birth of a new identity, which is affirmed through the adoption of new rituals and a new mythology to validate them. This last phase "may obscure all traces of the earlier history (or histories) of the population and even promote a belief in a miraculous origin or special creation" (Hickerson, 1996: 70). Manipulation of the historical past is one of the distinctive characteristics of the process of ethnogenesis. As Hill observes, "ethnogenesis is not merely a label for the historical emergence of culturally distinct peoples but a concept encompassing peoples' simultaneously cultural and political struggles to create enduring identities in general contexts of radical change and discontinuity" (1996: 1).

In the ebb and flow of populations after the arrival of the Europeans in the New World, ethnogenesis occurred many times as groups were physically dislocated from the areas they had traditionally exploited. During the sixteenth and seventeenth centuries, Tanoan-speaking people known as the Jumano, who were bison hunters and traders, were exploiting an area east of the Rio Grande in the southern Plains. As a

Mashantucket Pequot Tribal Nation dancers at a tribal powwow, or schemitzun.

consequence of unsuccessful warfare with the Apache over trade routes and access to trade centers, they appear to have dispersed, many moving north. The use of the name Jumano then declined, but subgroups with their own names continued. The term Kiowa later appeared as the label for these groups, now in their new homeland in the Platte-Arkansas River area. Today, the people of the modern Kiowa nation have an origin myth that begins with their ancestors' emergence from the underworld in a cold land far north—thought to be in the Yellowstone River Valley. The ancestors subsequently moved south and east to their historic territory (Hickerson, 1996: 83). Here we see a sequence in which the Jumano disappear and "die" and a new people, the Kiowa nation, are born, following the rites-of-passage pattern described above.

The process of ethnogenesis not only is applicable to the establishment of tribal or ethnic groups in the New World but also parallels the development of *ethnonationalism* in Europe. When European ethnonationalists are able to take control of the state, they co-opt the state's use of force, which they now turn to their own nationalistic purposes. Ethnogenesis in Europe has a long history. The French Revolution may be seen as "the expression of emerging French national self-identity" (Pickett, 1996: 12). Under the banner of "Liberty, Equality, and Fraternity," Napoleon brutally brought France's "civilizing principles" to the rest of Europe. Though pretending to spread universal principles, he was actually expanding the scope of French nationalism and hegemony. As often happened throughout history, one group's ethnogenic awakening produced a reaction among that group's neighbors. German ethnogenesis and the movement toward German unification in the latter half of the nineteenth century was a reaction to what was happening in France. This led Germany to develop a sense of its own special destiny. One may argue that nationalism's goals are diametrically opposed to the universalistic ideals of Christianity and more recently of socialism, which apply equally to all humanity. As Pickett points out, "ethnogenesis is hostile to knowledge" (1996: 16). Ethnogenesis ignores science in favor of its newly created myths; it denies history in order to distort it and control it. French hegemony under Napoleon—that is, nationalism under the guise of universal principles—proved ephemeral. In the same way, Soviet Russian hegemony—Russian nationalism under the guise of universal socialist principles—has also disappeared. In the next chapter, we will examine the various nations and ethnonational movements that have taken its place, as well as the ways ethnicity and nationalism have become battlegrounds all over the world.

Anthropologists over the past 50 years focused primarily on how cultures change, particularly in response to external forces. That meant dealing with the way colonialism had affected small-scale societies with particular regard to a number of different factors. The problem of land rights arose in the context of colonial settlement in such countries as Australia, the United States, Canada, and South Africa. Colonies in other parts of the world were established to obtain raw materials, which involved taking over land and exploiting the population as a source of labor. Missionaries often spearheaded the advance of colonial expansion in their zeal to convert souls and change the "heathen way of life." The history of New Ireland reveals the way the factors operated in a particular case, and the pressures that they placed on local cultures. In the colonial as well as postcolonial periods, anthropologists have been involved in governmentally instituted change, but not as makers of policy that dictated such changes.

Internal migration, transmigration, rural urban migration, and diasporas have marked both the colonial and postcolonial periods in many parts of the world. Though these terms are of recent vintage, the phenomena they describe have been the subject of anthropological investigation for a long period of time. The peoples living under colonial rule have responded to pressures with revitalization movements, nativistic movements, and cargo cults. Prophets arose to lead such movements, which combined traditional cultural ideas and the desire to gain access to the power of the colonial masters. These movements served to reassert cultural identity. Another response related to the reassertion of cultural identity is ethnogenesis, which parallels ethnonationalism (to be discussed in the next chapter).

Chapter Fourteen

Ethnicity, Race, and Nationalism: Anthropology for the Twenty-first Century

Independent nation-states are the successors of colonies in the contemporary world, as we noted earlier. Their goal has been to create a national culture that supersedes or incorporates "tribal peoples," who then are transformed into ethnic groups within the new nation-state. We have pointed out that culture is the integrating concept in anthropology, and cultural identity was the means by which individuals identified themselves. In today's pluralistic, multicultural world, the terms *ethnic* and *ethnic identity,* as a way of identifying oneself, are frequently used as alternatives to *culture* and *cultural identity.*

The word *tribe* was originally used by anthropologists to refer to cultural groupings, each of which spoke its own language. Anthropologists now understand that tribes were, in effect, created by colonial governments to enable them to deal more efficiently with groups with a common culture and language but whose most complex political groupings were villages or bands (Fried, 1975). For example, in the previous chapter we saw the way the German colonial government established a single political entity, New Ireland, where previously there had been independent, autonomous villages speaking different languages. In the new nation-states, identity can be framed in terms of a hierarchy in which the tribal identity, now ethnic identity, becomes less inclusive and national identity, more inclusive.

The terms *ethnic identity, ethnic group, ethnogenesis, ethnonationalism, nationalism, multiculturalism,* and *race* are not only conceptual tools used by anthropologists and other social scientists but also part of the language of television news programs and newspaper headlines—they are themes for our times. *Ethnic groups* share common cultural norms, values, identities, patterns of behavior, and language. Their members recognize themselves as a separate group and are so recognized by others. They may or may not be politicized. Ethnic identity, or ethnicity, is seen by some analysts as based on primordial sentiments, that is, sentiments that are conceptualized as going back to ancient times and that tie group members to one another emotionally, despite persistent attempts to assimilate them. To others, ethnic identity is entirely situational, utilized in some contexts but not in others. In Europe, ethnic groups were often also territorially defined. Influenced by ideas of ethnonationalism, they frequently sought political autonomy and even the freedom to form their own nation-states.

Religion is one of the important factors serving to distinguish one ethnic group from another. In a number of examples discussed below, we will see that in addition to ethnic differences, meaning cultural differences, there are also religious differences. When religious differences are present, the ethnic conflict is heightened and intensified. Fighting the other ethnic group, the "infidel," becomes a sacred mission. Each side finds support in the moral authority of its own religion for continuing the conflict and for using violent action against those whom it characterizes as heretics. The former Yugoslavia illustrates this very well. The dominant Serbs are an Orthodox population, who view themselves historically as Christian martyrs who suffered under the Muslim Ottoman Empire. Bosnians and Albanians, in Kosovo, are Muslims. Croatians, on the other hand, are Roman Catholics. Despite similarities in language and culture among these ethnic groups, their religious differences have exacerbated the ethnic conflict and are sometimes used today to justify even the raping of women of the other ethnic group.

Ethnic differences may also parallel class differences. In some societies, the underclass is a separate ethnic or racial group. Under those conditions, ethnic conflict may be characterized as class conflict. In addition, race and racial classifications often are a basis for making distinctions between ethnic groups. Many people tend to think of race as a scientific concept based on biological systems of classification. In reality the definition and form of the concept of race differs from one society to another. This means that race is socially constructed. For example, in Brazil, color of complexion, which is one aspect of the concept of race, forms an element in the conceptualization of status and group. In the United States, an individual, on the basis of complexion color, is categorized as either white or African American. In the United States, genealogy is also involved in the assignment of people to these two categories. A person with African-American ancestry whose complexion is indistinguishable from a white person's may decide to pass as a white person. If the African-American ancestors of such a person are then revealed, he or she can no longer pass as white and will be categorized by others as African American. The social construction of race is illustrated by the fact that while in Brazil race is a continuum, in the United States it is clearly a bipolar category. Forces of racism work to keep the two categories of white and African American separate. As anthropologist John Gwaltney's African-American informants in *Drylongso* expressed it, oppressed by the white majority, they were one of two "nations" in the United States (Gwaltney, 1993). Social scientists have echoed this point, from Gunnar Myrdal, who called America's treatment of African Americans *An American Dilemma,* to Andrew Hacker's view of *Two Nations: Black and White, Separate, Hostile, Unequal.* Later in this chapter we will see how African Americans, since the 1960s, have been creatively constructing cultural aspects of their identity.

The previous chapter ended with a discussion of ethnogenesis and nationalism. The idea of *nation-building* began in Europe, the *nation* being defined as a sovereign political state with a single national culture (Gellner, 1983; Hobsbawm, 1992). France, Italy, and England began to develop their nation-states before other European countries. The development of national cultures involved conscious culture-building on the part of the hegemonic group in political control of the state—the goal being the elimination of regional ethnic cultures in favor of a national culture. Anthropological research has revealed the way this process of conscious, national culture-building, in Africa, for example, takes place in various media such as radio, TV, and newspapers.

Even archaeology is utilized in the service of creating national identity, as is the case in Pakistan and Israel. States choose to emphasize one aspect of their archeological past rather than another, in keeping with the messages about the past, which the archaeological results are meant to support. Each state tells its own myth about its past. In Israel, archaeology has always served the function of conveying the Israeli myth about the rights of the Israelis to the land. Israel chooses to emphasize archaeological research related to religious rather than secular sites. It concentrates on the periods of the First and Second Temples, that is the Iron Age through early Roman times, ignoring earlier sites such as the Mount Carmel caves where Neanderthal skeletal material was found. Archaeological sites, like that of Masada, are used as the locations for national ceremonies to imbue Israeli national values. Emphasis on this particular archaeological information builds a mythic cultural past for Israel. In Pakistan, during the colonial period, Buddhist sites such as Taxila were important locations for archaeological investigation. When the Islamic state of Pakistan was established, there was no longer any scientific interest in these sites by the Pakistani state, which emphasized only its Muslim historical roots. As Kohl points out, "control of the past provides a source of legitimization for control of the present" (1999: 236).

The imposed national culture was usually that of the hegemonic group. In Great Britain, that meant that the language and culture of the English, the politically dominant group, were to supersede the Celtic cultures and languages of Wales, Scotland, and Ireland. Regional differences between the people of Cornwall and Yorkshire should disappear in favor of standard English language and culture. The same process occurred in France and somewhat later in Germany and in Eastern Europe. Despite attempts to impose a national culture emanating from the capital, London or Paris, regional cultural and dialect differences persisted and national identity never really fully penetrated the countryside, especially the more remote areas. More recently, in Great Britain, the Scottish people have moved beyond the assertion of their ethnic identity. The establishment of the Scottish Parliament is an expression of their movement to ethnonationalism. Wales now has its own national assembly, and the Welsh language is taught to youngsters in public schools and can be heard in radio broadcasts.

Sometimes the process of nation-building involves the breakup of older empires. For example, in the nineteenth century the intellectual elites in the Czech area of the Austro-Hungarian Empire sought the freedom to have their own nation-state. Through the process of ethnogenesis, they set out to rediscover and re-create a national cultural repertoire, consciously selecting cultural items, often from rural folk culture, that they identified as Czech. Some people went to the trouble of inventing a Czech ancestry using bogus early records, such as medieval manuscripts supposedly discovered in Bohemia in 1817 and 1818 (Lass, 1988). The French philosopher Renan has sarcastically defined the nation as a group of people held together by an erroneous view of the past and a shared hatred of neighbors surrounding them. Renan's remarks also relate to the idea of ethnocentrism, introduced in Chapter 1, the notion that one's own language and culture are superior to all others. Both nations and ethnic groups can be ethnocentric with regard to their neighbors. In the language of ethnocentrism, the people in the next valley are seen as practicing bizarre rituals, stealing babies, and copulating like animals.

The process of nation-building accelerated in Europe after World War I with the creation of several nations out of both the old Ottoman Turkish and Austro-Hungarian Empires. However, the new nations that resulted, such as Czechoslovakia, Poland, Romania, and Yugoslavia, ended up being multiethnic states. These states included one dominant ethnic group and several minority groups. For example, Poland included Germans, Ruthenians, Kashubians, and Jews as minority groups. In Czechoslovakia, the Czechs were the dominant group. Recently, they and the Slovaks decided that they wanted to be separate nation-states. Czechoslovakia was peacefully divided into the Czech and Slovak nations. However, even within the Czech Republic there are Moravian and Silesian people who demand a measure of autonomy and self-government (Bugajski, 1994: 306–310). Gypsies, present in considerable numbers in the former Czechoslovakia, are not welcome in either the Czech Republic or Slovakia. The mayor of the Slovakian town of Usti nad Labem in northern Bohemia had a wall built to separate the Gypsies from ethnic Slovaks. Yugoslavia was another nation-state created after World War I; its borders encompassed a congeries of ethnic groups lumped together at that time on the basis of the ethnogenesis of a South Slavic identity. The nation was under the hegemony of the Serbs. It was a union of several different ethnic groups speaking very closely related languages (Serbo-Croatian) but divided by religious and cultural differences. They never surrendered their distinct ethnic identities. The Yugoslavian Communist state, based on universal principles, began to fall apart after the death of Tito, the head of state under Communism. Croatia, Slovenia, and Bosnia, asserting their ethnonationalism, became separate states, with Serbian minorities. Only Serbia and Montenegro remain as Yugoslavia.

Both the process of nation-building and its obverse—in which nation-states, once created, then collapse—are to be found not only in Europe but also in Africa and Asia (Fox, 1990). These nation-states include the tribes, or Fourth World Peoples, whom anthropologists have been studying since the beginning of the discipline; but now the focus is on the adjustment of these societies to the penetration of the newly developed national culture. Nations are composed of one politically autonomous ethnic group, while *state* is the term used to refer to any politically autonomous entity, whether it is composed of one or many different ethnic groups. The term *nation-state* is used when nation and state are coterminous.

A multicultural state is composed of several ethnic groups, none of which is dominant. Instead, all are ideologically considered equal. In the nineteenth century, when the United States welcomed large numbers of immigrants seeking refuge from persecution, they became Americans, part of what was referred to as the "melting pot." American, as a national identity, was being constructed, and an American culture was developing. However, since the 1960s we have come to think of ourselves differently. We now view ourselves as a multicultural society. Other nations, for example, Great Britain, are reflecting on whether they are indeed multicultural states. The French state has officially rejected multiculturalism. However, as noted in Chapter 9, the French legal system has accepted Islamic law in cases involving family law. The Muslims from North Africa who have settled in France challenge the official suppression of ethnically based identity. While Germany does not consider itself a multicultural state, it is, in effect, beginning to move in that direction in an interesting manner. The Turkish migrant workers brought their cuisine to Germany when they migrated. Donner kebab, which consists of thin cuts of lamb laid on pita flat bread and steeped in *tsatsiki* sauce, a favorite Turkish dish, has now become a German fast food. The factories that mass-produce the German version of this dish for stalls and restaurants in many German cities surpass the sales of McDonald's and Burger King combined. For many Germans, eating donner kebab represents their first contact with Turkish culture. However, it does not seem to have moved the Germans to think about their country in multicultural terms. Multiculturalism is distinctly different from the characteristically European situation in which one ethnic group is the national core. In that case, the values of the dominant group constitute the national culture, politically and religiously, and that group dominates smaller minorities, creating two classes of citizenship.

As noted above, in Great Britain today, political power and linguistic recognition have now been given to the Scottish and Welsh people. However, those people who migrated to Great Britain from other parts of the Commonwealth have been dealt with in a different way. Earlier waves of people coming to England as conquerors, like the French, left marks of their culture and language, as described in Chapter 3. Other migrants, in later centuries, have been assimilated into mainstream English culture and life, so that by the middle of the twentieth century there was a widespread belief that British culture was homogeneous, though, in reality, it was dominated by English culture (Ellis and Khan, 1999: 38). After World II, large numbers of migrants from the Caribbean and, more particularly, from India and Pakistan came to Great Britain to better themselves economically, accepting work that the English no longer wished to do. Though it was originally thought that they would return to their homelands, instead, they sent for their families and settled permanently. Language and religious differences set apart the South Asians, especially, from the rest of the population. Islam provides its adherents with a communal way of life with separate religious institutions—mosques, separate schools, the right to wear their type of clothing and eat *halal* meat—all of which challenges assimilation. As we noted in

Chapter 5, Islamic Sufi adherents in Manchester periodically parade to demonstrate the way they have "conquered" new territory as well as their right of religious expression. Further, in terms of the ideas of Edward Said, "orientalist" concepts of the West have defined Muslims as perpetually the "other" in opposition to and inferior to the Christian white West—Europe and America. Though the British authorities have made concessions in the direction of multiculturalism, British Muslim activists have been challenging the Islamophobia, which has not diminished with time (Ellis and Khan, 1999: 45). State support for separate Muslim schools has been an especially thorny issue. Multiculturalism, as currently practiced in Britain, still does not allow for full participation in the society if one chooses a public Muslim identity rather than an accommodation that confines one's Muslim identity to the domestic and local community environments. Though the dialogue of multiculturalism is voiced, Britain has remained essentially a homogeneous, Western, Christian society rather than a pluralist society accepting of people who are significantly different in religion or race. Anthropological research has revealed that Muslims and immigrants from the Caribbean wish to retain a separate, hyphenated, identity while participating fully in the institutions of the society. This is what multiculturalism is all about.

Ethnicity and Nationalism after Communism

After the Russian Revolution in 1917, the Union of Soviet Socialist Republics was created out of the Russian Empire. This empire had been based on the conquest of many non-Russian peoples, just as the Ottoman Empire had included many non-Turkish people and the Austro-Hungarian Empire had incorporated peoples who were neither Austrians nor Hungarians. This example reveals the dialectic between hegemonic state culture and different ethnic cultures who desire to have their own nation-states. The Soviet government tried to construct a Soviet culture as the national culture of the Union of Soviet Socialist Republics. This Soviet culture included the idea that workers of the world should unite as a class and rise above national sentiments. The government's attitude toward the different "nationalities" vacillated between the celebration of ethnic differences and the suppression of ethnic national identity, which was seen as challenging Soviet identity. When the Soviet Union crumbled at the end of the 1980s, its 15 constituent republics—Lithuania, Armenia, Georgia, Uzbekistan, and the others, including Russia itself—became independent sovereign states. Ethnic minorities, who formerly had had their own autonomous republics or autonomous oblasts (districts) contained within the newly established independent states, now demanded self-determination in the form of cultural and political autonomy or independence. Such ethnic minorities exemplify ethnonationalism as they strive to establish independent sovereign states.

Under the freedom of Gorbachov's glasnost, ethnic identity and nationalist sentiment could be expressed. These identities, which had been suppressed during the Communist era, are what propel politics in all the areas of the former Soviet Union today. The newly independent republics must cope with the legacy of 70 years of

Soviet rule. This means that they must deal with larger or smaller numbers of individuals who are culturally Russian or members of other ethnic groups who migrated there or were moved there by the Soviet government. They must also contend with territorial borders, which were drawn by the Soviet state.

Joseph Stalin—who ruled the Soviet Union as a dictator from the mid-1920s to 1953, when he died—had borders drawn between Armenia and Azerbaijan in such a way as to prevent the emergence of a Transcaucasian Federation. The area has had a complicated history, having been under the Muslim rule of either the Ottoman or Persian Empires for centuries. The enclave of Nagorno-Karabakh, within the territory of Azerbaijan, had long been occupied by Armenians. The Azerbaijanis not only prevented the Armenians of Nagorno-Karabakh from culturally expressing themselves, but also discriminated against them because they were different in culture and in religion. Armenians speak an Indo-European language, are Christians, and are intellectually oriented toward the West, while Azerbaijanis, or Azeris, as they are also called, speak a Turkic language and are Muslims. Here, religious differences exacerbated ethnic differences. With glasnost and the lifting of Soviet repression, the Armenians of Nagorno-Karabakh began a campaign for the transfer of their territory to Armenia (Dudwick, 1992). There was also strong support for this in Armenia as part of a national movement expressing resentment at what was seen as the Russification of Armenian culture. The fact that Nagorno-Karabakh was the location of ancient Armenian shrines made it particularly significant in what became a resurgence of Armenian nationalism. Demonstrations by Armenians in Nagorno-Karabakh were met with anti-Armenian violence on the part of Azerbaijanis, and conflict between the two groups escalated. In the meantime Armenia and Azerbaijan became independent states when the Soviet Union fell apart. There was now open warfare over the fate of Nagorno-Karabakh between the armies of the two states. The recent assassination of the prime minister of Armenia has set back the delicate negotiations that have been taking place between Armenia and Azerbaijan over the future of Nagorno-Karabakh. Members of the Armenian-American diaspora support a nonviolent settlement, and recently, the Armenian government has enlisted their support to this end. This ethnic conflict, which began in 1988, has not yet been settled.

The new nation-state of Georgia, in the Caucasus Mountains south of Russia, contains several non-Georgian ethnic groups with sizable populations, such as the South Ossetians and the Abkhazians. In addition, Georgia has ethnic Russians, Armenians, and Azerbaijanis. Meskhetians originally lived in Georgia but were expelled by Stalin after World War II and sent to live in Uzbekistan. Under Soviet rule, the Abkhazians and Ossetians had some degree of political and cultural autonomy, though the Georgians were politically dominant in the Republic. The Abkhazians are linguistically and culturally distinct from the Georgians, though they are physically similar to West Georgians (Benet, 1974). Their mythic history stresses their distinctiveness. However, they have historically been oriented toward the Mediterranean since Abkhazia is on the Black Sea. Christianity entered Abkhazia in the sixth century, and Islam much later, in the fifteenth and sixteenth centuries. While most Abkhazians are nominally Muslim, a small minority have remained Christian. Abkhazians retain their cultural distinctiveness through their style of dress, dance, folklore, legends, kinship system,

Fighters for Abkhazian independence preparing for attack by Georgian forces who will reincorporate them into the Georgian state.

and other cultural items. Their exceedingly difficult language, which Russians, Georgians, and Armenians rarely learn, also serves to set them apart. Within the Abkhazian Autonomous Republic, the Abkhazians form only a quarter of the population; the other three-quarters are Russians, Georgians, Greeks, Turks, and Armenians.

The forces of ethnonationalism propelled the Georgian Republic to independence. However, the attempts of the Abkhazians and South Ossetians, with their own ethnonationalistic feelings, to gain their independence or autonomy were seen as threats to the Georgian state and Georgian political hegemony. Though political leadership at the local level was in the hands of Abkhazians and South Ossetians, they were overrepresented in low-class manual and rural occupations (Jones, 1992). The Georgians considered these people ethnic groups not entitled to their own sovereignty. In fact, all those who were not ethnic Georgians were seen as having no rights, as foreigners in Georgia. South Ossetians and others, such as Russians, were viewed as invaders who should return to where they came from. Government policy favored Georgian expansion into non-Georgian areas. The aim of the educational system was to indoctrinate all students in Georgian language and culture, regardless of their ethnic background.

The Abkhazians and Ossetians declared their independence, resulting in fighting on all sides. The Abkhazian fight for independence has become a subject for the international media, as shown by the accompanying photograph. The South Ossetians of Georgia would like to unite with the North Ossetians, who live in Russia, which is now a separate country. The Abkhazians have succeeded in gaining control over their territory. In fact, some 200,000 Georgians who fled Abkhazia claim that they

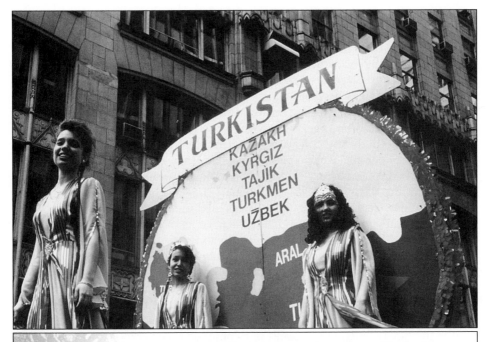

This float in the annual Turkish Day parade in New York City emphasizes the unity of all Turkish-speaking peoples, including the Uzbeks.

have been subjected to a policy of ethnic cleansing. Russia had continued to maintain several military bases in Georgia. The Gudauta base was situated in Abkhazia, and the Georgians had suspected that the Russians were aiding the Abkhazian separatists. Georgian officials negotiated for the closure of this base and have recently been successful. The Georgian case exemplifies a situation in which a politically dominant group's attempts to homogenize a population of different ethnic groups result in demands by those groups not merely for cultural autonomy but for complete political independence.

Like Georgia, the newly independent nation of Uzbekistan in Central Asia is ethnically diverse. The Uzbeks themselves, two-thirds of the population, are Muslims who speak a Turkic language. They are in the process of making decisions about which part of their historic past constitutes their true Uzbek heritage. This would then be used as a rallying point for building Uzbek national culture and developing an Uzbek national identity. Is the focus of Uzbek nation-building to be the heritage represented by Turkic Runic script and the Chaghatai Turkic language (Menges, 1967) or the Islamic tradition with its Arabic script, which the Arabs brought into the area when they overran the Turks in the seventh and eighth centuries? The question of whether to shift from Cyrillic, introduced by the Russians, to Arabic or Turkic Runic script represents the dilemma of whether Uzbek heritage is to be Islamic or pre-Islamic. The building of national identity is always a creative as well as a political process. This often involves choosing to emphasize one aspect rather than another from a very complicated multiethnic history. The choice of one script over another, as in this case, becomes an important political decision.

Most recently, the state institutions of Uzbekistan have been under attack by an Islamic fundamentalist insurgency, known as the Islamic Movement of Uzbekistan, which desires to purge the current government of corruption. It has set car bombs and in one incident killed 16 people in Tashkent, Uzbekistan's capital. The government has closed 900 mosques and arrested people suspected of antigovernment sentiments after the slaying of several policemen. The resurgence of Islam in Central Asia as a whole has led some people in this area to talk about an Islamic state—a revival of an earlier idea of a grand Turkestan, or, in more modern terms, a United States of Asia, which would join Uzbekistan with Kyrgyzstan, Kazakhstan, Tadzhikistan, and Turkmenia, all nations with Islamic backgrounds (Hall, 1992). The Uzbek Islamic fundamentalist movement has sent fighters from its bases in northern Tajikistan into Kyrgyzstan to use villages in an Uzbek enclave in that country as bases from which to attack Uzbekistan. Russia and Uzbekistan sent support to the Kyrgyzstan government to repel this attack. The Pan-Islamic movement has created turmoil in the newly independent states of Central Asia. The comparative perspective in anthropology involves examining Islamic fundamentalism as it is developing from Nigeria to Central Asia to look for what these movements have in common and the ways the particular local setting of each results in differences.

Ethnic Processes in Sri Lanka

The ethnic conflict that has continued in Sri Lanka for decades exemplifies the way ethnic identity is heightened and transformed under certain conditions: the role played by differences in religion and language, the economic factors operative, and the ways majority-minority relations can worsen to the point of civil war (see Tambiah, 1986, 1988). The conflict is between two ethnic groups: the Sinhalese, who speak an Indo-European language, and the Tamils, who speak a Dravidian language. Both languages have borrowed significantly from one another over the centuries. Since 74 percent of the population is Sinhalese, that language became the official language when Sri Lanka gained its independence from Britain. However, public education continued to be provided in parallel Tamil and Sinhalese tracks. The majority of the Sinhalese are Buddhist, with some Christians, mostly Roman Catholics; the Tamil are primarily Hindu, also with a Roman Catholic minority. There is, in addition, a small Muslim population descended from Arab, Persian, and Malay seafarers and people from the Malabar coast of India. There are many cultural similarities between the Sinhala and Tamil groups and no perceived racial differences, despite these differences in language and religion and different mythic charters.

The Tamils consider the northern part of the island of Sri Lanka their traditional homeland, though much of the Tamil population is scattered among the Sinhalese in the rest of the island. The two were separate ethnic communities until the advent of British colonial rule in 1796. The British developed a colonial economy on the island, which was then known as Ceylon, based on tea plantations. A small English-speaking elite, educated in English-style schools run by missionaries, included both Tamils and Sinhalese. However, for some time the Sinhalese have resented what they see as a Tamil monopoly of the white-collar and professional positions that were the rewards of such an education.

Sri Lanka became independent in 1948. During the postwar period, Sri Lanka went through the uneven economic development that characterized many Third World countries. It tried to organize a welfare state to improve the educational and health systems for its people, but its economy did not improve. The plantation economy declined, attempts to develop exports failed, living standards fell, and rising expectations went unfulfilled as young people left school educated but with no employment prospects. The underclass began to suffer, but protests were organized in terms of ethnic differences rather than along class lines. Earlier in this chapter, we described the way class differences may be expressed as ethnic differences. Animosity was directed by the Sinhalese majority, who saw themselves as the original population, against the Tamils, whom they characterized as outsiders.

From the beginning of the colonial period, a revival of Buddhism was spearheaded by Buddhist monks who borrowed the evangelical techniques of the Christian missionaries who had come to Ceylon under the colonial umbrella. While the urban, English-speaking elite had political power, a group of Sinhalese-speaking rural leaders, schoolteachers, indigenous medical practitioners, traders, and merchants began to see themselves as the conservators of Sinhalese language, culture, and religion. They joined forces with the monks in the 1950s in a Sinhala revival, which emphasized not only the Sinhalese language and Buddhism, but also a view of the Sinhalese as an Aryan race who were claimed to be different from the allegedly dark-skinned, Dravidian-speaking Tamils. This use of "Aryan" raised the "bogey of racist claims" (Tambiah, 1986: 5). It represented the imposition of a conceptualization from India, where "fair-skinned Aryans" were the invaders from the north who conquered the "dark-skinned" people of the south. The Sinhalese looked to a mythic history that saw their destiny as conquerors and rulers over the whole island for the glory of Buddhism and the expulsion of the Tamil invaders in the north.

The strength of this mythic history is seen as the reason the Sinhalese majority still persist in exploiting the Tamil minority, despite the fact that the alleged Tamil over-representation in education and employment was corrected. In recent years the consequence has been Tamil reprisals and violence, and the Sinhalese have responded in kind. The Tamil now demand self-determination, recognition as a nationality, and a guarantee that they will be able to continue to live in their traditional homeland. The government of India became involved when Prime Minister Rajiv Ghandi, who had originally sided with the Tamil separatists, tried in 1985 to broker a peace settlement between the Sri Lankan government and the Tamil rebels. When he sent Indian troops into Sri Lanka in 1987 as peacemakers, they clashed with Tamil guerrillas and the relationship soured. In 1991 Ghandi was assassinated, reputedly by a Tamil rebel group. As of this writing, active combat, including terrorist activity, continues between the two sides, with many casualties on both sides. During the summer of 1999, a distinguished Tamil legal scholar, who advocated negotiation, compromise, and a legislated settlement of the strife with the Sinhalese, was murdered by members of his own ethnic group, Tamil Tiger extremists who will settle for nothing less than independence. The Tamil rebel movement "maintains itself through an international network with offices in London and Paris and through the financial contributions of expatriate Tamils all around the world" (Eller, 1999: 139–40). Once again we have members of the diaspora supporting an ethnonationalist movement.

Anthropological comparison of the Tamil-Sinhalese conflict in Sri Lanka with similar conflicts in other parts of the world reveals the same militant, rampant ethnonationalism. In Sri Lanka, a resurgent Sinhalese Buddhism felt itself threatened by Tamil Hinduism from the north. Once again, class intersected with ethnicity, as resentment was expressed against Tamils, who were seen as educated and successful in greater numbers than they should have been. Although there were indeed real differences between Sinhalese and Tamils in Sri Lanka, their ethnic identities were invented and constructed, based on both mythic histories and differing views of recent history, as well as in oppositional terms—"we are the opposite of them." Each side defined itself in terms of its opponent. Another moral to this story is that troops sent in as peacekeepers do not always succeed in keeping combatants apart. In this case, Indians ended up fighting the Tamil insurgents. Both sides are always the losers in such fierce ethnic conflicts, and the militarily weaker side often faces genocide, whether it is the Tamils in Sri Lanka or the Kosavars who faced genocide at Serbian hands.

Ethnicity and Nationalism in Quebec

As French-Canadians began to see their culture being eroded by the penetration into Canada of popular American culture after World War II, they began to rally around a nationalist ideology. In this instance, feelings of cultural loss resulted not only in a reassertion of ethnic identity but in a political movement of ethnonationalism. They felt threatened by the possibility of political, cultural, and linguistic assimilation into the rest of Canada. Eastern Canada, Quebec in particular, was settled (Indians would say invaded) by the French when New France was established in the seventeenth century. Though the French lost political control over the area to the British as a consequence of the French and Indian War of 1754 to 1763, Quebec remained French in language and culture and Catholic in religion.

During the nineteenth and twentieth centuries, a sense of Canadian national identity began to be developed, in part to differentiate Canadian culture from the American culture of the United States. In Quebec, the response to this Canadian identity, which was essentially English-speaking and Protestant, took the form of renewed emphasis on French Canadian, or Quebeçois, culture. Later it turned into ethnonationalism, when political separation and independence from Canada became an issue.

Quebeçois culture was to be renewed by holding dance performances, folk handicraft exhibitions, fairs, and festivals that represented authentic Quebeçois culture (Handler, 1988). Quebeçois folk dancing, which was originally home entertainment, in the 1970s became public performance in an arena. Middle-class, white-collar Quebeçois tried to find their roots by going to stay with rural Quebeçois families during their vacations. They also attended events that attempted to re-create rural folk entertainments involving singing, dancing, telling of folktales, and even the creation of a farmhouse folk setting. Language was an important component of Quebeçois identity. There were purists who saw their language as French, while others saw a separate Quebeçois dialect, sometimes referred to as *jouval*, as the language of Quebec. During this period, many writers and musicians used *jouval* in their work as a demonstration of militant Quebeçois nationalism. To these Quebeçois, using *jouval* was a statement that they were more than just speakers of French, but were participants in the creation of an ethnic identity distinctly their own.

At the same time, the Quebec provincial government created the Department of Cultural Affairs to deal with provincial arts, historical monuments that emphasized links with French culture, and language and cultural relationships with French-speaking groups outside the province. The attempt was to promote a vision of a French-Canadian national culture. The bureaucratic fragmentation of this ministry was a consequence of its inability to come to decisions about what constituted French-Canadian culture. Some promoted an elitist view of culture, which would re-create a French-Canadian civilization. In the elitist view, the French language as spoken in France was seen as central to the task of preserving French-Canadian culture. The status of French was to be improved to make it the dominant language, and French was declared the official language of Quebec. Legislation was passed requiring all children to be schooled in French except those whose parents or siblings had been schooled in English. In fact, French took its place alongside English as an official language throughout Canada.

The Parti Quebeçois, which was founded in 1967, gradually gained political power in the province of Quebec; in 1976, the party won control of the provincial government. The vision of Quebec as an independent nation was one of the goals of the Parti Quebeçois, but even in 1976 this goal was played down since the party was unsure whether independence would be welcomed by the French-Canadian populace. Many Quebeçois were concerned that the province did not have the economic base to sustain itself as an independent nation. Sixty percent of the people of Quebec eventually voted against independence in a referendum in 1980. During the 1980s, the Canadian national government offered a number of plans to restructure the relationship between the provinces and the national government, and Quebec adopted a conciliatory attitude. Quebec had demanded special recognition of its French-speaking culture and threatened to break away from the Canadian confederation if this was not granted. After the 1993 election, polls showed that 60 percent of Quebec's population still did not want complete separation but rather, changes in the confederation giving them more self-determination and autonomy. They seek more of a say over their own destiny.

All this Quebeçois political activity produced a response on the part of the non-French-speaking minority in Quebec Province, making up 20 percent of the population, many of them immigrants from Eastern and Southern Europe and their descendants, and those who are English-speakers. Their minority status was a cause of concern. Would they become second-class citizens in an independent Quebec nation? For example, English-speaking members of the Quebec population, some 11 percent, are concerned about their ambiguous minority role in French-speaking Quebec. They are searching for an appropriate way to maintain their English identity in a monolingual Quebec. The same issue has been raised in all the newly created nation-states of Europe. Would Serbs living in the newly formed states of Croatia and Bosnia become second-class citizens? Would Russians have that second-class status in the newly created Baltic nations or Uzbekistan? Many English speakers living in Quebec were unwilling to see what the outcome would be and have emigrated to other provinces of Canada or to the United States (Esman, 1994: 165–167).

The Quebeçois case is an example of the resurgence of ethnic and national feeling that develops when a group feels it is being threatened with assimilation but desires to retain a separate identity. Once again, we see the central importance of maintaining language, music, and dance as symbols of a group's cultural distinctiveness. The Quebeçois national resurgence occurred on several fronts. Folk culture, the rural life of earlier times as embodied in music, dance, and performance, came to represent and reiterate national identity. At the same time, on the political level, government action involved developing programs to renew an elitist cultural definition of a Quebeçois national identity. Making Quebec a French monolingual province was also crucial. The Quebeçois have been extremely successful in making their voice heard at the national level.

In contrast, the French speakers in New Brunswick, 300,000 Acadians, continue to retain their French language and culture. Unlike the Quebeçois, their identification is as Canadians. While the Quebeçois have argued that the model of Canada as one country will inevitably lead to the extinction of French language and culture, the Acadians have retained their language and culture while compromising. Acadian history is quite different from that of the Quebeçois. When the French were defeated in Canada in 1759, British officials beyond Quebec ordered the mass expulsion of French settlers. Some returned to France, and some went to Louisiana, creating an Acadian diaspora (Cajun). The Acadians remaining in Canada have a perspective on Canadian identity different from that of the Quebeçois.

From Melting Pot to Multiculturalism in the United States

According to archaeologists, the first settlers of North America were the ancestors of the American Indians, as they now want to be called, who started coming across the Bering Strait perhaps as early as 25,000 years ago. The Indians, in their construction of their cultural past, as we have seen with the Kiowa in the previous chapter, view their mythic ancestors as having emerged from places in their native areas; hence they have always been in America. This is what their mythology tells them, tying them to the landmarks of their territories from time immemorial. They see the "story," told in American history books, of their crossing the Bering Strait as the white people's attempt to turn them into immigrants in America, like the white population itself. Today, members of American Indian tribes, with all that this category implies legally, as described earlier, may remain on the reservation as tribal members, move into urban areas and turn their tribal identity into ethnic identity, or lose themselves through assimilation in the general population.

The Europeans who came to North America in the 1600s as colonists called themselves English, Irish, Scottish, Dutch, Swedish, German, French, Spanish, and Russian. Slaves from Africa were imported by the colonists to work the plantations that had been established. An American culture began to develop from an English-Continental base, and earlier national identities merged to become an American identity. In the 1840s, American culture was portrayed by Alexis de Toqueville as emphasizing entrepreneurship, the "self-made man," personal advancement, individualism, restlessness, and the upholding of biblical tradition.

As immigration swelled in the late nineteenth and early twentieth centuries, the idea was that all who came to the United States would be assimilated into the emerging American culture. Ethnic differences were to disappear, certainly after the immigrant generation passed on. This idea is similar to the process of nation-building described above. The picture the United States had of itself was that of a melting pot, a receiver of people from many different cultures and societies who would learn the language of the country—English—and its culture, and assimilate into the developing American culture and society. Immigrants had chosen to come here because they saw it as a land of opportunity, and they were welcomed by the new society with open arms. America was industrializing. There was a great need for labor, and jobs were plentiful.

Many of the immigrants who came from Eastern Europe in the middle of the nineteenth century used ethnic terms, rather than terms referring to a nation-state, to identify themselves, demonstrating the weakness of national identity in some places in Europe at this time. They did not consider themselves Poles, but Silesians or Kashubians, since there was no independent Poland during the nineteenth century. These ethnic identities were maintained in the domestic realm and within the community, despite the ideology of the melting pot. In the communities they established in Pennsylvania, for example, they retained much of their Silesian and Kashubian language and culture as well as their religious affiliation. The Scotch-Irish have also maintained their ethnic identity, but their past is generally misunderstood. This group is commonly thought to be the result of intermarriage between Scottish and Irish peoples. In fact, they are descendants of a Protestant group from Scotland, moved by the conquering English into Ulster County in Northern Ireland, who subsequently emigrated to America in the eighteenth and nineteenth centuries. Many Scotch-Irish immigrants came from economically poor areas and moved into equally marginal frontier areas in the United States. The Scotch-Irish retained their ethnic identity in the economically less desirable border areas of Appalachia, providing us with the feuding Hatfields and McCoys, but they also gave us such self-made entrepreneurs as Andrew Mellon, patriots such as Patrick Henry, and five presidents of the United States—Polk, Buchanan, Jackson, Arthur, and Wilson.

Mexican Americans in Texas

We may consider the history of the Mexican Americans in one Texas town as an example of what happens to an immigrant group over a period of 150 years (Foley, 1988). It is a history of the way Mexican Americans become politically empowered to the point where they are able to elect one of their own as mayor, even though many first came to the area as sharecroppers. This section of Texas was owned by Mexico but became part of the United States after the Mexican-American War ended in 1848. Anglos, who were Civil War veterans, received land grants and established large cattle ranches, squeezing out the original Mexican landowners. By 1890 some of the large ranches were divided into smaller farms settled by Germans from central Texas, cotton farmers from the southeast, and others who practiced small-scale commercial farming. The town of North Town (the town studied by Foley) was established during this period. A number of Mexicans had been cowboys and wage laborers earlier, but larger numbers of Mexicans began to migrate to Texas to earn money because of the turmoil created by the Mexican Revolution.

Some of these immigrants lived in *Las Colonias* on one side of the town. A larger number lived in small hamlets with several Anglo families in cotton-growing areas. The hamlets were organized around a cotton gin and a store, owned by the Anglo rancher, plus a church and a school. Still other Mexican immigrants lived on individual farms and ranches, serving as clients of an Anglo *patron.* Many were sharecroppers who raised cotton and later, corn. The landlord provided the land and sometimes also animals, a plow, tools, and seed. The Anglo *patrones* took care of their Mexican workers in a paternalistic fashion, giving them credit, food, and tools in return for services such as labor on roads, domestic child care, and chores around the *patron's* house. Despite a superficial amiability between Anglo *patron* and Mexican client, the Mexicans were considered the "donkeys of the land," economically exploited and socially unequal. For Anglos, the churches and schools were their centers of social life from which Mexicans were excluded. Mexicans had their own churches and schools. The Anglos considered schooling for Mexicans to be useless, since they were destined to be only the underclass, the labor force.

The Mexican community was a lively and vibrant one, conducting a yearly round of ritual celebrations, fiestas, and dances. Large extended families were favored, with a strict division of labor in which women worked mostly at home. The Mexican Americans maintained a strong cultural tradition, completely segregated from Anglos. While Anglos could invade Mexican space, the reverse was not possible. Public buildings were considered Anglo space. The county government, the significant level of government until 1920, was run by an Anglo political machine. Though there were ethnic, religious, occupational, and political differences among the Anglos, as a group they saw themselves as racially superior to the Mexicans and devoted much energy to maintaining that separation and forcing the Mexicans to accept an inferior position. Mexicans had to assume a deferential posture and a respectful tone of voice in talking to Anglos, while Anglos could be familiar and derogatory, and joke at Mexicans. There was no pretense at a melting-pot ideology in this corner of Texas.

After 1930, the economic structure of the area began to change with the decline of cotton and spinach production as well as the erosion of the patron-client share-cropper relationship. The structure of farming changed with mechanization, the introduction of irrigation techniques, and the beginning of farm leasing, a process occurring all over the American South. The paternalistic system in south Texas broke down, to be replaced by absentee landlords and the use of seasonal wetback labor coming in from Mexico at harvest time. The Mexican families, who had been living in the area for many years, began to be recruited as families to work seasonally for growers, in west Texas and in the north. Mexican entrepreneurs organized these labor relations, becoming cultural brokers who earned enough money to become farmers in their own right, merchants, or even moneylenders. The experience of the Mexicans who periodically went north was broadening and economically productive, providing them with money to send their children to school or to buy and run retail stores. This enabled them to become socially mobile.

In the 1950s and 1960s, while the civil rights movement was gaining force in other parts of the country, the Mexicans were also beginning to push against the invisible wall of social segregation. The number of Mexicans voting greatly increased as a result of the penetration of new ideas about civil rights, political activism, and a more public recognition of the injustices that had been suffered at the hands of the Anglos. A cadre of new Mexican leaders began to create ethnic political organizations, such as the League of United Latin American Citizens and the G.I. Forum, a veterans' group for whom the war had been a learning experience, to challenge the earlier patterns of economic exploitation and social segregation. Mexicans then began to move into the political bureaucracy at the lower levels. Though schools were not fully desegregated until 1969, the general level of town schools improved as Mexicans pushed for educational opportunities for their children, since education was clearly the road for the socially mobile. School board elections became a political arena for Mexican Americans, and by 1960 political participation had increased to the point where there was a Mexican candidate for the city council. More moderate Anglo groups were recruiting Mexicans and attempting to form coalitions, though some of this activity represented tokenism.

As Mexican Americans moved into the modern Anglo world, there were greater aspirations, but also greater frustrations and resentment of Anglo society. Men begrudged the need for their wives to work as domestics in Anglo houses in order to have enough money to sustain a decent standard of life. They took to drinking in cantinas. The extended families in which Mexicans lived in the earlier period began breaking up when nuclear families moved into American-style homes and started to raise their children "the American way." Compadre relationships within the Mexican-American community were no longer important. Weddings and other rite-of-passage celebrations ceased being communal affairs; instead, they were now held in restaurants and clubs, with fewer guests invited. Musical tastes changed from mariachi music to popular American forms. While they retained their identity as Mexican Americans, the content of their culture was becoming Americanized.

By the end of the 1960s, the Mexicans were ready for public political confrontation with Anglos, complaining openly about the poor schools and the lack of streets and proper drainage facilities. The Mexican Americans had broken down the walls of their ethnic enclave and forced the adoption of a different set of rules for Mexican-American–Anglo dialogue, seeking to control more of their destiny than they had before. However, the Mexican-American community was not unified in its political aspirations. The threat to the development of Mexican-American ethnic unity and political power came in the form of factions which developed at the very time that Mexican Americans sought to make a common political front against the Anglos.

In 1964, the first city council and the first school board containing both Mexican Americans and Anglos were elected. A new, more liberal group of Anglo political leaders had emerged who were interested in cooperating with the local Mexican-American middle-class businesspeople, community leaders, and professionals. As a consequence of the national civil rights movement, students and other younger Mexican Americans also formed a group, the Raza Unita party, which was dedicated to the complete overthrow of Anglo rule. They considered Mexican culture to be at least as good as, if not superior to, the Anglo way of life. They were like the Black Panthers and other black-power groups of the time—aggressive and confrontational in demanding their rights. In reality, they were the college-educated sons and daughters of middle-class Mexican-American businesspeople and were critical of their elders for not being sufficiently active politically and for not militantly opposing the Anglos. Their candidate had already been elected to the city council. Though these Mexican-American groups were alienated from one another for a time, by 1973 they had joined forces and elected Mexican Americans to a majority of the city council seats. With Mexican Americans speaking out and in control, the Anglos began to feel threatened, resulting in frequent confrontations. However, many Mexican Americans stayed neutral, afraid of the economic consequences of taking sides. The formation of a biracial Better Government League was an attempt to counter both extremist Anglos and Mexican-American radicals. After a period of further polarization and conflict, a strengthened Better Government League, now 50 percent Anglo and 50 percent Mexican American, and the election of a Mexican-American mayor marked a subsequent period of ethnic accommodation. A new generation of Mexican Americans now demand to be recognized as full citizens, with economic, political, and social equality with Anglos while being able to maintain their Mexican-American identity. The content of their culture today, however, is more American than Mexican.

Culture Unassimilated, Reiterated, and Renewed

In retrospect, the idea of the melting pot was a myth for all Americans: Though people conformed to majority norms in the public spheres of work, school, government, and so on, ethnic cultural practices were often retained in the private spheres of life. While assimilation was being emphasized, the persistence of ethnic practices in any form was officially ignored and even denied, being revealed only in scholarly articles. Over the past 30 years the United States has recast its image and replaced the melting-pot symbol with that of a multiethnic, multicultural, pluralistic society. Americans are now enjoined to become more aware of and to respect the differing cultural backgrounds of ethnic groups other than their own. All the groups, taken together, are seen to constitute American culture today. The implications of this shift in our image of ourselves from assimilation to multiculturalism continue to reverberate in school curricula, in urban politics, on television and in the other media, as well as in many other aspects of our lives. Now that multiculturalism and multiethnic images occupy center stage, we are also paying more attention to cultural continuities with the past and to ethnic practices that continue from yesterday, in a reworked form.

There has been a defiant reiteration, strengthening, and redefinition of ethnic identity by various ethnic groups in recent years. This was in response to the civil rights movement in the 1960s, which gave birth to the idea of black power—the empowerment of African Americans—and the conscious construction of African-American culture. In the mid-1960s, African Americans proclaimed that "black is beautiful" and strengthened their African-American identity by reiterating their African traditions and constructing their African-American heritage anew.

Some had argued that the devastating effects of slavery had stripped African Americans of any of the elements of the African cultures of their ancestors (Frazier, 1963). Others saw African cultural practices perpetuated in the culture of African Americans (Herskovits, 1941; Turner, 1949). With today's emphasis on different ethnic traditions, scholars of African-American culture are again investigating continuities with African cultures. For example, rural African Americans in southern states such as Georgia, Alabama, and South Carolina had a tradition of cooking, washing, and sharing gossip in swept yards surrounding their houses. This custom is now found only among members of the older generation. Swept yards were the center of family activity during the slave period and after. This use of space has been linked by Westmacott to West African village practices (1992). Cultural continuities with both West African and Central African cultures have been traced in a number of other areas. African-American speech, discussed in Chapter 3, shows African retentions in verb tense usage (Asante, 1990) and the use of many lexical items from African languages (Herskovits, 1941; Turner, 1949). Some of these African words, like the terms *gumbo* and *goober,* have been borrowed by white speakers of English. Africanisms also survived in the various musical traditions that developed among African Americans, including the gospel tradition, jazz, and the blues (Maultsby, 1990).

The strengthening of African-American identity involved cultural creativity. Alex Haley's television miniseries *Roots,* first aired in the 1970s, graphically depicted the epic history of his family as he reconstructed it, beginning with his West African ancestor who was enslaved and transported to America. All America watched *Roots,* but it had an especially powerful impact on African Americans and their sense of ethnic identity. *Roots* served to directly connect African-American culture to West African culture. Learning Swahili, wearing Kente cloth, using African greetings, and learning to cook African foods were tied to a cognizance of a Pan-African heritage of historic accomplishments and greatness. The geographical location of ancient Egyptian civilization in the northeastern corner of the African continent led African-American intellectuals to characterize it as an African civilization in order to demonstrate the greatness of African cultures. This has provoked a debate about whether the ancient Egyptians were or were not African in physical appearance, language, and culture.

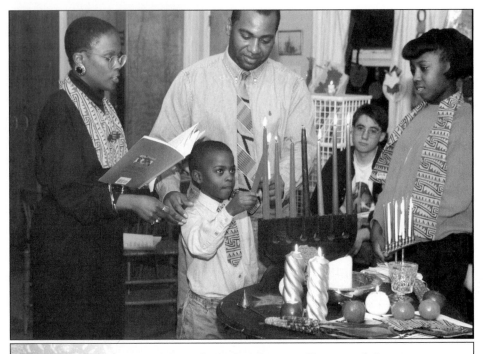

An African-American family light the candles to celebrate Kwanzaa.

The holiday of Kwanzaa is an example of cultural creativity that incorporates a number of African practices. It was developed in 1966 by a professor of black studies at California State University at Long Beach and is widely celebrated today all over the country with the sending of Kwanzaa cards and gift-giving. The seven-day cultural festival, held from December 26 to New Year's Day, is observed by African Americans of all faiths. The accompanying photograph shows one of the ceremonies of Kwanzaa. Like Kwanzaa, most holidays, religious and secular, were conscious cultural inventions, constructed at some point in the past. Christmas, which celebrates the birth of Christ, was originally a pagan rite celebrating the winter solstice, and the Christmas tree and Santa Claus are more recent inventions. We used to view ethnicity as a perpetuation of cultural traditions from the past. We now understand that the utilization of symbols of ethnic identity has always involved creativity and inventiveness (Sollars, 1989; Stern and Cicala, 1991). The question of authenticity of customs is frequently raised when they have been invented recently, but customs invented a century ago are accepted as authentic. The age of a custom or the number of years an event has been celebrated has nothing to do with its authenticity.

Other ethnic groups, following African Americans, began reasserting and reiterating their own ethnic identity and group solidarity and building their own hyphenated cultures in an increasingly public manner. Italians formed the Italian Anti-Defamation League, sponsoring a huge rally at Columbus Circle in New York City, on Columbus Day. Soon, instead of only a single Columbus Day parade dominated by Italian Americans, two parades were held in New York City on different days around Columbus Day, one sponsored by Italian organizations and the other by Hispanic organizations. The latter had contingents of hyphenated Americans from all the Latin American countries who marched in alphabetic order of their countries' names. Parades along Fifth Avenue in New York, occurring on many weekends, reflect the kaleidoscope of groups publicly displaying and reiterating their ethnic identity with floats, bands, costumes, and dignitaries. Among the ethnic parades during the year are the Irish, Greek, Indian (from India), Puerto Rican, Polish, German, and Turkish Day parade, as depicted in the photo. The largest ethnic parade of all is that of the West Indians, who march in Brooklyn on one of the days of the West Indian Labor Day celebration.

Recent immigrants from Korea, Japan, Vietnam, India, Haiti, and elsewhere place great emphasis on their ethnic identity and the maintenance of their cultural traditions in the food they eat, the music they play, the dances they perform, and the celebrations they commemorate. At the same time they are also adapting in many ways to American culture. Prejudice and discrimination against racially distinct groups—like Mexican Americans, as we have seen above, Chinese Americans, and Japanese Americans—have also prevented them from being absorbed into the larger society.

America is a nation based on religious freedom, and from the beginning, it attracted religious believers persecuted in their European homelands. Despite this, there is a strong streak of religious intolerance in the country, sometimes coupled with racism. The majority's intolerance of African-American Muslims, or Native American churches that practice the Peyote "cult," or Caribbean "sects" like Santeria, discussed earlier, seeking to carry out animal sacrifice, exemplifies this streak. The ritual practices of these religious groups offend the Christian majority, which legally tries to eliminate these practices.

How do third- and fourth-generation individuals with mixed ethnic heritages deal with ethnic identity today? Such Americans are now making choices regarding which of several ancestries they want to stress and which they will omit through selective forgetting (Waters, 1990). More and more of these people choose to be ethnic, though their ethnicity may be only situationally expressed. Those claiming Irish ancestry may demonstrate it only on Saint Patrick's Day. In similar fashion, people of multiracial backgrounds are celebrating their identity by marching in Washington, D.C., under the banner of the Multi-Racial Solidarity March. Though immigrants from Asia and their descendants still feel a strong sense of their ethnic identities as Chinese Americans, Filipino Americans, and Korean Americans, the racial attitudes of some Americans seem to be forcing them into an Asian American racial category.

The United States is now a multicultural, multiethnic, pluralist society. The ongoing debates regarding how to implement multicultural curricula in colleges, high schools, and elementary schools reflect our groping for new ways to symbolize and express the multiple aspects of our cultural traditions. The significance of these debates is that they have almost eclipsed the consideration of what remains of a shared

American culture and value system, which includes religious tolerance and the principles embodied in the Bill of Rights and the Constitution.

Over the past few decades the reassertion of ethnic identity has been one of the primary forces in the world. It has usually taken political form as ethnonationalism. Ethnonationalism and the assertion of ethnic identity may be coupled with ethnocentrism. Ethnic differences may also embody racial and class differences. When ethnic differences are paralleled by religious differences, animosity that may already exist is intensified. In Europe and later in Africa and Asia, the process of nation-building involved the cultural construction of a national culture embodying symbols and meanings identified with the nation.

In the United States in recent decades, we have moved from a vision of this country as a melting pot to a view of it as a multicultural, pluralistic nation. The ideal, when the Founding Fathers wrote the Declaration of Independence, the Constitution, and the Bill of Rights, was to have no one ethnic group dominant. In contrast, in other countries, such as Great Britain, France, and Germany, one religion was the state religion and the culture of one group was dominant. However, we must note that in the United States what was written on paper was not the case in reality. Immigrants who came here learned English, and Christmas, but not Hanukkah or the Prophet's Birthday, was a legal holiday. Today, in multicultural America, all holidays are recognized, many languages are the languages of instruction in school, and people can use Spanish ballots on election day. As in the United States, ethnic identity is being reasserted from Europe to Asia. Though countries like Great Britain, France, and Germany do not have a history of cultural pluralism and at present do not see themselves as multiethnic states, there are forces moving them in that direction.

Epilogue

The goal of anthropology is to demonstrate that there are many different cultures in the world and that our culture is but one of them. The mission of the anthropologist is to explore cultural differences among people to see the ways cultures are similar and the ways they differ. By gaining insight into other cultures, one is able to gain insight into one's own culture. Today, many people emphasize cultural relativism— that all cultures have uniquely different cultural traits and that cultural comparison will reveal only differences. We have shown in the various chapters of this book that cultural comparison reveals similarities as well as differences.

The fledgling anthropologist journeys to a culture very different from his or her own—to the Yanomamo or Kwakiutl—to gain an understanding of a way of life different from his or her own. This apprenticeship is a period during which the anthropologist learns how another culture works, and the different conceptualizations and ideas that guide its people.

Anthropology as a discipline is a product of Western culture. It is an outgrowth from the earlier Age of Exploration and a product of Enlightenment thinking and of European encounters with non-European peoples, their languages and cultures. To appreciate what anthropology is all about is to understand and respect cultural diversity. When we quoted Samuel Johnson, the English sage, as saying, "One set of savages is like another," we were citing the voice of ethnocentrism and of ignorance. To Johnson, the Yanomamo, the Tahitians, and even the Scots in the mountains bordering England were all the same—savages—in contrast to the civilized English like himself. But many philosophers of that time did read Cook's *Voyages* and Bougainville's *Voyages* and came to conclusions very different from those of Johnson. Montaigne and Diderot pointed out that a Tahitian might very well look at France and conclude that being drawn and quartered, as a punishment, was a barbarous custom indeed.

Respect for cultural diversity is one of the central messages of anthropology and of this book. It leads one to conclude that our culture practices are but one possible way of doing things, and that our way is not the "right way," the God-given way, the only way. Our form of the family is organized in a particular way for historical and functional reasons. The narrow, ethnocentric view of European settlers who came to America is exemplified by their idea that Native Americans should live in nuclear families like the Europeans, instead of in their own clans and extended families, and that each family should live on the property that it owned. Even today many Americans think ethnocentrically that our legal system is superior to all others. They wince when informed that under other legal codes present in the world today, a thief might have his right hand severed, which they consider barbaric. Yet America and Japan are the only advanced, industrialized nations with the death penalty. Other industrialized nations consider the execution of criminals barbaric.

Cultural diversity and cultural differences are linked to the central concept in anthropology, that of *culture*. The culture concept is a holistic idea, which forces one to consider the many aspects of culture as they relate to one other. Anthropologists do not examine the family structure or the legal system of society in isolation from the other aspects of culture. The focus is always on the way the family or the legal system is related to the economy, to religion, to morality, to ritual, to performance, and so on. The Trobriand family has a particular structure because it is part of the Trobriand economic system, political system, and religious system in particular ways.

The metaphor of the tapestry of culture, which we have used as the framework for this book, relates to the interrelationship, or interweaving, of these various aspects of culture or cultural institutions. Like the colors and designs of an enormous tapestry, every thread—meaning people's activities and individual behaviors as they live out their lives, observed by the anthropologist in the field—contributes to the pattern. However, not even the most elaborate medieval tapestry can approach the splendor and complexity of any single culture.

In this ever-changing world, decisions are constantly being made concerning the future direction of particular societies and ethnic groups. These decisions should be made by the people of these groups, and they should be informed decisions. This is where anthropology comes in. Basic anthropological knowledge can be provided by anthropologists from other places coming in to work with the members of the society, or it can be provided by trained anthropologists from that culture who have an understanding of culture change. The latter group themselves can act as policy makers. The late Jomo Kenyatta, who was president of Kenya, was such an individual with training in anthropology as well as great political skills.

In earlier chapters, we talked about globalization as a process that is having a significant impact on our world. Anthropology and its associated methodology is particularly well suited to explore the ways this global process affects the local scene. Anthropologists have always focused upon communities, upon the micro-analytic unit, concerned with the way it operates and the impact of outside forces, such as the penetration of external markets and national governmental agencies. As we have shown in many of the examples we have discussed, the anthropological perspective is able to reveal the ways people "on the ground" are reacting to the larger forces beyond their communities, which have greatly affected their villages and their lives. It can show the ways peoples' lives have been changed in response to the building of new factories locally, which are owned by multinational companies; or as a consequence of the introduction of new ways of growing crops, which have been developed in the laboratories of Western nations; or as a result of the availability of new products manufactured beyond the borders of their countries. This focus on the local level, where people live their lives, is central to the anthropological approach.

Cited References

Abotchie, Chris. *Social Control in Traditional Southern Eweland of Ghana: Relevance for Modern Crime Prevention.* Accra: Ghana Universities Press, 1997.

Abu-Lughod, Lila. "Shifting Politics in Bedouin Love Poetry." In *Language and the Politics of Emotion,* edited by Lila Abu-Lughod and Catherine A. Lutz. Cambridge, England: Cambridge University Press, 1990.

Adams, Kathleen M. "More Than an Ethnic Marker: Toraja Art as Identity Negotiator." *American Ethnologist 25* (1998): 327–351.

Alexander, Jennifer. "Women Traders in Javanese Marketplaces." In *Market Cultures: Society and Morality in the New Asian Capitalisms,* edited by Robert W. Hefner. Boulder, Colo.: Westview Press, 1998.

Anthony, David W. "Shards of Speech." *The Sciences* January/February 1996, pp. 34–39.

Appadurai, Arjun (ed.). *The Social Life of Things: Commodities in Cultural Perspective.* Cambridge, England: Cambridge University Press, 1986.

Arnold, Jeanne E. "Transportation Innovation and Social Complexity among Maritime Hunter-Gatherer Societies." *American Anthropologist 97* (1995): 733–747.

Asante, Molefi Kete. "African Elements in African-American English." In *Africanisms in American Culture,* edited by Joseph E. Holloway. Bloomington: Indiana University Press, 1990.

Atkinson, Jane Monnig. "How Gender Makes a Difference in Wana Society." In *Power and Difference: Gender in Island Southeast Asia,* edited by Jane Fishburne Collier and Sylvia Junko Yanagisako. Stanford, Calif.: Stanford University Press, 1990.

———. "Shamanisms Today." *Annual Review of Anthropology 21* (1992): 307–330.

Baillargeon, Morgan, and Leslie Tepper. *Legends of Our Times: Native Cowboy Life.* Seattle: University of Washington Press, 1998.

Barnes, Robert H. "Alliance, Exchange, and the Organization of Boat Corporations in Lamalera (E. Indonesia)." In *Kinship, Networks, and Exchange,* edited by Thomas Schweizer and Douglas R. White. New York: Cambridge University Press, 1998.

Bavin, E. L. "Language Acquisition in Cross-cultural Perspective." *Annual Review of Anthropology 24* (1995): 373–396.

Beal, E. Ann. "Consuming Women, Producing Men: The Gendered Construction of Elite Jordanian Shoppers." *Research in Economic Anthropology 19* (1998): 153–178.

Beattie, John. *Bunyoro: An African Kingdom.* New York: Henry Holt, 1960.

Benedict, Ruth. *Patterns of Culture.* Boston: Houghton Mifflin, 1934.

Benet, Sula. *Abkhasians: The Long-living People of the Caucasus.* New York: Holt, Rinehart and Winston, 1974.

Berlin, Brent, and Paul Kay. *Basic Color Terms: Their Universality and Evolution.* Berkeley: University of California Press, 1969.

Berman, Judith, "The Production of the Boas-Hunt Kwaw'ala Texts." In *Working Papers for the 26th International Conference on Salish and Neighboring Languages.* Vancouver, B.C.: University of British Columbia, 1991.

Berreman, Gerald D. "Sanskritization as Female Oppression in India." In *Sex and Gender Hierarchies,* edited by Barbara Diane Miller. Cambridge, England: Cambridge University Press, 1993, pp. 366–392.

Bettelheim, Bruno. *The Uses of Enchantment: The Meaning and Importance of Fairy Tales,* 1977. Reprint. New York: Vintage Press, 1989.

Bickerton, Derek. "Creole Languages, the Language Biogram Hypothesis and Language Acquisition." In *Handbook of Child Language Acquisition,* edited by William C. Ritchie and Tej K. Bhatia. New York: Academic Press, 1999.

Bird-David, Nurit. "Beyond 'the Hunting and Gathering Mode of Subsistence': Culture-Sensitive Observations on the Nayaka and Other Modern Hunters and Gatherers." *Man 27* (1992): 19–44.

Blacking, John. "Dance and Music in Venda Children's Cognitive Development: 1956–1958." In *Acquiring Culture: Cross Cultural Studies in Child Development,* edited by Gustav Johada and I. M. Lewis. London: Croom Helm, 1988.

Bloch, Maurice. *Ritual, History and Power: Selected Papers in Anthropology.* LSE Monographs on Social Anthropology, no. 58. London: Athlone Press, 1989.

Boas, Franz. Introduction to *Handbook of American Indian Languages,* 1911. Reprint. Lincoln: University of Nebraska Press, 1966.

———. *Kwakiutl Ethnography,* edited by Helen Codere. Chicago: University of Chicago Press, 1966.

Botiveau, Bernard. "Islamic Family Law in the French Legal Context." *Cambridge Anthropology 16* (1992/1993): 85–96.

Bott, Elizabeth. *Family and Social Network: Roles, Norms and External Relationships in Ordinary Urban Families.* London: Tavistock Publications, 1971.

Bourdieu, Pierre. *Outline of a Theory of Practice.* Cambridge, England: Cambridge University Press, 1977.

Brandon, George. "Sacrificial Practices in Santeria, an African-Cuban Religion in the United States." In *Africanisms in American Culture,* edited by Joseph E. Holloway. Bloomington: Indiana University Press, 1990.

Brown, Donald E. *Human Universals.* Philadelphia: Temple University Press, 1991.

Brown, Paula. "New Men and Big Men: Emerging Social Stratification in the Third World, a Case Study from the New Guinea Highlands." *Ethnology 26* (1987): 87–106.

Brown, Roger. "The Language of Social Relationship." In *Social Interaction, Social Contest, and Language,* edited by Dan Slobin, Jule Gerhardt, Amy Kyratzis, and Jiansheng Guo. Mahwah, N.J.: Lawrence Erlbaum, 1996.

Brunvand, Jan Harold. "Urban Legends." In *What's So Funny: Humor in American Culture,* edited by Nancy A. Walker. Wilmington, Del.: Scholarly Resources Books, 1998, pp. 145–154.

Buckley, Thomas, and Alma Gottlieb (eds.). *Blood Magic: The Anthropology of Menstruation.* Berkeley: University of California Press, 1988.

Bucko, Raymond. *The Lakota Ritual of the Sweat Lodge: History and Contemporary Practice.* Lincoln: University of Nebraska Press, 1998.

Bugajski, Janusz. *Ethnic Politics in Eastern Europe.* Armonk, N.Y.: M. E. Sharpe, 1994.

Carrillo, Jo (ed.). *Readings in American Indian Law: Recalling the Rhythm of Survival.* Philadelphia: Temple University Press, 1998.

Chagnon, Napoleon. *Yanomamo,* 4th ed. New York: Harcourt Brace Jovanovich, 1997.

Child, Irvin, and Leon Siroto. "BaKwele and American Aesthetic Evaluations Compared." *Ethnology 4* (1965): 349–360.

Chomsky, Noam. "On the Nature, Use, and Acquisition of Language." In *Handbook of Child Language Acquisition,* edited by William C. Ritchie and Tej K. Bhatia. New York: Academic Press, 1999.

Clerk, Christian. " 'That Isn't Really a Pig': Spirit Traditions in the Southern Cook Islands." In *South Pacific Oral Traditions,* edited by Ruth Finnegan and Margaret Orbell. Bloomington: Indiana University Press, 1995, pp. 161–176.

Coates, Jennifer. *Women, Men and Language: A Sociolinguistic Account of Gender Differences in Language,* 2d ed. New York: Longman, 1993.

Coates, Jennifer. *Women Talk: Conversation Between Women Friends*. Cambridge Mass.: Blackwell, 1996.

Cohen, Robin. *Global Diasporas: an Introduction*. Seattle: University of Washington Press, 1997.

Colloredo-Mansfield, Rudi. "The Handicraft Archipelago: Consumption, Migration, and the Social Organization of a Transnational Andean Ethnic Group." *Research in Economic Anthropology 19* (1998): 31–68.

Comaroff, Jean, and John L. Comaroff. "Christianity and Colonialism in South Africa." *American Ethnologist 13* (1986): 1–19.

Cooper, Frederick, and Ann L. Stoler. "Introduction: Tensions of Empire: Colonial Control and Visions of Rule." *American Ethnologist 16* (1989): 609–621.

Coplan, David. "Eloquent Knowledge: Lesotho Migrants' Songs and Anthropology of Experience." *American Ethnologist 14* (1987): 413–433.

Coyne, Michael. *The Crowded Prairie: American National Identity in the Hollywood Western*. New York: I. B. Tauris Publishers, 1997.

Davenport, William. "Sculpture of the Eastern Solomons." *Expedition 10* (1968): 4–25.

d'Azevedo, Warren. "Mask Makers and Myth in Western Liberia." In *Primitive Art and Society*, edited by Anthony Forge. London: Oxford University Press, 1973, pp. 126–150.

De Boek, Filip. "Of Trees and Kings: Politics and Metaphor among the Aluund of Southwestern Zaire." *American Ethnologist 21* (1994): 451–473.

Degh, Linda. *American Folklore and the Mass Media*. Bloomington: Indiana University Press, 1994.

Denniston, George C., and Marilyn F. Milos. *Sexual Mutilation: A Human Tragedy*. New York: Plenum Press, 1997.

Dietz, 1977 (in Pader, 1993: 18).

Donald, Leland. *Aboriginal Slavery on the Northwest Coast of North America*. Berkeley: University of California Press, 1997.

Douglas, Mary. *Natural Symbols: Explorations in Cosmology*. New York: Pantheon Books, 1970.

———. "Deciphering a Meal." In "Myth, Symbol and Culture." *Daedalus* (Winter 1972): 61–81.

———. "Witchcraft and Leprosy: Two Strategies of Exclusion." *Man 26* (1991): 723–726.

Draguns, Juris. "Psychological Disorders of Clinical Severity." In *Handbook of Cross-Cultural Psychology*, vol. 6, Psychopathology. Boston: Allyn and Bacon, 1980, p. 174.

Drummond, Lee. *American Dreamtime: A Cultural Analysis of Popular Movies, and Their Implications for a Science of Humanity*. Lanham, England: Rowman and Littlefield, 1996.

Drury, Nevill. *The Elements of Shamanism*. Longmead, England: Element Books, 1989.

Dudwick, Nora. "The Quest for Identity." *Cultural Survival 16*, no. 1 (1992): 26–29.

Duff, Wilson. *Images: Stone: B. C.* Seattle: University of Washington Press, 1975.

Dundes, Alan. "Into the Endzone for a Touchdown: A Psychoanalytic Consideration of American Football." *Western Folklore 37* (1978): 75–88.

Durkheim, Émile. *The Elementary Forms of the Religious Life,* 1915. Reprint. Translated by Joseph W. Swain. New York: Free Press, 1965.

Edwards, Jeanette, Sarah Franklin, Eric Hirsch, Francis Price, and Marilyn Strathern. *Technologies of Procreation: Kinship in the Age of Assisted Conception*. Manchester, England: Manchester University Press, 1993.

Eller, Jack David. *From Culture to Ethnicity to Conflict: An Anthropological Perspective On International Ethnic Conflict*. Ann Arbor: University of Michigan Press, 1999.

Engels, Frederick. *The Origin of the Family, Private Property, and the State,* 1884. Reprint. New York: International Publishers, 1942.

Erdoes, Richard, and Alfonso Ortiz. *American Indian Trickster Tales.* New York: Viking, 1998.

Erikson, Erik H. *Childhood and Society,* 2d ed. New York: W. W. Norton, 1963.

———. *Gandhi's Truth: On the Origins of Militant Nonviolence.* New York: W. W. Norton, 1969.

Errington, Shelly. "Recasting Sex, Gender and Power: A Theoretical and Regional Overview." In *Power and Difference: Gender in Island Southeast Asia,* edited by Jane Monnig Atkinson and Shelly Errington. Stanford, Calif.: Stanford University Press, 1990.

Esman, Milton J. *Ethnic Politics.* Ithaca, N.Y.: Cornell University Press, 1994.

Ewing, Katherine P. "Is Psychoanalysis Relevant for Anthropology?" In *New Directions in Psychological Anthropology,* edited by T. Schwartz, G. White, and C. Lutz. Cambridge, England: Cambridge University Press, 1992.

Farrell, Ann. "Gendered Settings and Human Rights in Early Childhood." In *Gender in Early Childhood,* edited by Nicola Yelland. New York: Routledge, 1998.

Feinberg, Richard. "Market Economy and Changing Sex Roles on a Polynesian Atoll." *Ethnology 25* (1986): 271–282.

Feld, Steven. "Dialogic Editing: Interpreting How Kaluli Read Sound and Sentiment." *Cultural Anthropology 2* (1987): 193–210.

Ferguson, R. Brian. *Yanomami Warfare: A Political History.* Santa Fe, N. Mex.: School of American Research Press, 1995.

Finckenauer, James O., and Elin J. Waring. *Russian Mafia in America: Immigration, Culture and Crime.* Boston: Northeastern University Press, 1998.

Fine, Gary Alan. *Manufacturing Tales: Sex and Money in Contemporary Legends.* Knoxville: University of Tennessee Press, 1992.

Firth, Raymond. *Elements of Social Organization.* London: Watts, 1951.

Fishman, Pamela. "Interaction: The Work Women Do." In *Language, Gender, and Society,* edited by B. Thorne, C. Kramarai, and N. Henley. Rowley, Mass.: Newbury House, 1983.

Foley, Douglas E. *From Peones to Politicos: Class and Ethnicity in a South Texas Town, 1900–1987.* Austin: University of Texas Press, 1988.

Forge, Anthony (ed.). *Primitive Art and Society.* London: Oxford University Press, 1973.

Foster, Robert. "Commoditization and the emergence of *Kastom* as a Cultural Category: A New Ireland Case in Comparative Perspective." *Oceania 62* (1992): 284–293.

Fox, Richard G. (ed.). *Nationalist Ideologies and the Production of National Cultures.* American Ethnological Society Monograph Series, no. 2, 1990.

Frazier, E. Franklin. *The Negro Church in America.* New York: Schocken Books, 1963.

Freud, Sigmund. *The Future of an Illusion.* London: Hogarth Press, 1928.

Fried, Morton. *The Notion of Tribe.* Menlo Park, Calif.: Cummings Publishing, 1975.

Fromm, Erich. "Individual and Social Origins of Neurosis." *American Sociological Review 9* (1944): 38–44.

Fuller, Chris. "Legal Anthropology, Legal Pluralism and Legal Thought." *Anthropology Today* no. 31 (1994): 9–12.

Gaidzanwa, Rudo. "Indigenisation as Empowerment? Gender and Race in the Empowerment Discourse in Zimbabwe." In *The Anthropology of Power: Empowerment and Disempowerment in Changing Structures,* edited by Angela Cheater. New York: Routledge, 1999.

Geertz, Clifford. "Deep Play: Notes on the Balinese Cockfight." *Daedalus 101* (1972): 1–37.

———. *The Interpretation of Cultures.* New York: Basic Books, 1973.

———. "From the Native's Point of View—On the Understanding of Anthropological Understanding." *Bulletin of the American Academy of Arts and Sciences 28,* no. 1 (1974).

Gellner, Ernest. *Nations and Nationalism.* Ithaca, N.Y.: Cornell University Press, 1983.

Ginsburg, Faye D. *Contested Lives: The Abortion Debate in an American Community.* Berkeley: University of California Press, 1989.

Gleason, Jean Berko, and Richard Ely. "What Color Is the Cat? Color Terms in Parent-Child Conversations." In *Perspectives on Language Acquisition,* edited by Ayhan Aksu Koc, Eser E. Taylan, A. S. Oasoy, and A. Kuntay. Istanbul: Bogazici University Printhouse, 1998.

Gmelch, George. "Baseball Magic." *Trans-Action 8* (1971).

Goldman, L. R. "A Trickster for All Seasons: The Huli *Iba Tiri.*" In *Fluid Ontologies: Myth, Ritual and Philosophy in the Highlands of Papua New Guinea,* edited by L. R. Goldman and C. Ballard. Westport, Conn.: Bergin and Garvey, 1998, pp. 87–124.

Good, Byron J. "Culture and Psychopathology: Directions for Psychiatric Anthropology." In *New Directions in Psychological Anthropology,* edited by T. Schwartz, G. White, and C. Lutz. Cambridge, England: Cambridge University Press, 1992.

Goodenough, Ward. *Description and Comparison in Cultural Anthropology.* Chicago: Aldine Publishing Co., 1970.

Graves, Robert. *The Greek Myths.* New York: George Braziller, 1955.

Greenberg, Joseph. *Language Universals.* The Hague: Mouton, 1966.

Groning, Karl. *Body Decoration: A World Survey of Body Art.* New York: Vendome Press, 1998.

Gudeman, Stephen. *Economics as Culture: Models and Metaphors of Livelihood.* London: Routledge and Kegan Paul, 1986.

Gunson, Neil. "Sacred Women Chiefs and Female 'Headmen' in Polynesian History." *Journal of Pacific History 22* (1987): 139–171.

Gwaltney, John Langston. *Drylongso: A Self-Portrait of Black America.* New York: New Press, 1993.

Hall, Michael. "From Marx to Muhammad." *Cultural Survival 16,* no. 1 (1992): 41–44.

Halpern, Joel M., and Barbara K. Halpern. *A Serbian Village in Historic Perspective.* New York: Holt, Rinehart and Winston, 1972.

Hamilton, Gary G. "Culture and Organization in Taiwan's Market Economy." In *Market Cultures: Society and Morality in the New Asian Capitalisms,* edited by Robert W. Hefner. Boulder, Colo.: Westview Press, 1998.

Hammel, Eugene. *Alternative Social Structures and Ritual Relations in the Balkans.* Englewood Cliffs, N.J.: Prentice-Hall, 1968.

Handler, Richard. *Nationalism and the Politics of Culture in Quebec.* Madison: University of Wisconsin Press, 1988.

Harley, George W. *Notes on the Poro in Liberia.* Papers of the Peabody Museum of American Archaeology and Ethnology, Harvard University, vol. 19, no. 2. Cambridge, Mass., 1941.

Harris, Marvin. "A cultural materialist theory of band and village warfare: the Yanomamo Test." In *Warfare, Culture and Environment,* edited by R. B. Ferguson. Orlando: Academic Press, 1984.

Headland, Thomas N., and Lawrence A. Reid. "Hunter-Gatherers and Their Neighbors from Prehistory to the Present." *Current Anthropology 30* (1989): 43–66.

Hefner, Robert W. "Introduction: Society and Morality in the New Asian Capitalisms." In *Market Cultures: Society and Morality in the New Asian Capitalisms,* edited by Robert W. Hefner. Boulder, Colo.: Westview Press, 1998.

Henderson, Mary. *Star Wars: The Magic of Myth.* New York: Bantam Books, 1997.

Hernsheim, Eduard. *South Sea Merchant.* Port Moresby: Institute of Papua New Guinea Studies, 1983.

Herskovits, Melville J. *The Myth of the Negro Past,* 1941. Reprint. Boston: Beacon Press, 1951.

Herzfeld, Michael. *A Place in History: Social and Monumental Time in a Cretan Village.* Princeton: Princeton University Press, 1991.

Hewitt, Kim. *Mutilating the Body: Identity in Blood and Ink.* Bowling Green, Ohio: Bowling Green State University Popular Press, 1997.

Hickerson, Nancy P. "Ethnogenesis in the South Plains: Jumano to Kiowa." In *History, Power, and Identity: Ethnogenesis in the Americas, 1492–1992,* edited by Jonathan D. Hill. Iowa City: University of Iowa Press, 1996.

Hill, Jonathan D. "Introduction: Ethnogenesis in the Americas, 1492–1992." In *History, Power, and Identity: Ethnogenesis in the Americas, 1492–1992,* edited by Jonathan D. Hill. Iowa City: University of Iowa Press, 1996.

Hobsbawm, E. J. *Nations and Nationalism since 1780: Programme, Myth, Reality,* 2d ed. Cambridge, England: Cambridge University Press, 1992.

Hodges, F. "A Short History of the Institutionalization of Involuntary Sexual Mutilation in the United States." In *Sexual Mutilation: A Human Tragedy,* edited by George C. Denniston and Marilyn F. Milos. New York: Plenum Press, 1997.

Hogbin, Ian. *The Island of Menstruating Men: Religion in Wogeo, New Guinea.* Prospect Heights, Ill.: Waveland Press, 1996.

Hovelsrud-Broda, Greta K. "Arctic Seal-Hunting Households and the Anti-sealing Controversy." *Research in Economic Anthropology 18* (1997): 17–34.

Humphrey, Caroline, and Stephen Hugh-Jones (eds.). *Barter, Exchange and Value: An Anthropological Approach.* Cambridge, England: Cambridge University Press, 1992.

Huntingford, G. W. B. *The Nandi of Kenya.* London: Routledge and Kegan Paul, 1953.

Huntsman, Judith. "Fact, Fiction and Imagination: A Tokelau Narrative." In *South Pacific Oral Traditions,* edited by Ruth Finnegan and Margaret Orbell. Bloomington: Indiana University Press, 1995, pp. 124–160.

Ingold, Tim. *Evolution and Social Life.* Cambridge, England: Cambridge University Press, 1986.

Jacobs, Jerry. *Fun City: An Ethnographic Study of a Retirement Community.* New York: Holt, Rinehart and Winston, 1974.

Jacobs, Sue Ellen, Wesley Thomas, and Sabine Lang. *Two-Spirit People: Native American Gender Identity, Sexuality and Spirituality.* Urbana: University of Illinois Press, 1997.

Jones, Stephen F. "Indigenes and Settlers." *Cultural Survival 16,* no. 1 (1992): 30–32.

Juillerat, Bernard. *Children of the Blood: Society, Reproduction and Cosmology in New Guinea.* New York: Berg, 1996.

Jules-Rosette, Bennetta. *Black Paris: The African Writers' Landscape.* Urbana: University of Illinois Press, 1998.

Kaberry, Phyllis. "The Abelam Tribe, Sepik District, New Guinea." *Oceania 21* (1940): 233–258, 345–367.

Kaeppler, Adrienne. "Structure Movements in Tonga." In *Society and the Dance,* edited by P. Spencer. Cambridge, England: Cambridge University Press, 1985.

Kearney, M. "The Local and the Global: The Anthropology of Globalization and Transnationalism." *Annual Review of Anthropology 24* (1995): 547–565.

Keating, Elizabeth. *Power Sharing: Language, Rank, Gender and Space in Phohnpei, Micronesia.* New York: Oxford University Press, 1998.

Keenan, Elinor. "Norm-makers, Norm-breakers: Uses of Speech by Men and Women in a Malagasy Community." In *Explorations in the Ethnography of Speaking,* edited by Richard Bauman and Joel Sherzer. Cambridge, England: Cambridge University Press, 1974.

Keesing, Roger M. "New Lessons from Old: Changing Perspectives on the *Kula.*" *Finnish Anthropological Society Transactions 27* (1990): 139–163.

Kendall, Laurel. "Korean Shamans and the Spirits of Capitalism." *American Anthropologist 98* (1996): 512–527.

Kenin-Lopsan, M. B. *Shamanic Songs and Myths of Tuva.* Los Angeles: International Society for Trans-Oceanic Research, 1997.

Kinoshita, Yasuhito, and Christie W. Kiefer. *Refuge of the Honored: Social Organization in a Japanese Retirement Community.* Berkeley: University of California Press, 1992.

Kipnis, Andrew B. *Producing Guanxi: Sentiment, Self and Subculture in a North China Village.* Durham, N.C.: Duke University Press, 1997.

Kleinman, Arthur, and Byron Good (eds.). *Culture and Depression: Studies in the Anthropology and Cross-Cultural Psychiatry of Affect and Disorder.* Berkeley: University of California Press, 1985.

Kluckhohn, Clyde. "Myths and Rituals: A General Theory." *Harvard Theological Review 35* (1942): 45–79.

Kluckholn, Clyde. "Universal Categories of Culture." In *Anthropology Today: an Enclyclopedic Inventory,* edited by A. L. Kroeber. Chicago: University of Chicago Press, 1953.

Kochanek, Stanley A. *Patron-Client Politics and Business in Bangladesh.* Newbury Park, Calif.: Sage Publications, 1993.

Kohl, Philip. "Nationalism and Archeology: On the Construction of Nations and the Reconstructions of the Remote Past." *Annual Review of Anthropology 27* (1998): 223–246.

Kondo, Dorinne. *Crafting Selves: Power, Gender, and Discourses of Identity in a Japanese Workplace.* Chicago: University of Chicago Press, 1990.

Koskoff, Ellen (ed.). *Women and Music in Cross-Cultural Perspective.* New York: Greenwood Press, 1987.

Kroeber, Alfred L. *Cultural and Natural Areas of Native North America.* Berkeley: University of California Press, 1939.

Labov, William. "Co-existent Systems in African-American Vernacular English." In *African-American English: Structure, History and Use,* edited by Salikoko S. Mufwene, John R. Rickford, Guy Bailey, and John Baugh. New York: Routledge, 1998.

Langmore, Diane. *Missionary Lives: Papua, 1874–1914.* Honolulu: University of Hawaii Press, 1989.

Lass, Andrew. "Romantic Documents and Political Monuments: The Meaning—Fulfillment of History in 19th-century Czech Nationalism." *American Ethnologist 15* (1988): 456–471.

Lattas, Andrew. "Sorcery and Colonialism: Illness, Dreams and Death as Political Languages in West New Britain." *Man 28* (1993): 51–78.

Lazarus-Black, Mindie. "Why Women Take Men to Court: Caribbean Kinship Ideology and Law." *Ethnology II 30* (1991).

Leach, Edmund. *Political Systems of Highland Burma: A Study of Kachin Social Structure,* 1954. Reprint. Boston: Beacon Press, 1965.

———. "Magical Hair." *Journal of the Royal Anthropological Institute of Great Britain and Ireland 88* (1958): 147–164.

———. "Anthropological Aspects of Language: Animal Categories and Verbal Abuse." In *New Directions in the Study of Language,* edited by Eric Lenneberg. Cambridge, Mass.: MIT Press, 1964, pp. 23–64.

Lee, Mee Sook. "Kinship Structure and Behaviors of Kin-Relatives in Modern Korea." In *Till Death Do Us Part: A Multicultural Anthology on Marriage,* edited by Sandra Lee Browning and R. Robin Miller. Stamford, Conn.: JA Press 1999.

Lepowsky, Maria. "Big Men, Big Women and Cultural Autonomy." *Ethnology 29* (1990): 35–50.

Lett, James W. *Science, Reason and Anthropology: the Principles of Rational Inquiry.* Lanham, Md: Rauman and Littlefield, 1997.

Lévi-Strauss, Claude. *Tristes Tropiques,* 1955. Reprint. Translated by John Russell. New York: Atheneum, 1961.

————. "The Structural Theory of Myth." Chapter 11 of his *Structural Anthropology*. New York: Basic Books, 1963, pp. 206–231.

————. *L'Homme Nu: Mythologique 4*. Paris: Plon, 1971.

————. *La Voie des Masques*. Paris: Plon, 1979.

Levine, Nancy E. "Fathers and Sons: Kinship Value and Validation in Tibetan Polyandry." *Man* 22 (1987): 267–286.

Lewin, Ellen. *Lesbian Mothers: Accounts of Gender in American Culture*. Ithaca, N.Y.: Cornell University Press, 1993.

Lewis, I. M. *Arguments with Ethnography: Comparative Approaches to History, Politics and Religion*. New Brunswick, N.J.: Athalone Press, 1999.

Lips, Julius. *The Savage Hits Back*, 1937. Reprint. New Hyde Park, N.Y.: University Books, 1966.

Lizot, Jacques. "Words in the Night: the Ceremonial Dialogue—One Expression of Peaceful Relationships among the Yanomami." In *The Anthropology of Peace and Non-Violence*, edited by Leslie E. Sponsel and Thomas Gregor. Boulder, Colo.: Lynne Rienner, 1994.

Loizos, Peter. "Disenchanting Developers." *Anthropology Today 7*, no. 5 (1991): 1–2.

Loker, William M. "Grit in the Prosperity Machine: Globalization and the Rural Poor In Latin America." In *Globalization and the Rural Poor in Latin America*, edited by William M. Loker. Boulder, Colo.: Lynne Reinner Publishers, 1999.

Louwe, Heleen. "Police-Reformers: 'Big Men' Failing Their Followers." In *Private Politics: A Multi-Disciplinary Approach to "Big Man" Systems*, edited by Martin A. Van Bakel, Renee R. Hogesteijm, and Pieter von de Velde, vol. 1, Studies in Human Society. Leiden, Holland: Brill, 1986, pp. 174–181.

Lowe, Kathy. "Gendermaps." In *Gender in Early Childhood*, edited by Nicola Yelland. New York: Routledge, 1998.

Lukanuski, Mary. "A Place at the Counter: The Onus of Oneness." In *Eating Culture*, edited by Ron Scapp and Brian Seitz. Albany: State University of New York Press, 1998.

Lutz, Catherine, and Lila Abu-Lughod (eds.). *Language and the Politics of Emotion*. Cambridge, England: Cambridge University Press, 1990.

Lynch, John. *Pacific Languages: An Introduction*. Honolulu: University of Hawaii Press, 1998.

Mackie, Jamie. "Business Success among Southeast Asian Chinese." In *Market Cultures: Society and Morality in the New Asian Capitalisms*, edited by Robert W. Hefner. Boulder, Colo.: Westview Press, 1998.

MacLaury, Robert E. "From Brightness to Hue: An Explanatory Model of Color Category Evolution." *Current Anthropology 33* (1992): 137–186.

Mageo, Jeannette Marie. "Male Transvestism and Culture Change in Samoa." *American Ethnologist 19* (1992): 443–459.

Mageo, Jeannette Marie. *Theorizing Self in Samoa: Emotions, Genders and Sexualities*. Ann Arbor: University of Michigan Press, 1998.

Malinowski, Bronislaw. *Argonauts of the Western Pacific*, 1922. Reprint. New York: E. P. Dutton and Co., 1961.

————. *The Sexual Life of Savages in Northwestern Melanesia*. New York: Harcourt, Brace and World, 1929.

————. *Coral Gardens and Their Magic: A Study of the Methods of Tilling the Soil and of Agricultural Rites in the Trobriand Islands*. New York: American Book Co., 1935.

————. "Introductory Essay." In *Methods of Study of Culture Contact in Africa*. International African Institute, Memorandum XV, 1938.

Manganaro, Marc (ed.). *Modernist Anthropology: From Fieldwork to Text*. Princeton, N.J.: Princeton University Press, 1990.

Mason, Mary Ann. "The Modern Step Family: Problems and Possibilities." In *All Our Families: New Policies for a New Century,* edited by Mary Ann Mason, Arlene Skolnick, and Stephen D. Surgarman. New York: Oxford University Press, 1998.

Maultsby, Portia K. "Africanisms in African-American Music." In *Africanisms in American Culture,* edited by Joseph E. Holloway. Bloomington: Indiana University Press, 1990.

Mauss, Marcel. *The Gift,* 1925. Reprint. Translated by Ian Cunnison. London: Cohen and West, 1954.

McCarthy, Mary. *The Group.* New York: Harcourt, Brace and World. 1963.

McDonough, Christian. "Breaking the Rules: Changes in Food Acceptability among Tharu of Nepal." In *Food Preferences and Taste: Continuity and Change,* edited by Helen Macbeth. Providence, R.I.: Berghahn Books, 1997.

McKnight, David. *People, Countries, and the Rainbow Serpent: Systems of Classification among the Lardil of Mornington Island.* New York: Oxford University Press, 1999.

Mead, Margaret. *Sex and Temperament in Three Primitive Societies,* 1935. Reprint. New York: Mentor Books, 1950.

Meggitt, Mervyn. " 'Pigs Are Our Hearts!' The Te Exchange Cycle among the Mae Enga." *Human Ecology 1,* no. 2. (1974).

———. *Blood Is Their Argument: Warfare among the Mae Enga Tribesmen of the New Guinea Highlands.* Palo Alto, Calif.: Mayfield Publishing, 1977.

Mehler, J., P. Jusczyk, G. Lambert, N. Halsted, and J. Bertoncini. "A Precursor to Language Acquisition in Young Infants." *Cognition 29* (1988): 143–178.

Meigs, Anna S. "Food Rules and the Traditional Sexual Ideology." In *Cooking, Eating, Thinking: Transformative Philosophies of Food,* edited by Deane W. Curtin and Lisa M. Heldke. Bloomington: Indiana University Press, 1992, pp. 109–118.

Meisch, Lynn A. "The Reconquest of Otavalo, Ecuador: Indigenous Economic Gains and New Power Relations." *Research in Economic Anthropology 19* (1998): 11–30.

Melton, J. Gordon. *Magic, Witchcraft, and Paganism in America: A Bibliography.* New York: Garland Publishing, 1982.

Menges, Karl H. "People, Languages, and Migrations." In *Central Asia: A Century of Russian Rule,* edited by Edward Allworth. New York: Columbia University Press, 1967.

Mertz, Elizabeth. "Legal Language: Pragmatics, Poetics, and Social Power." *Annual Review of Anthropology 23* (1994): 435–455.

Meshorer, Hank. "The Scared Trail to Zuni Heaven: A Study in the Law of Prescriptive Easements." In *Readings in American Indian Law: Recalling the Rhythm of Survival,* edited by Jo Carrillo. Philadelphia: Temple University Press, 1998, pp. 318–323.

Metcalf, Peter. *Celebrations of Death: The Anthropology of Mortuary Ritual.* New York: Cambridge University Press, 1991.

Miller, D. "Consumption and Commodities." *Annual Review of Anthropology 24* (1995): 141–161.

Mintz, Sydney W. *Sweetness and Power: The Place of Sugar in Modern History.* New York: Penguin, 1986.

Mitchell, J. Clyde. *The Kalela Dance: Aspects of Social Relationships among Urban Africans in Northern Rhodesia.* Manchester, England: Published on behalf of the Rhodes-Livingston Institute by Manchester University Press, 1956.

Moore, Omar Khayyam. "Divination: A New Perspective." *American Anthropologist 59* (1957): 69–74.

Morgan, Lewis Henry. *Ancient Society,* 1877. Reprint. New York: World Publishing, 1963.

Morgan, Marcyliena. "Theories and Politics in African American English." *Annual Review of Anthropology 23 (1994): 325–345.*

Mufwene, Salikoko S., John R. Rickford, Guy Bailey, and John Baugh (eds.). *African-American English: Structure, History and Use*. New York: Routledge, 1998.

Muhlhausler, Peter. *Linguistic Ecology: Language Change and Linguistic Imperialism in the Pacific Region*. New York: Routledge, 1996.

Munn, Nancy. "The Spatial Presentation of Cosmic Order in Walbiri Iconography." In *Primitive Art and Society*, edited by Anthony Forge. London: Oxford University Press, 1973.

Munroe, Ruth H., and Robert L. Munroe. "Child Development." *In Encyclopedia of Child Development*, edited by David Levinson and Melvin Ember. New York: Henry Holt and Company, 1996.

Murphy, Yolanda, and Robert F. Murphy. *Women of the Forest*, 2d ed. New York: Columbia University Press, 1985.

Nakamura, Keiko. "The Use of Polite Language by Japanese Preschool Children." In *Social Interaction, Social Context, and Language: Essays in Honor of Susan Ervin-Tripp*, edited by Dan Slobin. Mahwah, N.J.: Lawrence Erlbaum, 1996.

Nakanishi, Hisae. "Power Ideology and Women's Consciousness in Post-Revolutionary Iran." In *Women in Muslim Societies: Diversity within Unity*, edited by Herbert L. Bodman and Nayereh Tohidi. Boulder, Colo.: Lynne Rienner Publishers, 1998.

Nathanson, Paul. *Over the Rainbow: The Wizard of Oz as a Secular Myth of America*. Albany: State University of New York Press, 1991.

Neville, Gwen Kennedy. *Kinship and Pilgrimage: Rituals of Reunion in American Protestant Culture*. London: Oxford University Press, 1987.

Newman, Katherine. *Falling from Grace: The Experience of Downward Mobility in the American Middle Class*. New York: Free Press, 1988.

Obeyesekere, Gananath. *The Apotheosis of Captain Cook: European Mythmaking in the Pacific*. Princeton, N.J.: Princeton University Press, 1992.

Ochs, Elinor. "From Feelings to Grammar: A Samoan Case Study." In *Language Socialization across Cultures*, edited by Bambi Schieffelin and Elinor Ochs. Cambridge, England: Cambridge University Press, 1986.

O'Hanlon, Michael. *Reading the Skin: Adornment, Display and Society among the Wahgi*. London: British Museum Publications, 1989.

Orion, Loretta. *Never Again the Burning Times: Paganism Revived*. Prospect Heights, Ill.: Waveland Press, 1995.

Orlove, Benjamin. "Working in the Field: Perspectives on Globalization in Latin America." In *Globalization and the Rural Poor in Latin America*, edited by William M. Loker. Boulder, Colo.: Lynne Reinner Publishers, 1999.

Ortner, Sherry B. "Theory in Anthropology since the Sixties." *Comparative Studies in Society and History 26* (1984): 126–165.

O'Toole, Fintan. "The Many Stories of Billy the Kid." *The New Yorker*, vol. 74, no. 10, December 28, 1998–January 4, 1999, pp. 86–98.

Pader, Ellen J. "Spatiality and Social Change: Domestic Space Use in Mexico and the United States." *American Ethnologist 20* (1993): 114–137.

Palmie, Stephan. "Which Centre, Whose Margin? Notes Towards an Archaeology of U.S. Supreme Court Case 91-948, 1993 (*Church of the Lukumi vs. City of Hialeah, South Florida*)." In *Inside and Outside the Law: Anthropological Studies of Authority and Ambiguity*, edited by Olivia Harris. New York: Routledge, 1996, pp. 184–209.

Papataxiarchis, Evythymios. "Friends of the Heart: Male Commensal Solidarity, Gender, And Kinship in Aegean Greece." In *Contested Identities: Gender and Kinship In Modern Greece*, edited by Peter Loizos and Evythymios Papataxiarchis. Princeton, N.J.: Princeton University Press, 1991.

Parkin, Robert. *Kinship: An Introduction to Basic Concepts*. Malden, Mass.: Blackwell Publishers, 1997.

Peck, Catherine (compiler and annotator). *A Treasury of North American Folk-Tales.* New York: W. W. Norton, 1998.

Peters, Emrys. "The Proliferation of Segments in the Lineage of the Bedouin of Cyrenaica." *Journal of the Royal Anthropological Institute of Great Britain and Ireland 90* (1960): 29–53.

Pinker, Steve. *The Language Instinct.* New York: Harper Perennial, 1994.

Pitkin, Harvey. "Coyote and Bullhead: A Wintu Text." Native American Text Series. *International Journal of American Linguistics* 2.2, pp. 82–104. Chicago: University of Chicago Press, 1977.

Platt, Katherine. "Cognitive Development and Sex Roles on the Kerkennah Islands of Tunisia." In *Acquiring Culture: Cross-Cultural Studies in Child Development,* edited by Gustav Johada and I. M. Lewis. London: Croom Helm, 1988.

Podolefsky, Aaron. "Mediator Roles in Simbu Longfleet Management." *Ethnology 29* (1990): 67–82.

Powdermaker, Hortense. *Life in Lesu,* 1933. Reprint. New York: W. W. Norton, 1971.

Poynton, Cate. *Language and Gender: Making the Difference.* London: Oxford University Press, 1989.

Price, Richard. *First Time: The Historical Vision of an Afro-American People.* Baltimore: Johns Hopkins University Press, 1983.

Price, Sally. *Primitive Art in Civilized Places.* Chicago: University of Chicago Press, 1989.

Quinones, Maria. "Looking Smart: Consumption, Cultural History and Identity among Barbardian "Suitcase Traders." *Research in Economic Anthropology 18:* (1997): 167–187.

Radcliffe-Brown, A. R. *Structure and Function in Primitive Society.* Glencoe, Ill.: Free Press, 1952.
———, and Daryll Forde (eds.). *African Systems of Kinship and Marriage.* London: Oxford University Press, 1950.

Rapp, Rayna. "Reproduction and Gender Hierarchy: Amniocentesis in America." In *Sex and Gender Hierarchies,* edited by Barbara Diane Miller. Cambridge, England: Cambridge University Press, 1993, pp. 108–126.

Rappaport, Roy A. *Pigs for the Ancestors: Ritual in the Ecology of a New Guinea People,* 2d ed. New Haven, Conn.: Yale University Press, 1984.

Reichel-Dolmatoff, Elizabeth. "Foreword." In *Body Decoration: A World Survey of Body Art,* edited by Karl Groning. New York: Vendome Press, 1998.

Reyes, Adelaida. *Songs of the Caged, Songs of the Free: Music and the Vietnamese Refugee Experience.* Philadelphia: Temple University Press, 1999.

Richards, Audrey. *Land, Labour and Diet in Northern Rhodesia: An Economic Study of the Bemba Tribe.* London: Oxford University Press, 1961.

Rickford, John R. "The Creole Origins of African-American Vernacular English: Evidence from Copula Absence." In *African-American English: Structure, History and Use,* edited by Salikoko S. Mufwene, John R. Rickford, Guy Bailey, and John Baugh. New York: Routledge, 1998.

Riekse, Robert J., and Henry Holstege. *Growing Older in America.* New York: McGraw-Hill, 1996.

Ritchie, William C. "Child Language Acquisition: Introduction, Foundations, and Overview." In *Handbook of Child Language Acquisition,* edited by William C. Ritchie and Tej K. Bhatia. New York: Academic Press, 1999.

Rosaldo, Michelle. "Towards an Anthropology of Self and Feeling." In *Culture Theory: Essays on Mind, Self and Emotion,* edited by Richard Shweder and Robert A. LeVine. Cambridge, England: Cambridge University Press, 1984.

Roscoe, Will. *Changing Ones: Third and Fourth Genders in Native North America.* New York: St. Martin's Press, 1998.

Rosman, Abraham, and Paula G. Rubel. "Structural Patterning in Kwakiutl Art and Ritual." *Man 25* (1990): 620–640.

Rubel, Paula G., and Abraham Rosman. *Your Own Pigs You May Not Eat.* Chicago: University of Chicago Press, 1978.

Sahlins, Marshall. *Stone Age Economics*. Chicago: Aldine-Atherton, 1972.

———. *Islands of History*. Chicago: University of Chicago Press, 1985.

Sahlins, Marshall. "What Is Anthropological Enlightenment? Some Lessons of the Twentieth Century." *Annual Review of Anthropology 28* (1999): I-xxiii.

Salaff, Janet W. *Working Daughters of Hong Kong: Filial Piety or Power in the Family?* New York: Columbia University Press, 1995.

Saler, Benson. *Conceptualizing Religion: Eminent Anthropologists, Transcendent Natives, and Unbounded Categories*. Leiden, Holland: E. J. Brill, 1993.

Saussure, Ferdinand de. *Course in General Linguistics,* 1915. Reprint. New York: McGraw-Hill, 1966.

Scaglion, Richard. "Customary Law Development in Papua New Guinea." In *Anthropological Praxis—Translating Knowledge into Action,* edited by Robert M. Wulff and Shirley J. Fiske. Boulder, Colo.: Westview Press, 1987.

Schiefenhovel, Wulf, and Ingrid Bell-Krannhals. "Of Harvests and Hierarchies: Securing Staple Food and Social Position in the Trobriand Islands." In *Food and the Status Quest: An Interdisciplinary Perspective,* edited by Polly Wiessner and Wulf Schiefenhovel. Providence, R.I.: Berghahn Books, 1996.

Schieffelin, Bambi. "Teasing and Shaming in Kaluli Children's Interactions." In *Language Socialization across Cultures,* edited by Bambi Schieffelin and Elinor Ochs. Cambridge, England: Cambridge University Press, 1986.

Schieffelin, Bambi B., and Elinor Ochs. "The Microgenesis of Competence: Methodology in Language Socialization." In *Social Interaction, Social Context, and Language,* edited by Dan I. Slobin, Julie Gerhardt, Amy Kyratzis, and Jiansheng Guo. Mahwah, N.J.: Lawrence Erlbaum, 1996.

Schneider, David M. *American Kinship,* 2d ed. Chicago: University of Chicago Press, 1980.

———. *A Critique of the Study of Kinship*. Ann Arbor: University of Michigan Press, 1984.

Schulz, Dorothea E. "Morals of Praise: Broadcast Media and the Commoditization of Jeli Praise Performances in Mali." *Research in Economic Anthropology 19* (1998): 117–132.

Sebba, Mark. *Contact Languages: Pidgins and Creoles*. New York: St. Martin's Press, 1997.

Segal, Robert A. *Theorizing about Myth*. Amherst: University of Massachusetts Press, 1999.

Sherman, Suzanne (ed.). *Lesbian and Gay Marriage: Private Commitments, Public Ceremonies*. Philadelphia: Temple University Press, 1992.

Shott, Michael J. "On Recent Trends in the Anthropology of Foragers: Kalahari Revisionism and Its Archaeological Implications." *Man 27* (1992): 843–871.

Shweder, Richard, Manamohan Mahapatra, and Joan G. Miller. "Culture and Moral Development." In *Cultural Psychology: Essays on Comparative Human Development,* edited by James Stigler, Richard Shweder, and Gilbert Herdt. Cambridge, England: Cambridge University Press, 1990.

Skolnick, Arlene. "Solomon's Children: Psychological Parenthood, Attachment Theory, and the Best Interests Standard." In *All Our Families: New Policies for a New Century,* edited by Mary Ann Mason, Arlene Skolnick, and Stephan D. Sugarman. New York: Oxford University Press, 1998.

Smith, W. Robertson. *Lectures on the Religion of the Semites*. New York: D. Appleton, 1889.

Smitherman, Geneva. "Word from the Hood: The Lexicon of African-American Vernacular English." In *African-American English: Structure, History and Use,* edited by Salikoko S. Mufwene, John R. Rickford, Guy Bailey, and John Baugh. New York: Routledge, 1998.

Sollars, Werner (ed.). *The Invention of Ethnicity*. New York: Oxford University Press, 1989.

Spiro, Melford E. "Religion: Problems of Definition and Explanation." In *Anthropological Approaches to the Study of Religion,* edited by Michael Banton. A.S.A. Monograph, no. 3. London: Tavistock Publications, 1966, pp. 85–126.

Stacey, Judith. "Gay and Lesbian Families: Queer Like Us." In *All Our Families: New Policies for a New Century,* edited by Mary Ann Mason, Arlene Skolnick, and Stephan D. Sugarman. New York: Oxford University Press, 1998.

Stack, Carol B. *All Our Kin: Strategies for Survival in a Black Community.* New York: Harper and Row, 1974.

Starrett, Gregory. "The Political Economy of Religious Commodities in Cairo." *American Anthropologist 97* (1995): 51–68.

Stern, Stephen, and John Allan Cicala (eds.). *Creative Ethnicity: Symbols and Strategies of Contemporary Ethnic Life.* Logan, Utah: Utah State University Press, 1991.

Steward, Julian. *Theory of Culture Change.* Urbana: University of Illinois Press, 1955.

Stigler, James, Richard A. Shweder, and Gilbert Herdt (eds.). *Culture Psychology Essays on Comparative Human Development.* Cambridge, England: Cambridge University Press, 1990.

Stoller, Eleanor P. "Informal Exchanges with Non-Kin among Retired Sunbelt Migrants: A Case Study of a Finnish American Retirement Community." *Journal of Gerontology: Social Sciences 53B* (1998): S287–S298.

Stoller, Paul. "Ethnographers as Texts/Ethnographers as *griots.*" *American Ethnologist 21* (1994): 353–366.

Strathern, Andrew, and Marilyn Strathern. *Self-Decoration in Mount Hagen.* London: Gerald Duckworth, 1971.

Strathern, Marilyn. *Reproducing the Future: Essays on Anthropology, Kinship and the New Reproductive Technologies.* New York: Routledge, 1992.

Sullivan, Nancy. "Inside Trading: Postmodernism and the Social Drama of *Sunflowers* in the 1980s Art World." In *The Traffic in Culture: Refiguring Art and Anthropology,* edited by George E. Marcus and Fred R. Myers. Berkeley: University of California Press, 1995.

Sutherland, Anne. *Gypsies—The Hidden Americans.* Prospect Heights, Ill.: Waveland Press, 1986.

Swingewood, Alan. *Cultural Theory and the Problem of Modernity.* New York: St. Martin's Press, 1998.

Tambiah, S. J. "Animals Are Good to Think about and Good to Prohibit." *Ethnology 8* (1969): 423–459.

———. *Sri Lanka: Ethnic Fratricide and the Dismantling of Democracy.* Chicago: University of Chicago Press, 1986.

———. "Ethnic Fratricide in Sri Lanka: An Update." In *Ethnicities and Nations: Processes of Interethnic Relations in Latin America, Southeast Asia, and the Pacific,* edited by Remo Guidieri, Francesco Pellizzi, and Stanley J. Tambiah. Austin: University of Texas Press, 1988.

Tannen, Deborah. *Gender and Discourse.* New York: Oxford University Press, 1994.

Tatla, Darshan Singh. *The Sikh Diaspora: The Search for Statehood.* London: UCL Press, 1999.

Tattersall, Ian. *Becoming Human: Evolution and Human Uniqueness.* New York: Harcourt Brace, 1998.

Testart, Alain. "Game Sharing Systems and Kinship Systems among Hunter-Gatherers." *Man 22* (1987): 287–304.

Thomas, Wesley. *Two-spirit People: Native American Gender Identity, Sexuality, and Spirituality.* Urbana: University of Illinois Press, 1997.

Thomason, Sarah G. *Contact Languages: A Wider Perspective.* Philadelphia: John Benjamins Publishing, 1997.

Tollefson, Ted E. "Cinemyths: Contemporary Films as Gender Myths." In *The Soul of Popular Culture: Looking at Contemporary Heroes, Myths, and Monsters,* edited by Mary Lyn Kittelson. Chicago: Open Court, 1998, pp. 106–116.

Turino, Thomas. "The History of a Peruvian Panpipe Style and the Politics of Interpretation." In *Ethnomusicology and Modern Music History,* edited by S. Blum, P. Bohlman, and D. Neuman. Urbana: University of Illinois Press, 1991.

Turner, Lorenzo. *Africanisms in the Gullah Dialect,* 1949. Reprint. New York: Arno Press, 1968.

Turner, Victor. "Betwixt and Between: The Liminal Period in Rites de Passage." In his *The Forest of Symbols: Aspects of Ndembu Ritual.* Ithaca, N.Y.: Cornell University Press, 1967, pp. 93–111.

Tylor, Edward B. *Primitive Culture: Researches into the Development of Mythology, Philosophy, Religion, Language, Art and Custom,* 2 vols. London: John Murray, 1874.

Van Gennep, Arnold. *The Rites of Passage,* 1909. Reprint. Translated by Monika B. Vizedom and Gabrielle Caffee. Chicago: University of Chicago Press, 1960.

Wallerstein, Immanuel M. *The Modern World System: Capitalist Agriculture and the Origins of the European World Economy in the Sixteenth Century.* New York: Academic Press, 1974.

Waters, Mary C. *Ethnic Options: Choosing Identities in America.* Berkeley: University of California Press, 1990.

Weber, Max. *The Protestant Ethic and the Spirit of Capitalism.* London: Allen and Unwin, 1930.

Weiner, Annette B. *Women of Value, Men of Renown: New Perspectives in Trobriand Exchange.* Austin: University of Texas Press, 1976.

Weisgrau, Maxine K. *Interpreting Development: Local Histories, Local Strategies.* Lanham, Md.: University Press of America, 1997.

Werbner, Pnina. "Stamping the Earth With the Name of Allah: Zikr and the Sacralizing of Space among British Muslims." *Cultural Anthropology 11* (1996): 309–338.

West, C., and D. Zimmerman. "Women's Place in Everyday Talk: Reflections on Parent-Child Interaction." *Social Problems 24* (1977): 521–529.

Westmacott, Richard. *African-American Gardens and Yards in the Rural South.* Nashville: University of Tennessee Press, 1992.

Weston, Kath. *Families We Choose: Lesbians, Gays, Kinship.* New York: Columbia University Press, 1991.

Whalley, Lucy A. "Urban Minangkabau Muslim Women: Modern Choices, Traditional Choices in Indonesia." In *Women in Muslim Societies: Diversity within Unity,* edited by Herbert L. Bodman and Nayereh Tohidi. Boulder, Colo.: Lynne Reiner Publishers, 1998.

White, Leslie. *The Science of Culture.* New York: Farrar, Straus and Giroux, 1949.

———. *The Evolution of Culture.* New York: McGraw-Hill, 1959.

Wilson, Monica. *Good Company,* 1951. Reprint. Boston: Beacon Press, 1964.

———. *For Men and Elders: Change in the Relations of Generations and of Men and Women among the Nyakyusa-Ngonde People 1875–1971.* New York: Africana Publishing, International African Institute, 1977.

Wilson, Thomas C. "Urbanism and Kinship Bonds: A Test of Four Generalizations." *Social Forces 71* (1993): 703–712.

Wolf, Eric R. *Europe and the People without History.* Berkeley: University of California Press, 1982.

Woodbury, Anthony C. "A Defense of the Proposition, 'When a Language Dies, A Culture Dies.' " *Texas Linguistic Forum 33* (1993): 1–15.

Wright, Will. *Sixguns and Society: A Structural Study of the Western.* Berkeley: University of California Press, 1975.

Yai, Olabiyi Babalola. "In Praise of Metonymy: The Concepts of 'Tradition' and 'Creativity' in the Transmission of Yoruba Artistry over Time and Space." In *The Yoruba Artist: New Theoretical Perspectives on African Arts,* edited by Rowland Abiodun, Henry J. Drewal, and John Pemberton III. Washington, D.C.: Smithsonian Institution Press, 1994.

Young, Michael, and Peter Willmott. *Family and Kinship in East London.* Baltimore: Penguin Books, 1962.

Zicker, John P. "Kinship and Exchange among the Dolgan and Nganasan of Northern Siberia." *Research in Economic Anthropology 19* (1998): 191–238.

Suggested Readings

Chapter 1: The Anthropological Perspective

Borofsky, Robert (ed.). *Assessing Cultural Anthropology*. New York: McGraw-Hill, 1994.
A collection of theoretical articles presenting the viewpoints of leading anthropologists of the time.

Kuper, Adam. *Culture: The Anthropologists' Account*. Cambridge, Mass.: Harvard University Press, 1999.
A historical examination of the culture concept, along with an evaluation of its usefulness.

Layton, Robert. *An Introduction to Theory in Anthropology*. New York: Cambridge University Press, 1997.
A general introduction to anthropological theory, which takes into consideration the fragmentation of the subject over the past two decades.

Manganaro, Marc (ed.). *Modernist Anthropology: From Fieldwork to Text*. Princeton, N.J.: Princeton University Press, 1990.
A collection of papers dealing with modernism and postmodernism.

Chapter 2: The Anthropological Method

Bradburd, Daniel. *Being There: The Necessity of Fieldwork*. Washington, D.C.: Smithsonian Institution, 1998.
An account of fieldwork with the Komache nomads of southern Iran, which shows how direct interaction with another culture is essential for anthropological understanding, and documents the author's progress toward understanding another culture.

Codere, Helen. "Kwakiutl." In *Perspectives in American Indian Culture Change,* edited by Edward H. Spicer. Chicago: University of Chicago Press, 1961.
An account of Kwakiutl culture change from the time of the Indians' initial contact with white society to the contemporary period.

Jackson, Anthony (ed.). *Anthropology at Home*. London: Tavistock Press, 1987.
The methodological and theoretical problems involved when anthropologists study their own culture, in this case in Great Britain.

Rabinow, Paul. *Reflections on Fieldwork in Morocco*. Berkeley: University of California Press, 1977.
An anthropologist's account of the process of discovery involved in his Moroccan fieldwork, his penetration into the culture he is studying, and its effect upon him.

Sanjek, Roger (ed.). *Field Notes: The Makings of Anthropology*. Ithaca, N.Y.: Cornell University Press, 1990.
Selections of articles by anthropologists on the problems of analyzing their field notes.

Wolf, Diane L. (ed.). *Feminist Dilemmas in Fieldwork*. Boulder, Colo.: Westview Press, 1996.
A collection of essays that focus on the way gender, as well as ethnic identity, influences the data collected as a consequence of the ethnographic encounter.

Chapter 3: Language and Culture

Chomsky, Noam. *Language and Mind*. New York: Harcourt Brace Jovanovich, 1972.
The brilliant and provocative linguistic philosopher's statement of his position on the relationship between mind and language.

Fishman, Joshua (ed.). *Handbook of Language and Ethnic Identity*. Oxford, England: Oxford University Press, 1999.
A compilation of scholarly articles on the relationship between language and ethnicity, given the ethnic revival of the past 20 years.

Hardin, C. L., and Luisa Maffi (eds.). *Color Categories in Thought and Language*. Cambridge, England: Cambridge University Press, 1997.
A reexamination of the theories of Berlin and Kay about basic color terminology.

Kuipers, Joel C. *Language, Identity and Marginality in Indonesia: The Changing Nature of Ritual Speech on the Island of Sumba*. Cambridge, England: Cambridge University Press, 1998.
An analysis of the changes that have taken place in the tradition of ritual poetic speech in the Sumba language as a consequence of the rapid spread of Indonesian, the national language. The book also analyzes the new and hybrid forms of poetic expression that have developed, as well as the linguistic consequences of marginality.

Lutz, Catherine A., and Lila Abu-Lughod (eds.). *Language and the Politics of Emotion*. Cambridge, England: Cambridge University Press, 1990.
Sociolinguistic analyses of the relationship between language and emotions.

Salzmann, Zdenek. *Language, Culture, and Society: An Introduction to Linguistic Anthropology*, 2d ed. Boulder, Colo.: Westview Press, 1998.
A recent introduction, covering the major topics in linguistic anthropology.

Chapter 4: Learning Language and Learning Culture: Culture and the Individual

Bock, Philip K. *Rethinking Psychological Anthropology: Continuity and Change in the Study of Human Action*. New York: W. H. Freeman, 1988.
An excellent introduction to the history of psychological anthropology.

Hirschfeld, Lawrence A. *Race in the Making: Cognition, Culture, and the Child's Construction of Human Kinds*. Boston: MIT Press, 1996.
Explores the development of the child's notion of race and demonstrates the way race is not a product of the observation of physical differences, but is instead dependent upon the human capacity for classification.

Mageo, Jeannette Marie. *Theorizing Self in Samoa: Emotions, Genders, and Sexualities*. Ann Arbor: University of Michigan Press, 1998.
A psychological and historical ethnography of Samoa, which demonstrates the way Samoan understandings of the self are more sociocentric—accentuating the social roles that people play—than egocentric—emphasizing individual, interior feelings and perceptions.

Mead, Margaret. *Growing Up in New Guinea*, 1930. Reprint. New York: Mentor Books, 1960.
One of the earliest anthropological studies of how a child is socialized into a non-Western culture.

Ochs, Elinor. *Culture and Language Development: Language Acquisition and Language Socialization in a Samoan Village*. New York: Cambridge University Press, 1988.
How Samoan children are enculturated and learn the Samoan language.

Schieffelin, Bambi B. *The Give and Take of Everyday Life: Language Socialization of Kaluli Children*. New York: Cambridge University Press, 1990.
A study of the way Kaluli children in Papua New Guinea learn their language.

Valsiner, Jaan (ed.). *Child Development in Cultural Contexts*. Toronto: Hogrefe, 1989.
Selections examining child development in a number of different cultures.

Chapter 5: Symbolic Systems and Meanings

Counihan, Carol, and Penny Dan Esterik (eds.). *Food and Culture: A Reader*. New York: Routledge, 1997.
Articles that examine the meanings of food and eating across cultures, paying particular attention to the way men and women define themselves differently through their food ways.

Douglas, Mary (ed.). *Food in the Social Order: Studies of Food and Festivities in Three American Communities.* New York: Russell Sage Foundation, 1984.
Studies of the eating patterns of Lakota, Italian Americans, and rural Southern Americans, and their symbolic significance.
Feld, Steven, and Keith M. Basso (eds.). *Senses of Place.* Santa Fe, N. Mex.: School of American Research Press, 1996.
A series of essays dealing with the subject of space cross-culturally.
Geertz, Clifford. *The Interpretation of Culture.* New York: Basic Books, 1973.
———. *Local Knowledge: Further Essays in Interpretive Anthropology.* New York: Basic Books, 1983.
Two collections of essays by the leading proponent of the culture-as-symbols school.
Guttmann, Allen. *A Whole New Ball Game: An Interpretation of American Sports.* Chapel Hill: University of North Carolina Press, 1988.
A historical and sociological study of American sports that relates it to its cultural context.
Herzfeld, Michael. *The Social Production of Indifference: Exploring the Symbolic Roots of Western Bureaucracy.* Chicago: University of Chicago Press, 1993.
A provocative study that seeks to demonstrate that modern bureaucratically regulated societies are as symbolic as societies traditionally studied by anthropologists.
Turner, Victor. *The Ritual Process: Structure and Antistructure.* Chicago: Aldine, 1969.
A series of lectures by a leading proponent of symbolic analysis.

Chapter 6: Marriage, Family, and Kinship

Collier, Jane Fishburne, and Sylvia Junko Yanagisako (eds.). *Gender and Kinship: Essays towards a Unified Analysis.* Stanford, Calif.: Stanford University Press, 1987.
Gender viewed from the perspective of a redefined approach to kinship. Articles from a conference.
Edwards, Jeanette, Sarah Franklin, Eric Hirsch, Francis Price, and Marilyn Strathern. *Technologies of Procreation: Kinship in the Age of Assisted Conception,* 2d ed. New York: Routledge, 1999.
An analysis of the social and cultural implications of assisted conception, and the potential these create for parenthood, procreation, and kinship.
Fox, Robin. *Kinship and Marriage: An Anthropological Perspective.* Baltimore: Penguin Books, 1967. Reissued by Cambridge University Press, 1983.
A clear and wittily written introduction to the field of kinship, social structure, and marriage.
Godelier, Maurice, Thomas R. Trautmann, and Franklin E. Tjon Sie Fat (eds.). *Transformations of Kinship.* Washington, D.C.: Smithsonian Institution, 1998.
Essays demonstrating that the great variety of kinship systems in the world are variants of a limited number of classic types.
Holly, Ladislav. *Kinship, Honour, and Solidarity: Cousin Marriage in the Middle East.* Manchester, England: Manchester University Press, 1989.
Parallel cousin marriage among Middle Eastern societies is explored.
Mackey, Richard A., Bernard A. O'Brien, and Eileen F. Mackey. *Gay and Lesbian Couples: Voices from Lasting Relationships.* Westport, Conn.: Greenwood Publishers, 1997.
A well-documented study of the relationships between members of same-sex couples, focusing on what is actually involved in such relationships.

Chapter 7: Gender and Age

Bell, Diane, Pat Caplan, and Wazir Jahan Karim (eds.). *Gendered Fields: Women, Men, and Ethnography.* London: Routledge, 1993.
Essays exploring the effects of the anthropologist's gender on the process of fieldwork.

di Leonardo, Micaela (ed.). *Gender at the Crossroads of Knowledge: Feminist Anthropology in the Postmodern Era.* Berkeley: University of California Press, 1991.

Essays dealing with feminist research on biological anthropology, primate studies, global economy, new reproductive technologies, ethnolinguistics, race and gender, etc.

Eisenstadt, S. N. *From Generation to Generation: Age Groups and Social Structure.* Glencoe, Ill.: Free Press, 1956.

A classic comparative study of age grades and youth movements, using examples ranging from small-scale societies like the Nandi and the Nyakyusa to complex societies like Israel and Germany, in an attempt to specify the social conditions under which they arise.

Ginsburg, Faye, and Anna Lowenhaupt Tsing (eds.). *Uncertain Terms: Negotiating Gender in American Culture.* Boston: Beacon Press, 1990.

A series of articles concerning the different domains of American life in which definitions of gender are being contested and renegotiated, such as the family, the workplace, the clinic and hospital, and the school.

Jacobs, Sue-Ellen, Wesley Thomas, and Sabine Lang (eds.). *Two-Spirit People: Native American Gender Identity, Sexuality and Spirituality.* Champaigne: University of Illinois Press, 1997.

Empirical and theoretical essays revisiting the concept of the "North American berdache."

Kapchan, Deborah. *Gender on the Market: Moroccan Women and the Revoicing of Tradition.* Berkeley: University of California Press, 1999.

Describes the way Moroccan women challenge some of the most basic cultural assumptions of their society about honor and shame, privacy and modesty, obligation and hospitality, and particularly, power and authority.

Martin, Emily. *The Woman in the Body: A Cultural Analysis of Reproduction.* Boston: Beacon Press, 1987.

The relationship between women's views of menstruation, childbirth, and menopause and production metaphors in American culture.

Chapter 8: Provisioning Society: Production, Distribution, and Consumption

Bloch, Maurice, and Jonathan Parry (eds.). *Money and the Morality of Exchange.* Cambridge, England: Cambridge University Press, 1989.

Essays in economic anthropology concerned with monetary economies and questions of morality.

Chatty, Dawn. *Mobile Pastoralists: Development Planning and Social Change in Oman.* New York: Columbia University Press, 1996.

An account of how the nomadic pastoralists of Oman have shifted from camel to truck, from subsistence to salary, and from reliance on family labor to partial dependence on foreign workers, while maintaining other aspects of their traditional nomadic pastoral way of life.

Hann, C. M. (ed.). *Property Relations: Renewing the Anthropological Tradition.* New York: Cambridge University Press, 1998.

A series of essays considering the cultural, social, and symbolic aspects of property, as well as its material component, in a number of different societies.

Maclachlan, Morgan (ed.). *Household Economies and Their Transformations.* Monographs in Economic Anthropology, no. 3. Lanham, Md.: University Press of America, 1987.

How the household functions as a unit within the economic system, and how this has changed.

Plattner, Stuart (ed.). *Economic Anthropology.* Stanford, Calif.: Stanford University Press, 1989.

Coverage of the various subtopics of economic anthropology.

Chapter 9: Governing Society:
Politics, Government, Law, and Conflict

Lewellen, Ted C. *Political Anthropology: An Introduction,* 2d ed. Westport, Conn.: Bergin and Garvey, 1992.

A recent introduction to the concepts, theories, and methods of political anthropology.

Lindholm, Charles. *Charisma.* Cambridge, Mass.: Blackwell, 1990.

A discussion of the charismatic aspects of leadership.

Sponsel, Leslie E., and Thomas Gregor (eds.). *The Anthropology of Peace and Nonviolence.* Boulder, Colo.: Lynne Riener, 1994.

A series of articles about peacemaking in small-scale and complex societies. The authors examine nonviolent direct action, political action, and economic sanctions, which have been used as remedies to confront political and economic injustice.

Vincent, Joan. *Anthropology and Politics: Visions, Traditions and Trends.* Tucson: University of Arizona Press, 1990.

A critical review of the anthropological study of politics from 1879 to the present.

White, Geoffrey, and Lamont Linstrom (eds.). *Chiefs Today: Traditional Pacific Leadership and the Postcolonial State.* Stanford, Calif.: Stanford University Press, 1997.

Discussions of the ways the role of chiefs has been transformed within modern Pacific States, as well as the ways chiefs operate in fashioning national identities and managing the direction of political and economic development in 13 contemporary Pacific societies.

Chapter 10: Religion and the Supernatural

Becker, Penny E., and Nancy L. Eiesland (eds.). *Contemporary American Religion: An Ethnographic Reader.* Walnut Creek, Cal.: Altamira, 1997.

A series of ethnographic studies illustrating some of the new directions that religious beliefs and practices have taken in the United States.

Herdt, Gilbert, and Michelle Stephen (eds.). *The Religious Imagination in New Guinea.* New Brunswick, N.J.: Rutgers University Press, 1989.

Essays exploring personal expressions of religious fervor, such as dreams, trances, possession, sorcery, and shamanism, in Melanesia.

Hogbin, Ian. *The Island of Menstruating Men: Religion in Wogeo, New Guinea.* 1970. Reprint. Prospect Heights, Ill.: Waveland Press, 1996.

A fascinating account of the religious system of an island society off New Guinea in which men ritually "menstruate."

Klass, Morton. *Ordered Universes: Approaches to the Anthropology of Religion.* Boulder, Colo.: Westview Press, 1995.

A general introduction to the anthropology of religion.

Klass, Morton, and Maxine K. Weisgrau (eds.). *Across the Boundaries of Belief: Contemporary Issues in the Anthropology of Religion.* Boulder, Colo.: Westview Press, 1999.

A book of readings covering contemporary issues and major topics in the anthropology of religion.

Lewis, I. M. *Religion in Context: Cults and Charisma,* 2d ed. Cambridge, England: Cambridge University Press, 1996.

Examines various cultural contexts of manifestations of religious power, such as spirit possession, witchcraft, cannibalism, and shamanism.

Malinowski, Bronislaw. *Magic, Science and Religion,* 1948. Reprint. Prospect Heights, Ill.: Waveland Press, 1992.

Several essays by a pioneer anthropologist that discuss magic, science, and religion, using examples from the Trobriand Islands.

Saler, Benson. *Conceptualizing Religion: Eminent Anthropologists, Transcendant Natives, and Unbounded Categories.* Leiden, Holland: E. J. Brill, 1993.

A work considering religion as a universal category.

Stephen, Michele (ed.). *Sorcerer and Witch in Melanesia.* New Brunswick, N.J.: Rutgers University Press, 1987.

Essays on the cultural contexts of witchcraft and sorcery in Melanesia.

Chapter 11: Myths, Legends, and Folktales

Drummond, Lee. *American Dreamtime: A Cultural Analysis of Popular Movies and Their Implications for a Science of Humanity.* Lanham, Md.: Rowman and Littlefield, 1996.

A general consideration of themes in contemporary American films and their relationship to American culture.

Goldman, L. R., and C. Ballard (eds.). *Fluid Ontologies: Myth, Ritual, and Philosophy in the Highlands of Papua New Guinea.* Westport, Conn.: Greenwood Publishing, 1998.

A collection of essays discussing the relationship between myth, ritual, and ways of knowing in a number of Highland New Guinea societies.

Lévi-Strauss, Claude. *The Savage Mind.* Chicago: University of Chicago Press, 1966.

An exposition of Lévi-Strauss's structuralist theoretical framework for the analysis of myth, symbols, and systems of classification.

Traube, Elizabeth. *Dreaming Identities: Class, Gender and Generation in 1980s Hollywood Movies.* Boulder, Colo.: Westview Press, 1992.

A feminist perspective on the ways Hollywood has handled the frontier myth and the myth of American success in its presentations of gender and power.

Winniford, Lee. *Following Old Fence Lines: Tales from Rural Texas.* College Station: Texas A & M University Press, 1998.

Family stories, and the cultural context of their telling, collected by the descendant of the founders of a Texas town. Offers many glimpses into the folkways of cotton farmers as story-telling occasions, like picking cotton and killing hogs, are described.

Chapter 12: The Artistic Dimension

Boas, Franz. *Primitive Art,* 1927. Reprint. New York: Dover Publications, 1955.

A seminal volume on primitive art by a pioneer in the field, with emphasis on the art of the Pacific Northwest, where Boas did fieldwork.

Feld, Steven. *Sound and Sentiment: Birds, Weeping, Poetics, and Song in Kaluli Expression.* Philadelphia: University of Pennsylvania Press, 1982.

An innovative ethnography on the relationship between song and emotion among the Kaluli of Papua New Guinea.

Hatcher, Evalyn P. *Art as Culture: An Introduction to the Anthropology of Art,* 2d ed. Westport, Conn.: Bergan and Garvey, 1999.

A general introduction to the anthropological study of art.

Hiller, Susan (ed.). *The Myth of Primitivism: Perspectives on Art.* London: Routledge, 1991.

A series of essays exploring the concept of the "primitive" in modern Western and ethnographic art.

Meyers, Helen. *Music of Hindu Trinidad: Songs from the Indian Diaspora*. Chicago: University of Chicago Press, 1998.

An ethnomusicological study of Felicity, a town in the East Indian enclave of Trinidad, which deals not only with its musical culture, but also with the music brought by nineteenth-century North Indians when they came to Trinidad as indentured laborers.

Nettl, Bruno. *The Study of Ethnomusicology: Twenty-Nine Issues and Concepts*. Urbana: University of Illinois Press, 1983.

A general work by the foremost American authority in the field of ethnomusicology.

O'Hanlon, Michael. *Paradise: Portraying the New Guinea Highlands*. London: British Museum Press, 1993.

A study of a Highland New Guinea people whose aesthetic is expressed in the decoration of shields currently being used in warfare.

Philips, Ruth B., and Christopher B. Steiner (eds.). *Unpacking Culture: Art and Commodity in Colonial and Postcolonial Worlds*. Berkeley: University of California Press, 1998.

A series of essays providing a comparative perspective on the history, character, and impact of tourist art in colonized societies in Africa, Oceania, and North America. The global phenomenon of tourist art production is recognized as a significant and authentic expression of visual traditions.

Price, Sally. *Primitive Art in Civilized Places*. Chicago: University of Chicago Press, 1989.

A discussion of the relationship between Western viewers and non-Western art objects and their creators.

Chapter 13: The Colonial and Postcolonial Periods: Globalization, Migration, Diasporas, and Transnationalism

Appadurai, Arjun. *Modernity at Large: Cultural Dimensions of Globalization*. Minneapolis: University of Minnesota Press, 1996.

A postmodern discussion of modernization and globalization.

Chirot, Daniel, and Anthony Reed (eds.). *Chinese and Jews in the Modern Transformation of Southeast Asia and Central Europe*. Seattle: University of Washington Press, 1997.

A series of essays on the Chinese and Jewish diaspora populations and their entrepreneurial success, as well as the scapegoating and violence that these groups have encountered.

Comoroff, Jean, and John Comoroff. *Of Revelation and Revolution: Christianity, Colonialism, and Consciousness in South Africa,* vol. 1. Chicago: University of Chicago Press, 1991.

A history of British colonialism and missionary activity among the Tswana peoples of South Africa.

Cooper, Frederick, and Anne Laura Stoler (eds.). *Tensions of Empire: Colonial Cultures in a Bourgeois World*. Berkeley: University of California Press, 1997.

A series of essays that focus upon colonial encounters in various parts of the world and how they shaped ideas about imperialism in Europe and the politics of inclusion and exclusion in the colonies.

Dirks, Nicholas B. (ed.). *Colonialism and Culture*. Ann Arbor: University of Michigan Press, 1992.

Essays dealing with the culture of colonialism and its multifaceted nature.

Fabian, Johannes. *Language and Colonial Power*. Berkeley: University of California Press, 1986.

A study of the way Swahili was appropriated by the Belgian colonizers as the language of imperial domination.

Foster, Robert J. *Social Reproduction and History in Melanesia: Mortuary Ritual, Gift Exchange and Custom in the Tanga Islands.* Cambridge, England: Cambridge University Press, 1995.

An examination of Tangan mortuary rites that demonstrates the way Tangan participation in an expanding cash economy has resulted in the perception of these rites as customary and in opposition to the foreign practice of business.

Otto, Tom, and Nicholas Thomas. *Narratives of Nation in the South Pacific.* Amsterdam: Harwood Academic, 1997.

Efforts to develop national identity and national narratives, while grounding the newly developed nationhood in tradition, have been part of the modernization process in newly independent nations. The articles in this volume deal with the way these trends have operated in countries such as Papua New Guinea, Vanuatu, Samoa, and the Cook Islands.

Worsley, Peter. *The Trumpet Shall Sound: A Study of Cargo Cults in Melanesia,* 2d ed. New York: Schocken Books, 1968.

A comparative analysis of cargo cults that examines their history and relates them to the changing economic and political situation.

Chapter 14: Ethnicity, Race, and Nationalism: Anthropology for the Twenty-first Century

Daniel, E. Valentine. *Charred Lullabies: Chapters in an Anthropography of Violence.* Princeton, N.J.: Princeton University Press, 1996.

An examination of ethnic conflict and violence and the problems anthropologists have in conveying the experience of brutality in ethnographic texts.

Dominguez, Virginia, and David Y. H. Wu (eds.). *From Beijing to Port Moresby: The Politics of National Identity in Cultural Policies.* New York: Gordon and Breach, 1998.

The contributors to this volume illustrate the way culture and cultural construction operate in debates about national identity and national integration, and the way politics and cultural policy fashion a nation's heritage.

Grant, Bruce. *In the Soviet House of Culture: A Century of Perestroikas.* Princeton, N.J.: Princeton University Press, 1995.

A story of the Nivkhi of Sakhalin Island and how this ethnic minority constituted and reconstituted, restructured and dismantled its ethnic identity, from the time Russian missionaries tried to convert them, to Gorbachev's pronouncement, many decades later, that they could resume a "traditional" life.

Gregory, Steven, and Roger Sanjek (eds.). *Race.* New Brunswick, N.J.: Rutgers University Press, 1994.

Explores the way racial ideologies intersect with gender, class, nation, and sexuality in the formation of social identities and hierarchies.

Sollars, Werner (ed.). *The Invention of Ethnicity.* New York: Oxford University Press, 1989.

A collection of interdisciplinary essays considering the cultural construction of ethnicity.

Stack, Carol. *Call to Home: African Americans Reclaim the Rural South.* New York: Basic Books, 1996.

Describes the return of half a million black Americans from the cities of the north to their homes in the rural south, driven by lack of economic opportunities and consequent poverty.

Tambiah, Stanley J. *Buddhism Betrayed: Religion, Politics, and Violence in Sri Lanka.* Chicago: University of Chicago Press, 1992.

An examnation of Sinhalese Buddhism and the role it played in the Tamil-Sinhala ethnic conflict.

Glossary

acculturation   the process of culture change resulting from the contact between two cultures.

achieved status   position in a social structure dependent upon personal qualifications and individual ability.

adaptation   the process in which a population or society alters its culture to better succeed in its total environment.

affinal link   connections between kin groups established by marriage.

age grade   categories of individuals of the same age that are recognized by being given a name and that crosscut an entire society.

age set   a group of individuals of the same age that moves as a unit through successive age grades.

alliance   a linkage between kin groups established through marriage for the mutual benefit of the two groups.

allomorph   a variant form of a morpheme.

allophone   a variant form of a phoneme.

ancestor-oriented group   a social unit that traces kin relationships back to a common ancestor.

animism   a belief in the spiritual or noncorporeal counterparts of human beings.

ascribed status   an inherited position in the social structure.

authority   an institutionalized position of power.

avunculocal residence   a form of postmarital residence in which the bride goes to live with her husband after he has moved to live with his mother's brother.

band organization   a type of social group with a fixed membership that comes together annually for a period to carry out joint ritual and economic activities.

barter   an immediate exchange of unlike objects, which may involve bargaining.

berdache   Native American term for a man who assumes a woman's role and dresses as a woman.

Big Man structure   an achieved position of leadership in which the group is defined as the Big Man and his followers.

bilateral cross cousin   cross cousins through both the mother's and father's side.

bilateral societies   societies with kindreds but without unilineal descent groups.

bilocal residence   a form of postmarital residence in which husband and wife alternate between living with the husband's relatives for a period of time and then with the wife's relatives.

boundary maintenance mechanisms   the ways in which a social group maintains its individual identity by separating itself from the dominant society.

bride service   a custom whereby the groom works for the bride's family before marriage.

bridewealth payments   payments made by the groom's family to the family of the bride.

cargo cult   a particular type of revitalization movement that first appeared in the early twentieth century in Melanesia and represents a synthesis of old and new religious beliefs.

caste system   a grouping of economically specialized, hierarchically organized, endogamous social units.

chieftainship   a type of political organization in which fixed positions of leadership are present along with a method for succession to those positions.

clan   a social group based on common descent but not necessarily common residence.

clan totem   an animal from which members of a clan believe themselves descended and with whom they have a special relationship that may prohibit the eating of that animal.

cognate   a relative traced through either the mother's or the father's line.

cognatic rule of descent   a rule of descent in which group membership may be traced through either the father or the mother.

collateral relative   a relative not in the direct line of descent.

community   a naturally bounded social unit.

compadrazgo   ritual godparenthood found in Mediterranean Europe and Latin America.

components   the criteria used to characterize and differentiate any kind of category.

corporate descent group   a social group based upon common descent that owns property in common and extends beyond the lifetime of any one individual.

creole   a pidgin language acquired by children as their native language.

cross cousins   children of one's mother's brother or one's father's sister.

cultural relativism   the emphasis on the unique aspects of each culture, without judgments or categories based on one's own culture.

cultural rules   internalized rules of behavior covering all aspects of life.

cultural universals   cultural features which are to be found in all societies.

culture   the way of life of a people, including their behavior, the things they make, and their ideas.

dala   the Trobriand matrilineal subclan.

delayed exchange   the return of goods or of women a generation after their giving; associated with preference for marriage with father's sister's daughter.

demonstrated descent   descent in which kinship can be traced by means of written or oral genealogies back to a founding ancestor.

dialects   variations within a single language between one speech community and another.

diaspora   a population spread from its original homeland to other countries, which continues to maintain contact with that homeland.

diffusion   the process by means of which a culture trait that originates in one society spreads to another.

direct reciprocal exchange   a continuing exchange of like for like between two parties.

distinctive features   see *components.*

distribution   the manner in which products circulate through a society.

double descent   the presence of matrilineal and patrilineal descent rules in a single society.

dowry   goods that are given by the bride's family to the groom's family at marriage.

duolocal residence   a postmarital rule of residence in which husband and wife live with their respective kinsmen, apart from one another.

ebene   hallucinogenic substance used by the Yanomamo.

ego-oriented group   a kinship unit defined in terms of a particular ego.

enculturation   the process by which culture is learned and acquired by particular individuals.

endogamy   a rule requiring group members to marry within their own group.

ethnic groups   distinctive groups within a state who preserve cultural items from their past.

ethnocentrism   the idea that what is present in one's own culture represents the natural and best way to do things.

ethnogenesis   the creation of a new ethnic group.

ethnonationalism   the desire of ethnic groups within a state to have their own nation-state.

ethnosemantics   the anthropological investigation of native systems of classification.

exogamy   a rule requiring group members to marry outside their own social group.

extended family   several related nuclear families living together in a single household.

Fourth World peoples   oppressed tribal peoples living in Third World nations.

fraternal polyandry   a form of marriage in which a woman is simultaneously married to several brothers.

function   the way a particular unit or structure operates and what it does.

generalized exchange   a form of marriage in which women move from wife-givers to wife-takers but never in the opposite direction.

globalization   the worldwide connection between societies based upon the existence of global market connections and the spread of cultural items everywhere.

government   the process by which those in office make and implement decisions on behalf of an entire group in order to carry out commonly held goals.

grammar   the complete description of a language, including phonology, morphology, and syntax.

guardian spirit   among North American native peoples, an animal spirit that becomes the protector of an individual as a result of his quest for a vision.

gumlao   the egalitarian form of the Kachin political organization.

gumsa   the chieftainship form of the Kachin political organization, in which wife-givers are higher in rank than wife-takers.

hekura   small, humanlike supernatural creatures that are part of the Yanomamo religious belief system.

hortatory ritual   an exhortation to the supernatural to perform some act.

horticulture   a form of cultivation in which crops are grown in gardens without the use of a plow.

idiolect   the distinctive linguistic features or cultural features characteristic of an individual.

incest taboo   prohibition on sexual relations between certain categories of close relatives.

influence   the ability to persuade others to follow one's lead when one lacks the authority to command them.

innovation   the process of bringing about cultural change through the recombination of existing ideas into creative new forms.

joint family   a type of extended family in which married brothers and their families remain together after the death of their parents.

kaiko   a lengthy Maring religious ceremony.

kayasa   a competitive period of feasting, including a competitive giving of yams to the chief, and games like cricket among the Trobrianders.

kindred   a kin group oriented in terms of a particular individual.

kinship terminology   a set of terms used to refer to relatives.

kula   an exchange system involving one kind of shell valuables moving in a clockwise direction and another kind moving in a counterclockwise direction that links the Trobriand Islanders to a circle of neighboring islands.

levirate   a rule whereby the widow of a deceased man must marry his brother.

lewa   Wogeo spirits represented by masks.

liminal period   the in-between stage in a rite-of-passage ceremony when the individual has not yet been reincorporated into society.

lineages   unilineal descent groups in which descent is demonstrated.

lineal relative   a relative in the direct line of descent.

linguistic imperialism   the imposition by a dominant group of its language on minority speakers of other languages.

linguistic relativity   a point of view that emphasizes the uniqueness of each language and the need to examine it in its own terms.

malanggan   a term referring to New Ireland mortuary ritual, as well as the carvings displayed at such a ritual.

mana   belief in an impersonal supernatural force or power that is found in all aspects of nature.

manau   a Kachin religious ceremony consisting of a feast and sacrifice to the spirits.

markedness the process whereby a category (the marked category) is distinguished from a larger, more inclusive category (the unmarked category) by the presence of a single attribute.

matrilineal rule of descent a rule stating that a child belongs to his or her mother's group.

maximizing the concept in economic anthropology whereby individuals are seen as interpreting economic rules to their own advantage.

mayu/dama Kachin lineage categories; wife-giving lineages are *mayu,* and wife-taking lineages are *dama.*

metaphor an analytical concept in which one idea stands for another because of some similarity they are seen to share.

metonym the symbolic substitution of one of the constituent parts for the whole.

moieties a grouping based upon descent in which the entire society is divided into halves.

monogamy marriage with only one spouse at a time.

morpheme the smallest unit of a language conveying meaning.

nat spirits of the Kachin supernatural world.

nation a sovereign political state with a single national culture.

nation-state see *nation.*

nativistic movements religious cults that develop in periods of drastic cultural change and synthesize traditional cultural elements with newly introduced ones.

neolocal residence a rule of postmarital residence in which the newly married couple forms an independent household.

nibek Wogeo spirits represented by flutes.

nomadic pastoralists societies completely, or almost completely, dependent upon herds of domesticated animals.

nuclear family a family consisting of husband, wife, and their unmarried children.

numaym cognatic descent group of the Kwakiutl.

office a recognized political position.

parallel cousins the children of two brothers or of two sisters.

participant observation the anthropological method of collecting data by living with other people, learning their language, and understanding their culture.

patrilineal rule of descent a rule stating that a child belongs to his or her father's group.

patron-client relationship a hierarchical relationship in which the superior (the patron) acts as an intermediary and protector of the inferior (the client) vis-à-vis the national government.

phonemes the minimal sound units that make up a language.

pidgin a lingua franca developed when people speaking different languages but no common language need to communicate with one another.

political economy the interpretation of politics and economy.

politics the competition for political positions and for power.

polyandry marriage in which one woman has several husbands at one time.

polygamy marriage with plural spouses, either husbands or wives.

polygyny marriage in which one man has several wives at one time.

Poro Society secret society associated with the use of masks, found in Liberia and Sierra Leone.

postmarital residence rule a rule that states where a couple should live after marriage.

potlatch a large-scale ceremonial distribution of goods found among the indigenous peoples of the Northwest Coast of North America.

power the ability to command others to do certain things and get compliance from them.

primogeniture a rule of inheritance of property or office by the firstborn child.

private symbols symbols that individuals create out of their own experience and that they do not share with other members of their society.

production   the process whereby a society uses the tools and energy sources at its disposal and its own people's labor to create the goods necessary for supplying itself.

proto-language   ancestral form of a language arrived at by reconstruction.

public symbols   symbols used and understood by the members of a society.

reciprocal exchange   a type of exchange system in egalitarian societies in which women or material goods of equal value continue to be exchanged over generations.

revitalization movements   see *nativistic movements.*

rites of intensification   communal rituals celebrated at various points in the yearly cycle.

rites of passage   communal rituals held to mark changes in status as individuals progress through the life cycle.

sagali   a large-scale ceremonial distribution among the Trobriand Islanders.

segmentary lineage system   a descent system, typically patrilineal, in which the largest segments are successively divided into smaller segments, like branches of a tree.

serial monogamy   the practice of marrying a series of spouses, one after the other.

shaman   a ritual specialist whose primary function is to cure illness.

shifting cultivation   a type of horticulture in which new gardens are made every few years, when the soil is exhausted.

sister exchange   a marriage pattern in which two men marry each other's sisters.

situational leadership   a type of political organization in which there is no single political leader but rather leadership is manifested intermittently.

social organization   behavioral choices that individuals make in connection with the social structure.

social role   the behavior associated with a particular social status in a society.

social status   the position an individual occupies in a society.

social structure   the pattern of social relationships that characterizes a society.

society   a social grouping characterizing humans and other social animals, differentiated by age and sex.

sociolinguistics   the study of that aspect of language which deals with status and class differences.

sorcery   the learned practice of evil magic.

sororal polygamy   the marriage of a man to several sisters.

sororate   the custom whereby a widower marries his deceased wife's sister.

state   a type of political organization which is organized on a territorial basis and which is integrated through social stratification rather than through kinship.

status personality   the characteristic personality associated with a social position.

stem family   a two-generation extended family consisting of parents and only one married son and his family.

stipulated descent   a social unit, such as a clan, in which all members consider themselves to be related though they cannot actually trace the genealogical relationship.

structure   a description of parts or elements in relationship to one another.

style   a characterization of the component elements of art and the way those elements are put together.

suaboya   the single kinship term that the Yanomamo use for both female cross cousin and wife.

subcultural variation   cultural differences between communities within a single society.

swidden   see *shifting cultivation.*

syntax   that part of grammar which deals with the rules of combination of morphemes.

Te   the ceremonial distribution of pigs and pork among the Mae Enga of Papua New Guinea.

technology   that part of culture by means of which people directly exploit their environment.

total social phenomena   large-scale rituals that integrate all aspects of society—economic, political, kinship, religion, art, etc.

tribe   a unit used by colonial powers to refer to groups with a common language and culture.

tschambura   among the Abelam, partners who exchange long yams with one another.

ultimogeniture   a rule of inheritance of property or office by the last-born child.

unilineal descent group   a kin group, such as a clan, in which membership is based on either matrilineal or patrilineal descent.

urigubu   a Trobriand harvest gift given yearly by a man to his sister's husband.

uxorilocal residence   a rule of postmarital residence whereby the newly married couple resides with the relatives of the bride.

virilocal residence   a rule of postmarital residence whereby the newly married couple resides with the relatives of the groom.

vision quest   the search for a protective supernatural spirit through starvation and deprivation.

warabwa   large-scale ceremonial distribution in Wogeo.

witchcraft   a form of magic practiced by individuals born with this ability.

zadruga   a Yugoslavian virilocal extended family.

Photo Credits

260   (*Right*) By courtesy of the American Museum of Natural History
261   (*Top*) Franz Boas, *The Kwakiutl of Vancouver Island,* 1909
261   (*Bottom*) Franz Boas, *The Social Organization and Secret Societies of the Kwakiutl Indians,* 1897
267   Illustration from *Primitive Art* by Franz Boas (Oslo, 1927)
268   Abraham Rosman
269   Abraham Rosman
270   Abraham Rosman
275   Abraham Rosman
277   Abraham Rosman
287   From *Drawings Illustrative of Cook's First Voyage,* fol. 11. Reproduced by permission of the British Library, London
294   Library of Congress
303   Charles O'Rear/CORBIS
308   Grunzweig/Photo Researchers
311   Courtesy Mashantucket Pequot Tribal Nation
320   Reuters/Bettmann Archive
321   Don Levy/Gamma-Liaison
332   Image Works

Index

A

Abelam (New Guinea),
  Big Men, 185, 186
  eating symbolism, 76
  exchange system, 160–161
  horticulture, 152, 161
  marriage payments, 94
  moieties, 110
  organization of work, 161
  tshambura, 161
Abkhazians, 319–321
Abu-Lughod, Lila, 54
Acadians, 326
Achieved status, 186
Adolescence, initiation of (*see* Initiation rites)
Aesthetic impulse, 254
Affines and affinal links, 110
Afghanistan, 21
African-American, 331
  African language retention, 55, 331
  culture, 331
  language, 54
African-American English, 331
African-American folktales, 245
Age, categories based on, 137–141
Age grades, 138–139
Agriculture, 151–153
  irrigation, 153
  mechanization, 153, 302
'Aiga (Samoan), 203
"Airport art," 271
Algonquins (Northeast America), 66
Alliance, 110, 115
Allomorphs, 43
Allophones, 42
Allotment Act of 1887, 289
Aluund, 85, 189
Amazons, 240
American culture
  art in, 255
  bilateral society, 110
  body decoration, 264–265
  changing gender roles, 134–135
  ethnic differences, 330–331
  ethnic parades, 333
  family reunions, 126–127
  food in, 1, 78
  funeral in, 219–220
  international family, 126
  kinship relationships, 120–127
  kinship terminology, 116–117
  language acquisition, 58
  legends and folktales in, 244–252
  marriage in, 34–38, 38–40
  men's and women's speech styles,
    52–53, 60–61
  native culture and, as a plural
    society, 317
  race in, 314
  regional language usage, 54
  religion and, 207, 208, 209
  rites of intensification, 221
  rites of passage, 218–220
  shamanism, 228
  social space, 83
  sports symbolism, 87
  Wicca, 124, 207
American Indians (*see* Native Americans)
American kinship, 120–127
Amish, 177
Amok, 66
Ancestor-oriented kindred, 110
Ancestral spirits, 212
Animals
  classification of, 56
  domestication of, 153–158
  edibility of, 76, 82
  farm, 82
  game, 82
  stock reduction programs, symbolism
    of, 301
  totemic, 79
Animism, 213
Anthropological linguistics, 41–56
Anthropological practice, 300–302
Anthropological theory
  contemporary approaches, 16–20
  cultural evolution, 13–14
  functionalism, 15–16
  structuralism, 16
Anthropology
  basic concepts of, 1–12